Bouncing Back:

Critical reflections on the Resilience Concept in Japan and South Africa

Editors

Tamara Enomoto,
Marlon Swai,
Kiyoshi Umeya &
Francis B. Nyamnjoh

Langaa Research & Publishing CIG
Mankon, Bamenda

Publisher:

Langaa RPCIG
Langaa Research & Publishing Common Initiative Group
P.O. Box 902 Mankon
Bamenda
North West Region
Cameroon
Langaagrp@gmail.com
www.langaa-rpcig.net

Distributed in and outside N. America by African Books Collective
orders@africanbookscollective.com
www.africanbookscollective.com

ISBN-10: 9956-552-23-2

ISBN-13: 978-9956-552-23-8

Notes on Contributors

Maho ARAKI is a Ph.D. candidate at the Graduate School for Intercultural Studies, Kobe University, Japan, and a JSPS Research Fellow. She majors in anthropology, folklore and ethnomusicology. Her research interests revolve around the social relations between traditional folk music practitioners and communities in the southern islands of Japan. Her recent publications include 'Performing Arts on Iou Jima, Mishima Village under COVID-19 Situation' (2021, *Kagoshima Folklore* 159: 19–34, in Japanese, and 'The Development of Uchi-bayashi in Kesennuma, Miyagi Prefecture: Focusing on the Minato Matsuri Festival' (2021, *Tohoku Folklore* 55: 41–50, in Japanese).

Tamara ENOMOTO is Professor at the Organization for the Strategic Coordination of Research and Intellectual Properties, Meiji University. From 2003 to 2015, she worked at Oxfam where she was in charge of policy on humanitarian issues. Her recent publications include 'Demarcating Battle Lines: Citizenship and Agency in the Era of Misanthropy' in I. Hazama, K. Umeya and F. B. Nyamnjoh (eds), *Citizenship in Motion: South African and Japanese Scholars in Conversation* (2019, Bamenda: Langaa RPCIG), 'Overcoming the Dichotomy Between Africa and the West: Norms and Measures for Arms Transfers to Non-State Actors' in M. Endo, M. Neocosmos and A. K. Onoma (eds), *African Politics of Survival Extraversion and Informality in the Contemporary World* (2020, Bamenda: Langaa RPCIG), *Weapon Taboos: Genealogies of Pariah Weapons* (2020, Nihon Keizai Hyouronsha, edited book in Japanese) and *The Arms Trade Treaty: The Self, Sovereignty, and Arms Transfer Control* (2020, Kouyou Shobou, sole-authored book in Japanese).

Kolawole GBOLAHAN is a Nigerian by birth who has been residing in Cape Town for the past seven years. As a Mellon Fellow, Kola attained his Master's in music and is currently pursuing his Ph.D. at the College of Music, University of Cape Town. As a trumpeter, percussionist and poet, he has shared creative works and performance spaces with diverse musical collectives and creatives such as Mandla Mbothwe, Marlon Swai, Dizu Plaatjies and the UCT Symphony Orchestra. Some of his creative projects include founding the poetry-centered band Sounds & Words in 2016; a theoretical and performative project in 2019 which reclaimed the poetics of indigenous horns and; his 2021 co-founding of 'The Commons' (an experiment in the social). The thread that connects all of his work is a deep sense of responsibility for ability of art to facilitate sharing, healing and communing with the widest spectrum of people.

Toru HAMAGUCHI is a Ph.D. candidate at the Graduate School of Intercultural Studies, Kobe University. His main area of research is human migration, focusing on Filipinos who migrate to oil-producing countries in the Middle East, and especially on how their earnings from migrant work are situated in their social relations. His recent publications include 'The Relations between Migrant Worker, Migrant and Their Home: The Case of Filipino Specialist' (2019, *Shitennoji University Bulletin* 68: 369–386).

Itsuhiro HAZAMA is Professor of Anthropology at Toyo University in the Faculty of Sociology. In addition to thinking about the intersections between multispecies ethnography and citizenship studies, his current research involves an examination of the ways in which the machinations of global governance affect the ability of refugees to live with dignity in contexts such as Uganda. His recent publications include the co-authored 'Naturalography of Co-Existence among East African Pastoral Societies: An Introductory Overview of Japanese Scholarship' (2019, *African Study Monographs* 40(2-3): 45–75) and the co-edited *Citizenship in Motion: South African and Japanese Scholars in Conversation* (2019, Bamenda: Langaa RPCIG). Email: hazama@toyo.jp

Minga Mbweck KONGO is an anthropologist and fellow at HUMA with research interests in water sociality, mobility, urbanism, illness and climate change. He holds a Bachelor of Science degree in Biomedical Science and, from UCT, an Honours Degree in Social Anthropology and a Masters in African Studies. He has been a fellow of the Mastercard Foundation Scholars Program for undergraduate studies at UCT. Minga has served as a research assistant for several projects at UCT, has worked as tutor and teaching assistant and as curator at UCT's Centre for African Studies, and is a member of the Citizenship in Motion bilateral cooperation project between South African and Japanese scholars. He has worked widely in emergency medical services, the architecture, construction, arts and community development sectors. At HUMA, Minga's Ph.D. research in anthropology examines water, sociality and the navigation of dignified livelihoods in the Khayelitsha, Cape Town, South Africa.

Masayuki, KOMEYAMA is the Director-General of Hokudan Earthquake Memorial Park. He was born in Toshima, the epicentre of the Great Hanshin-Awaji Earthquake. At the time of the earthquake, as a member of the fire brigade, he engaged in rescue work. He has been giving lectures across the country as a *kataribe* (storyteller) of the experience of disaster to propagate the available lessons. Recently, he has been teaching younger generations under the principle that good storytellers can be grown even if they have not experienced the disaster directly.

Kharnita MOHAMED is a black feminist scholar who lectures in anthropology at the University of Cape Town (UCT). Her research is focused on epistemology, death, debility, disability, race and gender towards developing conceptual tools for thinking about death, disability and debility in and for the global South. In her teaching, she is passionate about developing pedagogies that open epistemic horizons. In 2020, she received the UCT Humanities Faculty's Dean's Teaching Award for her innovative curricula. Her 2018 debut novel, *Called to Song* received the 2020 UCT Meritorious Book Award, was shortlisted for the 2020 National Institute for the Humanities and Social Sciences Fiction Award and long listed for the 2019 *Sunday Times* Barry Ronge Fiction Prize.

Gaku MORIGUCHI is a part-time lecturer of Cultural Anthropology and African Politics at Tokyo University of Agriculture, Komazawa University and Waseda University. He has conducted fieldwork in Kampala, Uganda (2007–2011). During this time, he also served as external consultant to the Grant Assistant for Grass-Roots and Human Security Projects at the Embassy of Japan in Uganda. His recent publications include a chapter, co-authored with S. Kodamaya, 'Area Studies in the time of Globalisation: Introductory notes on comparative studies of two African nation-states' in S. Kodamaya, A. Sato and H. Shimada (eds) *Approaches to Area Studies: World Analysis from the Global South*, (2021, Kyoto: Minerva Shobō) and 'In and Out of Family: Family Affairs and Deep Play at Nightclubs in Kampala, Uganda' in I. Hazama, K. Umeya and F. B. Nyamnjoh (eds) *Citizenship in Motion: South African and Japanese*

Scholars in Conversation (2019, Bamenda: Langaa RPCIG).

Zuziwe MSOMI is a lecturer in the Centre for African Studies at the University of Cape Town. Her research interests include whiteness studies, language, discourse analysis, the constructions and deployment of race, higher education, the legal protection of indigenous knowledge and bioresources, privilege and inequality. Her areas of research share the common threads of domination, oppression and agency. She holds an M.A. in Political Studies from Rhodes University (referred by some as the University Currently Known as Rhodes). Her was doctorate, focusing on whiteness and whiteness studies, was awarded by the University of Cape Town. Zuziwe is currently writing a monograph, based on her Ph.D. thesis, titled 'Negotiating whiteness: a discourse analysis of students' descriptions of their raced experiences at Rhodes University, Grahamstown (now Makhanda), South Africa'.

Francis B. NYAMNJOH is Professor of Social Anthropology at the University of Cape Town, South Africa. He is the recipient of the 'ASU African Hero 2013' annual award by the African Students Union, Ohio University, USA, of the 2014 Eko Prize for African Literature and of the ASAUK 2018 Fage & Oliver Prize for the best monograph for his book *#RhodesMustFall: Nibbling at Resilient Colonialism in South Africa*. He is a B1 rated Professor and Researcher by the South African National Research Foundation (NRF), a Fellow of the Cameroon Academy of Science since August 2011, a Fellow of the African Academy of Science since December 2014, a Fellow of the Academy of Science of South Africa since 2016 and a Fellow of the College of Fellows of the University of Cape Town since December 2021. His scholarly books include *Drinking from the Cosmic Gourd: How Amos Tutuola Can Change Our Minds* (2017) and *Incompleteness: Donald Trump, Populism and Citizenship* (2022).

Berni SEARLE, born in Cape Town in 1964, is an artist who works with photography and the moving image. Often, but not exclusively, using herself in her work, she performs for the camera, producing works that explore issues of self-representation, the relationship between personal and collective identity and narratives connected to history, memory and place. Searle completed her undergraduate and postgraduate studies at the Michaelis School of Fine Art, at the University of Cape Town, where she was previously the Director and currently Professor in the department. She has won a number of awards including the Minister of Culture Prize at DAK'ART, 2000, the Standard Bank Young Artist Award for Visual Art, 2003, the Rockefeller Bellagio Creative Arts Fellow, 2014, and the Mbokodo Award, 2015. Her work was recently published in Phaidon's 'Great Women Artists' which features over 400 artists from throughout art history, from the 15th century to the present day.

Marlon SWAI is a writer, researcher and performance artist who lectures in Anthropology at the University of Cape Town. One aspect of his research evaluates how youth movements like hip hop simultaneously supplement and critique formal education. His work attempts to connect the dots between African-derived diasporic expressive practices like hip hop and reggae to explore their collective potential for galvanising Pan-African collaboration toward social justice, specifically with regards to issues around healthy/toxic masculinities, internalised oppression and the politics of representation. His recent publications include 'Mental Mobilities and Belonging to the Hip Hop Nation' in (eds.) Nyamnjoh, F., Umeya, K., & Hazama, I. (2019). *Citizenship in Motion: South African and Japanese scholars in conversation.* Langaa RPCIG. Swai's interest in transformative pedagogy was recognised with the University of Cape Town's honouring him with the 2020 Distinguished Teachers Award.

Noriko TAHARA is Professor of Social Anthropology at Shitennoji University in Osaka. In addition to having received her academic training in the sociology of medicine, she is also a practising pharmacist. Tahara has carried out fieldwork among the Asante people in central Ghana since 1993, as well as having conducted research with Alur communities in north-western Uganda since 2001. Among other projects at these sites, she has led an investigation into the value ascribed to personal archives and material inheritance among inhabitants of leprosariums. Her recent publications include 'Creation of Cooperativity through Memorial Rituals for the Dead: Ritual Citizenship among the Alur in the Republic of Uganda' in I. Hazama, K. Umeya and F. B. Nyamnjoh (eds), *Citizenship in Motion: South African and Japanese Scholars in Conversation* (2019, Bamenda: Langaa RPCIG) and 'Resilience of Healing: Infant's Disease of *Asram* in the Asante in Ghana' in *School of Global Humanities and Social Sciences, Nagasaki University* Vol. 6.

Toshiki TSUCHITORI is a Ph.D. candidate at the Graduate School for Intercultural Studies, Kobe University. He is also a JSPS Research Fellow and teaches part-time at Shitennoji University. He majors in cultural anthropology and folklore, and has been conducting research on contemporary folk religion in Sado Island, Niigata Prefecture, Japan. His recent publications include 'The Discussion about the Problem on the Return of Ashes through "The Human Bone Incident in Faculty of Letters, Hokkaido University": Colonialism and Academic Research' (2019, *Shitennoji University Bulletin* 68: 353–367, in Japanese), '"Tsukimono" and Marriage Discrimination:as Compared with Studies of Buraku' (2019, *Shitennoji University Bulletin* 67: 427-442) and 'A Research Note on the Intangible Culture Assets in Kesennuma City (III)', co-authored with Takuro Aizawa, Kiyoshi Umeya and Yukio Shyoji (2016, *Study and Education of Regional Design* 7: 75–83).

Kiyoshi UMEYA is Professor of Social Anthropology at the Graduate School for Intercultural Studies, Kobe University, and Visiting Professor at the University of Cape Town (2019–2020). He co-edited *Citizenship in Motion: South African and Japanese Scholars in Conversation* (2019, Bamenda: Langaa RPCIG). His recent publications include 'What is the Source of Power?: A Case of the Evangelized Witch in Eastern Uganda' (2019, *Journal of Intercultural Studies* 52: 29–52), 'The Gospel Sounds like the Witches' Spell: Ethnographic Accounts of Jopadhola, Eastern Uganda' (2019, *Kindai* 120: 1–44), 'Feast to Send-off the Dead: With Special Reference to the Jopadhola of Eastern Uganda.' in Bozena Gierek and Wojciech Kosior (eds) *Feast as a Mirror of Social and Cultural Changes* (2020, San Diego: AEcademic Publishing) and *The Gospel Sounds like the Witch's Spell: Dealing with Misfortune among the Jopadhola of Eastern Uganda* (2022, Bamenda: Langaa RPCIG). Email: umeya@people.kobe-u.ac.jp

Dedication

This book is dedicated to Professor Harry Garuba, our colleague, mentor and dear friend.

And, to all those who lost their lives in the Great Sendai Earthquake of 2011 and the Covid-19 pandemic.

Acknowledgement

The research that has resulted in this book was supported by the JSPS and NRF Bilateral Programme, 'Human Resilience in the face of man-made and natural disaster in Japan and South Africa: Ethnographic Perspective(2019-2021)'. The publication of this book was generously supported by KAKENHI (22H00920, 22H03828, 22H00035). Our appreciation goes to Mr Shigeru Sugawara, the mayor of Kesennuma City, and the officers of Kesennuma, who inspired the book. We are particularly grateful to Mr Yukio Shoji, the OB of the officer of Kesennuma, for arranging our excursion. The front cover image of the book is courtesy of Berni Searle (© Berni Searle).

Table of Contents

Chapter 1

Introduction: Towards Calmness after the Turmoil

Tamara Enomoto, Marlon Swai, Kiyoshi Umeya and Francis B. Nyamnjoh

I

This book grew out of our bilateral exchange project of JSPS (Japan Society for Promotion of Sciences) and NRF (National Research Foundation) of the Republic of South Africa. The project was conceived of at the tail end of another collaboration around the question of citizenship. At that time, South Africa's 'mother city', Cape Town, had just come into the global spotlight as being the first city in the world to almost run out of water, a crisis that exacerbated its plethora of socio-economic and environmental problems. Organically participants in this research collective began to reflect on the various points of overlap between Japan and South Africa with regards to how we deal with such massively impactful events, especially given the international reputation Japanese and South African people have earned for having survived some of the most catastrophic events in human history – man-made and natural disasters alike.

These conversations around surviving and contending with catastrophe crystalised during our visit to Kesennuma city, Miyagi prefecture, Japan, when we were at the final stage of a predecessor project (a bilateral exchange project led by Francis B. Nyamnjoh and Hazama Itsuhiro; see Hazama, Umeya and Nyamnjoh 2019) which involved the majority of the current project members. When visiting the city, Mr Sigeru Sugawara, the mayor of Kesennuma city, raised his concern about the use of the term 'resilience' by the Japanese government. 'The government has come to use "resilience" in the sense of '*kyojin* (fortitude),' he said.

Kesennuma is one of the areas hardest hit by the Great East Japan Earthquake. Extremely difficult policy disputes emerged immediately after the earthquake, including whether to build a high-tide embankment to protect the area from future tsunamis, whether to keep the tide embankment as low as possible (some even claimed that it was unnecessary) or whether to prioritise the livelihoods of people that have long lived with the sea (e.g., fishing). In such an atmosphere, the term '*kyojin*' seemed to align with the policy direction of the government at the time, which sought to raise the tide embankment as its primary objective. Moreover, the term '*kyojin*' seemed to somehow divert attention away from the enormous suffering that the people of Kesennuma had to face in the earthquake's aftermath. According to a survey conducted in 2017, about 150,000 evacuees had lost their homes and 50,000 were still living in temporary housing (still in February 2022, 38,139 evacuees and 15,516 live in temporary housing) (Reconstrution Agency 2022). To many, the term '*kyojin*' obscured the overwhelming damage and sense of loss that the Kesennuma residents still had to confront.

After returning from Kesennuma we began to seriously consider formulating another project, hinging on the idea of resilience. A rigorous debate ensued, with a general sentiment of scepticism around how the term gets deployed both by the state and in popular parlance. It was one of our graduate student contributors, Olivia Joanes in particular, who raised the concern that the notion of resilience and how it gets circulated is all too often experienced as an imposition that can exert unwanted and unjust pressure on communities struggling to contend with catastrophe that results in a double bind. To label communities' suffering from a man-made or natural disaster as resilient, argued Joanes, reproduces a form of violence especially against the backdrop of historical discrimination, systemic poverty, and disease and illness related to environmental racism and classism. What amplifies the violent nature of such an act of labelling is that the actors 'patting' such communities on the proverbial back, most often do so from a position of relative safety and security in terms of their proximity (physical and otherwise) to the impacts of the catastrophe. Therefore 'resilience' seemed to her a cruel word for those who find themselves facing insurmountable challenges precisely because the term is premised on the idea that such challenges can and should be overcome by individuals and collectives at the coalface of disaster. This move is often used as a way of relinquishing those people and institutions who are endowed with the means to add relief, or take charge of preventing crisis in the first place.

This critique resonated deeply with testimonies we heard in Kesennuma, many of which echoed a discomfort with the official rhetoric which tended to overemphasise the ability of the people of the city to restore it to its original state while simultaneously justifying the reduction of national and local government assistance toward these efforts. As a research collective we found several generative linkages between this set of tensions in Kesennuma and the predicament of the post-apartheid era most notoriously characterised by the set of discourses that burden the most vulnerable populations with having to overcome the 'trauma' caused by colonialism, anthropogenic violence or policies of apartheid. Similarly, the description of the black majority in South Africa as resilient has all too often been accompanied by an uncomfortable optimism that their trauma would be naturally healed without any substantive political economic resolutions. Ultimately, in the ensuing series of dialogues and debates resilience emerged as a complex and generative lens through which to think through some of the most salient questions of our time. Little did we know at the time that our forays into reflecting on 'resilience' were more prescient than we could even imagine as we were about to enter an era that would forever alter how we think about human responses to events of large-scale impact.

II

In *Rejiriensu No Shoso* (Aspects of Resilience: Challenge from the Perspective of Human History) (Nara and Inamura 2018) – a textbook of the Open University of Japan published in 2018, the two editors noted that the ambiguity of the word 'resilience' is a problem; even when limited to the field of disaster resilience, 'It is used with different meanings depending on the person ... However, there was a common understanding that resilience is an important concept in thinking about the future of a society. Therefore, we decided that for the time being, resilience should be broadly defined as "the flexible ability to survive crisis and adversity"' (Inamura and Nara 2018: 6).

Such a broad definition may be criticised by some, who argue that the term should be used only in the context of disaster-responsive social capital (Aldrich 2012), or by those who claim that academic terminologies should be defined as clearly and precisely as possible. However, constant indexicality and reflexivity exist as characteristics of language (Garfinkel 1967; Mehan and Wood 1975; Leiter 1980;

Hamamoto 1985: 114–117; Zeitlyn 1990). However, it is a common feature for a research project on a policy 'buzzword' to change the initial meaning of the term. New meanings and usages that were not originally imagined may be proposed, meanings of a term may be expanded or narrowed, and terms that originally had positive meanings may be used to indicate negative meanings. Occasionally, a phenomenon of reversal occurs in which the misuse of a term becomes accepted more widely.

Clifford Geertz wrote in his famous paper, 'Thick Description: Toward an Interpretive Theory of Culture', what often happens when certain ideas burst upon the intellectual landscape with a tremendous force. Although everyone at first 'snaps them up as the open sesame … crowding out almost everything else for a while' (Geertz 2000:3),

> After we have become familiar with the new idea, however, after it has become part of our general stock of theoretical concepts, our expectations are brought more into balance with its actual uses, and its excessive popularity is ended. …They try to apply it and extend it where it applies and where it is capable of extension; and they desist where it does not apply or cannot be extended. It becomes, if it was, in truth, a seminal idea in the first place, a permanent and enduring part of our intellectual armory. But it no longer has the grandiose, all-promising scope, the infinite versatility of apparent application, it once had. The second law of thermodynamics, or the principle of natural selection, or the notion of unconscious motivation, or the organization of the means of production does not explain everything, not even everything human, but it still explains *something* [our own]; and our attention shifts to isolating just what that something is, to disentangling ourselves from a lot of pseudoscience to which, in the first flush of its celebrity, it has also given rise (Geertz 2000: 3–4).

Resilience apparently seems to be what Geertz would say 'everyone snaps them up as the open sesame … crowding out almost everything else for a while' (Geertz 2000: 3). While it may take time for the debate to quiet down, it is also an opportunity to test the possibilities of the concept with respect to various themes and topics.

For this book, the editors did not ask the project members to share a detailed definition of the term 'resilience' and requested them to freely draw upon and discuss the topics that they are focused on using the term 'resilience'. In some chapters, it is generally assumed that 'most definitions emphasize a capacity for successful adaptation in the face of disturbance, stress, or adversity' (Norris et al. 2008: 129). However, other chapters suggest different usages of the term, such as 'resilience of witchcraft', 'resilience of postcolonial' and 'resilience of apartheid' in describing the situation in which something that may have been previously thought to be undesirable or have declined is persistently reinstated and revived. The reader is encouraged to assume that the concept of resilience may be used in different ways in each chapter and, if possible, scrutinise the scope of their usage that is implied.

III

This book consists of five parts. Part I presents competing genealogies of the resilience concept. It focuses in particular, firstly, on the discourse embedded in international policy because it is in this global political arena that we see the extent to which the concept of resilience matters to a great number of people around the world and, secondly, on interconnecting local and global hierarchies of resilient structures of inequalities and poverty at the service of power and privilege. In Chapter 2, Tamara Enomoto aims to introduce some basic criticisms of this concept in the development and humanitarian sector and to provide some points for discussion as to its use. Since the 2000s, the term 'resilience' has flourished in international policy documents in a wide range of areas, including development, disaster risk reduction, climate change adaptation, conflict resolution and peace building. Aid donors have created funding schemes to promote or improve the resilience of populations in the global South, including Africa, and local and international aid agencies have claimed to incorporate the idea of resilience into their operations. Academics in African studies have also been quick to develop research projects surrounding this concept, purporting to have expert knowledge on African people's potential to be resilient. As the global choir championing the idea of 'resilience' increased in volume, a body of studies criticising the resilience concept also emerged. Since the concept of resilience seems to have been mainstreamed as the dominant discourse in the development and humanitarian sector had been transformed by the end of the 1990s, Enomoto's chapter first examines in detail the transition of the dominant discourses of development, and then reflect on the criticisms of the term and suggest the possibilities and difficulties of using the concept. While affirming the critics' view that the resilience thinking tends to ignore structural injustices and material causes of suffering, and to legitimise measures to maintain a state of stability at lower material levels in the global South, and arguing that such thinking cannot escape the criticism that it is part of racist and racialised discourses and practices in the development and humanitarian sector, Enomoto questions critics' static view of the concept of resilience. She points out that based on such a static understanding of the concept, its diffusion is often perceived as a monolithic process, enabling the creation of resilient subjects and, hence, the possibility of various actors unconsciously transforming or consciously manipulating the semantic content of the concept tends to be overlooked. While the legitimacy of the term 'resilience' may be enhanced and the stability of semantic content may be strengthened through the process, there is also the possibility that the semantic content of this concept may be diffused or transformed by the conscious and unconscious actions of a wide range of actors. Conversely, the outcome of the battle over the semantic content of a particular concept depends on the power relations in the arena in which it takes place. In view of the post-Black Lives Matter move to rethink racist structures, systems, terminology, concepts, practices and attitudes in the areas of development, conflict resolution and peace building, she suggests that we may need to be conscious of our goals and the feasibility of achieving them in using the concept of resilience in our scholarly works.

In Chapter 3, Francis Nyamnjoh takes his cue from Enomoto's comprehensive exploration of the concept of resilience to draw attention to the resilience of systemic, structural or institutional inequalities and the interconnecting global and local hierarchies that sustain such inequalities and the tokenism of their transcendence despite repeated attempts by their victims to effectively undo them. He argues that a closer look at the production and institutionalisation of structures of inequality and skewed power relations is necessary in understanding how the ambitions of dominance and interests of the elite few seek to mitigate, neutralise or render invisible the otherwise valiant efforts or resilience of the subjugated and the marginalised majority against victimhood. Nyamnjoh uses Covid-19 as food for thought to critically review prevalent and conventional teleological modernist neoliberal assumptions about and usages of the notion of resilience. Such assumptions seem to take attention away from the power of resilient inequalities and injustices while deceptively encouraging the overdramatisation of the delusory power of ordinary folks to transform and transcend their circumstances with the benevolence and active assistance, supposedly, of the very same oppressive, repressive and suppressive elite, who, though not being a monolith, have structural power and privilege in common. The chapter argues that resilience as an empowerment or recognition of human agency for the overwhelming majority of ordinary folks the world over is possible not through mimicry, elite outsourcing of blame, prescriptiveness and trickledown munificence, but only to the extent that deeply embedded systemic – covert, tacit and everyday – inequalities are comprehensively and systematically excavated, deactivated and reconfigured in accordance with the logic and humility of incompleteness and conviviality. To transcend perennial elite domination that has effectively neutralised productive contestation by ordinary folks, the chapter calls for carefully negotiated and inclusive action, creativity, innovative and convivial modes of solidarity beyond the irrational ecstasy of ephemeral euphoria and exuberance.

Part II discusses the ways in which the notion of resilience emerges in the public discourses surrounding large scale disruptive events such as natural disasters and disease outbreaks.

In Chapter 4, Toru Hamaguchi's moving record of the rich discourse of storyteller in Awaji Island – that was narrated in front of the research team directly in the excursion by the man who actually experienced the fury of the natural disaster near the epicentre of the Great Hanshin-Awaji Earthquake – conveys both the sorrow and strength of human beings in the face of natural disasters.

The Hokudan Earthquake Memorial Park, located near the seismic centre of the Great Hanshin-Awaji Earthquake that occurred in 1995, was developed in an attempt to convey the experience of the earthquake. The storytelling is managed by *Kataribe* (storyteller), someone who was involved in the rescue operation as a volunteer fire brigade member for the affected Hokudan-cho, and his family members, including himself, who were victims of the earthquake. His discourse is focused on his experience as a disaster victim and his work in the volunteer fire brigade. He provides information on the local residents commonly shared by the volunteer fire brigade members about how the damage was minimised and the importance of the relationship between the volunteer fire brigade and the residents. However, the number of people joining the volunteer fire brigade is decreasing, which might be linked to the residents' decreasing consciousness. These reductions have a large impact on disaster resilience.

In Chapter 5, Noriko Tahara sheds light on struggles and pain experienced by patients with Hansen's Disease (HD), thereby highlighting the resilience of human-life dignity in weakness via the voice and imagination of 'different others'.

Modern society, originating in 17th-century Europe, began by alleviating and eliminating diseases and mental illness. It was an essential step to establish a civil society and a capitalist mode of production. Control of the spread of HD began in the early 20th century in Japan with forced quarantine and social isolation, which continued for about 90 years, contrary to global trends. HD is a chronic infectious disease where the skin and peripheral nerves are affected by Mycobacterium leprae. Excluding 'different others', such as those with an infectious disease, was a typical way of stabilising society. Moreover, it is challenging to resist the notion of 'protecting society from the dangerous'. The attitude of 'intolerance to different things' is prevailing, heightened by the exclusion of the sick during the COVID-19 pandemic. Thus, the chapter examines the activities of people with HD, deprived of various human rights under a compulsory quarantine policy. They engaged in various labour and cultural activities and interactions with the local community, thereby re-questioning their relationship with others.

Part III discusses social systems and resilience.

In Chapter 6, Minga Kongo examines the strategies residents of Khayelitsha township have employed to adapt to Cape Town's water crisis. Although the dreaded Day Zero was narrowly avoided, the chapter attempts to apprehend the ways in which the memory of the crisis continues to shape the community's understandings of and lived reality in relation to water. South Africa's challenges around water scarcity are daunting, and understanding adaptation practices in contexts in which communities are dependent on municipal water services is crucial. The chapter analyses the notion of adaptation as a heuristic through which to imagine resilience with regards to water access, particularly the ways in which adaptation prevails as the only route to survival in the face of the unequal distribution of water resources in informal settlements.

In Chapter 7, Gaku Moriguchi analyses the notion of African citizenship in the aspect of both resilience and resistance in the modern Ugandan societal context. He first explores the duality and multiplicity of African citizenship by critically looking at the Mamdani's text of *Citizen and Subject* (1996) and reflecting on the national and social condition of Uganda under the Museveni's regime. He then reviews three ethnographic studies on mourning the dead from the viewpoint of ritual citizenship, which were asserted by Tahara (2018). The notion of 'African resilience' will be discussed by referring to the African subjectivities which are ritually motivated and modified.

In Chapter 8, from an autoethnographic perspective, Kharnita Mohamed writes in an affective, vulnerable mode to explore resilience in the midst of COVID-19. The chapter finds resilience to be an inadequate concept, often used to describe continuity in the face of overwhelming privation, and Mohamed offers a meditation on the extent to which this concept places undue expectations on subjugated populations. The chapter exposes the fallacy of resilience theorising when expressed through the massification of grief and death, and it demonstrates painfully the ways that not everyone survives to be resilient. Paying attention to what it felt like to continue, to endure and become during the first few months of COVID-19, the essay interweaves themes such as pandemic subjectification, temporality, academic labour, love, embodiment, sociality, race and vulnerability.

Chapter 9 features a series of photographs by Cape Town visual artist Berni Searle. The photographs punctuate the volume with a moment of visceral archiving. The series was taken during the aftermath of one of the most devastating fires that the City of Cape Town has experienced in recent history. Particularly for the University of Cape Town community which sustained enormous damages, not least among those was the ruination of the beloved African Studies library. Searle went to great lengths to bring us to the coalface of that destruction and in her masterful capturing of a tower of knowledge brought to ash, beckons the audience to reckon with the fragility of the human pursuit to amass knowledge. It also forces us to take stock of the compoundedness of crises in this moment, considering that this event occurred in the midst of a global pandemic in a city that almost ran out of water just a few years prior. All of this on a campus that has not had a 'normal' academic year for the better part of a decade as it, just like to many of the institutions, cities and countries documented in this volume, seems to find itself in a constant state of disaster management. In this space of reimagining the artist asks serious questions about 'What it means to be the "custodians" of knowledge. Who builds and contributes to it? What is the meaning of heritage in the context of university architecture and its ruination? How can heritage be reconceptualized in this moment? What is knowledge and whose knowledge is given prominence especially as it pertains to archives from the continent represented in the African studies library?' Therefore, the collection of photographs presented midway through this book are riddled with the questions that permeate this volume just as they offer up opportunities to not only rebuild but reconceptualise the archive and its meaning to people far beyond the confines of the university.

Part IV discusses resilience in relation to art, ritual and agency.

In Chapter 10, Marlon Swai examines resilience in the context of educational justice struggles in South Africa. The chapter provides several historical precedents out of South Africa's long history of struggle for justice in education that showcase the ways in which artists and activists have brought about more equitable learning conditions for the country's most vulnerable student populations. The chapter contemplates the forms of resilience that are being demanded of students when continually being placed in the position to endure the kinds of learning barriers they encounter, especially in the face of stubborn forms of violence including structural inequalities in the education system which can be seen to culminate in several aspects of a general crisis confronting the country as a whole. Namely the environmental crisis, the global problem of race or anti-blackness, more specifically, and the pervasive and centuries-old catastrophe of gender-based violence to name but three. The chapter finally describes and analyses the work of a number of artist/activists who are responding to the current crises and leans on their work to ask whether the powerful anti-colonial movements of the past, which have enjoyed much needed resurgences in the last decades and which have inspired the current decolonial wave, can still adequately prepare our learners to face this current moment?

In Chapter 11, Maho Araki explores the tension between continuity and change in traditional Japanese folk performing arts. In

Japan, as is true elsewhere, the arts have always been influenced by external pressures as much as they have been reinforced by internal norms and values. Taking that this emic/etic delineation is heuristic at best, this chapter grapples with the ways in which communities of performance practitioners contend with this tension in the contemporary moment. The central objective of which is preservation and a commitment to tradition. Given the fierce debates around the encroachment of modernity on tradition around the world, this preoccupation is not surprising, especially amidst the rapid change currently taking place the world over. However, as we also understand from examples of tension between modernity and tradition around the world, these moments often represent a complex of gains and losses for individuals, communities and larger social formations. In many cases, the breaking of tradition gives way to an inclusivity not previously possible. For example, as is the case in Iou Jima and Kesennuma, where inclusion in certain dance and drumming schools was previously tied to familial lineage. Araki's chapter centres on the myriad implications of transformations that have taken place with regards to the ways in which folk performing arts knowledge and practice is transferred cross-generationally, and the strategies all stakeholders are adopting to make sense of and cope with that change by taking cues from discussions of community resilience, such as diversity of scales, unequal relationships in community and gradation of decision making and actions related to it.

In Chapter 12, Toshiki Tsuchitori considers what resilience towards depopulation entails; to this end, the case of the S Festival, held in the S Village on Sado Island in the Niigata Prefecture, Japan. In general, the term 'resilience' is often used to describe recovery and countermeasures concerning sudden shocks (e.g., natural disasters). The concept of resilience is used in several other contexts beyond natural disasters. This chapter explores depopulation as a form of long-term shock and discusses the recovery capacity necessary for any village system within a depopulated village.

In Japan, the phenomenon of depopulation has been expanding since the period of high economic growth in the 1960s. In the 1990s, Akira Ohno proposed the concept of 'marginal villages', which led to discussions in two different directions: regenerating depopulated villages or taking realistic measures after accepting the depopulation of villages. S Village is located in Sado City, Niigata Prefecture. In this study's survey site, it can aptly be called a marginal village because of its declining birth rate and ageing population. Under such circumstances, the people of S Village have included drum beating as a performing art at their festival. Why do these people make such seemingly pointless changes to the festival that have little effect on attracting tourists or migrants? It is thought that community values are enhanced by the establishment and maintenance of regional relationships in depopulated villages, even with those outside the villages.

The S Festival helps villagers maintain connections with people outside the village, and those that have left the village. The addition of drum-beating to the performing arts at the festival is considered a change that could strengthen the festival's effect. The importance of resilience to village depopulation lies not just in maintaining relationships between people but also in maintaining relationships centred upon the land within S Village. The relationships between the people of this land are considered an essential factor within the village system. Tsuchitori argues that the S Festival strengthens the resilience ability of village depopulation to maintain essential elements of the system even after the village disappears. In this case, the resilience towards depopulation is considered a function of maintaining regional ties, including with those outside the village, as a form of depopulation progresses.

In Chapter 13, Kolawole Gbolahan presents research on the socio-musical significance associated with labrosones (a generic term for lip-vibrated wind instruments, i.e., horns and trumpets) across various locations on the African continent. The term 'resilience, within the parameters of this chapter refers to the material strength and deeper layers of meaning associated with labrosones, their sounds, and how these associations have continuously contributed to their relevance unto the present'. The chapter scrutinises examples of labrosone instruments around the theoretical triad of socio-musical significance, cultural symbolism and material agency, tracking the historical journey of several specimens, considering the diverse ideas associated with them in different cultural traditions.

Part V builds on work in previous chapters that seek out conceptualisations of the resilience concept other than those deployed in the service of hegemony. Chapters in this section thereby delve into instantiations of the resilience concept which are taken up by communities of interest in order to critique hegemony by recognising and calling out the stubborn nature of oppressive and regressive cultural, socio-economic and political structurations.

In Chapter 14, Kiyoshi Umeya examines foreign workers in the Uber business in Cape Town, South Africa. Lockdowns that accompanied the spread of COVID-19 were catastrophic for the Uber business in Cape Town, causing it to shrink significantly. While several riots occurred and sporadic violent crimes were reported, organised xenophobic violent incidents, which were previously a cause of anxiety, decreased and no significant discrimination in government-sponsored testing or treatment was reported.

It appears that Uber drivers, while implementing various strategies, maintained their livelihoods by operating small businesses to transport local people to the extent permitted, sometimes eluding the law. In addition, they received food assistance from family members residing outside the country to whom they had previously sent remittances. While xenophobic elements persist, this chapter demonstrates the vitality of people desperately attempting to make a living. Although people employed various strategies during lockdowns, this could not be examined through fieldwork at the time of writing. What life will be like post-COVID-19 remained uncertain at the time of writing. In post-apartheid South Africa, the existence of social and psychological barriers to cultural others remains an issue. Foreign workers tend to cluster due to convenience, patron–client relationships, security reasons and economic factors, which contributed to the formation and maintenance of a characteristic ethnoscape with clear boundaries with others. Stereotyped categories in the ethnoscape tend to function as a wall between the two and, when turned negative, form an environment that fosters conflict and violence. Umeya finds that this situation was what was predicted in the Human Sciences Research Council's (HSRC) 2008 analysis on violence. Finally, the chapter examines resilience as a form of 'recuperative ability', investigating positive resilience and xenophobic resilience.

In Chapter 15, Itsuhiro Hazama focuses on the positive character of social communication. In situations where East African pastoralists are raiding outsiders, the improvisation of face-to-face identities transcends the formal ethnicity that encroaches on different cultural communities.

Ethnicity is a controversial issue. It is not limited to the ethnic generation of African pastoralists. Absolute loyalty to the community

– a homogeneous and hard sense of belonging that the people in the territory rely on – is the pillar and supports the system of rule even in the nation building of modern Europe. The state and ethnic group as a nepotism machine create formal ethnic identities, and begin a struggle against the outsider and a conflict of destruction. People put a brake on the obviousness of formal ethnic identities during coalitional lethal violence and engage in interpersonal negotiation over sparing enemies. Raiding is a momentum that makes it possible to re-soften ethnicity through the dehabituation of the sense of belonging based on territories. Identity generation in the face-to-face interaction East African pastoralists practice appears to open the door to possible solutions in the world of today full of struggles and destruction caused by identity politics.

In Chapter 16, Zuziwe Msomi, reflects on the emergence of critical whiteness studies as a contested field of enquiry in the South African scholarly terrain. The chapter examines the significance and implications of the shift in the academy to focusing on the socio-economically dominant group as the centre of its research agenda (dominant refers to those who are phenotypically and culturally white as those terms are understood in the South African context). This shift, which took root in the 1990s, was a necessary step toward understanding and ending racism because it dared to 'turn the camera' on the camera man. The chapter contends that, although foundational texts on what is now referred to as whiteness studies produced by black authors abounded long before, it is the 1990s academic shift from which most contemporary whiteness studies work draws, thus placing authorship under an equal amount of scrutiny. Resilience is invoked here both in terms of the staying power of exclusionary politics and ideologies within the whiteness studies field, but also the resilience of the intellectual works produced by invisibilised black authors. The chapter ultimately surfaces that hitherto excluded scholarship as a critical archive from which to draw in order to more deeply apprehend and thereby decolonise whiteness.

While editing this book, the COVID-19 pandemic struck the world. Among other things, the global pandemic highlighted the seemingly exponential increase in the intensity of global-scale events in the last half-decade. These global-scale events have also challenged the very resilience of the resilience concept itself and are necessitating a serious revision of how the idea gets deployed. The sheer diversity of themes and subject areas covered in this book is an indication of how pervasive the concept has become in our popular and professional discourses and, yet, the very conditions pressuring its utility are also bringing to the surface some of the deepest challenges facing humanity currently. For example, the insights provided in some of our chapters may offer a point of departure for thinking about why environmental disasters and exploitative political economies continuously expose inadequate responses to catastrophe on the part of states and other large power brokers. The critiques expressed by some of the authors, additionally, point to the fact that such inadequate ways of addressing disaster and suffering hinge on a demand for resilient individuals when a far more effective set of responses are proving to revolve around mass mobilisation and relations of solidarity as the internationalisation of the Black Lives Matter and #MeToo movements emphatically demonstrate. The sum of the parts of this book may ultimately point to the call for worlds that do not produce suffering but instead nurture social systems that celebrate resilient forms of care and creative resistance.

References

Aldrich, Daniel P. (2012) *Building Resilience: Social Capital in Post-Disaster Recovery*. Chicago: The University of Chicago Press. Garfinkel, Halord.

Garfinkel, H. (1967) *Studies in Ethnomethodology*, Englewood Cliffe: Prentice-Hall.

Geertz, Clifford (2000) *The Interpretation of Cultures*, New York: Basic books.

Hamamoto Mitsuru (1985) 'The cost of cultural relativism', *Risō*, Vol. 627, pp. 105–121 (in Japanese).

Hazama, Itsuhiro, Umeya, K. and Francis B. Nyamnjoh (eds) (2019) *Citizenship in Motion: South African and Japanese Scholars in Conversation*, Bamenda: Langaa RPCIG.

Inamura, Tetsuya and Nara, Yumiko (2018) 'Foreword', in Yumiko Nara and Tetsuya Inamura (eds) *Rejiriensu No Shoso: Jinruishiteki Shiten Karano chyosen* (Aspects of Resilience: Challenge from the Perspective of Human History) Hoso Daigaku, NHK Shyuppan (in Japanese).

Nara, Yumiko and Inamura, Tetsuya (eds) (2018) *Rejiriensu No Shoso: Jinruishiteki Shiten Karano Chyosen* (Aspects of Resilience: Challenge from the Perspective of Human History) Hoso Daigaku, NHK Shyuppan (in Japanese).

Norris, Fran H., Susan P. Stevens, Betty Pfefferbaum, Karen F. Wyche and Rose L. Pfefferbaum (2008) 'Community resilience as a metaphor, theory, set of capacities, and strategy for disaster readiness', *Am J Community Psychol* No. 41, pp. 127–150, DOI 10.1007/s10464-007-9156-6.

Leiter, K. (1980) *The Primer of Ethnomethodology,* Oxford: Oxford University Press.

Mamdani, M. (1996) *Citizen and Subject: Contemporary Africa and the Legacy of Late Colonialism*, Princeton, NJ: Princeton University Press.

Mehan, H. and Wood, H. (1975) *The Reality of Ethnomethodology*, New York: John Wiley and Sons.

Reconstrution Agency (2022) 'The number of the evacuees in the country, dated 25 February 2022', https://www.reconstruction.go.jp/topics/main-cat2/sub-cat2-1/20220225_kouhou1.pdf (last accessed 24 March 2022).

Zeitlyn, David E. (1990) 'Professor Garfinkel visits the soothsayers: Ethnomethodology and Mambila Divination', *Man* (n.s.), 25 (4): 654–666.

Part 1

Genealogies of the Resilience Concept

Chapter 2

Genealogies of Resilience in the Development and Humanitarian Sector: Potentials and Difficulties

Tamara Enomoto

1. Introduction

The term 'resilience' has been widely used in research and policy debate in the development and humanitarian sector since the 2000s. Government agencies, international organisations, non-governmental organisations (NGOs) and researchers have promoted resilience as a key concept in the sector, seeking to analyse the factors that may drive resilience and to devise measures to improve it. Some expect that the idea of resilience may have the potential to overcome existing problems of international policy debate, for example, the tendency to assume that people in the global South are powerless and helpless (Almedom and Tumwine 2008; FAO 2016).

The term has also been used extensively in domestic policy debates and practices in the global North in various fields, including disaster risk reduction (DRR – the resilience to bounce back after earthquakes, floods and nuclear power plant accidents), welfare (the resilience of care workers, of families of the mentally disabled and of abused children, etc.), education (educating children to become more resilient, etc.), business and labour (adapting to a changing business environment, adapting and recovering from stresses caused by a toxic work environment, etc.) and security and arms control (cyber-resilience against potential cyber-attacks, etc.). Although the meanings attached to the term are not always the same, they are often used to indicate some degree of ability to respond to, adapt to and recover from difficulties and suffering.

Much criticism of the concept of resilience has already emerged. For example, the United Kingdom's move to improve workers' resilience was criticised for its tendency to focus on the internal problems of individual workers while ignoring the fundamental structural factors that create the stress and difficulties to which workers are exposed (Bradley 2018; Traynor 2018). In the United

States, some have pointed out that calls for resilience in the face of racism became a coded way to shame people who speak out about injustice and to equate objecting to racism with weakness (National Public Media 2015).

This chapter focuses on the development and humanitarian sector and introduces some criticisms of the use of the resilience concept in the sector. It has been pointed out that the concept was mainstreamed in the sector in the 2000s, as the dominant discourse in policy debate in the sector had been transformed by the end of the 1990s. This chapter will first examine how the dominant discourses in the sector have been transformed since the mid-20th century, and seeks to understand how such transformation laid the foundation for the wide use of the term 'resilience'. It will then reflect on the criticisms of the term and suggest the potentials and difficulties of using the concept in the current critical juncture.

2. Changes in the Dominant Discourse in the Development and Humanitarian Sector

In 1946, roughly half a century before the concept of resilience took centre stage, the World Health Organisation (WHO) Constitution stated that the 'enjoyment of the highest attainable standard of health' was 'one of the fundamental rights of every human being without distinction of race, religion, political belief, economic or social condition' (WHO 1946). Underlying this assertion was the widely held view that science and modern medicine would ultimately modernise Southern states and populations (Pupavac 2008). The premise of modernisation was evident in the mainstream development theory in Western states in the 1950s and 1960s. Development was equated with economic development, urbanisation and industrialisation, while the spread of education and the penetration of liberal democracy were expected to transform pre-modern societies into modern ones. The lack of capital accumulation and technological innovation was seen as the main constraint to economic development, and state-led economic policies were devised to achieve import substitution industrialisation (Aghion and Bolton 1997; Pieterse 2009: 45–46). During the same period, Eastern countries also supported industrialisation under a state-led planned economy (Gilman 2003), and both the Eastern and Western blocks promoted state-led aid for economic development, especially selective aid to regimes close to their own blocs in order to expand their influence through aid (Gilman 2003).

However, by the 1970s, previous development theories began to be criticised for not matching reality. The Declaration on the Establishment of a New International Economic Order (NIEO), adopted by the United Nations Special Session on Natural Resources in 1974, included the need for a fundamental reorganisation of the world order in such areas as international trade, international finance and technology transfer.[1]

On the other hand, Western states and the World Bank argued that investments in human capital were important and that development assistance should meet 'basic human needs' (BHN), such as health, education, nutrition, safe water and housing (Kapoor 2008: 156–158). At the same time, criticism against modern society, industrialisation and its negative impact on ecosystems was growing, and structuralism and post-structuralism took root in various fields of study, prompting scholars to critically analyse modern ideas. Against this backdrop of scepticism about modernity and attention to environmental issues, it was widely asserted that development projects should not try to instil Western materialistic values in the global South and should not take the form of providing aid to Southern governments for material development but should focus instead on meeting the BHNs by utilising people's own knowledge, resources and capacities (Delgado 1995: 4–5). It was now deemed a priority to use local resources to ensure primary health care (PHC)[2] rather than providing materials and technology to construct advanced medical facilities. Moreover, the oil crises of 1973 and 1979 increased awareness of the possibility that economic development in the global South would lead to competition for and depletion of natural resources, and generated the idea that the entire world should not necessarily emulate the model of industrialised countries.

Later, in the 1980s, the idea of BHN was sidelined, as the accumulated debt problem was increasingly seen as an urgent and paramount development issue. In response to this situation, the structural adjustment policies promoted by the International Monetary Fund (IMF) and the World Bank began to dominate development assistance (Paloni and Zanardi 2006: 2–3). As Southern states lost influence in international politics, the establishment of the NIEO was increasingly overshadowed.

In the late 1980s, however, structural adjustment policies came under criticism for not having triggered the recovery of economic growth in the global South and for negatively affecting the lives of the poor. In 1987–1988, the report of the United Nations Children's Fund (UNICEF), 'Human-Faced Structural Adjustment' (Cornia et al. 1987, 1988), criticised structural adjustment for not paying enough attention to its negative impact on vulnerable people. In promoting 'structural adjustment with a human face', UNICEF advocated the idea of 'selective primary health care', which focused on increasing the survival of people (especially children) in crisis situations that resulted from structural adjustment policies (Pupavac 2008). This approach, however, focused primarily on mere survival, which was a lower-level goal than the PHC of the 1970s and far lower than 'the highest attainable standard of health' enshrined in the 1946 WHO Constitution (Pupavac 2008).

Criticism against economically defined development and concerns over increased poverty under structural adjustment were further intertwined with environmental concerns. The World Commission on Environment and Development (commonly known as the Brundtland Commission)[3] launched its report in 1987 and advocated the concept of sustainable development as development that meets the needs of the present without compromising the ability of future generations to meet their own needs (World Commission on Environment and Development 1987). The report argued that economic and social development goals should be defined in light of their sustainability and that values should be promoted that keep consumption levels within an environmentally compatible range. There was now widespread recognition that development should be promoted in a long-term sustainable manner while taking the poor into account rather than simply pursuing economic growth and promoting economic policies without regard to their impact on the poor.

Criticism of development policies that centred on material development, industrialisation and economic growth continued and were further reinforced after the end of the Cold War. In the early 1990s, under the influence of neo-institutionalist economics,[4] aid agencies began to share the view that the market could not function by merely correcting the government's economic policies and that the government should not be simply minimised but rather should play its role properly. Addressing institutional aspects through judicial and legislative reforms, democratisation, capacity building of those working in public institutions and anti-corruption measures were deemed necessary to make the market properly function and reduce poverty.

Part of the reason for this attention to the institutions of aid-recipient countries was that the collapse of the Soviet Union and the end of the Cold War made it possible for Western countries to advocate democracy as something of universal value. Western countries claimed that democratisation of aid-recipient countries would be essential for effective development aid and tried to promote their democratisation by making it a conditionality of bilateral aid, including democratic elections and multi-party systems (Singer 1994).

The World Bank also became actively involved in legal and administrative reform to bring about transformation within aid-recipient states, despite having a mandate[5] not to intervene in political matters (Inoue 2006: 69–70). The 'Governance and Development' report published by the World Bank in 1992 defined governance as 'the manner in which power is exercised in the management of a country's economic and social resources for development' (World Bank 1992: 1). The report argued that governance in this sense was not 'political' as long as it was recognised in the context of resource allocation and poverty reduction and set out its policy of involvement in the field of governance. Following this report, the World Bank produced a strategy for combating corruption in 1997 (World Bank 1997a) and the World Development Report 1997 on the role of the state in a changing world (World Bank 1997b) as well as a strategy for public sector reform and strengthening governance in 2000 (World Bank 2000a) and the World Development Report 2002 on building institutions for markets (World Bank 2002). The World Bank recognised the role of the state in addressing market failures and improving equity, and advocated ensuring aid effectiveness and reducing poverty by addressing legal, judicial and anti-corruption measures.

In this context, it was deemed necessary for Southern states to have the will and ability to voluntarily take ownership of the formation and implementation of poverty reduction policies in a manner appropriate to their national contexts. For example, 'Towards the 21st Century: Contributions through Development Cooperation' (OECD DAC 1996), adopted by the OECD DAC in

1996, set a development goal of halving absolute poverty by 2015 and emphasised the need for developing states to take ownership to achieve this goal. Based on the agreement reached at the IMF–World Bank Joint Development Committee and the Interim Committee in September 1999, the IMF and the World Bank also decided that aid-recipient states themselves should prepare three-year Poverty Reduction Strategy Papers (PRSPs) that would identify the causes of poverty and strategies for poverty reduction in their own states; donors, international organisations, civil society and the private sector were also expected to be involved in the preparation and monitoring of PRSPs. Some donor countries and international organisations adopted a policy of 'selectivity' (Hout 2007), by which they would selectively provide aid to countries that exhibited good governance, good PRSP documents and their proper implementation.

However, as Graham Harrison (2004) argued, the focus on institutions and the emphasis on 'ownership' and 'partnership' does not necessarily mean that aid-recipient states would be allowed to make independent decisions about the direction and content of their policies. Instead of implementing policies as instructed or ordered by external agencies, aid-recipient states were now supposed to formulate and implement 'appropriate' policies in partnership with domestic and foreign actors and to take ownership of them; aid was to be provided selectively and preferentially to countries that demonstrated the will and ability to do so. Aid-recipient states were expected to transform the values and behaviours of people within the government through the process, while aid agencies and external 'experts' were assumed to be deeply embedded in policy-making and monitoring processes.

Moreover, the attention to institutions for development has been extended not only to the judiciary, the legislature and the executive powers in the countries of the global South but also to the whole of society. In 1998, Joseph Stiglitz, Senior Vice President and Chief Economist of the World Bank, delivered a speech titled 'Towards a New Paradigm for Strategies, Policies and Processes of Development', in which he argued that past attempts to introduce certain economic policies into the global South had failed because they were based on too narrow a concept of development, and that future new development paradigms should aim at catalysing change and transforming whole societies, and should involve the transformation of institutions and the creation of new capacities (Stiglitz 1998). It was now argued that trying to force the transformation of society as a whole on Southern populations would not be effective, and that participation by the global South and their consensus and ownership would be the key (Stiglitz 1998: 16). Empowering people at every stage and transforming the entire society from the level of individual minds and behaviours under their participation and ownership came to be seen as the central themes of development. At the same time, global, external and structural factors, such as the unequal relationship between the global North and South, were increasingly overshadowed in international policy debate on the causes of underdevelopment.

The United Nations Development Programme (UNDP) also recognised the minds, attitudes, behaviours and relationships of Southern individuals as the key to development. The annual Human Development Report (UNDP 1990), which UNDP began publishing in 1990, relied on Amartya Sen's concept of capability (Sen 1992)[6] to define human development as a process of expanding people's choices and argued that the goal of development should be the expansion of choices, not economic growth or mere satisfaction of basic needs. The report also argued that human development itself should be the goal of development rather than being positioned as complementary to economic development and proposed the Human Development Index (HDI) – a composite of statistics on factors, including life expectancy, years of schooling and national income per capita – as an indicator to measure the degree of human development.

The Millennium Development Goals (MDGs),[7] based on the Millennium Declaration adopted at the United Nations Millennium Summit in September 2000, called for the cooperation of diverse actors to achieve its eight goals (eradicate extreme poverty and hunger, achieve universal primary education, promote gender equality and empower women, reduce child mortality, improve maternal health, combat HIV/AIDS, malaria and other diseases, ensure environmental sustainability, and develop a global partnership for development) by 2015. The MDGs were generally supported by governments, international organisations and NGOs, and poverty reduction was brought to a central place in the policy debate on development. As Vanessa Pupavac (2008: 183–184) points out, while the 1946 WHO Constitution declared that 'the highest attainable standard of health' was a basic human right, the MDGs' approach was primarily based on the recognition that the aforementioned 'selective primary health care' – originally conceived as the minimum level of health care to ensure the survival of people (especially children) in crisis situations caused by structural adjustment policies – was a human right.

In addition, concepts such as capability and human development in the 1990s increasingly emphasised happiness and fulfilment based on individual values and subjectivities. In the 2000s, such subjective aspects were further emphasised, and attempts were made to formulate indicators that incorporated subjective aspects. For example, the World Bank's 2000 report, 'The Voices of the Poor', argued that for the world's poor, '[w]ealth and wellbeing are seen as different, and even contradictory ... Wellbeing and illbeing are states of mind and being. Wellbeing has a psychological and spiritual dimension as a mental state of harmony, happiness and peace of mind' (Narayan et al. 2000: 21, emphasis in original), underscoring the importance of well-being rather than wealth. The 2011 UN General Assembly resolution 'Happiness: Towards a Holistic Approach to Development'[8] also recognised that 'the gross domestic product indicator by nature was not designed to and does not adequately reflect the happiness and well-being of people in a country'. It also stated that 'unsustainable patterns of production and consumption can impede sustainable development' and recognised 'the need for a more inclusive, equitable and balanced approach to economic growth that promotes sustainable development, poverty eradication, happiness and well-being of all peoples'. The resolution also invited UN member states to 'pursue the elaboration of additional measures that better capture the importance of the pursuit of happiness and well-being in development with a view to guiding their public policies'.

The 2012 report of the United Nations Secretary-General's High-Level Panel on Global Sustainability also included a recommendation that the international community develop new indicators for sustainable development beyond GDP (United Nations Secretary-General's High-Level Panel on Global Sustainability 2012: 7, 14, 63, 85). In response, the UNDP indicated its willingness to consider revising the HDI and to develop more comprehensive indicators (Clark 2012). These developments resonated with the debate on the 'post-2015' development agenda as the deadline for achieving the

MDGs approached. Goals that would encompass a broader range of themes than the eight MDGs mentioned above were considered, and the resulting Sustainable Development Goals (SDGs) were adopted at the UN Sustainable Development Summit in September 2015.

As we have seen, by the end of the 1990s, the dominant discourse in the development circle was no longer about GDP growth, material modernisation, macroeconomic stability or a fundamental reorganisation of the world order. A widely shared view was that, for development, governments should develop and maintain the will and capacity to formulate and implement 'appropriate' policies to reduce poverty and social and economic disparities while exhibiting ownership of such policies and demonstrating partnership with internal and external actors. At the same time, psychological, behavioural and relational transformation at the individual and community level was deemed necessary to reduce poverty, and individual households were now expected to maintain their livelihoods in a sustainable manner by managing resources sufficient to meet their food security and immediate social welfare needs. While this transformation does not mean that the GDP concept entirely lost its significance in the policy debate on development or that material improvements were now completely neglected, the dominant discourse of the policy debate focused on non-material elements, such as improved governance, empowerment, capacity building and the transformation of values and behaviours, and the level of material expectations for Southern populations was significantly lowered, as was seen in the change in recognition of a human right to health care.

Moreover, since the 1990s, poverty, underdevelopment and governance deficiencies have been problematised as the key factors that would increase the risk or likelihood of violence and armed conflict (Hillier and Wood 2003: 34–35; OI 2005: 14; UN Millennium Project 2005: 183).[9] Development, conflict resolution and peace building came to be seen as having interdependent relationships, as exemplified by the statement in a 2005 report published by the Commission for Africa that '[c]onflict is one of Africa's classic vicious circles. There can be no development without peace, but there can be no peace without development' (Commission for Africa 2005: 25).[10] It was also widely argued that poverty reduction and transformation of Southern states and populations into partners in creating peaceful social change was essential to address the root causes of violence and conflicts in the global South.

The World Development Report 2000/2001 (World Bank 2000b) also linked development and peace issues, and supported the idea of development oriented towards the transformation of the values and capacities of Southern people and governments. The report made combating poverty a major theme and set out a policy to fight poverty in three dimensions: opportunity, empowerment and security. Here, too, the logic to put empowerment and the expansion of opportunity, rather than materialistic development, at the centre of the fight against poverty and to link it to security is explicitly expressed. A similar logic is evident in a 2005 report by the United Kingdom's Department for International Development (DFID 2005). The report stated that '[t]he most important functions of the state for poverty reduction are territorial control, safety and security, capacity to manage public resources, delivery of basic services, and the ability to protect and support the ways in which the poorest people sustain themselves' (DFID 2005: 7). It further argued that fragile states which could not or would not deliver core functions to the majority of their people were more likely to descend into instability and perpetuate regional conflicts (DFID 2005: 7, 10).

As pointed out by Vanessa Pupavac, understanding of war and social conflict as arising from internal problems in the global South had not prevailed internationally in the Cold-War period (Pupavac 2004: 153). Rather than personal or cultural attitudes, it was the actions of the First World that had been blamed for conflict in UN debates, dominated by the views of the communist bloc and the newly independent countries (Pupavac 2004: 153). In stark contrast to much of the Cold War policy debate, the view that internal problems of the global South are the root causes of conflict was more strongly proposed by Western policy circles from the 1990s onwards. As the Soviet bloc dissolved and the Non-Aligned movement lost much of the leverage it was once able to exert, a tendency to seek the source of violence and armed conflict in the global South within the internal problems of states, communities and individuals became increasingly prominent in the international arena (Pupavac 2004: 154–156).

The lines between development aid, humanitarian aid and political policy became blurred as 'peacetime' and conflict and post-conflict policy issues came to be seen as overlapping and interrelated. It was argued in the 1990s that humanitarian assistance should be planned and implemented in coordination and collaboration with development assistance and other policies to contribute to desired consequences such as peace and sustainable development, and that humanitarian aid based on the existing humanitarian principles such as neutrality, impartiality and independence could have negative impacts on achieving such consequences (Curtis 2001). The 'new humanitarianism', which held that humanitarian assistance should be provided with the utmost calculation and care so as not to harm the achievement of desired consequences and should be even withheld when it is likely to harm such achievement started to gain support among major aid organisations and donors (Curtis 2001).

3. Wide Use and Criticisms of the Resilience Concept

It was in the post-Cold War period that the concept of resilience started to gain traction in the development and humanitarian sector. The year 1990 also heralded the beginning of the International Decade for Natural Disaster Reduction (IDNDR) which focused on the role of vulnerability in disaster reduction. Although the Final report of the Scientific and Technical Committee of the IDNDR made no mention of the term 'resilience',[11] its Programme Forum, held in 1999, adopted the International Strategy for Disaster Reduction (ISDR), whose Secretariat extensively used the term 'resilience' in its preliminary report released in 2002 (ISDR 2002) and its final version of the report published in 2004 (ISDR 2004a, 2004b). While the preliminary version defined '[r]esilience/resilient' as '[t]he capacity of a system, community or society to resist or to change in order that it may obtain an acceptable level in functioning and structure. This is determined by the degree to which the social system is capable of organising itself, and the ability to increase its capacity for learning and adaptation, including the capacity to recover from a disaster' (ISDR 2002: 24), the final version defined '[r]esilience/ resilient' slightly differently, as '[t]he capacity of a system, community or society potentially exposed to hazards to adapt, by resisting or changing in order to reach and maintain an acceptable level of functioning and structure. This is determined by the degree to which the social system is capable of organizing itself to increase its capacity for learning from past disasters for better future protection and to improve risk reduction measures' (ISDR 2004a: 16–17, 2004b: 6). In

2005, the Hyogo Framework for Action 2005–2015: Building the Resilience of Nations and Communities to Disasters, agreed upon at the World Conference on Disaster Reduction, refereed to the definition adopted in the ISDR's final report in 2004.[12]

These definitions and similar ones have been widely used in policy circles in the development and humanitarian sector ever since,[13] and a great number of policy and scholarly documents have promoted resilience as one of the key concepts in addressing matters such as human development, poverty reduction, disaster risk reduction, peace building and provision of humanitarian aid. For instance, UNDP's 'Human Development Report 2014: Sustaining Human Progress: Reducing Vulnerabilities and Building Resilience' stated that resilience underpins any approach to securing and sustaining human development (UNDP 2014: 5). The report problematised vulnerabilities of '[h]undreds of millions of poor, marginalized or otherwise disadvantaged people', argued that 'failures to protect people against vulnerability are mostly a consequence of inadequate policies and poor or dysfunctional social institutions' (UNDP 2014: 16), called for the need to reduce vulnerability through creating more-responsive states, better public policies and changes in social norms, and argued that '[r]esponsive institutions and effective policy interventions can create a sustainable dynamic to bolster individual capabilities and social conditions that strengthen human agency – making individuals and societies more resilient' (UNDP 2014: 10).

Since its major debut in international policy debate in the development and humanitarian sector in the 2000s, the concept of resilience has received a wide range of criticism until today. Critics generally argue that the wide use of the concept of resilience since the 2000s was precipitated by the aforementioned shift in the dominant discourse in policy debate in the development and humanitarian sector from the GDP growth, material modernisation, macroeconomic stability or a fundamental reorganisation of the world order to internal and non-material transformation, such as improved governance, empowerment, capacity building and the transformation of norms, values and behaviours of individuals, communities and governments in the global South. The term 'resilience' started to gain traction in the development and humanitarian sector, exactly when such a shift had already materialised and the idea that the transformation of the whole of societies of Southern states had come to be seen as necessary not only to reduce poverty but also to prevent violence and conflict in the global South. Thus, the criticism against this concept has been accompanied by a critical examination of the dominant discourse on which it supposedly rests.

For example, Mark Duffield (2005, 2007, 2009, 2010) points out that concepts such as sustainable development and resilience are based on fundamentally different thinking from the 1960s pursuit of material development and modernisation and that the focus in resilience thinking is on enabling people of the global South to maintain a state of stability at lower material levels through self-reliance and to acquire and maintain resilience that enables them to respond and adapt to such events as disasters and conflicts. The anti-modernist and anti-materialist ideas behind the resilience concept has led to an excessive focus on non-material aspects and has diverted attention away from material causes of suffering. Coupled with the tendency in the international policy circle since the 1990s to seek root causes of underdevelopment and violence in internal dysfunctions, resilience thinking tends to focus and problematise the day-to-day of Southern individuals, communities and states and may lead to overly intrusive interventions into non-material elements, such as the hearts, minds, values and cultures of Southern populations. The resilience concept ignores or downplays global, structural, political and material causes of suffering, and its orientation is to shift the responsibility away from the state to the individuals and communities and thereby legitimise measures focused on pacification and containment without ensuring significant material development.[14]

Some critics also argue that although resilience thinking at first glance seems to focus on people's capability and power, it is in fact based on an assumption of general human vulnerability and tends to seek root causes and solutions in internal problems of states and populations. As mentioned in the Introduction section of this chapter, some advocates of this concept claim that the concept of resilience may enable an approach that overcomes the limitations of imagining Southern populations as powerless and that respects their autonomy and potential (Almedom and Tumwine 2008; FAO 2016). In contrast, some critics point out that the view that sees humans as vulnerable and the idea to seek to strengthen resilience are two sides of the same coin, and they problematise the logic that runs through both. For example, Frank Furedi (2007: 180–183) and Vanessa Pupavac (2012) argue that the concept of resilience assumes general human vulnerability and legitimises interventions into people's values, culture and social relationships. David Chandler (2014) and Brad Evans and Julian Reid (2014) also argue that the resilience concept reflects a transformation from the idea of the self as capable of judging one's own goals and interests and changing the environment to emancipate oneself to a vulnerable self whose capacity to do so is dubious.

According to Chandler (2014), the resilience concept is fundamentally based on the denial of human agency in changing the world we live in. While the concept ostensibly appears to pay attention to the power and capability of humans, it assumes the fundamental vulnerability of humans. The concept is not based on classical liberal subjects who emancipate themselves through growth and the transformation of their circumstances, and therefore there is no longer the starting assumption of a transformative subject who drives progress and emancipation. The ontology underlying the concept of resilience is the view that humans are inherently and fundamentally vulnerable and that in such an idea, the ability of humans to anticipate crises, ensure safety and transform the external environment is doubted, which is why crises and dangers are assumed to be unavoidable and ever-present. Citizens are now imagined as unable to change the world; they are ever-vulnerable to risk and dysfunction and are therefore only expected to learn to cope with crisis and suffering. In this thinking, the principle of non-interference in the internal affairs of states and the private lives of individual citizens is fundamentally questioned. Once the rational capacity to make choices is denied to the human subject, there is no basis for liberal representative political and legal theory, and concepts, such as citizenship, are hollowed out and lose their political meaning. This thinking is fundamentally anti-modern and is based on fundamental doubts about the bases of modern thoughts and institutions, such as the human ability to think, create and change the world we live in. Human agency is doubted, political possibilities are closed off and (modern) aspirations for material development are denied and even stigmatised. Critics argue that such 'resilient subjects' are not imagined as political subjects capable of judging and acting to transform the environment and free themselves from dangers but rather as subjects who can only adapt to immutable situations and alleviate suffering. Such a view is fundamentally anti-modernist and nihilistic.[15]

4. Potentials and Difficulties of Using the Resilience Concept in the Development and Humanitarian Sector

As shown in the previous sections, there have been numerous criticisms of the concept of resilience in the development and humanitarian sector. What, then, are the implications for using the concept in the sector? This section analyses the critical literature introduced in the previous section and suggests the potentials and difficulties of the use of this concept in the development and humanitarian sector.

The criticisms are convincing and seem to be based on a detailed examination of international policy debate. The tendency of resilience thinking to ignore structural injustices and material causes of suffering and to legitimise measures to maintain a state of stability at lower material levels in the global South is evident. Other points – such as the concept of resilience being based on an assumption of general human vulnerability and justifying interventions into people's values, culture and social relationships – seem to be well exemplified by major documents, including the Human Development Report series. For example, the aforementioned report published by the UNDP in 2014, titled 'Human Development Report 2014: Sustaining Human Progress: Reducing Vulnerabilities and Building Resilience', argued that while everyone is in principle vulnerable to some extent, some people are more vulnerable than others (UNDP 2014: 18–20). It asserted that '[c]onceptions of security require a view of the human person that includes physical and psychological vulnerability, strengths and limitations, including limitations in the perception of risk' (UNDP 2014: 77). The report claimed that everyone is fundamentally vulnerable to varying degrees and cannot always be fully aware of risk and that '[p]rogress has to be about fostering resilient human development' (UNDP 2014: 1). Diverse issues – including provision of basic social services, full employment, social inclusion and early childhood development – were proposed to holistically build resilience to a wide range of risks.

At the same time, we may need to avoid the tendency that is seen in many of the critics' argument – the tendency to view the concept of resilience as stable and static. Critics of this concept often interpret its use as accepting more or less the same meaning, the same framework of thought and the same underlying concept of the self as generally imparted by agencies in the global North. The diffusion of this concept is often perceived as a monolithic process, enabling the creation of resilient subjects, and, hence, the possibility of various actors interpreting or localising the concept – unconsciously transforming or consciously manipulating the semantic content of the concept – tends to be ignored. In fact, the concepts used by actors of the global North – such as civil society, empowerment and trauma – have been diversely interpreted and utilised by local actors to justify and receive political and financial support for a wide range of policies and practices which might not have otherwise been supported (Enomoto 2011). Like these concepts, the concept of resilience also has the possibility of facing tensions between diverse actors over meaning in individual contexts (Wandji, Allouche and Marchais 2021). Different meanings may be assigned to the term in translation, and its meaning may be transformed by the conscious use of the term as a rhetorical tool.

In fact, there have been some scholarly efforts to utilise the term 'resilience' to critically analyse the situation in which structural injustices and causes of suffering, such as colonialism, apartheid and xenophobia are persistently reinstated and revived (Nyamnjoh, 2016; Umeya 2020). While the legitimacy of the term 'resilience' may be enhanced through the process, there is also the potential that the semantic content of this concept may be diffused or transformed by the conscious and unconscious actions of a wide range of actors. Thus, it is hard to conclude that the use of this concept necessarily leads to legitimation of the discourse that expects Southern populations to respond to, adapt to and recover from difficulties and suffering without significant material development and without addressing political and structural matters.

Conversely, the outcome of the battle over the semantic content of a particular concept depends on the power relations in the arena in which it takes place. For example, the convergence of the semantic content of certain concepts and phrases in international treaty negotiations has generally been heavily influenced by political, economic and military power relations in the international society of each era. The legitimacy of any discourse at the level of the state or community can be greatly influenced by the position of those who speak it, the space in which it is spoken, the strategies of those who speak it and their relationships with other actors.

Recently, criticisms against resilience thinking have been resurging as part of the move to challenge racism embedded in the development and humanitarian sector as the Black Lives Matter movement spread across continents and sectors following the killing of George Floyd by Minneapolis police officer, Derek Chauvin, in the United States on 25 May 2020. Although a number of development and humanitarian aid organisations initially issued statements and articles to support the movement and to educate the public about racism, this was soon followed by a cascade of critical comments on racism prevalent in the sector itself (Bruce-Raeburn 2020; Peprah 2020; Slim 2020). As the Black Lives Matter movement brought to the fore the systemic, structural and widespread nature of racism, a logical conclusion was that the sector may not have been immune to it. While the criticism provoked resistance and discomfort in some quarters of the sector, others claim that continuing to ignore the ubiquity of race and racism is no longer a choice they have (Nwajiaku-Dahou and Leon-Himmelstine 2020). Structural racism, racist concepts and racist behaviours and attitudes that have long been overlooked in the sector have now been discussed in social media using hashtags – such as #DecolonizeDevelopment, #AntiRacistInAid, #RethinkingHumanitarianism, #AidToo – and humanitarian aid and advocacy organisations have been openly called out (Adelman 2020; Majumdar 2020; Oppenheim 2020). Past critical comments against the dominant theories, ideas and practices that used polite terms, such as 'structural causes of suffering' and 'power imbalances', have been revaluated, and more explicit and less polite terms, such as racism, white supremacy and white privilege, are used with less hesitation. Attitudes, values and norms that are underpinned by racist and racialising ideas are also being critically examined, and resilience is no exception. Some criticise the tendency of resilience thinking to seek to pacify the populations in the global South at lower material levels without addressing material causes or wider structural and political causes of suffering as a part of racist thought in the sector. Such criticism is well summed up by Angela Bruce-Raeburn, who argued that we should 'stop enabling the use of words such as "resilient" and "resilience" when referring to people who live every day with uncertainty'. She points out that these words 'serve to perpetuate inequalities while telling vulnerable people how strong they are – and therefore changing absolutely nothing in their lives' (Bruce-Raeburn 2020).

As was made clear through the post–Black Lives Matter debate, the development and humanitarian sector has long been deeply imbued with structural racism and power imbalances between the global North and South. Ideologies and practices of the powerful have been routinely normalised and legitimised, and the triumph of the term 'resilience' in the sector may be understood precisely as a result of resilience of such structural racism and power imbalances. Concurrently, recognising racism in the development and humanitarian sector overall has now shed light on a tough question for practitioners and researchers – how should we address Northern-centric, Western-centric or racist structures, systems, practices, terminology and concepts including 'resilience'?

As terms such as decolonisation of aid and anti-racism have quickly become buzzwords since 2022, have already been co-opted and utilised by organisations situated in or originating from the global North and may be in danger of becoming catch-all terms for any change initiative, the sector is clearly at a crossroads as to which path to take. At this critical juncture, we are currently more than ever confronted with the difficult choice as to whether and how to use the term 'resilience' and may need to be conscious of our goals, the feasibility of achieving them and the strategies we must take in achieving them if we are to use the term.

Acknowledgements

This work was supported by the JSPS KAKENHI Grants 22H00920, 22H03828, 18H03606, 16H06318, 16H05664, 16K17075 and 21K13250.

Notes

[1] UN Document. A/RES/S-6/3201. Declaration on the Establishment of a New International Economic Order.

[2] At a joint meeting of the WHO and the United Nations Children's Fund (UNICEF) in 1978, PHC was defined as follows: 'Primary health care is essential health care based on practical, scientifically sound and socially acceptable methods and technology made universally accessible to individuals and families in the community through their full participation and at a cost that the community and country can afford to maintain at every stage of their development in the spirit of self-reliance and self-determination' (WHO and UNICEF 1978: 3).

[3] The commission was established the following year in accordance with a UN General Assembly resolution in 1983 and was chaired by Norwegian politician Glo Harlem Brundtland.

[4] New institutionalist economics generally believes that human rationality is incomplete (limited rationality) and that human beings subjectively recognise the real world and act on it, while their ability to collect, process and communicate information is limited; it focuses on institutional aspects, such as social norms that support this recognition and action. For instance, Douglas North et al. (North, Wallis and Weingast 2009) argue that social norms and social institutional frameworks play an important role in shaping individual behaviour and thinking, that economic development is correlated with the kind of social norms and social institutional frameworks which make democracy work, and that this correlation needs to be examined regarding the question of why poor countries remain poor.

[5] IBRD Articles of Agreement, Article IV, Section 10 (Political Activity Prohibited).

[6] Sen considered capability a set of selective functions representing a variety of being and doing that a person can achieve under economic, social and personal qualities, arguing that poverty is a lack of capability and that development is the expansion of an individual's capability.

[7] UN Document. A/RES/55/2. United Nations Millennium Declaration.

[8] UN Document. A/RES/65/309. Happiness: Towards a Holistic Approach to Development.

[9] UN Document. A/59/565. A More Secure World: Our Shared Responsibility. Report of the High-level Panel on Threats, Challenges and Change, paras. 22–23; UN Document. A/59/2005. In Larger Freedom: Towards Development, Security and Human Rights for All. Report of the Secretary-General, para. 16.

[10] Similar arguments can be found, for example, in Collier et al. (2003: 1).

[11] UN Document. A/54/132/Add.1 – E/1999/80/Add.1. International Decade for Natural Disaster Reduction, Report of the Secretary-General, Addendum, Final report of the Scientific and Technical Committee of the International Decade for Natural Disaster Reduction.

[12] UN Document. A/CONF.206/6. Report of the World Conference on Disaster Reduction. Kobe, Hyogo, Japan, 18–22 January 2005, Resolution 2, Hyogo Framework for Action 2005–2015: Building the Resilience of Nations and Communities to Disasters, p. 9.

[13] For instance, the Sendai Framework for Disaster Risk Reduction 2015–2030, the successor instrument to the Hyogo Framework for Action (HFA) 2005–2015: Building the Resilience of Nations and Communities to Disasters, uses a slightly different definition of resilience as '[t]he ability of a system, community or society exposed to hazards to resist, absorb, accommodate to and recover from the effects of a hazard in a timely and efficient manner, including through the preservation and restoration of its essential basic structures and functions'. See UN Document. A/CONF.224/L.2. Sendai Framework for Disaster Risk Reduction 2015–2030, p. 2.

[14] Some authors point out its similarities with colonial discourses or with Nazi discourse to encourage adaptation and non-resistance in concentration camps (see Reid 2012).

[15] Chandler also points out that the concept of resilience seems to legitimise intrusive interventions into the everyday lives of Southern populations while human rationality is universally degraded and doubted (Chandler 2014). As the

result, no one, not even those who intervene, is assumed to have the moral capacity to conceptualise the good, and no one is expected to provide a universal solution or linear path towards resilience. Thus, attempts are made to shift responsibility to local populations under the name of participation and ownership, yet these very local populations are also assumed to lack human agency.

References

Adelman, L. (2020) 'I've seen first-hand the toxic racism in international women's rights groups', *The Guardian*, 17 August 2020 [online], available: <https://www.theguardian.com/global-development/2020/aug/17/ive-seen-first-hand-the-toxic-racism-in-international-womens-rights-groups> (accessed 30 April 2022).

Aghion, P. and Bolton, P. (1997) 'A theory of trickle-down growth and development', *Review of Economic Studies,* Vol. 64, No. 2, pp. 151–172.

Almedom, A. M. and Tumwine, J. K. (2008) 'Resilience to disasters: a paradigm shift from vulnerability to strength', *African Health Sciences*, Vol. 8, No. S, pp. 1–4.

Bradley, K. (2018) 'Resistance not resilience: Ruling class and radical approaches to mental health', *Revolutionary Socialism in the 21st Century* [online], available: <https://www.rs21.org.uk/2018/11/18/ruling-class-and-radical-approaches-to-mental-health/> (accessed 30 April 2022).

Bruce-Raeburn, A. (2020) 'Opinion: the hustle—white saviors and hashtag activism', *Devex*, 12 June 2020 [online], available: < https://www.devex.com/news/opinion-the-hustle-white-saviors-and-hashtag-activism-97463> (accessed 30 April 2022).

Chandler, D. (2014) *Resilience: The Governance of Complexity*, Abingdon and New York: Routledge.

Clark, H. (2012) *Beyond GDP: Measuring the Future We Want.* Opening statement at UNDP event on measurement of sustainable development at Rio+20, Rio Centro, Brazil, 20 June.

Collier, P., Elliot, L., Hegre, H., Hoeffler, A., Regnal-Querol, M. and Sambanis, N. (2003) *Breaking the Conflict Trap: Civil War and Development Policy*, Washington DC and Oxford: World Bank and Oxford University Press.

Commission for Africa (2005) *Our Common Interest: Report of the Commission for Africa.*

Cornia, G. A., Jolly, R. and Stewart, F. (eds) (1987) *Adjustment with a Human Face, Volume 1: Protecting the Vulnerable and Promoting Growth*, Oxford: Oxford University Press.

__________(1988) *Adjustment with a Human Face, Volume II: Ten Country Case Studies.* Oxford: Oxford University Press.

Curtis, D. (2001) 'Politics and humanitarian aid: Debates, dilemmas and dissension', *Humanitarian Policy Group (HPG) Report*, No, 10.

Delgado, C. L. (1995) 'Africa's changing agricultural development strategies: Past and present paradigms as a guide to the future', *Food, Agriculture, and the Environment Discussion Paper*, No, 3.

DFID (Department for International Development) (2005) *Why We Need to Work More Effectively in Fragile States*, London: DFID.

Duffield, M. (2005) 'Getting savages to fight barbarians: Development, security and the colonial present'. *Conflict, Security and Development*, Vol. 5, No. 2, pp. 141–159.

__________ (2007) *Development, Security and Unending War: Governing the World of Peoples*, Cambridge and Malden: Polity Press.

__________ (2009) 'Liberal internationalism and the fragile state: Linked by design?', in M. Duffield and V. Hewitt (eds), *Development and Colonialism: The Past in the Present*, Woodbridge and Rochester: James Currey, pp. 116–129.

__________ (2010) 'The liberal way of development and the development–security impasse: Exploring the global life–chance divide', *Security Dialogue*, Vol. 41, No. 1, pp. 53–76.

Enomoto, T. (2011) 'Revival of tradition in the era of global therapeutic governance: The case of ICC intervention in the situation in Northern Uganda'. *African Study Monographs*, Vol. 32, No. 3, pp. 111–134.

Evans, B. and Reid, J. (2014) *Resilient Life: The Art of Living Dangerously*, Cambridge and Malden: Polity Press.

FAO (Food and Agriculture Organization) (2016) *Evaluation of FAO Strategic Objective 5: Increase the Resilience of Livelihoods to Threats and Crises.* Rome: FAO.

Furedi, F. (2007) *Invitation to Terror: The Expanding Empire of the Unknown*, London and New York: Continuum.

Gilman, N. (2003) 'Modernization theory, the highest stage of American intellectual history', in D. C. Engerman, N. Gilman, M. Haefele and M. E. Latham (eds), *Staging Growth: Modernization, Development, and the Global Cold War*, Amherst: University of Massachusetts Press, pp. 47–89.

Harrison, G. (2004) *The World Bank and Africa: The Construction of Governance States*, Abingdon and New York: Routledge.

Hillier, D. and Wood, B. (2003) *Shattered Lives: The Case for Tough International Arms Control,* Amnesty International and Oxfam International.

Hout, W. (2007) *The Politics of Aid Selectivity: Good Governance Criteria in World Bank, U.S. and Dutch Development Assistance*. Abingdon and New York: Routledge.

Inoue, J. (2006) 'Policies of the UN system and the EU promoting "Good Governance" and "Anti- Corruption" in developing countries: for fighting against poverty', *Keio Law Journal*, Vol. 4, pp. 63–101.

ISDR (International Strategy for Disaster Reduction) (2002) *Living with Risk: A Global Review of Disaster Reduction Initiatives, Preliminary Version*, Geneva: ISDR.

___________ (2004a) *Living with Risk: A Global Review of Disaster Reduction Initiatives, 2004, Volume I*, Geneva: ISDR.

___________ (2004b) *Living with Risk: A Global Review of Disaster Reduction Initiatives, 2004, Volume II*, Geneva: ISDR.

Kapoor, I. (2008) *The Postcolonial Politics of Development*, Abingdon and New York: Routledge.

Majumdar, A. (2020) 'Bearing witness inside MSF', *The New International*, 18 August 2020 [online], available: <https://www.thenewhumanitarian.org/opinion/first-person/2020/08/18/MSF-Amsterdam-aid-institutional-racism> (accessed 30 April 2022).

Narayan, D., Chambers, R., Shah, M. K. and Petesch, P. (2000) *Voices of the Poor: Crying out for Change*, New York: Oxford University Press.

National Public Media (2015) *How 'Resilience' is Misunderstood When Talking about Racism*, 6 December, [online], available: <https://www.npr.org/2015/12/06/458662021/how-resilience-is-misunderstood-when-talking-about-racism> (accessed 30 April 2022).

North, D. C., Wallis, J. J. and Weingast, B. R. (2009) *Violence and Social Orders: A Conceptual Framework for Interpreting Recorded Human History*, Cambridge: Cambridge University Press.

Nwajiaku-Dahou, K. and Leon-Himmelstine, C. (2020) How to Confront Race and Racism in International Development, *Overseas Development Institute*, 5 October 2020 [online], available:

<https://www.odi.org/blogs/17407-how-to-confront-race-and-racism-international-development> (accessed 30 April 2022).

Nyamnjoh, F. B. (2016) *#RhodesMustFall: Nibbling at Resilient Colonialism in South Africa*, Bamenda: Langaa.

OECD DAC (Organisation for Economic Cooperation and Development, Development Assistance Committee) (1996) *Shaping the 21st Century: The Contribution of Development Co-operation*, Paris: OECD.

OI (Oxfam International) (2005) *Paying the Price: Why Rich Countries Must Invest Now in a War on Poverty*, Oxford: Oxfam International.

Oppenheim, M. (2020) 'Nobel women's initiative leaders "profoundly shaken" as seven staff step down', *Independent*, 7 August 2020 [online], available: <https://www.independent.co.uk/news/world/nobel-womens-initiative-staff-resign-laureates-diversity-a9659571.html> (accessed 30 April 2020).

Paloni, A. and Zanardi, M. (2006) 'The IMF, World Bank and policy reform: introduction and overview', in A. Paloni and M. Zanardi (eds), *The IMF, the World Bank and Policy Reforms*, Abingdon and New York: Routledge, pp. 1–23.

Peprah, D. (2020) 'Opinion: we must translate anti-racism statements into action', *Devex*, 30 June 2020 [online], available: <https://www.devex.com/news/opinion-we-must-translate-anti-racism-statements-into-action-97591> (accessed 30 April 2020).

Pieterse, J. N. (2009) *Development Theory*, 3rd ed., London, Thousand Oaks, New Delhi and Far East Square: Sage.

Pupavac, V. (2004) 'War on the couch: the emotionology of the new international security paradigm', *European Journal of Social Theory*, Vol. 7, No. 2, pp. 149–170.

___________ (2008) 'Changing concepts of international health', in D. Wainwright (ed.), *A Sociology of Health*, London, Thousand Oaks, New Delhi and Far East Square: Sage, pp. 173–190.

___________ (2012) 'Global disaster management and therapeutic governance of communities', *Development Dialogue*, Vol. 58, pp. 81–97.

Reid, J. (2012) 'The disastrous and politically debased subject of resilience', *Development Dialogue*, Vol. 58, pp. 67–79.

Sen, A. (1992) *Inequality Re-examined*, Oxford: Clarendon Press.

Singer, H. W. (1994) 'Aid conditionality', *IDS (Institute of Development Studies) Discussion Paper*, No, 346.

Slim, H. (2020) 'Is racism part of our reluctance to localise humanitarian action?', *Humanitarian Practice Network*, 5 June 2020 [online], available: <https://odihpn.org/blog/is-racism-part-of-our-reluctance-to-localise-humanitarian-action/> (accessed 30 April 2022).

Stiglitz, J. E. (1998) *Towards a New Paradigm for Development Strategies, Policies, and Processes.* Paper given at the 1998 Prebisch Lecture at United Nations Conference on Trade and Development (UNCTAD), Geneva, Switzerland, 19 October.

Traynor, M. (2018) 'Guest editorial: what's wrong with resilience', *Journal of Research in Nursing*, Vol. 23, No. 1, pp. 5–8.

Umeya, K. (2020) 'The resilience of apartheid and xenophobia: From a glimpse on the ethnicity and citizenship in "Uber" business in South Africa', *Tabunka Shakai Kenkyu*, Vol. 6, pp. 317–338 (in Japanese).

UN Millennium Project (United Nations Millennium Project) (2005) *Investing in Development: A Practical Plan to Achieve the Millennium Development Goals.*

UNDP (United Nations Development Programme) (1990) *Human Development Report 1990*, New York and Oxford: Oxford University Press.

___________ (2014) *Human Development Report 2014: Sustaining Human Progress: Reducing Vulnerabilities and Building Resilience*, New York: UNDP.

United Nations Secretary-General's High-Level Panel on Global Sustainability (2012) *Resilient People, Resilient Planet: A Future Worth Choosing*, New York: UN.

Wandji, D., Allouche, J. and Marchais, G. (2021) 'Vernacular resilience: an approach to studying long-term social practices and cultural repertoires of resilience in Côte d'Ivoire and the Democratic Republic of Congo', *STEPS Working Paper*, No, 116.

WHO (World Health Organization) (1946) *Constitution of the World Health Organization.* [online], available: <http://apps.who.int/gb/bd/PDF/bd47/EN/constitution-en.pdf> (accessed 30 April 2022).

WHO and UNICEF (World Health Organization and United Nations Children's Fund) (1978) *Primary Health Care: Report of the International Conference on Primary Health Care, Alma-Ata, USSR, 6–*

12 September 1978, Geneva: World Health Organization [online] available:
<http://whqlibdoc.who.int/publications/9241800011.pdf> (accessed 30 April 2022).

World Bank (1992) *Governance and Development*, Washington DC: World Bank.

__________ (1997a) *Helping Countries Combat Corruption: The Role of the World Bank*. Washington DC: World Bank.

__________ (1997b) *World Development Report 1997: The State in a Changing World*, New York: Oxford University Press.

__________ (2000a) *Reforming Public Institutions and Strengthening Governance: A World Bank Strategy*, Washington DC: World Bank.

__________ (2000b) *World Development Report 2000/2001: Attacking Poverty*, New York: Oxford University Press.

__________ (2002) *World Development Report 2002: Building Institutions for Markets*, New York: Oxford University Press.

World Commission on Environment and Development (1987) *Our Common Future*. Oxford: Oxford University Press.

Chapter 3

Covid-19 and the Resilience of Systemic Suppression, Oppression and Repression[1]

Francis B. Nyamnjoh

Introduction

This chapter is about the resilience of systemic, structural or institutional inequalities (informed by real or imagined categories such as race, ethnicity, culture, geography, class, gender, sex and age) and the interconnecting global and local hierarchies that sustain such inequalities and the tokenism of their transcendence despite repeated attempts by their victims to effectively undo them. The Covid-19 pandemic offers a commanding kaleidoscopic prism through which to examine resilience, not so much from the vantage point of the valiant investments by ordinary people and their advocates to resist, overcome and get by despite their precarities and the overwhelming forces that seek to subject, numb, blame, neutralise and co-opt them, their rights, entitlements, freedoms, creative endeavours and their very existence. This is not to downplay the power and successes of social movements by and on behalf of the systematically suppressed, oppressed and repressed. Rather, the paper looks at resilience from the angle of the often hidden and invisible underpinnings (re)engineered by the dominant (elite) interests/order (North, South, East and West, global and local) to disguise or camouflage their power, influence, privileges and suffocating grip on resources, opportunities and the minds, bodies, souls and humanity of dependent others, while speaking the language of autonomy, inclusivity and accessibility. The chapter digs deep into the structural foundation of human relations across races, ethnicities, geographies, classes, genders, sexualities and generations, among other factors, to show how resilient inequalities, injustices, poverty and underinvestment in critical social services, for instance, systematically continue to undermine and neutralise the efforts of the most vulnerable and dispossessed majority of humanity globally to organise, mobilise, assert and fulfil themselves in meaningful ways.

Covid-19 offers much food for thought to critically review prevalent and conventional teleological modernist neoliberal assumptions about and usages of the notion of resilience. Such assumptions seem to take attention away from the power of resilient inequalities and injustices while deceptively encouraging the overdramatisation of the delusory power of ordinary folks to transform and transcend their circumstances with the benevolence and active assistance, supposedly, of the very same oppressive, repressive and suppressive elite, who, though not being a monolith, have structural power and privilege in common. The paper argues that resilience as an empowerment or recognition of human agency for the overwhelming majority of ordinary folks the world over, is possible not through mimicry, elite outsourcing of blame, prescriptiveness and trickledown munificence, but only to the extent that deeply embedded systemic – covert, tacit and everyday – inequalities are comprehensively and systematically excavated, deactivated and reconfigured in accordance with the logic and humility of incompleteness and conviviality. To transcend perennial elite domination that has effectively neutralised productive contestation by ordinary folks, the chapter calls for carefully negotiated and inclusive action, creativity, innovative and convivial modes of solidarity beyond the irrational ecstasy of ephemeral euphoria and exuberance.

Covid-19: Symbol of Globalisation as a Process of Flows and Closures

In its early stages, especially prior to May 2020, Covid-19 was presented as the ultimate symbol of globalisation as a homogenising process devoid of all trappings of hierarchies and inequalities. Every TV channel, radio station, press release, blog and Facebook post, and WhatsApp forward that fed my anxious and eager palate in those early days of the pandemic sought to reassure with sobering words. Reassurances well captured by Zou Yue, CGTN anchor, in a viral WhatsApp video clip[2] thus: 'Covid-19 respects no national borders, no social bounds, no political systems and no cultural values. It hits us just as hard. It levels the world.' A sentiment echoed in March 2020 by Mike Ryan, executive director of the World Health Organization (WHO) Health Emergencies Programme: 'Viruses know no borders and they don't care about your ethnicity, the color of your skin or how much money you have in the bank.'[3]

Really? Yes, and No.

To what extent is Covid-19 no respecter of national borders? It may have been first identified in Wuhan, China,[4] but Covid-19 has rapidly proven, through its invisible nimbleness of feet and wings, that it is *not only* a Chinese or a Wuhan virus. Its giant compressor ambition is no respecter of walls, real or imaginary. It has spread at lightning speed, metamorphosing almost at the blink of an eye into a truly global crisis that requires nothing short of a well-coordinated global response.

In this regard, it is regrettable that whilst it has spread rapidly and sparing no corner of the globe, effective public health responses have remained rather local and national. This poses the 'danger that Covid-19 will do long-term damage to migrant rights, as states continue to adopt inward-looking policies' partly to contain the movement of 'people seeking better economic opportunities' as well as to keep out 'those fleeing political persecution'.[5] In terms of compression of time and space, neoliberalism in its various guises and disguises runs the risk of losing out to the virus, bringing about a new global order, if current rates of transmission are not contained with imagination, creativity and innovation.

As bubbly in generosity as it seems, Covid-19, just like neoliberalism, thrives on hierarchies and their interconnections, globally and locally. It follows, celebrates and is encouraged by the same orifices of cosmopolitan fertility, melting pots and triumphs.

Outside of Wuhan, even as it has hit major cities of Europe and the Americas more than anywhere else, it has not exactly ignored (nor can it afford to, given its global ambitions of dominance) the underdeveloped and the underprivileged North and South, East and West, urban and rural.

It is true – thanks largely to its invisibility and insensitivity to various technologies of containment and regimes of detection, detention, and deportation – that the coronavirus is more aggressive at border crossings than capital, privileged forms of labour, the frequent flyer elite, consumerism or any world religion has ever been.

Like a cockroach in the perforated luggage of an undocumented and underprivileged wayfarer at a heavily policed border crossing, Covid-19 has a debilitating ability to neutralise borders (physical, social, cultural, bodily and ideological) that others hold in awe with norming ease and deadening silence. Notwithstanding its invisibility, Covid-19's mode of travel and privileged crucibles of self-activation remain human. This is not unique to Covid-19, argues Howard Philips, as many other diseases, HIV, TB and past pandemics inclusive, are equally invisible and share similar modes of self-propagation in a manner that makes history instructive in a time of plague.[6]

Curiously, without much ado and almost with the press of a button, the virus has humbled strongmen of politics, and their penchant for hubris and for power without responsibility. It may have much in common with fake news in the digital age of post-truths. But it is far more real and potent than any digitally driven fake news virus. The vectors and vehicles that transmit Covid-19 are humans hungry for sociality, intimacy and *ubuntu*. Hence the insistence on policies and practices of physical and social distancing, though as Hassan Yosimbom observes, these forms of sociality and conviviality are not easy to unlearn or suspend, especially in densely populated places and spaces of poverty, vulnerabilities and precarity, where the only physical and social distancing possible is the ever-widening gap between the rich and the poor.[7] As Chambi Chachage rightly observes, this reality is not to imply that social and physical distancing are impossible, if and when Africans see a need for it.[8]

Those who propagate the virus unknowingly do not need manipulation to desire and seek to be desired through relationships of interconnection with fellow humans. Being human in tune with the humanity of others does not require engineering or inducement to do what should come naturally to humans as social beings.

Unlike fake news viruses, Covid-19 does not need the hidden hand of tech giants, hackers or spyware manufacturers to activate its potency as an efficacious malicious agent. Like Dracula, all it requires is our schooled taste and hunger for human warmth and connectivity as social beings to lure us, one and all, to its vampirish inferno of appetites. In typical vampire fashion, Covid-19 opportunistically insinuates its fangs into our intimacies, by preying on our sociality, comparative disadvantages, pre-existing precarities and related physical frailties that feed from and into debilitating hierarchies of systemic inequality and poverty. Jair Bolsonaro, the President of Brazil, the second most coronavirus-afflicted country globally, after the USA, with over 1,670 infections, and nearly 67,000 Covid-19-related deaths as of 8 July 2020, callously remarks, 'I'm sorry, some people will die, they will die, that's life,'[9] Two Brazilian researchers, Carolina Parreiras and Viviane Mattar, note that:

> All the government needs to do is to let certain forces operate without constraints, so that they can cause suffering and death. In this instance, a biological entity (Covid-19) works together with the pre-pandemic structural factors that already thwart the possibility to live and prosper for many people – an under-resourced public health system, higher rates of pre-existing medical conditions caused by structural racism, and so on. The government lets people die by not enforcing more effective regulations to curb the spread, and by not doing enough to strengthen and expand the capacity of the public health system.[10]

Globally, no sooner have economies reopened than they have reported surges in infections and deaths, leading some countries or regions/provinces/states within countries to reintroduce states of disasters, suspend or slow down plans to reopen their economies. The repeated insistence by leaders such as Trump and Bolsonaro that economies should reopen despite the enormity of deaths and continued surges in coronavirus infections, reflects a perplexing resilient investment in a zero-sum economistic logic of suppression, oppression and repression that undermines the need to focus both on saving lives by curbing the spread of Covid-19 and keeping economies alive in a responsible manner that does not simply throw Covid-19 a lifeline with sighs of resignation such as Trump's: 'Something I don't like saying about things, but that's the way it is.'[11] As some have argued in favour of such a balance of the tension between saving lives and saving livelihoods, while livelihoods lost can be regained, lives lost are lost forever.

New Kinds of Connectivity and Effective Leadership are Necessary to Defeat Covid-19

(a) A different type of connectivity

Paradoxically, defeating the virus requires a different type of connectivity – one that is not necessarily physical, but certainly social and emotional. Policy options and prescriptions such as physical and social distancing, handwashing and sanitisation, to be effective, cannot afford to downplay, as Jess Auerbach reminds us, that human beings are inherently social, and cannot thrive without communities of trust, belief and practice.[12] As Katrien Pype illustrates in her study of 'consolation, compassion, and the digital during Covid-19 in Kinshasa',[13] humans must harness a virtual form of solidarity to enable coming together while staying apart. For, as it is aptly and repeatedly stressed, coronavirus does not spread itself, people spread it. To discipline, punish and curb its excesses, in turn, demands of us discipline enough to suspend our immediacy in the senses of touch, taste and smell by embracing technologies of presence in absence and absence in presence. This, of course, is not to deny the serious threat Covid-19 poses to the livelihoods of all those who depend exclusively on in-person presence in particular places and spaces to be effective in the services they deliver and/or seek. As Anna Lekas Miller, communications manager at the Media Diversity Institute in London remarks, it soon became evident to her that Covid-19 'was going to be impacting people that couldn't necessarily stay home and work from home' and that these were mostly working-class people of colour, who have suffered disproportionately from inequalities and poverty.[14] Of South Africa, Pumla Dineo Gqola observes that, while it is possible for employers to socially distance by working from home, 'this does not extend to the women who clean their houses, who are not able to work away from the physical sites of their jobs. Working-class black women in domestic work and similar employment are obliged to travel long distances almost daily.'[15] Hence, far from radically disrupting established hierarchies of inequalities in livelihoods, Covid-19 has mostly preyed upon and, in some instances, exacerbated existing victimhood and vulnerabilities.

(b) Leadership

Defeating the virus requires leadership in the production and sharing of quality research to inform evidence-based decision making, policies and practices. It is gratifying to know that almost without exception the scientific community is stepping up to provide such leadership, notwithstanding distractions by peddlers in conspiracy theories.[16] There are initiatives afoot to 'align research funders towards a coordinated effort for supporting high-quality research for the most pressing global needs … around Covid-19 and for future epidemics and pandemics', the aim being to 'improve relevant research outputs, ensure outputs are shared rapidly to permit consolidation and review, inform policy and practice and ensure lessons are learned to improve responses within this pandemic and for future epidemics and pandemics'.[17] Even a cursory surfing of the internet with keyword Covid-19-related searches would evidence that the WHO, in collaboration with centres for disease control at national and regional levels are actively involved in promoting such research, reaching in and reaching out to universities and research institute for relevant expertise in fostering such scientific collaboration.[18]

The scientific findings and knowledge require political leadership at local and global levels to inform policy and practice. Unfortunately, such leadership has been slow at coming. While most contemporary heads of state are men, the Covid-19 pandemic appears to have 'revealed the weakness of strongmen' in power,[19] with female leaders seemingly more successful at managing it. As Henley and Eleanor Ainge Roy of *The Guardian* remark, 'Plenty of countries with male leaders have also done well. But few with female leaders have done badly.'[20]

In general, globally, leaders have, regardless of gender, actually used their individual leadership potential and national resources to combat the pandemic. While they have not achieved full liberation from the rampaging virus, they have demonstrated a human effort to tackle the virus. Masks and the wearing of masks have been presented by health experts as a means of preventing the spread of Covid-19 and, almost everywhere, masks have acquired a significance, symbolism and potency beyond the simple but important fact of their relevance in fighting Covid-19. In Cameroon, for instance, according to Divine Fuh, masks have been 'deployed for generating prestige, to navigate belonging, to lampoon the state and the international community, and ultimately to seek to survive in a context where every country had retreated to themselves, leaving Covid-19 to everyone'.[21] Some male leaders have, however, been far more preoccupied with how much of their macho masculinities would be drained out of them if they were to venture to wear a mask in public. These tensions are captured by Helier Cheung in a BBC article about why some male leaders who had resisted wearing masks in public, finally yielded to doing so. Of Donald Trump and Boris Johnson, Cheung writes:

> In the past few days, both US President Donald Trump and UK Prime Minister Boris Johnson have been seen wearing masks in public for the first time.

> It's a dramatic turnaround – Mr Trump previously mocked others for wearing masks, and suggested some might wear such personal protective equipment to show their disapproval of him, even after the US Centers for Disease Control recommended face coverings.
>
> Meanwhile, the UK government was initially reluctant to advise the general public to wear face coverings, even as other countries in Europe did.
>
> It introduced rules requiring people to wear face coverings on public transport in June, and now says people in England must wear face coverings in shops or face a fine.[22]

Despite Trump's very reluctant concession to be seen wearing a mask in public, he, contrary to the recommendation by the top US infectious diseases expert Dr Anthony Fauci that everyone should use masks, rejects mandatory masks nationwide, insisting: 'I want people to have a certain freedom.'[23] Even as in an apparent volte-face – of appearing to care at long last, in the hope, perhaps, that the electorate would forget his initial inertia and failure to rise to the occasion and provide leadership[24] – on July 21 Trump claimed wearing masks a show of 'patriotism'; warned that the coronavirus pandemic 'will probably unfortunately get worse before it gets better'; appealed to everybody to 'wear a mask, get a mask' when 'not able to socially distance'; and admitted that masks 'have an impact' and 'an effect' regardless of one's attitude towards wearing them.[25] His position contradicts the urgency of the situation, with over 6,896,274 people in the USA having tested positive for Covid-19 and at least 200,807 having died from the disease by 23 September 2020.[26] Trump may have reluctantly yielded on masks, but he still self-consciously believes mask wearing somehow diminishes one's masculinity. On 3 September 2020 Trump mocked his opponent, Democratic party nominee, Joe Biden, for wearing a mask. A Paul LeBlanc of the CNN reports, 'Speaking to a largely mask-less crowd in Pennsylvania, Trump asked his supporters if they know "a man that likes a mask as much as Biden. It gives him a feeling of security," the President said. "If I was a psychiatrist, I'd say this guy has some big issues."'[27]

Trump may vacillate on masks, but he has continued, with remarkable consistency, to promote and defend the use of hydroxychloroquine as a cure, retweeting a video of and praising a controversial Cameroon-born Houston-based medical doctor-cum pastor, Dr Stella Immanuel, who has actively touted the efficacy of the drug and who is said to believe 'demons cause illnesses'.[28] Describing her as 'very impressive', President Trump speaks of Dr Stella Immanuel as someone who has had 'tremendous success with hundreds of different patients', adding: 'I thought her voice was an important voice but I know nothing about her.'[29] President Trump's endorsement of the unproven cure contradicts his own public health officials, including Dr Anthony Fauci, a leading member of the White House coronavirus task force, who maintains that 'every single good study [...] has shown that hydroxychloroquine is not effective in the treatment of Covid-19', and 'regulators warn it may cause heart problems'.[30] The situation is further complicated by allegations that even renowned and authoritative journals as the *Lancet* and the *New England Journal of Medicine*, are sometimes pressured to accept for publication papers with contested conclusions by 'financially powerful' pharmaceutical companies interested in promoting or taking attention away from a particular drug.[31] The *Lancet* reformed its editorial policy three months after retracting a controversial peer-reviewed study it published in May 2020, 'which concluded that Covid-19 patients who received the drug hydroxychloroquine were dying at higher rates', although 'figures on the number of deaths and patients in hospital cited by the authors did not match up with official government and health department data'.[32]

Indeed, as Tara McKelvey reports, 2020 being an election year in the USA, '[t]he wearing of masks has become a catalyst for political conflict, an arena where scientific evidence is often viewed through a partisan lens.' While '[m]ost Democrats support the wearing of masks' ... '[m]ost Republicans do not. The Republicans are following the lead of the president: Trump has been reluctant to wear a mask, saying that it did not seem right to wear one while he was receiving heads of state at the White House.'[33] Trump's exploitation of presidential power to settle political scores and secure political advantage against his opponents by denying them the necessary resources or deploying America's financial abilities to commandeer personal protective equipment (PPE), is largely seen to have encouraged the spread of the virus in the USA. Trump's vacillations have been condemned in general, including even from within the ranks of his governing Republican party. In 'Fighting Alone', an opinion piece in *The Washington Post* on 16 July, Larry Hogan, the Republican governor of Maryland, criticises Trump for not providing timely federal leadership to mitigate the high number of Covid-19-

related deaths in the USA. Governor Hogan writes: 'So many nationwide actions could have been taken in those early days but weren't. While other countries were racing ahead with well-coordinated testing regimes, the Trump administration bungled the effort.'[34] To Joe Biden, Trump's Democratic party opponent for the presidency in the 2020 election, 'It is long past due for President Trump to listen to somebody other than himself in how to fight this virus, because after six straight months of deadly mismanagement it is spiralling even more out of control.'[35] To Jeremy Konyndyk, a senior policy fellow at the Center for Global Development who contributed actively to US government response to Ebola in 2014, the Trump administration's response to the coronavirus is 'one of the greatest failures of basic governance in modern times' – 'a leadership failure of astounding proportions'.[36] Critical of leaders who have downplayed and sabotaged collective efforts to tackle the pandemic, UN Secretary General Antonio Guterres calls for humility and global solidarity. He regrets the 'total lack of coordination among countries' in response to the pandemic, criticising the world's biggest powers in particular for failing to work together, and thereby 'creating the situation that is getting out of control'.[37] Yet, only such creative and innovative forms of solidarity, at local and global levels, could encourage and build on experiences such as reported in *Business Insider SA*, where South Africa came to the rescue by exporting 800,000 masks to Italy in the early days of Covid-19 in Europe, when no fellow European Union country would assist.[38] As Sanne van der Lugt remarks, Italian hospitals, running out of stock of medical protection gear and desperate, naturally 'asked their European partners for help. However, the first reaction from the rest of Europe was to stockpile face masks and other equipment to help their own citizens and not one European country came to the rescue. Instead, it was South Africa that sent the first batch of face masks to Italy.'[39]

On Friday 2 October 2020, President Donald Trump, 'being 74, a man and someone categorised as obese' and 'in a higher-risk category for Covid-19'[40] tweeted: 'Tonight, @FLOTUS and I tested positive for COVID-19. We will begin our quarantine and recovery process immediately. We will get through this TOGETHER!'[41] Two days after he was admitted for treatment to the Walter Reed National Military Medical Center close to Washington DC, Trump sought to reassure the American public: 'I came here, wasn't feeling so well, I'm much better now,' he said, later adding: 'Over the next period of a few days I guess that's the real test. We'll be seeing what happens over those next couple of days.'[42] Speaking in on CBS's Face the Nation, House Speaker Nancy Pelosi, a Democrat, was critical of the president's 'anti-science' attitude to the virus, which she said was shared by Republicans in congress. She expressed hope that following his positive Covid-19 diagnosis, President Trump's 'heart will be open to the millions of people who have been affected' and 'signal that we really have to do better in preventing the spread of this virus'.[43] Determined to continue downplaying the deathly virus, on Monday 5 October, 'feeling really good', Trump tweeted he would be releasing himself from hospital later that day, with these defiant words: 'Don't be afraid of Covid. Don't let it dominate your life. We have developed, under the Trump Administration, some really great drugs & knowledge. I feel better than I did 20 years ago!!'[44]

In Africa, while many countries have responded favourably with strict lockdowns that have surprised many a doom and gloom prediction[45] of the continent being a '"timebomb" waiting to explode' or 'to fall apart under the weight of a public health emergency' like the coronavirus,[46] some leaders have been equally opportunistic and indifferent to the risks posed by Covid-19, in their pursuit of personal power. Some have gone ahead to conduct presidential elections, ignoring the prevention measures, leading to a spike in Covid-19 positive cases and deaths of numerous leading personalities. There was an allegation that former president of Burundi died at a time he was diagnosed Covid-19 positive and that death led to a short-lived constitutional crisis.[47] In Malawi as well, elections were held in June, and two weeks thereafter the country witnessed a spike and a number of notable public figures died, including a member of parliament, a district commissioner, senior academics in public universities and politicians both in the ruling and opposition parties.[48] Another curious case is Tanzania that suspended testing if not just reporting of cases ostensibly to allow for upgrade of its testing capacity which had been producing mixed results. The number of reported cases in that country were frozen at 509 for three months, thereby feeding the illusion that there was no Covid-19 or that it had been controlled.[49] President John Magufuli reportedly told worshippers in a church in Dodoma: 'Coronavirus, which is a devil, cannot survive in the body of Christ ... It will burn instantly,'[50] and claimed that 'The corona disease has been eliminated thanks to God.'[51] Tanzania was heading to the polls in October 2020, and it could be argued that for political expediency the incumbent president, who had been seeking a second term, would not like news of rising cases and deaths as it may affect his re-election at the polls.[52]

Towards the quest for compassionate, decisive, selfless, principled and foresighted leadership beyond the resilient diktats of dominant masculinities and strongman politics, the following words by Helen Lewis, a London-based staff writer at *The Atlantic*, offer food for thought in contemplating the gendered dynamics of leadership in an interconnected world that yearns for the humility of incompleteness and conviviality: 'Women leaders aren't the cause of better government. They are a symptom of it.'[53]

Covid-19 in Connivance with Systemic Inequalities and Hierarchies

It is true that Covid-19 is humbling leaderships, economies and predictabilities globally. But that is the story at a general level. At a structural and layered level, the story is much more complex and nuanced. The more closely one looks, the clearer the pictures of power, privilege and hierarchies become, at sub-national, national, regional and global levels.

Globally, the coronavirus has gained a reputation as a pandemic that kills without negotiation, mercy or remorse, making of everyone a potential victim. Stories of death and dying are truly horrendous. As Father Mario Carminati from a small town in northern Italy, an area hard hit by the virus, put it: 'Authorities didn't know where to put the coffins.'[54]

However, while every social category is affected, not everyone is affected to the same degree. Everywhere, elderly people are dying disproportionately to the young. Could this turn out to be Africa's saving grace as a youthful continent, where three-quarters of the population is aged below 35?

There are also gender differences in how the virus affects humans. Writing for BBC Future, a science site, Martha Henriques observed: 'In the US, for example, twice as many men have been dying from the virus as women. Similarly, 69% of all coronavirus deaths across Western Europe have been male. Similar patterns have been seen in China and elsewhere.'[55] On the other hand, with the confinement measures, women are losing jobs at higher rates and 'were making less money to begin with'.[56] In terms of gender identities, Miriam

Aurora Hammeren Pedersen argues that the transgender community is being hit especially hard. As she observes:

> Lockdown in South Africa and elsewhere has meant that queer meeting places such as bars and cafés have had to close their doors. The ban on social gatherings has put a stop to queer events and social gatherings. LGBTQ+ rights and support organisations have had to move their meetings online.
>
> As universities have closed their doors, students all over the world have been sent home, supposedly, to their families to complete the term through online studies. This poses problems and potential risks for those trans people who are now forced to move back in with less accepting families or into less accepting communities.
>
> Trans people, especially trans women of colour, are at high risk of harassment, violence and homicide. Covid-19 has provided little relief.[57]

In Cape Town, such inequalities generated a response by seven queer activists operating under the name #WeSeeYou, who occupied an Airbnb mansion at Camps Bay to draw attention to the plight of LGBTQI communities by linking home, homelessness, lack of housing, land repossession and sexual identity.[58]

There is discrimination along racial lines as well. In Europe and North America, racialised people are dying in inverse proportions to their white counterparts. In Chicago, for example, blacks 'account for half of all coronavirus cases in the city and more than 70% of deaths, despite making up 30%' of the city's population.[59] Indigenous populations have a higher risk as well, leading some experts to speculate that Covid-19 could destroy whole nations and communities of indigenous peoples. 'In the US, one in every 2,300 indigenous Americans has died, compared to one in 3,600 white Americans – making them the second most at-risk ethnic category in the US after black Americans.'[60] Brown people are equally at higher risk than white people. At face value, the higher risk experienced by black, brown and indigenous populations in the US reflects the inaccessibility of affordable and quality healthcare as well as systemic exclusion from other societal services and benefits. It also reflects their lowly positions on the hierarchy of socioeconomic and political visibility that neoliberalism and legacies of the institution of enslavement have enshrined and perpetuate even in camouflage.[61] Hence, former President Barack Obama's comment: 'A disease like this just spotlights the underlying inequalities and extra burdens that black [brown and indigenous] communities have historically had to deal with in this country.'[62]

Ethically, how does one negotiate and navigate the delicate balancing act of representing these disproportionalities, scientifically, journalistically, politically and otherwise, without implying that the lives of those most adversely affected matter less?[63] Thomas Cousins, Sabina Leonelli, Michelle Pentecost and Kaushik Sunder Rajan, in their conversation on Covid-19 and the implications for democracy of the epidemiological and political challenges it poses, suggest that such a delicate balance is attainable through 'a community-driven approach [that] provides a more democratic mechanism, which leads not only to more salutary political outcomes, but also to better epidemiological ones'.[64]

While the economic effects globally are devastating for most as the virus drives productivity into hibernation, some people are losing their businesses and jobs faster than others. In many an African country and turgid democracies where citizens have mostly failed over the years to jolt the reigning dictatorships out of their slumber of inaction and complacency, Covid-19 has succeeded in attracting, at the level of hollow rhetoric at least, the attention of governments to the urgency of the moment. Even if only to regret, or appear to regret, the deplorable public health systems they have ignored or underfunded with impunity for decades – preferring, as they often have, to head elsewhere for more prestigious healthcare for themselves and their immediate families. That not even the health systems of Africa's most competitive economies are spared the brutish embarrassment of being overwhelmed by the coronavirus, is exemplified by 'An exclusive, weeks-long BBC investigation inside filthy hospitals in South Africa' that 'exposed an extraordinary array of systemic failures showing how exhausted doctors and nurses are overwhelmed with Covid-19 patients and a health service near collapse.'[65] Despite imposing one of the world's strictest lockdowns, South Africa, by July 2020 – with an official Covid-19 infection rate of over 470,000 and a death toll above 7,500 – had risen to the fifth highest case count in the world behind the USA, Russia, Brazil and India, and the government had reportedly 'begun digging large, makeshift cemeteries in preparation for more deaths'.[66]

Africa's Covid-19 Predicament

Compared to Europe, Asia and the Americas, Covid-19 cases and deaths in Africa have been much lower, with barely1,569,680 cases and 38,196 deaths reported in a population of 1.3 billion, on the continent,[67] compared to a global total of 36,754,395 confirmed cases and 1,064,838 deaths, by 9 October 2020.[68] Commenting on this state of affairs, British politician and former UK Prime Minister, Tony Blair, suggests that this could be attributed to Africa having a more resilient and immune population, the youthfulness of the population, the possibility that Africa is not recording all of its Covid-19-related deaths, the fact that Africa is not doing enough testing, or that the worst is yet to come.[69] Kevin Marsh and Moses Alobo of the African Academy of Sciences Covid-19 research team provide substantiation for some of Blair's hunches.[70] Others, like Karen Attiah of the *Washington Post*, rightly draw attention to the timely action taken by African governments to impose strict lockdown measures, as well as to the pre-existing pandemic response infrastructure in some African countries from the Ebola outbreak of late 2013 to 2016, as well as from the management of past pandemics and viral diseases.[71] It could be argued, however, how surprising it is, for anyone remotely connected with power and privilege in Europe – a region that has for centuries excelled at underdeveloping Africa and at policing the mobility of Africans with repressive policies and practices of detection, detention and deportation, mobilising Africans strictly on terms dictated by the whims, caprices and narrow self-interests of the European state involved – to express surprise that a disease like Covid-19 which thrives on flexible and accelerated mobility of people should not find fertile ground in Africa, despite Africa's unenviable reputation as an underdeveloped continent of doom and gloom.

Whatever the reasons for its failure to find traction in Africa, the growing threat of Covid-19 is particularly challenging for the continent where 'health-care systems are already stretched' and 'Conventional social distancing is next to impossible'. Added challenges include 'prevalence of already life-threatening conditions such as malaria, tuberculosis and acute malnutrition', compromised immunity in persons living with HIV/AIDS, 'acute shortages of trained medical staff, medical supplies and crucial equipment',[72] as well as long-term consequences on health and beyond. If aggressive and massive testing is necessary to contain the ravages of Covid-19, how do African countries of preponderantly modest means and underfunded public health services afford the testing and personal protective equipment needed by medical and public health practitioners to do justice to such an expectation? And what will be the long-term impacts that 'the huge focus' on the virus has had on 'other health issues being neglected'[73]? The answer, in part, is for African states and government to seek inspiration from popular traditions, practices and wisdoms that African communities have accumulated endogenously, before, during and after the continent's encounters with European colonialism and its resilient zero-sum logic of superiority and orthodoxy in everything human.[74]

(a) Covid-19 catalysed risks of dying of hunger

The potentially devastating economic effects, especially those on the African continent rendered economically poor by poor practices and policies, are frightening to contemplate. The reports of ordinary folks driven to disarmingly horrendous levels of desperation are widespread and surging. In Kenya for example, Peninah Bahati Kitsao, a Mombasa-based widow, was reportedly 'cooking stones for her eight children to make them believe she was preparing food for them', hoping 'they would fall asleep while they waited for their meal'.[75] While her story caught the attention of many Kenyans who apparently rallied to her aid, it is not impossible to imagine thousands or even millions of fellow Kenyans and Africans in similar positions not being as lucky, as they run the risk of dying as much from hunger as from Covid-19. Kenya is not alone. In South Africa, where a hard lockdown was enforced on 27 March 2020, a national survey in July, four months on, showed 'large groups of households' were experiencing 'tremendous hardship' such as job and income losses and mounting household food insecurity as a direct result of the lockdown, despite social protection measures instituted by government to safeguard livelihoods.[76] Indeed, warns Oxfam, the coronavirus could push an estimated 122 million of the world's poorest people to the brink of starvation, with 12,000 people a day dying from hunger rather than from Covid-19 itself.[77] Paradoxically, amidst such risks of chronic hunger and risk of starvation, and the disturbing reality of underfunded and overwhelmed public health systems, are reports of some rich and high profile Kenyans 'rush[ing] to install ICU beds in their homes, complete with all the required equipment' and with 'arrangements for standby private doctors and nurses',[78] notwithstanding nationwide 'major shortages in chest specialists, hospital physicians and emergency care nurses'.[79] Resilient coloniality, power, privilege and unequal distribution of resources informed by hierarchies of humanity are all too evident in these accounts of the unfolding ramifications of Covid-19 in Kenya and the rest of Africa.

(b) Victim of perennial racism and neocolonialism

African scientists, working through universities and research institutes as well as under the auspices of national, regional and continental academies of sciences, centres for disease control and other advocacy groups and networks, have contributed significantly to studying the coronavirus and its ramifications. They have been actively involved with various initiatives, from the several different quick tests that were developed (in countries such as Senegal and Ghana, for example) and rolled out really quickly at the beginning of the pandemic, to provision of expert advice on managing pandemics, involvement in vaccine trials as scientists and constitution of myriad research projects.[80] Such contributions and similar initiatives by African intellectuals more broadly[81] have tended to be overshadowed by certain controversies around resilient racism and neocolonialism.

The controversies have provoked questions such as the extent to which African governments are committed to resisting the pressure to simply handing over the African populace to be used as guinea pigs and experimented upon to guarantee salvation for the lives of others higher up the reigning hierarchies of humanity. Would it be proper for Africans to come last in terms of access to and prioritisation of personal protection equipment, only to be prioritised and privileged in testing for the effectiveness of various vaccines on trial? This would be unwise, as suggested by the racism row provoked by two French doctors suggesting on a TV show in a rather condescending manner that virus vaccines be tested 'in Africa where there are no masks, no treatment or intensive care'.[82] Being critical of vaccine trials that seek to take advantage of Africans by devaluing their humanity is not to deny the need for Africans to volunteer and avail themselves for vaccine trials along with volunteers of other continents and races, as the race for a cure to Covid-19 intensifies. As Richard Fisher, a volunteer in the trial of a Covid-19 vaccine developed by Oxford University remarks, the 'vaccine trial may not turn out to be the success that many wish for. It may not meet the safety and efficacy threshold that takes us out of these difficult times. But that's how science works – it's long-term, collective and filled with wrong turns – and right now I've never been more glad that we have it.'[83] Finding a Covid-19 vaccine is of such preoccupying urgency that organisations in the UK, USA and Canada trying to develop a coronavirus vaccine had been reportedly targeted by hackers 'highly likely with the intention of stealing information and intellectual property relating to the development and testing of Covid-19 vaccines'.[84]

There are legitimate concerns about a lingering 'colonial mentality' in Europe and North America,[85] an attitude that has drawn widespread condemnation as well as suspicion and the circulation of rumour and conspiracy theories among Africans towards trials for 'a vaccine that works worldwide – and not just for richer nations'.[86] Beyond conspiracy theories, Carmen Paun reported in *Politico* that 'across Africa, health officials are growing increasingly concerned they won't be able to afford the potentially life-saving therapies currently under development'.[87] A concern reiterated in an open letter published in *The Washington Post* by eight world leaders, including the leaders of three African countries (Cyril Ramaphosa of South Africa, Sahle-Work Zewde of Ethiopia and Elyes Fakhfakh of Tunisia), calling for 'global solidarity' for fairness in distributing any Covid-19 vaccine that may be developed. Maintaining that 'Where you live should not determine whether you live', the leaders called for strategic action to ensure benefits for countries across the world for any vaccine developed:

> At this point in time, with almost 200 potential Covid-19 vaccine candidates currently at different stages of development, there is hope that soon one or more will prove to be both safe and effective.
>
> What happens next is equally important. This cannot be a race with one winner. When one or more vaccines are successful, it must be a win for all of us.
>
> We cannot allow access to vaccines to increase inequalities within or between countries – whether low-, middle- or high-income.[88]

A related concern stirred by the controversy around Covid-Organics, a 'herbal cure' proposed by the Malagasy Institute of Applied Research (IMRA) and promoted by President Andry Rajoelina of Madagascar as a 'herbal tea [that] gives results in seven days',[89] poses the additional problem of the unresolved tensions between the competing and often conflictual healthcare traditions on the continent – one generally termed 'plant-based', 'traditional', 'African' or 'endogenous' and the other roughly equated with being 'medical', 'scientific', 'orthodox', 'Western' and 'colonial' in origin.

According to President Rajoelina, people would not be so sceptical if a European country had discovered the remedy. As he told France 24's Marc Perelman and RFI's Christophe Boisbouvier in an interview: 'What if this remedy had been discovered by a European country, instead of Madagascar? Would people doubt it so much? I don't think so.'[90] Following President Rajoelina expression of scepticism on France 24, an announcement on 20 July 2020 that a vaccine developed by Oxford University had shown promising results in trial was widely and favourably reported across the world, despite the cautious reaction of medical experts such as Dr Sarah Pitt, a virologist at the University of Brighton, who cautions that although the Oxford University vaccine has been proven to induce an immune response, 'we don't necessarily know that it will protect us from infection, which is the next stage of their investigations'.[91] Such caution has not stopped governments from rushing to place orders for AZD1222, as the vaccine is called. 'The UK has ordered 100 million doses of the vaccine, while a number of other governments around the world, including the US, France and Germany, have entered into supply deals' with AstraZeneca the company with which Oxford University has partnered to produce the vaccine, should the vaccine 'prove effective and gain regulatory approval'.[92]

The President of Madagascar is categorical about what is truly in question about Covid-Organics as a 'preventive and curative remedy' is the assumption that nothing good can originate from Africa: 'What is the problem with Covid-Organics, really? Could it be that this product comes from Africa? Could it be that it's not OK for a country like Madagascar, which is the 63rd poorest country in the world ... to have come up with (this formula) that can help save the world?'[93] While there is clearly reason to be concerned about the resilience of a colonial mentality in Europe's relations with Africa, it must be said as well that African leaders have often been quick to mobilise anti-imperialist rhetoric when faced with accountability pressures. Reports in July 2020 that Madagascar's coronavirus cases and deaths were increasing rapidly, and overwhelming hospitals are an indication that the efficacy of the concoction is not good enough.[94]

Equally, the rising infections and deaths reiterate the need to watch against opportunistic deployment of anti-imperialist rhetoric in order not to throw the baby of scientific accountability out with the colonial bathwater. In this regard, it is a step in the right direction that the WHO and the Africa Centres for Disease Control and Prevention (Africa CDC) on 22 July 2020, in a joint effort, 'launched an expert advisory committee/panel to provide independent scientific advice and support to countries on the safety, efficacy and quality of traditional medicine therapies', by conducting in collaboration with the countries concerned, 'clinical trials of traditional medicines in compliance with international standards'.[95]

Not unrelated, African governments also need to protect their citizenry from the proliferation of fake cures, by paying particular attention to fighting opportunistic fake pharmaceutical drugs, especially given the 'lack of regulatory oversight' that makes parts of the continent 'so attractive to criminals in the business of falsifying medicines' to prey upon vulnerable health-seeking Africans in under-resourced health systems.[96] Even as some African governments have invited Christian, Muslim and endogenous religious authorities to help spiritually in combating the pandemic,[97] they have been called upon as well, to protect their citizens from false hope churches and related religious and spiritual outfits and false prophets that offer prayer as both prevention and antidote, with promises of miracle cures through divine intervention, on the continent and from beyond.[98]

Reminiscent of the way Chinese and other East Asians were treated in other parts of the world in the beginning of the pandemic, reported resurgence in prejudice, stereotyping, discrimination, and physical and social distancing from Africans in China[99] is worrying, and another test of whether African governments truly care beyond declarations of intent. Covid-19 has indeed exposed that African governments and states have a persistent challenge of rendering meaningful the citizenship and humanity of their nationals in a manner that buttresses the self-confidence and dignity of their people, especially in relationships with peoples of other races, ethnicities and continents.

(c) Coping with attendant economic downturns and recessions

The International Monetary Fund (IMF) and World Bank are predicting downturns and recessions for economies globally and especially on the African continent,[100] where by 30 July 2020, at least 33 countries had already received approval of millions of US dollars in IMF loans – with South Africa having the lion's share of US$4.3 billion – to redress the severe economic impact of the Covid-19 crisis.[101] Concomitantly, the United Nations Secretary-General, António Guterres, in his Nelson Mandela Annual Lecture 2020 speech, has called for a more critical attitude towards certain 'fallacies and falsehoods' perpetrated by these same institutions. Among these untruths, he lists: 'The lie that free markets can deliver healthcare for all; The fiction that unpaid care work is not work; The delusion that we live in a post-racist world; [and] The myth that we are all in the same boat.' That these are falsehoods, fallacies and myths is evidenced by the fact that the 'legacy of colonialism still reverberates [...] in economic and social injustice, the rise of hate crimes and xenophobia; the persistence of institutionalised racism and white supremacy.' To Guterres, only a major reform of the UN security council, the IMF and the World Bank, could begin the process of meaningfully addressing systemic inequalities exposed by the coronavirus pandemic.[102]

Even the Big Tech companies (Amazon, Facebook, Apple and Google), largely reported as winners in the Covid-19 era,[103] have been negatively affected by the economic fallout of the coronavirus pandemic, reporting either less than expected profits or marginal declines.[104] More generally, the economic effects of the pandemic are likely to be sweepingly devastating. According to some estimates, because of Covid-19, extreme poverty in the world is estimated to rise to affect about 50 million people in 2020, undoing all the progress made in poverty reduction since the launch of the Sustainable Development Goals (SDGs) in 2015.[105] A survey conducted for the BBC World Service in 27 countries by GlobeScan in June 2020, revealed that the Covid-19 pandemic 'has had a more severe impact on people in poorer countries and has exacerbated existing inequalities' and 'opened up a gulf between young and old', with younger generations claiming 'they have experienced a tougher time than older generations'.[106] Calls for intelligent, rigorous and robust responses by African governments are greeted with the proverbial beggars' bowl, outstretched, unscrupulously and unashamedly, and not without dubious intentions in some cases, West and East, notwithstanding that these regions are facing their own worst economic nightmares. With 36,754,395 confirmed cases of Covid-19, including 1,064,838 deaths worldwide as of October 9 2020,[107] and with many of the traditional countries Africa usually relies on for aid reported as having the most deaths, it is easy to see that reprioritisation of resources would likely affect Africa negatively.[108] In addition, the African Union has hurriedly put in place a committee to seek urgent assistance from developed economies towards addressing the crisis.[109]

If the rest of the world has in the past and under relatively normal times not been that generous or effusive in their *ubuntu* towards Africa, there is little to suggest that, plagued by their own problems under the coronavirus tsunami, they are suddenly going to become evangelists of selfless philanthropy. Even as every country and everyone worldwide is challenged to lend each other a hand in order to survive Covid-19 and its devastations,[110] how amenable are countries and individuals cultivated to dramatise zero-sum articulations of autonomy and survival to a logic, ethic, morality and practice of inclusivity, looking out and being there for one other in sickness or in health? Africans must do more to disabuse themselves of the complacency that feeds stereotypes of dependency and helplessness among predators and treasure-hunters disguised as benevolent and selfless saviours. If Africans have not been sure about what to do with the neo-colonial and neoliberal umbilical cord that ties them and their continent to a fantasy of Western philanthropy, it could be argued that the Covid-19 pandemic is an opportunity for African leaders and people to think and realise that dependency may be a very convenient option, but a debilitating one. Beg, borrow or repatriate misappropriated funds, one thing is certain: Fighting Covid-19 requires not rhetoric and vacillation but appropriate action, creativity and innovative modes of solidarity.

The Challenge of Resilient Covid-19

Innovative modes of solidarity are a global imperative, as Covid-19 continues to defy popular and political impatience with scientific rigour, magical thinking and our human propensity to hope. The world is far from getting a handle on the virus. Very much like the proverbial elephant and the blind men, each who experiences the virus and lives to tell the tale adds to the growing understanding of just what untold havoc the virus is capable of wreaking. This is what we gather from Richard Quest of CNN, who is one of the lucky ones to have recovered from an attack of Covid-19. The terror in his description of Covid-19 is evident:

> I got infected back in mid-April. The onset of symptoms came quickly. I suddenly noticed I was feeling very tired and I had a new cough. I got tested and the morning after I received a phone call from the medical center, I had tested positive for coronavirus.
>
> The virus is like a tornado. When it lands, it swirls through the body, causing chaos, confusion, coughs, wreaking damage to each organ it touches. Some won't survive its visit. For those that do, when it has gone, one surveys the damage to the human landscape and realizes it's much greater than first thought. My symptoms were on the milder side: I never had breathing difficulties, or loss of sense or smell. I was wiped-out tired and I always had 'the cough,' which has now returned.[111]

To recover in the immediate and short term, might not say much about the real impact of the virus on a victim's person. The coronavirus affects the entire human body. It 'damages not only the lungs, but the kidneys, liver, heart, brain and nervous system, skin and gastrointestinal tract'. Other effects include 'causing the blood to clot, the heart to lose its healthy rhythm, the kidneys to shed blood and protein and the skin to erupt in rashes. It causes headaches, dizziness, muscle aches, stomach pain and other symptoms along with classic respiratory symptoms like coughing and fever'.[112] Although Quest has supposedly recovered from the virus, it is difficult to be categorical. As Quest puts it:

> The cough has come back, without warning and seemingly for no reason; so has the fatigue. True, neither are as debilitating as when I had the actual virus, but they are back.
>
> Like many others, I am now coming to realize that I am living and suffering from the long tail of Covid-19.[113]

He adds:

> I am also discovering new areas of damage: I have now become incredibly clumsy. I was never the most lissom person, no one ever called me graceful, but my clumsiness is off the chart. If I reach for a glass, or take something out of a cupboard, I will knock it, or drop it on the floor. I have tripped over the curb and gone flying. I fall over furniture. It is as if that part of my brain, which subconsciously adjusts hand and movement to obstacles it sees, isn't working.
>
> At times there's a sense of mild confusion. The micro delay in a thought, the hesitation with a word. Nobody would notice but me.
>
> My digestive system is peculiar, to say the least.
>
> It doesn't matter whether I call them symptoms, traits, or wreckage – my body doesn't feel quite right.[114]

These potentially long-term ramifications of Covid-19 on humans, along with the extended effects of Covid-19 induced pollution of the environment,[115] make the case for global unity in the service of humanity even more compelling. UN Secretary General, Antonio Guterres, who delivered the 2020 Nelson Mandela Foundation Lecture on 18 July 2020 via video link from New York, used the opportunity to reiterate his call for global solidarity and leadership in tackling 'the inequality pandemic'. He maintained that the Covid-19 'pandemic has demonstrated the fragility of our world', and 'laid bare risks' which the powerful and privileged few 'have ignored for decades' despite the critical voices that have sought to draw attention to such realities as: 'inadequate health systems; gaps in social protection; structural inequalities; environmental degradation; the climate crisis'. He appealed for a 'New Social Contract and a New Global Deal that create equal opportunities for all, and respect the rights and freedoms of all.' Such a contract and deal should 'enable young people to live in dignity; [...] ensure women have the same prospects and opportunities as men; and [...] protect the sick, the vulnerable, and minorities of all kinds.' It should ensure that we 'right the wrongs of the past and move forward together, for the good of all.'[116]

Conclusion

The coronavirus has without doubt proven itself to be a truly global pandemic, and in the process has drawn fresh attention to a proliferation of excruciatingly resilient local and global infrastructure of inequities and inequalities. No geographical region or social category has escaped devastation by Covid-19. In some regards, it could be argued that some countries usually categorised in a taken-for-granted manner as rich, industrialised, technologically advanced, pacesetters in modernity and at the apex of civilisation have been the most afflicted by the virus. The USA, renowned for its litany of systemic racism and related inequalities, belongs in this category and is arguably the world's leading economy, is leading as the worst-affected country in the world by coronavirus infections and deaths. Brazil, a giant of the Global South, a country with 'a long legacy of racism' and the last country in the Americas to abolish slavery, follows closely. As Djamila Ribeiro observes, while Brazil may not have resorted to 'a legal apartheid like the US or South Africa', the state has done little in public policy to desegregate society institutionally and structurally since slavery was abolished in 1888.[117] While it is true that the situation in both Brazil and the USA has been exacerbated by the incompetent, ignorant and arrogant leadership of their respective presidents, it has also revealed Covid-19 to be particularly savagely drawn to preying upon resilient systemic inequalities, injustices and hierarchies of humanities in both societies. Due to similar structural inequalities inherited from the apartheid era and compounded by corruption and lip service to transformation under the ruling African National Congress (ANC) government,[118] in South Africa, timely national state of disaster and prolonged lockdown measures taken under the active leadership of President Cyril Ramaphosa may have mitigated the explosive proliferation of Covid-19, but with over 646,398 positive cases and more than 15,378 deaths as of 11 September 2020,[119] the country has still emerged as having the most cases and the most deaths in Africa so far. Dr John Nkengasong, director of the Africa CDC, is very concerned that the virus is seeping into vulnerable populations around big cities, the less-privileged areas and the slums in South Africa.[120] There is concern, as well, that a newly approved IMF loan to mitigate the negative economic effects of Covid-19 might only compound the precarious situation of the South African poor, for a range of reasons, amongst which, the IMF's notoriety as a cure that is often more dangerous than the disease.[121] Indeed, moved by nationwide outrage at reports of corruption in his ANC government's response to the coronavirus pandemic, President Ramaphosa wrote a letter to fellow members of the ANC in which he expressed his support for the popular anger and disillusionment in these terms:

> I write this letter to you, my fellow ANC member, as our movement and our country face one of the greatest challenges since the advent of democracy.
>
> I am sure that you are aware that across the nation there is a sense of anger and disillusionment at reports of corruption in our response to the coronavirus pandemic.
>
> This anger is understandable and justified. In recent weeks, we have heard stories of tenders for personal protective equipment that have been given to individuals associated with ANC leaders and of public servants flouting the law in issuing tenders.
>
> What has caused the greatest outrage is that there are private sector companies and individuals (including civil servants) who have exploited a grave medical, social and economic crisis to wrongfully enrich themselves. This is an unforgivable betrayal for the millions of South Africans who are being negatively affected by the impact of Covid-19, experiencing hunger daily, hopelessness and joblessness.[122]

Almost everywhere, regardless of geography, the fact of a resilient racialised configuration of the world has meant that black and brown people have borne the brunt of coronavirus infections and deaths, as Covid-19, in its globalised nimble-footedness, has opportunistically insinuated itself into intimacies, by preying on sociality, comparative disadvantages, pre-existing precarities and related physical frailties that feed from and into debilitating hierarchies of systemic inequality and poverty. The fact of racial and ethnic hierarchies of humanity has meant that while Chinese and other East Asians have been stereotyped and unfairly victimised as vectors in other parts of the world in the beginning of the pandemic, in China for instance, Africans have, in turn, been subjected to similar prejudice, stereotyping, discrimination and physical and social distancing by Chinese. To what extent, in our post-covid-19 world, will we in positions of power and privilege have learnt to exercise greater accommodation of those we tend to dehumanise, and either to immobilise or to mobilise purely on our own terms? If and when borders and airports closed down in a bid to police the spread of Covid-19 are reopened, what lessons in global solidarity and tolerance will we have learnt and how generous to strangers, foreigners and migrants are we prepared to be, regardless of race, geography, class, gender, sexuality, culture, religion and related categories that inform our judgement, policies and decisions on who belongs or not?[123]

In other respects, the virus has adopted and, in certain instances, reinforced pre-existing hierarchies of race, class, space, gender and age as loci of vulnerabilities. While every social category is affected, not everyone is affected to the same degree. Everywhere, people aged 55 and above are dying more than their younger counterparts, despite reports that 'People in their 20s, 30s and 40s account for a growing proportion of the cases in many places, raising fears that asymptomatic young people are helping to fuel the virus's spread.'[124] There are also gender differences in how the virus affects humans, with men more likely to be infected and to die of the virus than women, and women, in turn, more likely to suffer disproportionately from loss of economic and academic opportunities and from gender-based violence as a result of being physically and socially confined in the same spaces and places with men under prolonged lockdown in contexts of patriarchy and insensitivity to the rights and humanity of women.[125] There is discrimination along racial lines as well, in racialised societies (like the UK, USA, Brazil and South Africa) that privilege whiteness and its system of values, where black and brown people are dying in inverse proportions to their white counterparts. Such disproportionate deaths, at face value, reflect the inaccessibility of affordable and quality healthcare as well as systemic exclusion from other societal services and benefits. They also reflect the preponderant, albeit contested, positions of servitude, subservience, subjugation and invisibility of black and brown people on the hierarchy of socioeconomic and political visibility that neoliberalism and legacies of the institution of enslavement and racialism have normalised, actively maintained and reproduced in various guises and disguises.[126]

While the economic effects globally are devastating for most as the virus drives productivity into hibernation, some regions and social categories are more acutely affected than others because of the systemic hierarchies of inequalities. In Africa, the attention to Covid-19 by governments is severely mitigated by deplorable under-staffed and overwhelmed public health systems, where health workers are disproportionately testing positive for Covid-19 due to shortages of personal protective equipment.[127] There is the added risk of dying as much from hunger and poverty as from Covid-19. If the rest of the world has in the past and under relatively normal times not been that generous to or in solidarity with Africa and its claim to human equality and dignity, there is little reason to be optimistic that plagued by their own Covid-19-imposed challenges, they would maintain or enhance their philanthropy towards the continent. Yet, it is precisely innovative modes of solidarity that are needed to tackle what the UN Secretary General, Antonio Guterres, has rightly termed 'the inequality pandemic' that has opened the floodgates to an opportunistic pandemic like Covid-19 to prey upon a racialised Eurocentric male-dominated world of crippling inequalities and insensitivities.[128] It is significant that Guterres, in his Mandela lecture, is on the side of victims of systemic exclusion, especially given that the UN as the institutional locus of his enunciation is a contributor to the problem. The world cannot continue to appeal to victims of systemic inequalities and injustices to bend over backwards to the point of contortion to demonstrate resilience while simultaneously turning a blind eye on the pernicious resilience of the very same structural injustices and inequalities at the roots of the savage trinity of repression, suppression and oppression that continues to neutralise their dignity and determined pursuit of fulfilment.

Notes

[1] A 1,200-word summary of this chapter was published as a paper entitled 'Covid-19: The Humbling and Humbled Virus with much to Say about Resilience' in *Corona Times*, www.coronatimes.net/covid-19-humbling-humbled-virus.

[2] 'What works against the virus?' 19 March 2020, https://news.cgtn.com/news/2020-03-19/What-works-against-the-virus--OZBF7I0PiU/index.html.

[3] 'WHO official warns against calling it "Chinese virus," says "there is no blame in this"', by Morgan Gstalter, 19 March 2020, https://thehill.com/homenews/administration/488479-who-official-warns-against-calling-it-chinese-virus-says-there-is-no.

[4] A point Donald Trump reiterates repeatedly for political effect, insisting that China be held accountable for having 'unleashed this plague on to the world', a message he repeated on 22 September 2020 in a virtual speech at the UN General Assembly, that coincided with the US death toll for coronavirus, a disease he has often downplayed, rising to more than 200,000, the highest in the world. See 'UN General Assembly: US-China tensions flare over coronavirus', by BBC, 22 September 2020, https://www.bbc.com/news/world-54253408; see also 'Trump's

UN speech was a bizarre feat of gaslighting and fantasy', by Michael H. Fuchs, 24 September 2020, https://www.theguardian.com/commentisfree/2020/sep/24/trumps-un-speech-was-a-bizarre-feat-of-gaslighting-and-fantasy.

[5] 'Letter from Africa: Spare a thought for stranded migrants', 17 May 2020, www.bbc.com/news/world-africa-52645702.

[6] See Howard Phillips, 'More eyes on COVID-19: Perspectives from History: The need for history in a time of plague'. *South African Journal of Science*, 2020: 116(7/8), Art. #8495, 1 page. https://doi.org/10.17159/sajs.2020/8495.

[7] 'The myth of physical and social distancing in Cameroon', by Hassan M. Yosimbom, 15 April 2020, https://www.coronatimes.net/myth-social-physical-distancing.

[8] 'Social distancing and "flatten the curve": Africa can do it', by Chambi Chachage, 30 March 2020, https://www.coronatimes.net/social-distancing-africa-can-do-it/.

[9] 'Bolsonaro's politics of death, Covid-19 and racial inequality in Brazil', by Carolina Parreiras and Viviane Mattar, 8 July 2020, https://www.coronatimes.net/bolsonaro-politics-death-covid-19-race-brazil/.

[10] Ibid.

[11] 'Trump concedes pandemic to "get worse before it gets better"', by Anthony Zurcher, 22 July 2020, https://www.bbc.com/news/world-us-canada-53494766.

[12] 'More eyes on COVID-19: Perspectives from Anthropology – What people believe is a lot less important than that they believe it', by Jess Auerbach, 29 July 2020, *South African Journal of Science*, 2020: 116(7/8), Art. #8491, 1 page, https://doi.org/10.17159/sajs.2020/8491.

[13] 'Consolation, compassion, and the digital during Covid-19 in Kinshasa', by Katrien Pype, 16 June 2020, https://anthrocovid.com/2020/06/16/consolation-compassion-and-the-digital-during-covid-19-in-kinshasa/.

[14] 'Key quotes: Covid-19 and reporting on communities of color', by Taylor Mulcahey, 2 July 2020, https://ijnet.org/en/story/key-quotes-covid-19-and-reporting-communities-color.

[15] 'On movement, human rights and Covid-19', by Pumla Dineo Gqola, 26 March 2020, https://www.newframe.com/on-movement-human-rights-and-covid-19/.

[16] 'John Oliver on coronavirus conspiracy theories: "People are going to get burned"', by Adrian Horton, 20 July 2020, https://www.theguardian.com/tv-and-radio/2020/jul/20/john-oliver-coronavirus-conspiracy-theories-people-are-going-to-get-burned.

[17] 'Strengthening the global effort on Covid-19 research', by Alice Norton, Jeffrey Mphahlele, Yazdan Yazdanpanah, Peter Piot and Marta Tufet Bayona, 16 July 2020, https://www.thelancet.com/action/showPdf?pii=S0140-6736%2820%2931598-1; see also, 'Funder principles for research in epidemics', by the United Kingdom Collaborative on Development Research and the Global Research Collaboration for Infectious Disease Preparedness, https://www.ukcdr.org.uk/resource/funder-principles-for-research-in-epidemics/?preview=true.

[18] For example, in July 2020 the South African Academy of Science *South African Journal of Science* (Vol 116 No 7/8, 2020) published a special compilation – 'More eyes on COVID-19' (https://www.sajs.co.za/issue/view/809) – that brought together a series of invited commentaries to provide 'more eyes' on the Covid-19 pandemic by drawing in perspectives from experts in the social sciences and humanities.

[19] 'The Pandemic Has Revealed the Weakness of Strongmen', by Helen Lewis, 6 May 2020, https://www.theatlantic.com/international/archive/2020/05/new-zealand-germany-women-leadership-strongmen-coronavirus/611161/.

[20] 'Are female leaders more successful at managing the coronavirus crisis?', by Henley and Eleanor Ainge Roy, 25 April 2020, https://www.theguardian.com/world/2020/apr/25/why-do-female-leaders-seem-to-be-more-successful-at-managing-the-coronavirus-crisis.

[21] 'The time of masks: everyone to themselves and Covid-19 for us all', by Divine Fuh, 8 May 2020, http://publicanthropologist.cmi.no/2020/05/08/the-time-of-masks-everyone-to-themselves-and-covid-19-for-us-all/.

[22] 'Coronavirus: Why attitudes to masks have changed around the world', by Helier Cheung, 14 July 2020, https://www.bbc.com/news/world-53394525.

[23] 'Coronavirus: Donald Trump vows not to order Americans to wear masks', 18 July 2020, https://www.bbc.com/news/world-us-canada-53453468.

[24] Watch 'Trump again says Covid-19 will "disappear" in first virus briefing in months, The 11th Hour, MSNBC', by Brain Williams, 21 July 2020, https://www.youtube.com/watch?v=3JV5LuqCm90&feature=youtu.be.

[25] 'Trump concedes pandemic to "get worse before it gets better"', 22 July 2020, https://www.bbc.com/news/world-us-canada-53494766.

[26] 'Tracking Covid-19 cases in the US', by Sergio Hernandez, Sean O'Key, Amanda Watts, Byron Manley and Henrik Pettersson, 23 September 2020, https://edition.cnn.com/interactive/2020/health/coronavirus-us-maps-and-cases/#!

[27] 'Trump mocks Biden for wearing mask: "Did you ever see a man that likes a mask as much as him?"', by Paul LeBlanc, 3 September 2020, https://amp.cnn.com/cnn/2020/09/03/politics/trump-biden-coronavirus-mask/index.html.

[28] 'Trump retweeted a video with false covid-19 claims. One doctor in it has said demons cause illnesses', by Travis M. Andrews and Danielle Paquette, 29 July 2020, https://www.washingtonpost.com/technology/2020/07/28/stella-immanuel-hydroxychloroquine-video-trump-americas-frontline-doctors/.

[29] 'Stella Immanuel – the doctor behind unproven coronavirus cure claim', by Dickens Olewe, 29 July 2020, https://www.bbc.com/news/world-africa-53579773.

[30] 'Coronavirus: Hydroxychloroquine ineffective says Fauci', by BBC, 29 July 2020, https://www.bbc.com/news/world-us-canada-53575964.

[31] 'Lancet Editor Spills the Beans and Britain's PM Surrenders to the Gates Vaccine Cartel', by Alliance for Human Research Protection (AHRP), 5 June 2020, https://ahrp.org/lancet-editor-spills-the-beans-and-britains-pm-surrenders-to-the-gates-vaccine-cartel/; see also, 'Surgisphere: mass audit of papers linked to firm

behind hydroxychloroquine Lancet study scandal', by Melissa Davey and Stephanie Kirchgaessner, 10 June 2020, https://www.theguardian.com/world/2020/jun/10/surgisphere-sapan-desai-lancet-study-hydroxychloroquine-mass-audit-scientific-papers.

[32] 'The Lancet changes editorial policy after hydroxychloroquine Covid study retraction', by Melissa Davey, 22 September 2020, https://www.theguardian.com/world/2020/sep/22/the-lancet-reforms-editorial-policy-after-hydroxychloroquine-covid-study-retraction.

[33] 'Coronavirus: Why are Americans so angry about masks?', by Tara McKelvey, 21 July 2020, https://www.bbc.com/news/world-us-canada-53477121.

[34] 'Fighting alone: I'm a GOP governor. Why didn't Trump help my state with coronavirus testing?', by Larry Hogan, 16 July 2020, https://www.washingtonpost.com/outlook/2020/07/16/larry-hogan-trump-coronavirus/?arc404=true.

[35] 'My statement on Donald Trump's continued failure to control Covid-19', by Joe Biden, 19 July 2020, https://medium.com/@JoeBiden/my-statement-on-donald-trumps-continued-failure-to-control-covid-19-1d0bddb9504f.

[36] 'After 200,000 coronavirus deaths, the US faces another rude awakening', by Ed Pilkington, 22 September 2020, https://www.theguardian.com/world/2020/sep/22/us-coronavirus-deaths-trump-autumn.

[37] 'UN chief criticizes lack of global cooperation on Covid-19', by Edith M. Lederer, 24 June 2020, https://abcnews.go.com/US/wireStory/chief-criticizes-lack-global-cooperation-covid-19-71417094.

[38] 'SA exports 800 000 masks to Italy, as the WHO warns of a global mask shortage due to Covid-19', by Jay Caboz, 5 March 2020, https://www.businessinsider.co.za/the-world-faces-a-mask-shortage-due-to-covid-19-the-who-warns-as-sa-exports-800-000-to-italy-2020-3.

[39] 'Taking back responsibility: A joint effort to increase the production of medical masks in Europe', by Sanne van der Lugt, 2 April 2020, https://www.clingendael.org/publication/joint-effort-increase-production-medical-masks-europe.

[40] 'Trump Covid: President criticised over drive-past', by BBC, 5 October 2020, https://www.bbc.com/news/election-us-2020-54415532.

[41] 'Trump Tests Positive for the Coronavirus', by Peter Baker and Maggie Haberman, 2 October 2020, https://www.nytimes.com/2020/10/02/us/politics/trump-covid.html.

[42] 'Trump says he is doing well, but next couple of days the "real test"', by the BBC, 4 October 2020, https://www.bbc.com/news/election-us-2020-54405734.

[43] 'Trump health monitored after weekend of confusion', by BBC, 5 October 2020, https://www.bbc.com/news/election-us-2020-54413536.

[44] 'Trump to leave hospital on Monday after weekend Covid treatment', by BBC, 5 October 2020, https://www.bbc.com/news/election-us-2020-54427390.

[45] 'How to Talk about COVID-19 in Africa', by Nanjala Nyabola, 15 October 2020, http://bostonreview.net/global-justice/nanjala-nyabola-how-talk-about-covid-19-africa.

[46] 'Africa has defied the covid-19 nightmare scenarios. We shouldn't be surprised', by Karen Attiah, 22 September 2020, https://www.washingtonpost.com/opinions/2020/09/22/africa-has-defied-covid-19-nightmare-scenarios-we-shouldnt-be-surprised/.

[47] 'Burundi's president died from COVID-19: reports', by Ahmet Emin Donmez, 16 June 2020, https://www.aa.com.tr/en/africa/burundis-president-died-from-covid-19-reports/1878252; 'Burundi president dies of illness suspected to be coronavirus', by Jason Burke, 9 June 2020, https://www.theguardian.com/world/2020/jun/09/burundi-president-dies-illness-suspected-coronavirus-pierre-nkurunziz.

[48] 'Malawi lawmaker dies of COVID-19', by Moses Miachael-Phili, 17 July 2020, https://www.aa.com.tr/en/africa/malawi-lawmaker-dies-of-covid-19/1913615; "Malawi Confirmed Coronavirus Cases Are Rising Faster - Death Toll At 8", by Osman Faiti, 18 June 2020, https://allafrica.com/stories/202006190052.html.

[49] 'Is Tanzania covering up the real number of coronavirus deaths?', by Jaclynn Ashly, 12 May 2020, https://www.aljazeera.com/news/2020/05/tanzania-covering-real-number-coronavirus-deaths-200511054304751.html; 'Coronavirus in Tanzania: What do we know?', by Peter Mwai and Christopher Giles, 19 June 2020, https://www.bbc.com/news/world-africa-52723594.

[50] 'Tanzania President John Magufuli: The man who declared victory over coronavirus', by Basillioh Mutahi, 22 October 2020, https://www.bbc.com/news/world-africa-54603689.

[51] 'Coronavirus: John Magufuli declares Tanzania free of Covid-19', by BBC, 8 June 2020, https://www.bbc.com/news/world-africa-52966016.

[52] 'Tanzania President John Magufuli: The man who declared victory over coronavirus', by Basillioh Mutahi, 22 October 2020, https://www.bbc.com/news/world-africa-54603689.

[53] 'The Pandemic Has Revealed the Weakness of Strongmen', by Helen Lewis, 6 May 2020, https://www.theatlantic.com/international/archive/2020/05/new-zealand-germany-women-leadership-strongmen-coronavirus/611161/.

[54] 'Italy small town priest deals with death on industrial scale', by Flavio Lo Scalzo, 28 March 2020, www.reuters.com/article/us-health-coronavirus-italy-coffins-idUSKBN21F0M6.

[55] 'Why covid-19 is different for men and women', by Martha Henriques, 13 April 2020, www.bbc.com/future/article/20200409-why-covid-19-is-different-for-men-and-women.

[56] 'Why covid-19 is different for men and women', by Martha Henriques, 13 April 2020, www.bbc.com/future/article/20200409-why-covid-19-is-different-for-men-and-women.

[57] 'Trans people have been hit hard by Covid-19 disruptions – here is why', by Miriam Aurora Hammeren Pedersen, 9 June 2020, https://www.coronatimes.net/trans-people-hit-hard-covid-19-disruptions.

[58] 'Camps Bay Mansion Occupiers: Who's Who and their Mission', by Refilwe Pitjeng, accessed 16 October 2020, https://ewn.co.za/2020/09/28/camps-bay-mansion-occupiers-who-s-who-and-their-mission; 'Camps Bay Airbnb saga: Occupiers leave mansion, as second group yells at them not to', by Jenni Evans, 8

October 2020, https://www.news24.com/news24/southafrica/news/camps-bay-airbnb-saga-occupiers-leave-mansion-as-second-group-yells-at-them-not-to-20201008.

[59] 'Coronavirus wreaks havoc in African American neighbourhoods', 7 April 2020, www.bbc.com/news/world-us-canada-52194018.

[60] 'How Covid-19 could destroy indigenous communities', by Terri Hansen, 30 July 2020, https://www.bbc.com/future/article/20200727-how-covid-19-could-destroy-indigenous-communities.

[61] 'Opinion: The hustle — white saviors and hashtag activism', by Angela Bruce-Raeburn, 12 June 2020, https://www.devex.com/news/opinion-the-hustle-white-saviors-and-hashtag-activism-97463.

[62] 'Coronavirus: Obama criticises Trump administration's virus response', 17 May 2020, www.bbc.com/news/world-us-canada-52694872.

[63] 'How to Talk about COVID-19 in Africa', by Nanjala Nyabola, 15 October 2020, http://bostonreview.net/global-justice/nanjala-nyabola-how-talk-about-covid-19-africa.

[64] 'Situating the biology of Covid-19: A conversation on disease and democracy', by Thomas Cousins, Sabina Leonelli, Michelle Pentecost and Kaushik Sunder Rajan, 3 July 2020, https://www.theindiaforum.in/article/situating-biology-covid-19.

[65] 'Coronavirus in South Africa: Inside Port Elizabeth's "hospitals of horrors"', by Andrew Harding, 15 July 2020, https://www.bbc.com/news/world-africa-53396057.

[66] 'South Africa braces for more coronavirus deaths as cases surge', by Max Bearak and Marco Longari, 30 July 2020, https://www.washingtonpost.com/graphics/world/2020/07/30/south-africa-coronavirus-deaths/.

[67] 'Coronavirus Disease 2019 (COVID-19): Africa CDC Dashboard Region', by Africa CDC, 11 October 2020, https://africacdc.org/covid-19/.

[68] 'WHO Coronavirus Disease (COVID-19) Dashboard', by WHO, 9 October 2020, https://covid19.who.int/.

[69] 'Forecasting Covid-19 for Sub-Saharan Africa', by Tony Blair, 10 July 2020, https://www.facebook.com/watch/?v=1325632400972592 ; see also, 'Planning for the worst and hoping for the best: Forecasting Covid-19 for Sub-Saharan Africa', by O.B. Sesay, Maryam Abdullah and Elizabeth Smith, 10 July 2020, https://institute.global/advisory/planning-worst-and-hoping-best-forecasting-covid-19-sub-saharan-africa?fbclid=IwAR2SmCm-8Tlhf1yoi00T0XSGF67O9qF7c3_nyf127zLQkcuL7xTqdOCJ96U.

[70] 'COVID-19: examining theories for Africa's low death rates', by Kevin Marsh and Moses Alobo, 7 October 2020, https://theconversation.com/covid-19-examining-theories-for-africas-low-death-rates-147393.

[71] 'Africa has defied the covid-19 nightmare scenarios. We shouldn't be surprised', by Karen Attiah, 22 September 2020, https://www.washingtonpost.com/opinions/2020/09/22/africa-has-defied-covid-19-nightmare-scenarios-we-shouldnt-be-surprised/.

[72] 'African nations must urgently prepare to confront Covid-19', by Tony Blair, 28 March 2020, https://institute.global/tony-blair/african-nations-must-urgently-prepare-confront-covid-19.

[73] 'Coronavirus in Africa: Contained or unrecorded?', 20 May 2020, www.bbc.com/news/world-africa-52702838.

[74] 'Social distancing and "flatten the curve": Africa can do it', by Chambi Chachage, 30 March 2020, https://www.coronatimes.net/social-distancing-africa-can-do-it/.

[75] 'Coronavirus: Kenyans moved by widow cooking stones for children', 30 April 2020, www.bbc.com/news/world-africa-52494404.

[76] 'South Africa faces mass hunger if efforts to offset impact of COVID-19 are eased', by Gabrielle Wills, Leila Patel, Servaas van der Berg and Bokang Mpeta, 26 July 2020, https://theconversation.com/south-africa-faces-mass-hunger-if-efforts-to-offset-impact-of-covid-19-are-eased-143143?

[77] 'Covid-19 could kill more people through hunger than the virus itself, warns Oxfam'by Harriet Barber, 9 July 2020, https://www.telegraph.co.uk/global-health/science-and-disease/covid-19-could-kill-people-hunger-virus-warns-oxfam/.

[78] 'Covid-19: Race against time as rich Kenyans install ICU beds in homes', by Eric Wainaina, 10 July 2020, https://www.pd.co.ke/news/covid-19-race-against-time-as-rich-kenyans-install-icu-beds-in-homes-43404/.

[79] 'Covid-19 exposes weaknesses in Kenya's healthcare system. And what can be done', by Abdu Mohiddin and Marleen Temmerman, 27 July 2020, https://theconversation.com/covid-19-exposes-weaknesses-in-kenyas-healthcare-system-and-what-can-be-done-143356?

[80] See for example, 'Resources: Documents and publications from Africa CDC', https://africacdc.org/resources/, accessed 19 October 2020.

[81] See for example, 'African intellectuals write Covid-19 letter to continent's leaders', by APA-Banjul (The Gambia), 19 April 2020, http://apanews.net/en/news/african-intellectuals-write-covid-19-letter-to-continents-leaders/.

[82] 'Racism row as French doctors suggest virus vaccine test in Africa', by Rebecca Rosman, 4 April 2020, https://www.aljazeera.com/news/2020/04/racism-row-french-doctors-suggest-virus-vaccine-test-africa-200404054304466.html.

[83] 'Coronavirus: What I learnt in Oxford's vaccine trial', by Richard Fisher, 22 July 2020, https://www.bbc.com/future/article/20200721-coronavirus-vaccine-trial-what-its-like-to-participate.

[84] 'Coronavirus: Russian hackers target Covid-19 vaccine research', 16 July 2020, https://www.bbc.com/news/technology-53429506.

[85] 'Africa has defied the covid-19 nightmare scenarios. We shouldn't be surprised', by Karen Attiah, 22 September 2020, https://www.washingtonpost.com/opinions/2020/09/22/africa-has-defied-covid-19-nightmare-scenarios-we-shouldnt-be-surprised/.

[86] 'Coronavirus: Why Africans should take part in vaccine trials', by Anne Mawathe, 18 May 2020, www.bbc.com/news/world-africa-52678741.

[87] 'In race for vaccine, African countries fear coming in last', by Carmen Paun, 31 July 2020, https://www.politico.com/news/2020/07/31/african-governments-fear-losing-out-in-vaccine-distribution-389213.

[88] 'The international community must guarantee equal global access to a covid-19 vaccine', by Justin Trudeau, Sahle-Work Zewde, Moon Jae-in, Jacinda Ardern, Cyril Ramaphosa, Pedro Sánchez Pérez-Castejón, Stefan Lofven and Elyes Fakhfakh, 15 July 2020, https://www.washingtonpost.com/opinions/2020/07/15/international-community-must-guarantee-equal-global-access-covid-19-vaccine/.

[89] 'Coronavirus: Caution urged over Madagascar's "herbal cure"', 22 April 2020, www.bbc.com/news/world-africa-52374250.

[90] 'Exclusive: Madagascar's president defends controversial homegrown covid-19 cure', 12 May 2020, www.france24.com/en/africa/20200512-exclusive-madagascar-s-president-defends-controversial-homegrown-covid-19-cure.

[91] 'Possibility of several vaccines – or none', by Kaye Adams, BBC Radio Scotland, 21 July 2020, https://www.bbc.com/news/coronavirus.

[92] 'Coronavirus vaccine: Oxford trial is "safe" and produces immune reaction, first study results show', by Samuel Lovett, https://www.independent.co.uk/news/health/coronavirus-vaccine-oxford-university-study-trial-result-covid-19-safe-a9628491.html?

[93] 'Exclusive: Madagascar's president defends controversial homegrown covid-19 cure', 12 May 2020, www.france24.com/en/africa/20200512-exclusive-madagascar-s-president-defends-controversial-homegrown-covid-19-cure.

[94] 'Coronavirus: Hospitals in Madagascar "overwhelmed"', by Felix Tih, 23 July 2020, https://www.aa.com.tr/en/africa/coronavirus-hospitals-in-madagascar-overwhelmed/1919657.

[95] 'WHO, Africa CDC in joint push for Covid-19 traditional medicine research in Africa', by Africa CDC, 22 July 2020, https://africacdc.org/news-item/who-africa-cdc-in-joint-push-for-covid-19-traditional-medicine-research-in-africa/.

[96] 'Fake pharmaceutical industry thrives in West Africa', 14 July 2020, https://www.bbc.com/news/world-africa-53387216.

[97] 'Fighting Covid-19: Interventions from Ghana's Traditional Priests', by Samuel Aniegye Ntewusu and Samuel N. Nkumbaan, 13 May 2020, https://religiousmatters.nl/fighting-covid-19-interventions-from-ghanas-traditional-priests/.

[98] 'Now more than ever, Ghana's Christians don't need false prophets', by Joseph Oduro-Frimpong, 27 June 2020, https://www.coronatimes.net/ghana-christians-dont-need-false-prophets-covid-19/.

[99] 'Victimisation of Africans in China threatens Afro-Sino relations', by Mills Soko and Mzukisi Qobo, 14 April 2020, www.dailymaverick.co.za/article/2020-04-14-victimisation-of-africans-in-china-threatens-afro-sino-relations.

[100] 'Coronavirus: "World faces worst recession since Great Depression"', by Szu Ping Chan, 14 April 2020, www.bbc.com/news/business-52273988, and 'Sub-Saharan Africa faces R1.4-trillion output loss and food crisis due to covid-19, says World Bank', by Bekezela Phakathi, 13 April 2020, www.businesslive.co.za/bd/national/2020-04-13-sub-saharan-africa-faces-r14-trillion-output-loss-and-food-crisis-due-to-covid-19-says-world-bank.

[101] 'Covid-19 Financial Assistance and Debt Service Relief', by IMF, 30 July 2020, https://www.imf.org/en/Topics/imf-and-covid19/COVID-Lending-Tracker#AFR; 'IMF Executive Board Approves US$4.3 Billion in Emergency Support to South Africa to Address the COVID-19 Pandemic', by Geoffrey W.S. Okamoto, 27 July 2020, https://www.imf.org/en/News/Articles/2020/07/27/pr20271-south-africa-imf-executive-board-approves-us-billion-emergency-support-covid-19-pandemic.

[102] 'Tackling the inequality pandemic: A new social contract for a new era', United Nations Secretary-General António Guterres's Nelson Mandela Annual Lecture 2020, 18 July 2020, https://www.nelsonmandela.org/news/entry/annual-lecture-2020-secretary-general-guterress-full-speech.

[103] 'How Big Tech got even bigger in the Covid-19 era', by Robin Wigglesworth, 1 May 2020, https://www.ft.com/content/d2e09235-b28e-438d-9b55-0e6bab7ac8ec; 'As Covid-19 surges, the world's biggest tech companies report staggering profits', by Rani Molla,30 October 2020, https://www.vox.com/recode/2020/10/30/21541699/big-tech-google-facebook-amazon-apple-coronavirus-profits.

[104] 'Amid the Covid-19 pandemic, Big Tech companies report mixed earnings', 31 July 2020, https://www.livemint.com/companies/company-results/amid-the-covid-19-pandemic-big-tech-companies-report-mixed-earnings-11596154637567.html.

[105] 'Turning back the poverty clock: How will covid-19 impact the world's poorest people?', by Homi Kharas and Kristofer Hamel, 6 May 2020, www.brookings.edu/blog/future-development/2020/05/06/turning-back-the-poverty-clock-how-will-covid-19-impact-the-worlds-poorest-people/?preview_id=804150.

[106] 'Coronavirus: BBC poll shows stark divide between rich and poor countries', https://www.bbc.com/news/world-54106474, accessed 11 September 2020.

[107] 'WHO Coronavirus Disease (COVID-19) Dashboard', by WHO, 9 October 2020, https://covid19.who.int/.

[108] According to the BBC, as of 29 June 2020, 'More than 501,000 people have died after contracting coronavirus, according to a tally by Johns Hopkins University in the US. Here are 10 countries reporting the highest number of deaths: United States: 125,803; Brazil: 57,622; United Kingdom: 43,634; Italy: 34,738; France: 29,781; Spain: 28,343; Mexico: 26,648; India: 16,475; Iran: 10,508; Belgium: 9,732', https://www.bbc.com/news/live/world-53216079.

[109] 'Trevor Manuel in bid to find international support for Africa', by Linda Ensor, 13 April 2020, www.businesslive.co.za/bd/economy/2020-04-13-trevor-manuel-in-bid-to-find-international-support-for-africa.

[110] 'Covid-19 as a global challenge: towards an inclusive and sustainable future', by Helen Lambert, Jaideep Gupte, Helen Fletcher, Laura Hammond, Nicola Lowe, Mark Pelling, Neelam Raina, Tahrat Shahid and Kelsey Shanks, https://www.thelancet.com/pdfs/journals/lanplh/PIIS2542-5196(20)30168-6.pdf.

[111] 'I got Covid-19 two months ago. I'm still discovering new areas of damage', by Richard Quest, 7 July 2020,

https://edition.cnn.com/2020/07/07/health/richard-quest-covid-wellness-intl/index.html?

[112] 'How coronavirus affects the entire body', by Maggie Fox, 11 July 2020, https://edition.cnn.com/2020/07/10/health/coronavirus-entire-body-effects-columbia/index.html.

[113] Ibid.

[114] Ibid.

[115] As reported on the BBC, with the advent of the Coronavirus and the need for protection against it, 'The masks you throw away could end up killing a whale', as 'more and more protective equipment is ending up in the sea.' According to Ocean Conservancy, 'We are putting 129 billion face masks and 65 billion plastic gloves into the environment every month, according to Ocean Conservancy', 8 July 2020, https://www.bbc.com/news/av/science-environment-53287940/coronavirus-the-masks-you-throw-away-could-end-up-killing-a-whale. It is worth noting that the environmental issues are greater than this. Other effects include increased use of detergents, sanitisers, alcohol-based substances that enter water ways and seas with as yet under-assessed implications; there is some research suggesting covid is entering sea through waste water systems, again with unknown consequences for marine life; increased use of medications, which, as waste, enter waterways etc.

[116] 'Tackling the inequality pandemic: A new social contract for a new era', United Nations Secretary-General António Guterres's Nelson Mandela Annual Lecture 2020, 18 July 2020, https://www.nelsonmandela.org/news/entry/annual-lecture-2020-secretary-general-guterress-full-speech.

[117] 'Brazil's racial reckoning: "Black lives matter here, too"', by Katy Watson, 25 July 2020, https://www.bbc.com/news/world-latin-america-53484698.

[118] 'A king's allowance and almost a king's ransom in tenders for presidential spokesperson's husband', by Ferial Haffajee, 28 July 2020, https://www.dailymaverick.co.za/article/2020-07-28-a-kings-allowance-and-almost-a-kings-ransom-in-tenders-for-presidential-spokespersons-husband/#gsc.tab=0.

[119] 'Latest confirmed cases of covid-19 in South Africa (11 sept 2020)' by the National Institute for Communicable Diseases, 11 September 2020, https://www.nicd.ac.za/latest-confirmed-cases-of-covid-19-in-south-africa-11-sept-2020/.

[120] 'Covid-19 Lessons from South Africa: Africa warned about dangers of pandemic taking root in vulnerable communities', by Peter Fabricius, 23 July 2020, https://www.dailymaverick.co.za/article/2020-07-23-africa-warned-about-dangers-of-pandemic-taking-root-in-vulnerable-communities/#gsc.tab=0.

[121] 'The IMF's $4bn loan for South Africa: the pros, cons and potential pitfalls', by Danny Bradlow, 28 July 2020, https://theconversation.com/the-imfs-4bn-loan-for-south-africa-the-pros-cons-and-potential-pitfalls-143553?

[122] 'Let this be a turning point in our fight against corruption', by Cyril Ramaphosa, 23 August 2020; see also 'End of Cyril Ramaphosa "The Consensus Man"?' by Stephen Grootes, 23 August 2020, https://www.dailymaverick.co.za/article/2020-08-23-end-of-cyril-ramaphosa-the-consensus-man/; 'Read the full letter Ramaphosa sent to the ANC on

corruption', https://ewn.co.za/2020/08/23/read-the-full-letter-ramaphosa-sent-to-the-anc-on-corruption, accessed 24 August 2020.

[123] See 'Writing about "that kind of country" in a time of coronavirus', by Jess Auerbach, 19 March 2020, https://africanarguments.org/2020/03/19/writing-about-that-kind-of-country-in-a-time-of-coronavirus/; 'Convivial networks: how migrants cope with the pandemic in South Africa', by Tamuka Chekero and Helidah Refiloe Ogude, 14 September 2020, https://www.coronatimes.net/convivial-networks-migrants-pandemic-south-africa/; 'The Corona Virus and Migration Governance in South Africa: Business As Usual?', by Franzisca Luise Zanker and Khangelani Moyo, 20 May 2020, https://journals.sagepub.com/doi/full/10.1177/0002039720925826.

[124] 'As Virus Surges, Younger People Account for "Disturbing" Number of Cases', by Julie Bosman and Sarah Mervosh, 23 July 2020, https://www.nytimes.com/2020/06/25/us/coronavirus-cases-young-people.html.

[125] The full psychological and social impact of prolonged periods of lockdown are still a matter of speculation. See, 'How lockdown may have changed your personality', by Christian Jarrett, 29 July 2020, https://www.bbc.com/future/article/20200728-how-lockdown-may-have-changed-your-personality.

[126] See Faye Harrison interview, 'ODVV interview: Systemic racism in the US assumes a variety of covert and overt forms', by Kourosh Ziabari, 25 June 2020, http://www.odvv.org/blog-3049-ODVV-interview-Systemic-racism-in-the-US-assumes-a-variety-of-covert-and-overt-forms.

[127] 'Coronavirus "disproportionately hit African health workers"', by Rhoda Odhiambo, 23 July 2020, https://www.bbc.com/news/live/world-africa-47639452?

[128] 'Tackling the inequality pandemic: A new social contract for a new era', United Nations Secretary-General António Guterres's Nelson Mandela Annual Lecture 2020 speech, 18 July 2020, https://www.nelsonmandela.org/news/entry/annual-lecture-2020-secretary-general-guterress-full-speech#search-form.

Part 2

Resilience in Public Discourse in Contexts of Calamity

Chapter 4

Attempts to Promote Resilience at the Great Hanshin Awaji Earthquake Seismic Centre: Based on *Kataribe* Story Telling

Toru Hamaguchi
(*Kataribe*: *Masayuki Komeyama*)

1. Introduction: Conveying Past Lessons to the Present

Twenty-six years have passed since the occurrence of the Great Hanshin Earthquake, and memories of the earthquake have become diluted. However, some of the people who experienced this earthquake are attempting to convey their experiences in different ways. The Hokudan Earthquake Memorial Park is located adjacent to the seismic centre and consists of facilities such as The Nojima Fault Preservation Museum, the Seminar House, a restaurant and a local product sales office. The Nojima Fault Preservation Museum was established to exhibit and provide information on the earthquake damage, Nojima Fault and earthquake preparation efforts. Additionally, *Kataribe* (storyteller) events are continuously held to convey the experiences of the earthquake to younger generations. The present *Kataribe* is Mr Komeyama, who was affected by this disaster and, at the same time, participated in rescue activities as a member of the volunteer fire brigade (*Shouboudan*) in Hokudan-cho. This analysis uses the stories of the *Kataribe* to review the activities of the volunteer fire brigade and their relationship with the community residents, which was the cornerstone of the town's resilience.

The Home page of the Fire Disaster Management Agency (FDMA) said that the firefighting and rescue operations are done by full time firefighters who are the staff of FDMA and members of *Shouboudan*. The members of *Shouboudan* are part-time, special-purpose local officials who rush to the scene of a fire or major disaster from their homes or workplaces and use their local experience to carry out firefighting and rescue operations. *Shouboudan* is the municipality's emergency fire-fighting organisation and its members have other main jobs (FDMA Home page).

2. The Great Hanshin Awaji Earthquake

The Southern Hyogo Prefecture Earthquake occurred on 17 January 1995 at 5:46:52 am. It led to 6,433 deaths, and more than 100,000 buildings were destroyed. The name above used to refer to this earthquake was created by the mass media arbitrarily, but the government decided that a unified name was necessary for future restoration. Subsequently, the earthquake was named the Great Hanshin-Awaji Earthquake because the Hanshin region centring on Kobe City and the northern part of Awaji Island were the most affected areas. As this earthquake occurred directly beneath urban areas, the range of the damage was extensive, with severe damage to people and infrastructure, including houses and buildings.

Hokudan-cho is located in the north-west part of Awaji Island, which is close to the seismic centre of the earthquake, and the Nojima Fault that caused this earthquake runs beneath this town. Consequently, the Great Hanshin-Awaji Earthquake caused extensive damage in Hokudan-cho: 39 people were killed, 59 people were severely wounded and 811 were injured, and 3305 buildings collapsed.

Among the six districts in Hokudan-cho, Toshima District was the most damaged area, and 26 people in the district were killed, representing 67% of the total deaths in the town. In Toshima District, 80% of the houses were totally or partially destroyed (Hokudan Town Office 1997). By 22 January 1995, five days after the earthquake, 1,077 people in Toshima District, representing 45% of the town's total population, had been evacuated (Urano 1999).

Mr Komeyama's discourse is mainly focused on his experience of receiving support as a disaster victim and participating in the rescue operations as a volunteer fire brigade member. In his blog, Mr Komeyama says that he will share his experiences with future generations to ensure that the regrettable and sad outcomes of the disaster are not repeated.

3. Story Telling by Mr Komeyama (*Kataribe*)

This chapter will introduce the story told by Mr Komeyama in Japanese at The Hokudan Earthquake Memorial Park on 15 July 2019:

From the earthquake at Hokudan-cho, 38 out of 39 died immediately from being crushed to death or suffocation. The remaining person died in hospital four months after the incident.

In this town, more than 90% of the houses collapsed or were damaged by the earthquake.

At that time, there were 3,700 houses in Hokudan-Cho. However, out of those, 3,300 houses collapsed or were partially damaged.

Because of the relationship of mutual trust between the residents and the volunteer fire brigade, the rescue activities could be started soon after the occurrence of an earthquake. The persons who were involved in the rescue activities knew the residents. For example, which older person was staying in a particular house.

Because of the community in the local area, the residents and volunteer fire brigade members who were involved in the rescue activities knew the family situation of damaged houses. For example, whether older people or small children were among the family members or not, in which room of the damaged house these family members were sleeping.

Such knowledge was quite important because the earthquake occurred at 5:40 am early in the morning when most of the residents were sleeping. (Because of the knowledge of the people involved in the rescue activities, they could take necessary actions quickly).

Because of that, even in a collapsed house, the rescue team could anticipate the location of the residents. As a result, about 300 people buried alive were rescued from collapsed houses.

By the afternoon of that day, we had rescued everyone (who were trapped inside the collapsed houses) and declared zero missing persons. The rescue team could confirm the location of all residents by around 5 pm that day.

During that period, 565 persons were registered as members of the volunteer fire brigade among the total population of 11,000 residents in Hokudan-Cho. Compared with other townships, the ratio of the volunteer fire brigade members in Hokudan-Cho was quite high.

In addition to 565 active members, about 500 ex-volunteer fire brigade members participated in the rescue activities. They cooperated with the active members to conduct these activities.

I was among the 565 members and participated in the rescue activities.

On that day, I was in bed with my two-month-old baby girl and my wife.

I was woken up by the sudden loud sounds, the shock that pushed me up, and my wife shouting.

I noticed that my wife covered my daughter to protect her. I then covered my wife and daughter. At first, the shake occurred horizontally with short intervals, and the intervals became longer and longer.

When the earthquake happened, I lived on the fourth floor of a four-storey apartment located along the road in Toshima District of Hokudan-Cho. Toshima District was the most severely damaged area by this earthquake.

As I have never experienced such a large earthquake before, at first, I could not believe that the intense shaking was due to the earthquake. I thought that a huge truck had crashed into our apartment.

Some of my friends thought that the shock was from an airplane crash at Kansai International Airport, which is located on the opposite side of Awaji Island because the airport had begun operations just one year before, in 1994.

I experienced a loud sound and furious shaking. In my apartment, a cabinet fell, and the tableware was broken into pieces. I could not move but covered my wife and daughter for some time. When the shaking stopped, I tried to see what had happened outside the apartment, but the shaking started again because of the aftershocks.

The shaking probably continued for only 40 seconds, but it felt as long as five minutes. Eventually, the shaking stopped for a while, and I tried again to see outside. However, it was 5 am in January, and it was still dark outside. However, I could see that it was snowing outside.

After I checked that my daughter and wife were not hurt, we tried to escape from the apartment before it collapsed, but the entrance door was deformed by the earthquake and could not be opened.

It seemed that the apartment building had deformed a bit. The door to the next room was difficult to open because some of the furniture in the next room blocked the doorway. A cupboard had fallen and leaned against a table. The tableware was broken into pieces, the things stored in the refrigerator had fallen out, and bottles of sake and other seasoning bottles were broken. Due to the leaked seasoning mixed with other liquids, the room was full of unpleasant smells.

The microwave oven that was on a 1.5m-high shelf fell onto the floor, landing 2 meters away.

I tried to check another tatami room where I had been sleeping apart from my family because I had the flu until the day before the incident. I found that the TV had fallen on the tatami where I had been sleeping. If I had slept in that room for another day, the TV would have fallen on me.

I was frightened by the situation and tried to run away from the apartment as soon as possible. I held my baby daughter, who was covered with a blanket, and held my wife's hand so we could escape from the site and go to the gym hall of the elementary school that was located about 100 meters away from my place.

When I arrived at the gym hall, several people had already been sheltered. Among these people, I could see an older man with an injured leg and an older woman with a towel wrapped around her head covering an injury on her head.

As soon as I arrived at the gym hall, an older woman shouted to me, 'your parents' house collapsed!' My father's house was also located in Toshima District. I was anxious about my father and other family members, so I hurried to my father's house, leaving my baby daughter and wife at the shelter.

When I came out of the shelter, the house located next to the shelter had a damaged roof, and there were many collapsed houses on the way to my father's house. The damage became worse as I approached my parents' house.

I ran into my parents' house at full speed. As I arrived in front of the house, I saw my father, mother, grandfather and grandmother, all of my family members, standing there absentmindedly.

When I saw them, I was very glad that they were still alive! They were OK. My parents' house was a double story house, but the second floor was not at full height as the house had a mezzanine floor. As the main roof on the top of the house had collapsed, there was a large hole in that roof, and because of this large hole, the main roof did not cover the whole of the second roof. Although the entire house was damaged, all four of my family members had escaped from the house without injury. My father was sleeping on the first floor next to a wardrobe, which could be detached through the upper and lower portions. Although the upper portion of the wardrobe fell, it was stopped by the lower portion, creating a triangle-shaped gap. He was caught in the gap and thus could escape without any injuries.

While I talked with my father and congratulated him on his survival, my uncle and aunt, whose single-storey house was located just behind my parents' house, shouted something at us. However, I could not understand what they were saying because they were panicking. I could guess from their explanation that most of their house's roof tiles had fallen into their house. This was because their house had collapsed into two parts from the centre of the roof as the big houses on both sides of their house had swayed and put extraordinary pressure on their house.

My uncle and aunt were in the room close to the entrance so that they could easily escape from the house. When I checked the inside of their house, a cupboard fell, and all of the tableware that was stored in the cupboard broke into many pieces and scattered around on the floor.

In the most inner room, I found an 80-year-old woman who had difficulties moving and was stuck under a low table with a heater (a *kotatsu* in Japanese). She blinked her eyes as she was terrified. I addressed her and asked her to lean onto my shoulder, then I carried her to a shelter about 300 metres from the house. While I carried her, I did not feel any tiredness or her weight. I might have run over heaps of rubble on the road on the way to the shelter; however, I cannot remember how I did it even now.

As I was a member of the volunteer fire brigade, after I dropped off the older woman at the shelter, I went to the fire brigade office and put on my uniform, rubber boots and safety hat to join the rescue activities in Toshima District.

When I arrived at the site, the residents and members of the volunteer fire brigade had already begun rescue activities. We started the work that we could do by ourselves as we did not have time to wait for help from other towns or ambulances. We had only one chain saw in our team, but that could not be used as the blade of the chain saw could be easily damaged by iron bars or iron nails. We used a manual saw, scoop, hoe, blanket and crowbar, which we brought from our houses and a jack from a car. We used these tools that were available in our daily life for the rescue activities.

Members of the volunteer fire brigade have everyday jobs. Some of the members are carpenters who know the houses' structures, so they can advise the other members of the team on what is essential to support the structure of the house. Some other members are electricians who can quickly repair electric cables.

On Awaji Island, we use gas cylinders to provide gas to each house. As the volunteer fire brigade members and the residents had closed the valves of the gas cylinders, there were no fire accidents in Toshima District. It would be the end of the story if we had had a fire under those circumstances, and those words became a slogan among the members of the rescue team.

The rescue work was a tough job. There was a lot of work for the fire brigade. One task was patrolling the area. After the main earthquake with a seismic intensity of 7 occurred, aftershocks with a seismic intensity of 5 or 4 continued for several days. We had difficulties in convincing the victims to evacuate their homes and move to the shelters. Some victims insisted that they wanted to remain in their houses, which were totally collapsed, and some insisted that they would stay in their house even though a neighbouring house had collapsed on top of their house.

We had to convince the victims and guide them to the shelter. These victims complained that they did not want to stay in the shelter with a cold floor or did not want to sleep next to strangers. Thus, the fire brigade team repeatedly went from house to house to convince them to evacuate their places and stay in the shelter. During the patrol, we checked whether the damaged houses could collapse and if the access road used before the earthquake was still accessible.

The distribution of relief supplies was also an important task for the volunteer fire brigade. At the peak, 3,650 people stayed at the 19 different shelters in the area. We received many relief supplies from all over Japan. These supplies were delivered to the Hokudan-cho town office and sorted in an open-air space located in front of the office, and the task of the fire brigade was to distribute the sorted supplies to each shelter.

For the first or second day after the earthquake, people were supposed to help each other or cooperate with each other; however, after a few days, mindsets gradually changed to be more egocentric and more family-first attitudes. In the beginning, when we distributed food supplies, people said we should prioritise small children to have the food supplies; however, as time passed, their attitude changed and became more egoistic, and some people came to pick up supplies repeatedly. They fought each other over the food.

During the first several days in the shelter, nobody cared about where they slept, who slept next to them, about snoring, about children running around the shelter, or about how frequently older people went to the toilet. There were no complaints from the people in the shelter. However, after several days, they gradually began to complain about their situation in the shelter and started quarrelling with each other or fighting each other over their situation in the shelter. In the shelter, people used cartons or books to make a partition to maintain their space and privacy. The height of such partitions gradually increased daily. At that time, newspapers and TV programmes only reported the good side of the situation; however, as part of the real story, I was obliged to see such a bad side of human beings.

Mr Komeyama showed us the movies.

These movies are from Kobe City, in the Nagata area, and because of this earthquake, 6,434 persons passed away. The authorities suspect that over 500 people among this figure died from fires.

In Kobe City, so many people passed away because of fires. I suspect that the leading cause of fires in Kobe City was the automatic recovery system for the electricity supply. When the earthquake occurred, the electricity supply, water supply and gas supply systems through pipelines were automatically shut down because of the strong movements of the buildings. However, when the building sway was not very strong, an automatic recovery system for the electricity supply was first activated. Due to the earthquake, gas leakages occurred and caught a spark from damaged electric cables after the electric supply was reactivated, and this caused a big fire. It seems that more than half of the fires in Kobe City were caused by this situation.

As I said earlier, there were no fire accidents in Toshima District during this earthquake. Apart from Toshima District, there were two cases of fire in Hokudan-cho.

One of the cases occurred because of the ignition of chemical agents at a junior high school. This was extinguished at the very early stage of the fire, so the damage was limited.

There was another severe fire incident at a private house in the Hirabayashi area located about 5 km away from here, toward the Akashi Kaikyo Bridge. In this house, one family consisted of a grandfather, father, mother, the eldest daughter who was a university student living outside of Awaji Island, the eldest son who was a high school student and a second son who was a junior high school student. When the incident happened, five persons, except the eldest daughter, were staying in the house.

When the earthquake occurred, the mother was preparing a lunch box for the family in the kitchen. While she was cooking, she felt a big shock, immediately recognising that it was an earthquake and hastily tried to wake up the family members who were still sleeping, but the house collapsed instantly. After that, the father, eldest son, second son and grandfather escaped from that collapsed house. However, their mother could not. While she was trapped inside the house, she was still alive, and her voice was heard. Then, the fire started.

When the Hirabayashi volunteer fire brigade received information about this family, they prepared to rescue the mother trapped inside the house. When the fire brigade noticed the fire, they immediately connected the fire hose from the fire engine to the fireplug; however, the water did not flow because the earthquake had destroyed the water pipeline to the plug.

Six months before this earthquake, there were no fire plugs in Hirabayashi, and instead, a water tank for firefighting was available. The Hirabayashi volunteer fire brigade used the water from this tank for firefighting. As they tried to speed up the firefighting activities, they built fire plugs instead of a water tank for firefighting. However, the fireplug was not usable at all on this day, so they tried to use old water tanks and seawater to extinguish the fire, and it took a long time.

... My close friend was a member of the Hirabayashi volunteer fire brigade and participated in their firefighting activities. According to him, at first, he could hear her screaming, 'Help me,' but this screaming became 'Help me, [it's] very hot,' and gradually, her voice became weaker and weaker. Finally, he could not hear her voice, and because of the firefighting activities, he was quite sure that he would gradually approach her, but he could not reach her. He still remembered his regret ....

The recording is suspended.

So, four people were rescued, but one person died because of this fire incident. Furthermore, one year after this incident, the father of this family committed suicide. After the incident, this family always took care of each other and talked to each other, which was how they could survive; they should be united, but the father committed suicide. It seems that this father suffered so much by losing his beloved wife and had some mental health problems.

Mr Komeyama showed some photos.

This is a photo taken in Kobe City. The tour bus almost fell off Hanshin Express Road (this morning, after we checked out from the hotel in Kobe, we used this highway on the way to this place, and this photo showed a part of that highway). Before the earthquake, Kobe Police Authority planned to use only the express road for emergency vehicles. As this express road was damaged so much by this earthquake, the plan was paralysed.

This photo illustrates the situation near the toll gate at Ashiya; the elevated Hanshin express road was damaged for about 635 meters. Although the Hanshin express road was damaged so much, the entire road resumed operations in September 1996 (one year and eight months after the earthquake). I think this is amazing.

Immediately after the earthquake, a company from the Shikoku area provided portable toilets for all of the shelters. About 20–25 toilet units were provided to the large-scale shelters, and at least five toilet units were provided to small-scale shelters.

As the damage from the earthquake was not so much in the southern part of Awaji Island, the town office contracted a cleaning company in that area to clean the toilets every morning. This was a good measure.

(Showing the photo) This is the building of the Hokudan-cho Town office. Initially, we stored relief supplies from all over Japan in the open air in front of this building. Then, we arranged tents to cover these things to prevent rainwater damage. However, soon after, there was a shortage of storage space. We tried to utilise space inside the shelters, but soon, there was a space shortage again. A group of carpenters from the Kochi prefecture of Shikoku voluntarily came to build five storage houses in the middle yard of a junior high school in the town.

Soon after, again, these spaces were not enough to store the relief supplies. The group of local carpenters built a storage unit in Hokudan-cho. Although there was no bridge between the mainland (Honshu, Kobe side) and Awaji Island built yet, there was a bridge between Awaji Island and Shikoku Island; thus, many relief supplies came from Shikoku. As the name of Hokudan-cho was reported in the media as an area affected by the earthquake, most of the relief supplies were delivered to the Hokudan-cho town office.

Every morning about 20 large post-office delivery trucks delivered supplies to the office. So many relief supplies were delivered from all over Japan.

In *Kobe* City, to get one rice ball (*onigiri*), the victims queued in extremely cold weather. In Hokudan-cho, relief supplies were distributed to the victims without a queue, which really helped our situation.

The arrival of the Japanese self-defence forces was unexpectedly fast. At 4:00 pm, the main troops had already arrived at our place.

To manage such a massive natural disaster, the ability of the local government and fire brigade are limited. When the local residents become panicked, they depend on local people too much. However, the self-defence forces can utilise the means from the land, sea, sky and the directive order system, making them a reliable organisation during disasters. I really appreciate their attendance.

Many volunteers were coming to us. Based on the data, it was said that a maximum of 215 persons per day came as volunteers; however, I believe that about 300 people came to us on some dates as volunteers. Not only private persons but also members of citizen groups, enterprises, professionals and religious groups participated as volunteers.

Among the volunteers, we could recognise many younger people who are said to be indifferent to volunteer activities, and many students participated as private persons for a long period.

This was the organisation chart that they used during the volunteer activities.

The year of 1995 (Heisei 7), when this earthquake occurred, was named the first year of volunteering in Japan. Before this earthquake, it was rare to hear the word volunteer, and it was quite rare to meet a person who had experience of volunteer activities.

In the case of Hokudan-cho, most people who participated in the volunteer activities were inexperienced in such activities. Therefore, they did not know what they should do. They had the idea that the victims were pitiful, and they lost their loved ones or houses. Due to this understanding, they believed that the victims of Hokudan-cho should not do anything, and they (the volunteers) tried to do everything using all means. Even simple work, such as cleaning work in the shelter, cleaning the bathrooms and helping the preparation and distribution of emergency food was done by the volunteers.

Hokudan-cho depended on them and did nothing. This was a bad aspect of the activities. Basically, an important thing for the volunteers was to arrange their own food and their sleeping bags to not place an extra burden on the victims.

In addition to this, an important point about conducting volunteer activities was that the volunteers should not insist on their own opinions, but they should face the victims to listen to their opinions and help them do the things they could do. I learned from this experience that volunteers should encourage the victims to be independent.

In Hokudan-cho, although a total of 39 people passed away, about 300 people who were buried alive could be rescued. The major factors limiting the damage were, first, that the earthquake occurred early in the morning when the daily activities had not started.

We knew who slept where; however, if someone had already woken up, we could not locate them so easily. As most of the people were sleeping, our work to confirm their safety could be easily done.

(The second factor that minimised damage) Besides the water supply, two lifelines, the electric supply and gas supply, were available immediately after the earthquake. Even the water supply was recovered at 19 shelters with the help of water supply repair people from Shikoku four days after the earthquake.

(The third factor that minimised damage) As I mentioned earlier, we experienced only one big fire. Although the Hokudan-cho area was famous for its strong winds during winter, there was no wind on that day, by chance, and so large fires did not affect the neighbouring houses. This was also a good point.

(The fourth factor that minimised damage) I believed that you passed route 31, which runs beside the sea. On that date, although there was damage on the road such as cracks and swells, we could still use it. There was a space to let one vehicle pass.

These four points were the beneficial factors that minimised damage. If we did not have these good factors that I have explained, the situation of our town would have been beyond the imagination.

Mr Komeyama showed a document.

In this paper, the possibility of disaster prevention is mentioned. Is *Gensai* (disaster reduction) the only word available in Japan? There was the term *Gensai* (disaster reduction). I understood that all kinds of natural disasters could not be prevented; therefore, we tried to make an effort to reduce the damage from the disaster using the unity of the people, by helping each other. I understand that this attitude is the basic foundation of *Gensai*.

This paper said that anti-seismic measures were important. Although there are points to be overcome, such as technical aspects and cost factors, it is better to arrange anti-seismic measures within the possible range. If you can prevent the instant collapse of your house, your chance to save your life could be increased, although you might lose your house. Please apply anti-seismic measures to your house as much as possible.

To store water, this paper recommended having three litres of water per person per day and storing it for three days. I believe that storing water is very important during a disaster. When you plan to store water, do not store all of the stock of water in one place. It is better to store the water in different places such as several bottles in the kitchen, while others can be stored in the entrance hall. Based on the consideration of severe damage to the house, I recommend storing the water near windows that can be accessed from outside the house.

This is the photo of the shelter. It is better to discuss with your family members and decide how to access the shelter from your house. I recommend you consider not just one access route but at least three alternative plans to access the shelter. With your friends or family members, why don't you take a walk in your town? See your town with your own eyes. You could obtain valuable information by doing so.

This is a photo of how to anchor a wardrobe using metal fittings. In some Japanese books published in Japan, the books recommend not putting wardrobes in your bedroom. However, during the earthquake in our town, not only one but several persons survived because of furniture that fell. This furniture that fell supported collapsed columns and provided evacuation space.

So, I cannot agree 100% with what the book said; however, basically, you should anchor your furniture to prevent it from falling.

If you fix the chain to hold the ceiling lights, the chain can prevent ceiling lights from falling. This photo shows a film on the window glass. If you put the film on window glass, you can prevent broken glass from scattering around.

This is the photo of a pair of slippers. I used the slippers when I encountered an earthquake. (Protecting your feet is quite important for evacuation.)

In your daily life, you should arrange your shoes or slippers within reach to evacuate in case of an emergency. When an earthquake occurs, you definitely will be in panic mode; so, it is important to remember the location of your necessary items.

You especially have to arrange protection for your body, feet and head. You should not evacuate empty-handed. You should bring bed sheets, blankets, shirts, jackets ... whatever can be used for protection.

Now, I always have this whistle. When the earthquake occurred, some people were buried alive with no injuries, but they could not call for help loudly. The whistle can be blown with a little breath to get the attention of the rescue team, and so you should bring a whistle with you.

Whenever you go to bed, you should place your whistle, torch and radio close to your bed. However, they need to be placed carefully. Remember, when an earthquake occurs, even a microwave can be moved 2 meters. Therefore, small items should be placed near you carefully. In my case, I put a chain or cord on these items and fixed them to my bed sheet with a safety pin so that I would not have to look for these small items in case of an emergency.

Once I start to comment on preparing against disasters, there will be no limit.

In Japan, we have a proverb. Providing is preventing. If you prepare the countermeasures well, you will have less sorrow. Until the rescue operation starts, you do not have any other choice, but you must depend on yourself and your preparation. Therefore, please prepare whatever you think can help during a disaster as much as you can.

I suggest that you should start a workshop. Workshops are arranged at town offices or schools. You should start the workshop with a small group of people and ask about their anxieties, and ask them to discuss their problems, worries and anxieties, even small ones. Then, these should be categorised into items that can be handled by an individual person, items that can be handled by family members and items that can be handled by community members. By categorising each item, I would like the residents to recognise that they will not be able to protect their town unless they consider the disaster by themselves. They should always have such ideas in their minds.

Here, in these documents, is the name list. Nowadays, in Japan, people are concerned about privacy when someone prepares a name list. However, I believe that human life is more important than privacy. If central control (done by the town office using a name list) is hard, at least necessary information should be exchanged between people who need help and the people who can help (who can participate in the rescue activities) during the disaster.

Please utilise the information for disaster prevention. To utilise this information, there should be a common understanding between the government as the sender of the information and the residents as the recipients of the information. Otherwise, the information cannot be useful. If the recipients cannot understand the meanings of the words in the message sent by the sender, such messages cannot be adequately understood.

One example is the water disaster in 2001 that occurred at the Maruyama River, which is located in the northern part of Hyogo prefecture (Heisei 16). As the river water was about to reach a dangerous level, the town office issued an 'evacuation advisory'. The water level soon exceeded a dangerous level, and the town office issued an 'evacuation order'. However, the residents understood that the risk of the 'evacuation order' was less than an 'evacuation advisory'. As a result, several residents failed to escape in time.

There is an interval in the recording.

Human beings try to believe that they are the only ones who will be OK, even if they encounter a massive natural disaster. The result of such an understanding is that they fail to escape in time.

Suppose that the emergency bell in this hall is rung now. I believe that it would be difficult for everyone to escape smoothly. Some of you will try to believe that the emergency bell does not apply to this place, or some of you will be embarrassed to run away because of an emergency bell.

It is quite difficult for an individual person to take extraordinary action. Therefore, daily communication with neighbours and having a firm connection with these people are essential (to have a third-party opinion about your situation). You have to create an atmosphere with your surrounding people to escape together when a disaster occurs.

So far, I have been talking about the disaster; however, the basic line of preventing disaster, the most important point for preventing disaster is that your life should be protected by yourself. You should have this idea always in your mind, which is the most important point. Second, your area should be protected by the residents of the area. Residents' participation is an essential factor in protecting your area. Once you can protect your area, you can be protected. I want you to always have the consciousness of protecting your own life and the consciousness of protecting your own region.

Here is a letter. The family consisted of a father, mother and two daughters in Kobe. As a result of this earthquake, their eldest daughter passed away. Ten years after the earthquake, the mother wrote a letter to her late daughter. I would like to introduce this letter to you.

The contents of the letter were read by Mr Komeyama.

To Nozomi, thank you, Nozomi. Thank you for being born as my daughter. Although the five years I could spend with you were too short, our daily life with four family members, including you, were very happy.

Nozomi, you were a very nice and helpful elder sister, and you were our precious daughter. Since you left us behind and went to Heaven, I have had an aching heart. However, with the help of your loving father and many people I know because of you, I did not give up on my life. Since that day, ten years have passed. Nozomi, now you would be 15 years old; what kind of girl would you be now? Although the number of candles on your birthday cake is increasing annually, Nozomi in the photo is still five years old. Although the

Nozomi in my heart has grown every year, I cannot imagine your grown-up face. This is very sad to me. Now, Nozomi, what do you like? What are you interested in now? Please tell me. I would like to ask you. I would like to hug you now and tell you I am sorry. Beside your bed in the hospital, although the medical doctor in charge told us there was no hope for you to recover, I talked to you about various things. However, the miracle never happened.

You said good night to me, and I replied to you, good night and sleep well. This conversation was the last word I exchanged with you. Why could I not say I love you that night? Nozomi, I love you. Nozomi, so many people care for you. You are still surviving in the heart of so many people. As many people have such tenderness, I believe that your life in Heaven is full of happiness. One day I will see you in Heaven, and so I try my best to fulfil my life and tell you that I could achieve it. Nozomi, please watch me from there. From your mother.

Due to the earthquake, many cases similar to this family happened. I know one family that consisted of a 22-year-old father, a 20-year-old mother, a two-year-old son and an 11-month-old son. The father and the two sons, three people, passed away because of this earthquake.

On the day of the earthquake, mass funeral services were conducted at the Hokudan-cho residents' centre. The 20-year-old mother attended this funeral service. However, she could not walk and stand, so other people supported her from both sides of her body. She was continuously crying until no tears came from her eyes. I still remember this scene clearly. I do not want to see such a person with deep sorrow any more.

Previously, I had a chance to participate in a TV programme. I received a call from a man in Osaka who watched the programme and worked at a crematorium. He explained that usually, a dead body was sent by a funeral coach to the crematorium; however, because of the earthquake, not only funeral coaches but also ambulances, police cars and self-defence force vehicles brought the bodies, one after another. About 70 to 80 dead bodies were brought to the crematorium, and he continuously attended the cremations for 24 hours.

On the day of the earthquake, one child of around 11 to 12 years old visited him with a social worker. His parents, grandfather and grandmother, all of his family members, had passed away because of this earthquake, and their bodies were sent to this crematorium. This boy cried so much, but he tried to behave bravely in front of him. He put his hand in his pocket to take out his money and said, 'Though I only have this much money with me now, please cremate them,' and tried to hand the money to him. 'You should keep that with you, do not worry,' he said to this boy. We should not let such a small boy do this.

The number of disaster orphans who lost their parents was 573 as far as the government body knows. I do not want to have such children anymore; I do not want to have such an affected family again.

Several months after the earthquake, I was told by the town mayor, Mr Kokubo at the time, 'What sort of repayments could we, the residents of Hokudan-cho, make to the people from all over Japan who did so much for us, such as sending relief supplies and volunteers?' He told me that one way was to recover from this situation was to rebuild our town to reactivate our normal daily life as soon as possible. The other was to share the situation of this earthquake, our experiences and the necessity of daily preventive or reduction activities against natural disasters to the next generation.

I quite agree with his idea. If we forget what this earthquake caused us to suffer, we may repeat our mistakes again. As a person who experienced this great earthquake, I believe that we should not forget it. We should not waste the valuable lives of the victims. As a person who encountered this earthquake, and as a person who survived this natural disaster, I know that we should pass on our experiences to the next generation.

Now, I would like to close my presentation. I hope that some of the points that I explained to you today can be useful references for your life.

Thank you for your listing.

Q&A Session: Any questions?

Q1. How many people became disabled because of the earthquake?

Answer to Q1: No answer was available to this question.

Q2 (By Professor Nyamnjoh). You just said that this is the very moving account about something that we are almost all concerned about, and as he was speaking, I wished I had come with a tape recorder and recorded everything because we would like to share the story in the project we are doing, and then if we could transcribe it and eventually have it as one of the documents in our project, that would be wonderful because it has all of the elements of the things we are researching. Thank you again for this wonderful story; I am happy to hear from you today.

Answer to Q2: It is OK to use what I speak today for your project.

Q3. What happened to the children, the orphaned children?

Answer to Q3: In the case of Awaji Island, how do I say ... Awaji Island is a rural area. The best way to answer this question is that the residents protect orphaned children. I know one case that is close to me. In his case, his relatives, maybe more than his relatives; his neighbors have been taking care of the children, and now the children are fine.

Talking about the children, I have heard that two and a half to three years after the Great Hanshin Awaji Earthquake, the atmosphere at the school – most of the cases were in the elementary school on Awaji Island and even in Kobe – were desolated due to the earthquake. A similar case was experienced during the Great East Japan Earthquake.

I talked with school teachers and told them that continuous mental health care for children who experienced the disaster for years afterward was quite important. During the earthquake or immediately after the occurrence of an earthquake, these children were patient with handling specific situations in their own way (controlling their emotions); however, their patience came to the fore after a certain period, I believe.

Q4. (Professor Harry Garuba).Thank you very much. I just want to ask. Do you know whether there are novels, performances and poems based on the Hanshin Awaji Great Earthquake but non-fiction or newspaper stories? Whether these were translated or not?

Answer to Q4: I made a picture story to show children, although I do not know about others.

Q5 (Professor Nyamnjoh). I just want to come back to the point I mentioned; fortunately, Noriko has recorded, and I know that people here say that Noriko has done very good work. Would it be

OK if one of us works on this recording and comes back to him to cross-check so that eventually, if we publish this, his account will be recounted as respectfully as possible so we can document it.

Answer to Q5: In the Japanese version? Check the figures or so .... It is OK by me.

Q6. After 1995, was there another earthquake? What was the highest magnitude that happened?

Answer to Q6: There were cases in the Niigata and Tohoku areas. In this area, we had the Awaji Island Earthquake about six years ago (2013), but this earthquake was not related to the Great Earthquake.

Q7. Where did the Awaji Island Earthquake happen?

Answer to Q7: Close to Sumoto City, which is located approximately 30 km from here. The scale of this earthquake was smaller than the Great Hanshin Awaji Earthquake.

Mr Komeyama showed us the picture of the picture story show he had created.

This is a picture story that I prepared for children. Although the person's name in this story is not real, the story was prepared based on a real story. I wrote the story, and the drawings were drawn by my friend.

This ends Mr Komeyama's storytelling.

4. The Volunteer Fire Brigade's Activities

In Mr Komeyama's discourse, he repeatedly explained the activities of the volunteer fire brigade. To understand Mr Komeyama' s discourse more precisely, I would like to introduce the significance of volunteer fire brigades in Japan again.

In his discourse, the Japanese word *shouboudan* was translated to volunteer fire brigade. *Shouboudan* was institutionalised by the Japanese government and is called the Fire and Disaster Management Agency (FDMA). In this organisation, firefighting agencies comprise regular fire prevention services and non-conventional volunteer fire brigades, *shouboudan*. Both these agencies are established under the responsibility of regional municipalities and controlled under the jurisdiction of municipal mayors.

Volunteer fire brigades in every town and city in Japan have mobilisation and response capabilities. Every member of the volunteer fire brigade has an everyday job, but they are actively protecting their town by themselves. Their mindsets are deeply rooted in the spirit of their devotion to their hometown.

While they are involved in firefighting activities, they also protect residents' lives and properties from natural disasters such as earthquakes, and wind and water damage through rescue efforts, warning patrols and evacuation guidance.

Even when there is no disaster, volunteer fire brigades organise numerous community-based activities designed to improve fire and disaster prevention capabilities and rejuvenate their local community. Female volunteer fire brigade members participate in activities including home visits to older people, fire prevention for people living alone and holding fire prevention classes at kindergartens and elementary schools (FDMA n.d.).

5. Analysis

From Mr Komeyama's discourse, the activities of the volunteer fire brigade in Hokudan-Cho at the time of the earthquake can be understood. Mr Komeyama said that the earthquake damage in Hokudan-cho was minimised not only because of the volunteer fire brigade's skills but also because the fire brigade members understood the residents' lives. Mr Komeyama believes that because the volunteer fire brigade is close to the local community and has knowledge of the residents, such knowledge is helpful in the event of a disaster.

However, the number of people belonging to the volunteer fire brigade is decreasing annually, and FDMA statistics indicate that, in 1965, there were 194 million volunteer fire brigade members but, by 2019, this was about half, at 83 million.

According to the FDMA's 'Current Situation and Issues', the decrease in the volunteer fire brigade members in 2017 was for two reasons. The first is resignations due to relocation because of jobs or schools. The second reason is retirement due to age and limited physical strength (FDMA 2017).

According to an opinion poll conducted in Sagamihara City, Kanagawa Prefecture in 2011, there were two reasons for the decrease in the number of volunteer fire brigade members: first, it seems difficult to maintain the balance between work and the fire brigade activities, and second, the consciousness of the residents toward the community has decreased (Sagamihara City Office 2011). If we associate the decrease in volunteer fire brigade personnel with a decrease in the local community's consciousness, the knowledge volunteer fire brigade members have about the residents, which was thought to have been useful in the Great Hanshin-Awaji Earthquake, will not be utilised in future disaster countermeasures.

6. Conclusion

As for disaster resilience, Yoshioka illustrated how Vanuatu recovered from the typhoon damage. Yoshioka demonstrated that mutual help among the people in Port Villa in Vanuatu contributed to the effectiveness of the disaster recovery (Yoshioka 2017).

Helping others during a disaster in Vanuatu and Mr Komeyama's discourse on the activities of the community-based volunteer fire brigade has something in common that contributes to disaster recovery. However, according to statistics, the number of volunteer fire brigade members has decreased annually because of a change in residents' consciousness.

In the future, volunteer fire brigade members who have changed their consciousness will need to participate in rescue operations. Would they be able to engage in community-based firefighting activities like that which Mr Komeyama experienced? To answer this, it is necessary to analyse the experiences of the Great Hanshin-Awaji Earthquake to ascertain the reliability and future of volunteer fire brigade activities as a countermeasure to disasters.

References

Fire and Disaster Management Agency (FDMA) (2017) Current Status of the Fire Brigade and Their issue (in Japanese), https://www.fdma.go.jp/singi_kento/kento/items/kento206_03_shiryo2.pdf. (accessed on 17 August 2022).

Fire and Disaster Management Agency (FDMA)(n.d.) Fire and Disaster Management Agency. https://www.fdma.go.jp/en/post1.html (accessed on 17 August 2022).

Hokudan-Cho Municipality Office (1997) *The Great Hanshin Awaji Earthquake: The record of Hokudan-Cho*. Hokudan-Cho Municipality Office (in Japanese).

Fire and Disaster Management Agency (FDMA) https://www.fdma.go.jp/relocation/syobodan/ (in Japanese, accessed on 17 August 2022).

Sagamihara City Office (2011) Public opinion polls on city administration—Reasons for the decrease in firefighters, https://www.city.sagamihara.kanagawa.jp/shisei/shisei_sanka/yoron_survey/100519/1005204.html(accessed on 17 August 2022).

Urano, Masaaki (1999) 'Confusion of and Readjustment Project on Awaji Island: Case of Toshima, Hokudan-Cho', *Sociology of The Great Hanshin Awaji Earthquake*, Vol. 3, in Nobuhiko Iwasaki, Kouzou Ukai, Masaki Urano, Katsuji Tsuji, Kamon Nitagai, Takashi Noda and Takeo Yamamoto (eds.) Showadou (in Japanese).

Yoshioka, Masanori (2017) 'Towards the anthropology of resilience: a case study of the cyclone disaster in Vanuatu', *Japanese Society for Oceanic Studies Newsletter*, p. 115.

Chapter 5

Conviviality Created through Resilience: Cultivating the Imagination of 'Different Others' in the Leprosaria of Japan

Noriko Tahara

Introduction

At present, there is a prevailing attitude of intolerance to 'different others' under the expansion of neoliberalism, highlighted by the exclusion of the sick during the coronavirus (COVID-19) pandemic. This is reminiscent of the historical ostracisation of Hansen's Disease (HD) patients in Japan. Kazuo Mori, the Chairman of the National Council of Hansen's Disease Leprosarium Residents said:

> When I heard that a car with an out-of-prefecture license plate had been damaged, it reminded me of the days of forced quarantine. When a new infectious disease appears, prejudice and discrimination like the one we suffered will appear. Discrimination against the families of infected people with COVID-19 and medical personnel engaging in the treatment for COVID-19 is also linked to the issue of Hansen's Disease (Asahi Shimbun 29 June 2020).

Kazuo Mori was born in June 1940 and entered the National Leprosarium, Oshima Seishoen, in 1949. His brother had difficulties getting married because he and his sister were in a leprosarium. We can understand their difficulty if we consider the current COVID-19 pandemic that is devastating our lives. Excessive risk hedging is creating challenges for people. Nyamnjoh (2022) described COVID-19 as a kaleidoscopic prism and wrote that 'COVID-19 offers much food for thought to critically review prevalent and conventional teleological modernist neoliberal assumptions about and usages of the notion of resilience'.

For a hundred years since the enactment of the Infectious Disease Prevention Law in 1897, infectious disease control in Japan had generally focused on mass prophylaxis despite global trends indicating a transition from mass prophylaxis to person-centred treatment in the latter half of the 20th century. Based on the recommendation of the Public Health Council, a new law for infectious disease control was established in 1999, centred on personal treatment (Ministry of Health, Labour and Welfare 2004: 43).

Hansen's Disease (HD) control in Japan has seen the following milestones.

First, in 1907, Act No. 11 on Leprosy [Law 1907] was enacted to build leprosaria that could accommodate vagrant people with HD, thereby avoiding communal discrimination against their families. Thereafter, a strict segregation policy continued for almost 90 years, until 1996, even after HD was deemed curable in the 1940s. The law was revised to the 'Leprosy Prevention Law' in 1931 [Law 1931] which strictly prescribed isolating all HD patients in leprosaria, even those who could be taken care of at home. HD patients continued to be admitted into these institutions, with no legal accommodation for patients to leave or return home. This policy was continued until 1996; though HD had become a curable disease after the invention of Promin in the 1940s, there was no regulation to allow patients who were cured to leave the leprosarium. The total number of HD patients accommodated from 1909 to 2010 was estimated to be 56,575 (Mori et al. 2019). Second, the nationwide campaign 'Movement for Leprosy-free Prefecture' was carried out twice, before and after World War II, with the first movement starting in 1929 before World War II and the second in 1947, with the official notice of Director General of Public Health, Ministry of Health and Welfare. With the support of the local government, these campaigns encouraged the community to find HD patients living in their own homes and pushed prefectures to compete over the number of HD patients they could find, often motivating the betrayal of patients by their neighbours.

After the incarceration of HD patients, members of the public health centre thoroughly disinfected the homes of the patients, sometimes with police officers present. These public scenes constructed a horrific image of HD, promoting prejudice and discrimination. In the leprosaria, patients were forced to use pseudonyms to prevent each other, and the outside world, from knowing their identities. The term 'leprosy' still aggrieves survivors of HD, reminding them of the discrimination and prejudice they suffered owing to the compulsory quarantine policies. Leprosy is officially called Hansen's Disease in Japan, and the term 'leprosy' can only be used in a medical or legal context.

The leprosarium was not a place in which patients were taken care of by medical staff. Patients had to manage their own lives to survive. Based on their symptoms, they cooked, washed clothes or built roads; the relatively healthier patients took care of those who were seriously ill. Some of them lost fingers and limbs as their injuries worsened without them realising it. Their activities were reconfigured in accordance with the logic and humility of incompleteness and conviviality.[1]

As Enomoto (2022) notes in Chapter Ten, the term 'resilience' is criticised for its tendency to over-emphasise internal causes of suffering without addressing political and structural causes. 'Resilience', used as a highly agent-centric concept, perpetuates inequalities towards vulnerable people without addressing political and structural matters. Therefore, we should consider social conditions when studying the framework of resilience. This is an important point. Describing the patients' resilience will reveal how the Japanese government excluded them from their own communities and expose deeply embedded systemic inequalities against patients with HD in the society. They were not allowed to have children even after marriage as HD was mistakenly thought to be inherited, and the government sought to provide eugenic protection. Men were operated on to prevent them from having children and women were subjected to abortion if they became pregnant.

Although there were movements of HD survivors to challenge the segregation policy, most residents chose to remain in the leprosarium and adopted convivial practices in their daily lives. We can observe that resilience was undertaken not only personally, but also collectively, in an attempt to create solidarity with fellow patients in the leprosaria. This can be thought of as resilience at the existential level. This study attempts to explore the nature of resilience through the lives of people with HD, deprived of human rights under a compulsory quarantine policy. Section 1 clarifies the social and historical background of the exclusion of people with HD. Section 2 traces their lives in the leprosarium via interviews and art, showcasing the trials they face.

1. Forced Quarantine and Long-term Isolation for HD Convalescents

Foreign missionaries began to protect and care for people with HD after Japan's post-seclusion opening in 1885. The first leprosarium for people with HD, Koyama Fukuseien, was opened in Shizuoka by the Father of the Paris Foreign Missions Society in 1889. Another leprosarium was opened by the sisters of the Anglican Church in 1895 in Kumamoto. Masanao Makino, Emeritus Director-General of the National Leprosarium, Oku-Komyoen, reviewed the medical policy for HD and stated the following:

> At that time, the existence of HD patients on the streets was considered a national shame and evidence of underdevelopment relative to the Western cultured countries. Japanese people and the government were hypersensitive to such notoriety, especially from Western countries. Some doctors, politicians, and bureaucrats were really concerned about the situation and made great efforts to establish the HD separation law (Makino 2010: 36).

In the process of establishing a modern nation, a quarantine policy for HD was put into place with the enactment of Act No. 11 on Leprosy [Law 1907]. Under the law, prefectural allied leprosaria were established in each of the nation's five territories in 1909 to accommodate HD patients, those without medical care and the poor. These facilities were built away from the towns, in remote areas or on islands, to prevent infection and to protect society. This attitude of intolerance to different others is not a recent neo-liberalism trend; it has existed for more than a century in Japan. The government, through its laws, and the community, through its movements, worked in tandem to eliminate people with HD.

1-1. Leprosy Prevention Law

The first law, i.e., Act No. 11 on Leprosy [Law 1907], was enacted in 1907. At that time, there was no effective treatment for HD and people with the disease were subjected to discrimination and prejudice. For this reason, many people left their home towns fearing harassment towards their families, and wandered from place to place. The first leprosarium was built to accommodate such people. Law 1907 was amended in 1916, and the director of the leprosarium was given a 'disciplinary inspection right' to discipline residents who attempted flight or were rebellious, without trial. Law 1907 was replaced by the Leprosy Prevention Law in 1931 [Law 1931]. The quarantine range was extended in Law 1931 regarding patients 'who are a danger to society', with the aim of isolating all patients into leprosaria, even those cared for at home (Nakamura 2019). In the culmination of the isolation policy, in 1941, all public leprosarium facilities were transferred to the jurisdiction of the Ministry of Health. Further, 80% of HD patients were confined in leprosarium facilities in 1945.

In 1943, Promin was discovered as a cure for HD in the USA. The Promin acquisition campaign emerged among the HD patients in Japan around 1948. Finally, they received proper treatment at the leprosaria and HD became a curable disease. As they awoke to the strength of unity, they formed a federation to connect with fellow patients across Japan's leprosaria in 1951 and to seek better treatment. They also tried to abolish Law 1931 but that was in vain. Law 1931 was revised in 1953 [Law 1953]; the policy of long-term isolation at the leprosarium continued. Behind the decision was a statement in 1951 by the three directors of the National Leprosarium at the Diet in support of the continuation of the isolation policy.

In 1958, the 7th International Leprosy Conference recommended the abolition of forced leprosy quarantine to its Japanese members. In 1959, the World Health Organization's Committee of Leprosy Experts recommended abolishing compulsory quarantine and stated that leprosy treatment should be conducted as a general treatment. However, all these recommendations went unheeded (Uchida 2006: 560–565). The policy did not change, and most patients had to spend their life in the leprosarium, as there was no provision for discharge in the law.

Finally, Law 1953 was abolished in 1996 via two revisions, but it was too late. The convalescents in the leprosaria had been isolated for too long and had lost connection with their family, friends and communities. The bond with their home was severed, and there were also after-effects of HD. Persistent discrimination and prejudice against HD remained. Given the extensive isolation policy, survivors remained in the leprosarium even after the abolition of the law; they were afraid that these shelters would be shut due to the abolition of the Leprosy Prevention Law.

Currently, the number of leprosarium residents (in 13 national facilities and one private facility) is decreasing, and the population is ageing. There are 1,333 residents (622 males, 711 females) at the National Hansen's Disease Leprosarium (13 facilities), with an average age of 85.5 years (May 2018).

1-2. Nationwide 'Campaigns for Leprosy-Free Prefecture'

For about 90 years, a sequestration policy was conducted by the government and medical professions, as well as the society, promoted by the 'Campaigns for Leprosy-Free Prefectures', a movement to improve community lives. The term 'Leprosy-Free Prefecture', denoting a prefecture whose HD patients are isolated in leprosarium facilities, was first used in Aichi Prefecture in 1929 (Verification meeting of the HD problems 2005: 171). The campaign was strengthened after the onset of the '20 Year Eradication Plan of Leprosy' in 1936, as 10,000 people were segregated in 1940. Miyasaka (2006) noted that the campaign employed a top-down management design to seek out patients hidden from administrative agencies. This campaign was unique to Japan and symbolised the harshness of Japan's HD policy (Study Group of Campaign of Leprosy-Free Prefecture 2014: 57).

1-2-1. Pre-WWII

The absolute segregation policy was implemented via the promulgation of Law 1931, and the Leprosy Prevention Association was established in the same year by the Minister of Internal Affairs, Kenzo Adachi, and Eiichi Shibusawa. The association's funds were covered by a gift from the Empress, the national treasury subsidy, membership fees and donations. 'Leprosy Prevention Day' was established on the Empress's birthday, 25 June, for enlightening activities. Lectures and movies were held at 180 venues nationwide, with about 135,000 participants in 1933; the number of participants nationwide reached 200,000 in 1934 (Aoyama 2013: 83–86).

Patients were gradually abducted from their homes. Though the leprosarium was advertised as a haven for socially persecuted patients, the actual situation was severe, requiring hard labour from patients. The new patients were indispensable for securing a labour force in the leprosaria, increasing the number of residents in the 1930s and 1940s (Study Group of Campaign of Leprosy-Free Prefecture 2014: 68). The leprosarium facilities were situated on islands or in isolated areas, and there was a strong sense of repulsion towards such facilities.[2]

All tasks in the general leprosarium life, from daily routines to patient care, were conducted by patients, including woodwork, metalwork, construction work, rice milling, nursing, laundry, animal breeding, food manufacturing, sewing, agriculture, delivery of goods, assistance for treatment, activities such as hairdressing, purchase of goods, meal transportation, clerical work and sanitary management. Given the demanding work, many patients exacerbated their symptoms, had sequelae and developed other illnesses (Kawasaki 2016: 46).

In 1940, the Ministry of Health and Welfare issued the following instructions to prefectures: 'The prevention of leprosy can be achieved at least by isolation, and the most urgent task is to accommodate the patient in the leprosarium' (Kumamoto District Court 'Leprosy Prevention Law' Opinion Judgement of State Liability Claim 2001). For the seamless isolation of patients, 'Campaigns for Leprosy-Free Prefectures' was necessary as it encouraged each prefecture to disseminate the leprosy prevention idea among its people.

1-2-2. After WWII

After the war, Promin treatment started in 1947, and HD became a curable disease, though the isolation policy for HD patients continued under the new Constitution of Japan. In 1947, the government issued the Leprosy Policy Implementation Guidelines. The implementation policy comprised 'measures to prevent Japan's epidemics, which is the basis of the reconstruction of Japan as a civilised country, to ensure complete leprosy prevention, and to make it a country without leprosy'. It encouraged the 'Campaigns for Leprosy-Free Prefectures', seeking general cooperation (Ko 2014: 223).

The ideology that promoted the 'Campaigns for Leprosy-Free Prefectures' changed from ethnic cleansing to social defence. HD patients were considered a national shame and barrier to ethnic cleansing before and during WWII, and a threat to society after WWII. As relief initiatives accompanied social defence to save patients, it then made it easier for people to report suspected patients to the administrative personnel (Tokuda 2014: 207–208).

The role of local residents was thoroughly emphasised, and the capacity of HD leprosarium facilities expanded despite the international trend of individual treatment of HD patients in their communities. Under the Eugenics Protection Act (enacted in 1948), sterilisation and abortion were promulgated and implemented legally at each leprosarium. 'Campaigns for Leprosy-Free Prefectures' unveiled the modus operandi that resulted in HD patients being expelled from society by neighbours, relatives and schoolteachers, thereby promoting the stigma attached to HD.

Michihiro Ko (former chairman of the National Council of HD Leprosarium Residents) said that the campaign stopped patients from living at home in their communities. He was born in Fukuoka Prefecture and developed HD at the age of 16. He left high school in 1951 and entered the leprosarium at the age of 17. Afterwards, he was forced to live under the leprosarium pseudonym for 45 years until the abolishment of the law. The campaign stopped people from thinking about HD patients who were forcibly quarantined. People were forced to not think about the patients' future after isolation (Ko 2014: 223–237).

Most family members of patients who were forced into a leprosarium faced challenges in continuing their lives. Some were ostracised in their own neighbourhoods while others were forced to relocate to other lands. The national and prefectural governments never assumed responsibility for the 'Campaign for Leprosy-Free Prefecture' until the Leprosy Prevention Law was filed as an unconstitutional law in 1998.

1-3. Studies of Incarcerated People

Various studies have been conducted on such situations, especially in the area of social history, focusing on human rights aspects regarding eugenics (Fujino 2006); clarifying the activities of people leading to the abolition of the Leprosy Prevention Law in 1996; trying to verify the legal defects in leprosarium facilities (Miyasaka 2006; Narita 2015); investing in the local community and politics (Hirokawa 2011; Study Group of Campaigns for Leprosy-Free Prefectures 2014; Kawasaki 2016); focusing on the daily activities in the leprosarium (Araragi 2017; Arizono 2017); and charting out the life histories of the survivors of HD (Fukuoka and Kurosaka 2015). However, Hirata (2015) noted that historical elucidation is insufficient to ascertain why and how HD convalescents were forced to quarantine for 90 years, deviating from international trends and resulting in irreversible mistakes (human rights violations or life damages).

The National Institute of Infectious Diseases, Tokyo, Japan (Mori, Department of Mycobacteriology of the HD Research Centre) examined all medical reports of national leprosarium facilities, and traced and totalled the number of individuals entering and leaving the numerous facilities from 1909 to 2010. Their study reveals the number of people in detail:

> The number of general residents was 56,575, and the number of general out-going persons was 54,047 (death: 25,200; change of leprosarium: 4,350; formal discharge: 7,124; informal discharge including escape: 12,378; wrong diagnosis: 310; others: 4,685) (Mori et al. 2019).

This study reveals in detail the little-known fact that some people were discharged with the support of the leprosarium under the isolation policy, and some escaped or were transferred from one leprosarium to another.[3]

2. The Lived Reality of the People in Leprosaria

People with HD tried to establish their lives in the leprosarium while under the oppression of the nation-state and the society outside. This section consists of interviews with HD survivors Towao Takita, Masao Kitagawa, Haruo Tanaka, Ayako Hamano and Akira Negishi, focusing on life in Matsuoka Hoyoen, a leprosarium in northern Japan.[4] They are a diverse set of people in terms of their homeland, relationships with family and profession. Takita noted that 'People may think I am a poor person, for I have been isolated in a leprosarium all my life. But the leprosarium is also a type of society of human beings, and we have made our lives here'. Their way of life provided an opportunity to think about the existential resilience of convivial lives that connected with others and shared solidarity.

2-1. Northern Leprosarium, Matsuoka Hoyoen

Matsuoka Hoyoen in Aomori City was established in 1909 as the Northern Leprosarium of the second territory, a federation of the six prefectures in Tohoku and Hokkaido Island, under the Department of the Interior of Meiji government. The leprosaria were transferred under the Ministry of Health and Welfare in 1941, and the Northern Leprosarium was renamed Matsuoka Hoyoen.

There are three sections (for an inpatient ward, a ward for people with disabilities and a dormitory for those who can live without support) in an area of approximately 240,000 square metres. Promin treatment began in 1950 here; the number of inhabitants, at a peak of 824 in 1942, steadily decreased. An earth embankment once surrounded the leprosarium to prevent residents from fleeing. It is now maintained as a promenade, as of 2018. The Social Communication Hall, which keeps documents and enlightens people about the lives and history of the leprosarium, was opened in 2018. The current number of residents is 56 and the average age is 86.8 years (2020).

Until the 1950s, the residents of Matsuoka Hoyoen had to perform all work by themselves to maintain their lives. This involved nursing other patients, carrying meals, feeding blind patients, teaching young patients, growing food, sewing clothes, keeping pigs for food, burying the dead and taking care of children who were not infected.

Residents were also engaged in various cultural activities, such as literary activities, growing bonsai (potted Japanese dwarf plants), playing music and painting. The magazine *Koda no Suso* was first published in December 1930 as a patient magazine, and it continued for 90 years. This study highlights the lives of these people through interviews and art, such as their paintings and *tanka* (a Japanese verse form in five lines of five, seven, five, seven and seven syllables).[5] These activities are highly valued as they portray lives with HD that are infused with literary and fine arts.

2-2. Escape to Quarantine

The 'Heaven and Hell' illustration (Fig. 1) depicts the experience of isolation in a leprosarium. The artist Yutaka Naruse was born in Fukuoka in 1922 and developed HD at the age of 18 in 1940. In 1952, he entered the national leprosarium, Kikuchi Keifuen. He founded and participated in a painting group comprising residents (Matsuoka Hoyoen 2013). He moved to Matsuoka Hoyoen in 1957 and continued to paint the life of the leprosarium in his spare time. He died in 2013 at the age of 91.

This is a cat, but the title is 'Heaven and Hell' because the cat cornered the mouse, blocking its escape, and the mouse jumped into the mousetrap. No matter how angry the cat was, it could not enter. Therefore, the mouse is singing songs with peace of mind. This situation is peace. Although it is heaven, entering here is the ultimate hell. There is no help. I drew this picture in that sense (Matsuoka Hoyoen Syooukai 2020 31–32).

This feeling, the agony of being chased by a cat (others) and living in a mousetrap (leprosarium), is a common feeling among those who live in a leprosarium.

Figure1. Heaven and Hell

(Matsuoka Hoyoen Syououkai, 2016:30)

Towao Takita was born in Fukushima Prefecture in 1924 and was infected around 1935 after his father became ill with HD.[6] Takita later expressed his feelings at the time through a *tanka*.

My father got leprosy
Our family were blamed for his sickness
I was alone by the river and put a leaf boat on the surface of the river to drift away (Takita 1956: 9).

In those days, doctors were obliged to report those who had HD to the police, who, in turn, were tasked with admitting them to a leprosarium. Takita said the police officer of his village told villagers not to go to their house or they would be infected. Moreover, children jeered at them. Takita could not go to primary school and spent his time taking care of his younger brother. On 21 September 1937, at the age of 12, he and his father went to Aomori to be admitted to the leprosarium. The *tanka* he wrote at that time is as follows.

> Even on the day we leave for the leprosarium
> We depart at midnight
> Minding not to expose our leprous bodies to villagers (Takita 1956: 13)

Takita said he could not forget how the prefecture hygiene staff member,[7] who recommended hospitalisation, came to see him off at the station early in the morning and gave him a box of candy as a souvenir. They got on the special train, called the 'royal train', which was meant to transport only HD patients, accompanied by police officers. They arrived at the Northern Leprosarium in 24 hours.

In Osaka in the 1930s, some doctors were influenced by Dr Noboru Ogasawara (Kyoto Imperial University), who objected to the forced isolation of those who had HD and provided outpatient treatment for HD patients (Hirokawa 2011: 187–223). Outpatient treatment was legally acceptable if the doctor reported their treatment of patients to the police.

Masao Kitagawa was born in Osaka in 1928. He received outpatient treatment at the HD treatment building in the annexe of Osaka University in the 1940s, while attending night classes at the school of commerce.[8] The doctor said it was not necessary to go to the leprosarium, as he gave the same treatment to outpatients. Kitagawa was grateful for his words. However, around 1948, when he was 20 years old, he was threatened by frequent letters from the Ministry of Health in Osaka Prefecture, which recommended that he go to a leprosarium. The letter always ended with the same sentence, 'If you won't do what we say, we will visit you at your house.' Mr Kitagawa was horrified as he had never told his family and friends about his condition. He said, 'That is what we are most afraid of. I cannot help getting sick. However, it would be hard if it was known to my family, friends, and people around me. This is because the prejudice is terrible. All relationships as members of society are cut off.'

Kitagawa says the difference between HD and other illnesses is that you cannot say the name of this disease to people close to you without being worried about what they may think. He tried to argue with the person in charge of the Ministry of Health but in vain. The people in the Ministry of Health became stricter than he thought; he said, finally, 'I couldn't help it, and I had no choice but to escape to the leprosarium.' He decided to be admitted into a leprosarium far from Osaka, although there were three nearby, located on islands isolated by the sea. He chose one with an access road, because he was not good at swimming. When he entered, he was relieved.

> I was relieved as soon as I entered the leprosarium because I had company. I have been oppressed in many ways. I could not say what I wanted to say. I could not say it out loud. However, after entering the leprosarium, I was relieved because they all had the same illness and had similar patients. That is why I was so excited and enjoyed every day. I think it's funny to get sick and have fun, but it's a real feeling (Masao Kitagawa).

Life at the leprosarium was inconvenient, with no money, little food and clothes sent from his home. Kitagawa was blessed with the opportunity to learn from Teiichi Suzuki, the secretary-general of the National Council of Patients at the National Leprosy Leprosarium (currently the National Council of HD Leprosarium Residents [All Patients' Association]), who opposed the HD compulsory isolation policy and improved the life of leprosarium residents while fighting prejudices in society. Kitagawa wanted to further his studies and enrolled in the high school near the leprosarium. However, one of his best friends committed suicide; thus, he decided to leave the leprosarium to avoid the 'dangerous' situation, which he did not explain in detail.

> I chose this place [Matsuoka Hoyoen] because I thought few who knew me would come to this place. Well, there was another leprosarium in Kusatsu, but there was strong prejudice around it. When people in Japan hear the name of Kusatsu, they link the name to HD and think

about you as an HD patient. Therefore, coming here was the best to eliminate your past (Masao Kitagawa).

Kitagawa rode on a night train with his wife, who had been his pen pal at the time, and migrated to Matsuoka Hoyoen around 1954. Sociologist Edward Kirumira says that mobility does not mean freedom from others, boundaries or power; however, freedom, whether it is coerced or chosen, means the determination and desire to be free (Kirumira, 2016).

For these people, escape from home to a leprosarium and migration to another leprosarium were a means of coping with social risks and living better. Patients tried to construct their own world by choosing the time and place of the escape and interacting with others on the run.

2-3. Escape from Quarantine

Despite the situation, some people tried to re-enter society, as previously mentioned. The leprosaria tried various methods to prevent escapes, such as earthen walls, uniforms and the use of leprosarium currency.

The first time Takita arrived at the leprosarium, all the money he had was replaced with leprosarium currency. He said, 'With this currency, you cannot shop outside, because it does not work anywhere else but the shops here. Thus, they do not have to worry about our escape anymore.'

After graduating from primary school at the leprosarium in 1940, Takita shifted to a room where people could move by themselves, to work in the leprosarium. He took care of patients with severe conditions, helped out with other things such as diet, defecation, urination and treating wounds. He despaired when the people he took care of ended their lives alone with no connection to their families. He felt that they were an augury of his future. He decided to escape and make some money off the clothes left by his father. In 1941, he escaped with his four roommates by train.

He stayed at a cheap hotel, made a toilet odour remover with naphthalene and started peddling it with his roommates. They travelled around the northern area as peddlers for several months, but the work was over when the winter season set in. When he came home for the new year, a police officer in the village was waiting for Takita. Though the policeman visited frequently and urged him to go to a new leprosarium known as Tohoku Shinseien, Takita thought, 'I cannot give up and escape again,' for he did not appear sick with HD and had only some flecks at that time.

He succeeded in escaping the police and was hired as a precision mechanic at a factory. He went to work at a munitions factory situated away from Tokyo; he did not want to bother his brother and sister working in the city. After winter, he lost sensation in his hands and began to drop tools such as spanners. The symptoms of HD appeared, and he requested a vacation from the factory to 'go home to cure' himself; he directly admitted himself to the leprosarium, Tohoku Shinseien. In 1945, he visited an acquaintance from Matsuoka Hoyoen and decided to stay there. He contributed to the leprosarium activities, such as receiving proper treatment, acting as the secretary of the blind people with HD and organising followers of the Catholic Church. Takita tried to be resilient in the face of isolation.

Haruo Tanaka was also resilient against the power of isolation. He was born in Kochi and noticed the onset of HD when he hurt his thumb and bled while working in a rice field but did not feel pain.[9] His mother would offer rice in exchange for his medicine, and he recuperated at home for about three years. However, the hygiene police visited his home and pressed for his admission into a leprosarium. He refused several times but finally decided to go, as his mother was frightened by the frequent visits. He went to a leprosarium, but not the one that was recommended to him. He chose it by himself in 1949.

> I avoided Oshima Aiseien, which is too close to my hometown, and entered Nagashima Aiseien at the age of 17, spending 8 years there until the age of 25.

Tanaka was getting bored with life at Nagashima Aiseien and decided to travel to Hokkaido, a northern island. With a short-term exit pass from the leprosarium, he headed to the north while stopping at other leprosarium facilities. Before going to Hokkaido, he stopped at Matsuoka Hoyoen to visit and stayed there in 1954, as it looked better than other leprosarium facilities.

Until then, some people moved from one leprosarium to the other. I knew some people hung around moving in and out. Some explored all leprosariums. I was relatively stable, but I was one of them. However, I was told that it was the last time, and that such movement would no longer be permitted unless there was an appropriate reason.

Tanaka married Ayako Hamano, whom he met at Matsuoka Hoyoen. Hamano was born in Hokkaido and felt something wrong with her body around 1952. Some spots appeared on her face around 1955, so she entered Matsuoka Hoyoen at the age of 23 in 1956.

In the late 1960s, Tanaka and Hamano healed and returned to Kochi; they lived by farming and selling crops in the city. 'I would really have wanted to stay there if I was healthy. The work was quite interesting,' says Tanaka. However, about a year and a half later, Tanaka's foot burns did not heal, and the bandages and medicine cost a lot. 'I washed and dried the bandage, but I could not make it in time. I feel we were burdening his mother, so we came back here,' said Hamano. Tanaka was 35 or 36 years old when they returned to the leprosarium.

If there had been appropriate treatment options for Tanaka in the community, they would not have needed to go back to the leprosarium. The re-admission of HD patients into leprosaria is often due to injuries caused by nerve paralysis, which is a sequela of HD, and other physical conditions unrelated to HD.

Currently, more hospitals are accepting treatment for other illnesses of HD patients in the local area around Matsuoka Hoyoen. Residents at Matsuoka Hoyoen can receive appropriate treatment at other hospitals and local orthopaedics as needed.

2-4. Constructing Solidarity

Patients in Matsuoka Hoyoen organised several clubs, such as 'Love and Help' in 1939, for the mutual aid of residents, and 'Friends of Cane' in 1953, established by a group of blind persons. They built their lives helping each other. To earn some money, they tried many things together, such as pig farming, cattle farming, poultry farming (around 1931–65), carp farming (1951–58, 1976–81) and grape orchards (1954–76).

They also formed a poetry group, interacting with poets in other leprosarium facilities and those in regular society through literary activities through Matsuoka Hoyoen's magazine *Koda no Suso*. On the recommendation of poetry editors, Takita published his book of poetry *Milky Way* in 1956, presenting it to local libraries and public health centres. He said: 'I thought that *tanka* was the only proof that I lived in this world. I tried as much as possible to leave something.'

Residents of the HD leprosaria formed the National HD Leprosarium Patients' Council (currently the National HD Leprosarium Residents' Council) in 1951. They conducted protests against the Leprosy Prevention Law by convening at the National Diet and in each leprosarium. The residents of Matsuoka Hoyoen also joined the protests, and Akira Negishi (1930–2018) sang a *tanka* about their solidarity (1953):

> Marching around with placards
> Appealing our hope against the law
> Our wish ended in the narrow leprosarium.

Negishi was born in 1930 in Akita as the second of four siblings.[10] In 1944, when he was in the second year of high school, his father took him for a medical examination at the leprosarium. However, he had to support his family when his father was drafted into the army; he worked in the factory and cleared bushes for cultivation. At the end of the war, his brother returned and took his place to support the family. Negishi then entered Matsuoka Hoyoen; he was 18 at the time.

In 1953, the Leprosy Prevention Law was enacted in the Diet, and the isolation policy continued despite protests. The campaigners never gave up cooperating and established a proper medical treatment system in each leprosarium in the 1960s. In those days, some people with improved conditions were permitted to leave the leprosarium facilities; 45 people left during the 10 years from 1955 to 1965. It was the highest number of people to leave Matsuoka Hoyoen (Negishi 2020: 109).

According to Negishi, the director of Iwao Arakawa (in the period 1978–86) used to urge residents to leave Matsuoka Hoyoen and return to society if they were in better health, encouraging them that they would be fine. 'Farewell ceremonies' were usually performed. Residents' music bands would play a march with instruments such as clarinets, drums and accordions.

When the economic boom started in 1955 (lasting until 1973), the possibility to do 'outside labour' was introduced. Residents with better health conditions could go out to make up for the labour shortage in the local community, with permission, after consultation with the director. This measure became popular as wages outside the leprosariums were 10 times more than the wages inside. However, most residents engaged in earthworks, which often exacerbated their condition. Negishi sang the following *tanka*, describing the situation, in 1967 (Matsuoka Hoyoen 1967: 18):

> You work sweating in the leprosarium
> The fee of earthworks is less than one-tenth outside work
> What can we do, I wonder?

'Outside labour' also brought other problems to the leprosarium, as healthier residents were supposed to attend to the more seriously ill residents. Thus, the residents' association agreed with the leprosarium that 'outside labour' would only be allowed for half the day.

The Leprosy Prevention Law was finally abolished in 1996. This was achieved through the tireless efforts of the residents. Of course, those who had already passed away could not enjoy this news, and few people appreciated the efforts of the National HD Leprosarium Residents' Council (Negishi 2020: 87–88):

> Leprosy Prevention Law was abolished at last
> Hope to share my great joy with comrades
> Though my comrades passed away already.

The patient associations had made requests to amend the law in 1963, 1984, 1988 and 1991. However, as already highlighted, residents had ambivalent feelings regarding abolishing the law, because most of them were unsure of their relationship with their homeland and family as they had lived in the leprosarium for a long time. Some had sequelae of HD, and discrimination and prejudice against those with HD persisted in society. However, the patients had tried hard to make their lives better in the leprosarium and to establish their community with proper medical treatment systems through the movement of the National HD Leprosarium Residents' Council.

Matsuoka Hoyoen was surrounded by earthen walls that raised the foundation, and acacia was previously planted on it. The earthen walls were left as they were even after the abolition of the Leprosy Prevention Law, and eventually collapsed. At the end of December

2016, Negishi paved the way for the project of removing the earthen walls as a symbol of isolation and constructing a promenade as a symbol of living in harmony. He went to see the sports festival of Shinjo Junior High School alone in an electric wheelchair a few years before the project. Director Kawanishi (the school's director during 2013–20) said the following to the students of Shinjo Junior High School:

> For residents who have been isolated for a long time, it was never easy to go to the athletic festival alone. Think carefully about the courageous actions of one resident as an opportunity to open up the earthen walls and create a new promenade. Akira Negishi may have shown a new way to live together after overcoming 70 years of separation due to isolation (Kawanishi 2018).

The social community hall opened in 2018. There were visual exhibitions of the history and life of Matsuoka Hoyoen, including a display of the magazine *Koda no Suso*, the *Braille Matsuoka* and other literary works by the residents, and a kitchen for the 'memorial dining room' where one could enjoy cooking nostalgic dishes with the residents. Currently, the grand design of the *Matsuoka no Mori* [The Forest of Matsuoka] is being preserved to prevent the recurrence of human rights violations.

2-5. The Trial to Reclaim Lives

Francis Nyamnjoh (2018) posits that 'conviviality emerges out of the necessity to earn one's living, to surmount the tensions and divisions of inequality with attempts at flexibility propelled by the need to get by. Conviviality, in many ways, results from compliances with cultural implications of power. Its intricacies in everyday life are, in fact, steeped in tensions'.

We observed the conviviality of people's activities that enriched their lives. The visually impaired, who lived the most difficult life in the leprosarium, formed an association and learned acupuncture and moxibustion to treat other residents. Their activities were an attempt to fulfil the notion of 'we will do what we can do ourselves' (in the words of Negishi). It was a convivial practice based on free will and enriching lives together, with which began the trial to reclaim the lives based on the community in leprosaria.

In those days, Tanaka and other residents planned a tour. They prepared 10 motorcycles and a used car that they purchased collectively, when it was difficult to get out of the leprosarium. Tanaka recalled the time:

> I took everyone who had never been outside, being seriously ill and too weak. When the nuclear ship on the Shimokita Peninsula arrived in 1969, we all went to see it at Mutsu and camped on the beach.

Figure2. Shout

(Matsuoka Hoyoen, 2013: Cover)

These convivial practices were created by imagining the feelings of others and trying to make them happy. Naruse's masterpiece 'Shout' was derived from his experience of cooking fish (Fig. 2). When he cut off the head of a fish to cook, it opened its mouth slightly and the round eyes of a fish stared at his eyes. Naruse told the fish:

> Ah, you are also an unlucky fish. You were killed by me because you were caught in a small net when you swam in such a big ocean. But if I

can say some words as a human being, I have something to shout. You and I are the same (Matsuoka Hoyoen Syououkai 2016).

Naruse identified with the fish in his thoughts and wanted to shout to the world, as he felt the fish was doing. Embracing the pain of others is a capacity he cultivated during his time at the leprosarium as an HD patient. Takita also created a *tanka* to respond to the people in South Africa under apartheid and described his feelings of being close to those who were oppressed by the racial segregation policy, calling HD patients as 'black in Japan' (Takita 1982). Discrimination and slander against people with infectious diseases have been repeated throughout history. Negishi sang a *tanka* as follows:

Newspaper reveals
People with O-157 [an infectious disease] are discriminated against
I saw myself in the article.

The HD convalescents developed the ability to imagine others' pain and connect with their memories. Protection against infectious diseases often manifests itself as excessive risk hedging, although everyone is at equal risk.

The residents of Matsuoka Hoyoen have experienced living in a leprosarium, fleeing, negotiating and, sometimes, struggling with national isolation policies and exclusion from the society. They have cultivated fields, created orchards, raised pigs and chickens, and planted cherry blossoms. They have organised the 'dance of the dead' festival, athletic festivals, sumo competitions and several other events that every resident could participate in with conviviality. They tried to establish new lives and reclaim the dignity of being human. Shortly after the relocation of the leprosarium in October 1909, cherry trees were planted by residents who could not return to their home towns; these are now over 100 years old. A cherry blossom viewing party is held by the residents' association with the local people annually (albeit it was cancelled in 2020 and 2021 due to COVID-19).

3. Conclusion: Movement Created by Resilience

Isolation policies have formed a social structure of exclusion in society. Initially, they were conducted by the sanitation and security police and involved threatening people, from Law 1907 through Law 1931. Due to the isolation policy, HD patients and their families were deprived of the right to live as citizens in society. Through the 'Campaigns for Leprosy-Free Prefectures', people were mobilised to report suspected patients in the name of sanitary environment and modernisation.

This paper describes the trials of people with HD to study the nature of resilience in those lives deprived of human rights under a compulsory quarantine policy. Their resilience is undertaken not only personally, but also collectively, to create solidarity with fellow patients in the leprosarium. It can be thought of as resilience at the existential level. However, this attempt does not condone the Japanese isolation policy or the distress enforced in the leprosarium facilities. Describing their resilience is expected to reveal how the Japanese government excluded people with HD from their own communities and expose the deeply embedded systemic inequalities in the community against people with infectious diseases.

After the abolition of the Leprosy Prevention Law in 1996, 13 HD survivors filed a lawsuit against the government for its unconstitutional acts in 1998. The Kumamoto District Court pronounced the plaintiffs victorious, finalised by the government's abandonment of an appeal in 2001. The government acknowledged the responsibility for violations of human rights against HD patients and their families, and announced that the national and local governments would work on enlightening the public on the challenges faced by HD convalescents and their families, to eliminate discrimination and prejudice through dialogue. The 'Law concerning the promotion of the resolution of leprosy problems' was enforced in 2009 (Study Group of Campaign for Leprosy Free Prefecture 2014). It obliged the government to establish medical systems for residents in leprosaria and provide support for societal rehabilitation and restoration of dignity of the people with HD. The following regulations were also included: local governments could open up the old leprosarium facilities and surrounding land to local residents to formulate plans for future sanatoria or outreach facilities. The government has been working to raise awareness, but the road to a solution is still in its infancy.

HD survivors are still living in leprosaria using pseudonyms, as they fear that using their real names will cause trouble for their families. In fact, prejudice and discrimination against HD is not only directed at the patients, but also at their families; in fact, it grew out of the segregation policy and divided the families.

Those who had been separated from their HD-afflicted family members and faced challenges due to the isolation policy of Law 1953 filed a lawsuit against the government in 2016, which they won in 2019. The district court decision in June 2019 acknowledged the responsibility of the state and ordered it to provide compensation. The state abandoned its appeal, thus finalising the decision. The families of HD patients described their damages as 'life damages'.

The victories of the plaintiffs – of the HD survivors in 1998 and of their families in 2019 – revealed the challenge of societal living in Japan. About 400 HD survivors with the right to claim compensation gave up on the application, despite the appeal of the Ministry of Health, Labour and Welfare. It can be assumed that these people never narrated their experiences to their families, or were advised to not apply by their families, because applying for the compensation becomes a confirmation of their condition. Among the families of HD survivors, only 10 out of 561 plaintiffs acted in public; the others did not reveal their names or faces due to fear of discrimination (Asahi Newspaper 29 June 2020). According to the Ministry of Health, Labour and Welfare, approximately 24,000 people qualified for the compensation for HD survivors' families, under a law enacted in November 2019. By July 2020, only 20% (5,368 people) had applied for compensation. The attorney, Naito Masayoshi, noted that the reluctance to proceed with the application was due to a fear of being stigmatised. Moreover, in some cases, people have remained unaware that they had HD patients in the family.

The notion of 'protecting society from the danger of infectious diseases' leads to 'protecting society from the dangerous', in other words, people with infectious diseases (like HD); this easily becomes linked to the prevalent repulsion and exclusion of sick 'different others. At present, slanderous attacks on people with COVID-19, people without masks and the families of frontline workers reminds HD survivors of their past.

Matsuda cites the rapid growth of nationalist political parties in Europe and the emergence of violent groups trying to eliminate Koreans and Chinese in Japan. He noted, 'The intolerance in the modern world is expanding and progressing today, which resonates with the spirit of trying to restore "order" and "stability" by attacking and eliminating "different others" to "purify" ourselves' (Matsuda 2017: 497).

'Different others' describes people, things and creatures at the fringes of society. Sickness drives people to that boundary and makes them 'different others'. This study examined the voice of those forced into the role of 'different others' by society through the interview and arts of HD recuperators, and reveal cooperative resilience in the leprosarium. Everyone can be excluded from society for being 'different' with regard to not only sickness, but also ethnicity, nationality and gender. HD recuperators have known that everyone has the chance of being branded as such, and understand the pain of being deprived of their social lives. Their resilience continued into the next generation to create a movement to sue the government for compensation and reclaim their own lives.

Acknowledgements

This work was supported by JSPS KAKENHI Grant Numbers JP18H03606, JP22H00920 and JSPS Joint Research: South Africa–Japan 'Human Resilience in the face of man-made and natural disaster in Japan and South Africa: Ethnographic Perspective'.

Notes

[1] Conviviality arises out of the necessity for flexible continuity of life, with an order of inclusion and attraction of the 'different others' through dialogue (Nyamnjoh, 2018).

[2] The leprosarium in the third territory in Osaka was destroyed by the storm surge of the Muroto typhoon in 1934. About 30% of the residents at that time, i.e., 196 people (173 patients, 3 staff members, 11 family members of staff, and 9 construction workers), were killed. Due to the opposition movement of the residents in the third territory, no land was found to restore the leprosarium. It was rebuilt in 1938 on the island, which is the fourth territory.

[3] About 35,000 people were placed in isolation. Some of these tried to go back to society; 3,357 people were reintegrated into society from 1930 to 1975 (Sakata, 2012).

[4] Since my first visit to Matsuoka Hoyoen in September 2015, I continued to interview those who recovered from HD in February 2016; April and June 2018; March, September, and November 2019; and March 2020.

[5] *Tanka* is one form of *waka* (Japanese poetry) consisting of five lines of five, seven, five, seven, and seven syllables each. It is said that this style is the most natural length for a lyric poem expressing emotion in Japanese. The first three lines of five, seven, and five syllables are termed the *kami no ku* ('upper poem') and the remaining two lines of seven syllables each are called the *shimo no ku* ('lower poem'). As a short form of lyric poetry, *tanka* stresses the beauty of life and nature, and a feeling of yearning is an important element. What is sought within this simple form is to express the essence of this yearning with a depth in which all the emotions are intermingled. The vivid expression of that which touches the heart has the power to evoke a wealth of association. This allusive feeling contained in these thirty-one syllables is referred to as *yojo*. In content, a *tanka* poem should include this *yojo* (Nittetsu Gijutsu Joho Senta, 2016:307).

[6] Interviews with Towao Takita were conducted in September 2015 and February 2016. Takita died on August 17, 2016, at the age of 91. The farewell ceremony was held at the Matsuoka Catholic Church on August 19, attended by relatives, many friends, residents, and staff at Matsuoka Hoyoen. The director at the time, Kawanishi, said it was a good farewell ceremony for Takita.

[7] The words 'hygiene staff', 'hygiene department', 'special hygiene department', and 'hygiene-related person' appeared in each person's narrative. Under the isolation policy during pre-war times, the Sanitation Division of each prefectural police department in cooperation with private organisations, such as Japan MTL, and medical institutions, treated HD patients (Sakata, 2012:128). In Osaka Prefecture, the Health Division of the Police Department (Ministry of the Interior since 1942) was in charge (Hirokawa, 2011:215). The narrative reflects this situation.

[8] An interview with Kitagawa was conducted at Matsuoka Hoyoen in September 2015 and February 2016. The last time I greeted Kitagawa, who was wearing an oxygen mask, was in April 2018. I am inclined to pray for his soul.

[9] Interviews with Haruo Tanaka and Ayako Hamano were conducted in September 2015, February 2016, April 2018, and June 2018. I visited them last in March 2019; they were confined to their beds in serious conditions and could only speak a few words.

[10] Interviews with Akira Negishi were conducted in September 2015, February 2016, and April 2018. In July 2018, Mr. Negishi passed away while receiving adequate nursing care.

References

Aoyama, S. (2013) 'Campaigns for leprosy-free prefectures', in Kinjo Gakuin University Graduate School of Letters, *Aichi Prefecture before World War II*, Vol. 19, pp. 75–96.

Araragi, Y. (2017) *Listening to 'Experience of illness': Life history of Hansen's Disease [New Edition]*, Seikatsu-Shoin.

Arizono, M. (2017) *Living in a Hansen's Disease leprosarium: Creating an isolation wall as a fort*, Sekai-Shisosya.

Asahi Newspaper (2020) *Evening Paper*, 29 June, p. 7.

___________ (2020) *Morning Paper*, 27 June, p. 31.

Enomoto, T. (2022) 'Genealogies of resilience in the development and humanitarian sector: Potentials and difficulties', *Bouncing Back: Critical Reflections on the Resilience Concept in Japan and South Africa*, Langaa RPCIG (in print).

Fujino, Y. (2006) *Hansen's Disease and Postwar Democracy: Why Isolation has Strengthened*, Iwanami-shoten.

Fukuoka, Y. and Kurosaka, A. (2015) 'Struggling to win the segregation policy unconstitutionality lawsuit: Interview with a Hansen's Disease Ex-patient', *Journal of Japanese & Asian studies*, Vol. 12, pp. 147–185.

Gold Coast Colony (1908) The Infectious Diseases Ordinance: An Ordinance to Make better Provision for the Prevention of the Spread of Infectious and Contagious Diseases, and for the Settlement of Claims for Compensation and Damages in Connection with Measures Taken to Prevent the Spread of Such Disease.13th April, 1908. No.2. Gold Coast Colony, CO97/5, National Archives in UK.

Hirata, K. (2015) 'A Study on History of Social Work for Hansen's Disease Patients in Japan (7)', *Bulletin of Faculty of Education*, Nagasaki University 1, pp. 65–76.

Hirokawa, W. (2011) *Hansen's disease problems and local communities in modern Japan*, Osaka University Humanities and Social Sciences Series.

Ishi, N. (2019) 'To understand Hansen's Disease properly', *Fureai Welfare News*, Vol. 16, pp. 5–8.

Kawanishi, T. (2018) 'Transforming the earthen wall segregating leprosy patients into a walkway uniting the community', *Koda no Suso*, No. 695, pp. 6–7.

Kawasaki, A. (2016) 'Campaigns for leprosy-free prefectures during pre WWII and post WWII and Hansen's Disease Leprosarium', *Journal of the Faculty of Sociology,* Ryutsu Keizai University, Vol. 26, No. 2, pp. 45–59.

Kirumira, E. K. (2016) 'African Potentials: creating for an interrogative and comparative discourse beyond conflict resolution – indigeneity revisited', paper presented at the 6th

African Forum, *African potentials to develop alternative methods of addressing global Issues*, Dec. 9–11, 2016, Kampala, Uganda.

Ko, M. (2014) '"Campaign for leprosy free prefecture" and forced detention/absolute isolation', in *Civic Association of Hansen's Disease* (eds.) *Identify the proof of life*, Kaiho Shuppansya, pp. 223–237.

Kumamoto District Court, (2001) '"Leprosy Prevention Law" Opinion Statement of State Redress Proceedings', [online], available: <https://www.mhlw.go.jp/topics/bukyoku/kenkou/hansen/kanren/dl/4a2.pdf> (accessed 8 February 2021).

Makino, M. (2010) 'Learning from the history of leprosy: Looking back at one hundred years of medicine at the leprosaria', *Japanese Journal of Leprosy*, Vol. 79, No. 1, pp. 25–36.

___________ (2017) 'How can we overcome intolerance to different others?', in K. Watanabe, C. Ishida and K. Tomita (eds) *Contemporaries of Differentities*, Ibunsha. pp.495–524.

Matsumoto, S. (2017) 'Problems concerning Hansen's Disease policy and the families after World War II: Focusing on the lawsuits brought by the families of the patients', *Bulletin of the Social Work Education Center*, Vol. 14, pp. 107–122.

Matsuoka, Hoyoen Syououkai (2016) *Naruse Yutaka Collection of pictures and essays*, Human Rights Fukuoka.

Matsuoka Hoyoen (1967) *Kouda no suso*, 351, Matsuoka hoyoen syooukai.

___________ (2013) *Kouda no suso*, 678, Matsuoka hoyoen syooukai.

Ministry of Health, Labour and Welfare (2004) *White Paper*.

Miyasaka, M. (2006) *Record of Detention for Hansen's Disease Patients*, Syueisya Sinsyo.

Mori, S., Ato, M. and Ishii, N. (2019) 'A study on the entering and out-going trends at Japan's National Hansen's Disease Leprosariums: An investigation from 1909 to 2010, *Japanese Journal of Leprosy*, Vol. 88, No. 2, pp. 53–75.

Nakamura, B. (2019) 'Sociological consideration on the legal relationships between two prevention laws for "leprosy" and its legal influences to the patients with Hansen Disease in Okinawa society', *Archives of Yamaguchi Prefectural University*, Vol. 12, pp. 51–87.

Narita, M. (2015) 'Consideration regarding the heavy ward: the special sickroom (revised and expanded edition)', *National Hansen's Disease Museum Research Bulletin*, Vol. 5, pp. 1–16.

Negishi, A. (2020) *Collection of poems: shining green leaves*, Matsuoka hoyoen syououkai.

Nittetsu, Gijutsu Joho Senta (2016), *Nippon: The Land and Its people*, Nittetsu sumikin soken kabushiki gaisha.

Nyamunjoh, F. B. (2018) 'Rethinking citizenship in 21st century Africa: some conceptual considerations', *Japanese Journal of Cultural Anthropology*, Vol. 83, No. 2, pp. 180–192.

__________ (2021) 'Covid-19 and the resilience of systemic suppression, oppression and repression', *Bouncing Back: Critical Reflections on the Resilience Concept in Japan and South Africa*, Langaa RPCIG (in print).

Sakata, K. (2012) *Life history of Hansen's Disease People: Living in Isolation*, Seikyusya.

Study Group of Campaign for Leprosy Free Prefecture (2014) *Incarceration policy for Hansen's Disease patients and Japanese society: Research on Campaign for Leprosy Free Prefecture*, Rikka Shuppan.

Tahara, Noriko (2007) *Knowledge of Inclusion and Candour: Through the Everyday Life Practice in the Asante World*, Sagano Syoin.

Takita, T. (1956) *Collection of poems: Milky way*, Publishing Department of National Leprosarium Hansen's Disease Patients Association.

__________ (1982) *Collection of essays: star festival*, Aomori colony.

Tokuda, Y. (2014) 'Campaign for leprosy free prefecture after WWII and Kikuchi incident', in Study Group of Campaign for Leprosy Free Prefecture (eds), *Incarceration policy for Hansen's Disease Patients and Japanese Society: Research on Campaign for Leprosy Free Prefecture*, Rikka Shuppan, pp. 207–226.

Uchida, H. (2006) Record of the Hansen's Disease verification meeting, Akashi syoten.

Verification meeting on the HD problem, (2005) Final report of the verification meeting on the leprosy problem, Japan Law Foundation. [online] available: https://www.mhlw.go.jp/topics/bukyoku/kenkou/hansen/kanren/4a.html

Web Resources

Human Rights Awareness Video 'Understanding the Issue of Hansen Disease: Thoughts of Former Patients and Their Families' https://www.youtube.com/watch?v=gPH5b_CDwto&t=29s (Viewed on 25 December 2021.

Part 3

Resilient Social systems/Resilience against Anti-Social Systems

Chapter 6

Resilience in a Complex Adaptive Environment: Water Scarcity and Adaptation in Khayelitsha, South Africa

Minga Mbweck Kongo

Part One

> 'I am 54 years of age, male; I live with my daughter, my son in law and my two granddaughters. No, the government does not give us appropriate access to water. The government does not give us enough water for us to live comfortably. We walk to get water due to the lack of taps inside the yard. Yes, water causes many diseases, especially in the areas that have communal taps_one can get sick anytime. Eish, brother, nkuzima (it's tough), I do not know what can happen without this business.'

This above excerpt is from an intense conversation that took place in 2018 with Sive during fieldwork in Khayelitsha. Our conversation took 60 minutes and ranged from food to water usage, and many other topics. In passing, Sive raises several issues concerning service delivery. Perhaps the most pertinent was the question of water – which is increasingly becoming an element of contestation specifically in an informal settlement. The issues arising from the conversation undeniably represent the focus of this chapter. This chapter provides much illumination into people adaptation; the challenges residents are confronted with as well as vulnerabilities when it comes to access water specifically through a communal tap.

1 Introduction

Despite the effort to flatten the curve and the engagement between the government and residents of informal settlements, the global indicators imply that Covid-19 continues to threaten global social and economic structures and water management in many instances remains a pipe dream. With the global economic crisis, the overstaying at home due the lockdown and the rise in infection, and the uncertainty of global change, water access through communal taps with or without proper sanitation is no longer simply about reducing negative impacts imposed by the Covid-19 pandemic but rather the ability of residents to negotiate, reconcile and operate in an environment which enables them to survive and remain resilient over time. A paradigm shift is needed by which President Ramaphosa calls for the South African government to better understand its role in the system in which it operates in terms of its interactions within/between social and environmental elements to better ensure that the water provision does not deteriorate beyond certain thresholds where it can no longer recover from risk events.

In August 2021, President Ramaphosa announced changes to his cabinet arguing that 'water is our country's most critical natural resource' and decided to separate the water and sanitation ministry which will ensure that all citizens have access to water. According to the World Wildlife Fund (WWF), water demand is set to reach 17.7 billion m^3 by 2030 – up from 13.4 billion m^3 in 2016 which outstripped the country's capacity to secure and provide to its citizens. Furthermore, Covid-19 has forced the municipalities and the Department of Human Settlements, Water and Sanitation to re-look at free essential water provision to its people and ensure that everyone has access to this most basic of rights. Also, to provide the necessary infrastructure for said provision. Conversely, the announcement by President Ramaphosa demonstrates that after 27 years into a democratic the government's efforts were failing to encourage the long-term adoption of improved practices. Instead, it appears to be perpetuating the same challenges without addressing the root causes of why the government is failing to achieve long-term activity change. The South African National Development Plan and researchers agree on the shaping of a coherent policy and urge the City authorities to engage with residents to assist them better understand the functioning and impact that they have on the social environment in which they operate.

Covid-19 has again exposed the lack of infrastructure and the supply of water and adequate sanitation facilities to the most vulnerable people living in the informal settlements and has continually changed the way residents see, understand and consume water. Based on the assumption that it will be possible to achieve better results with a couple of adjustments, one of the most severe challenges facing South Africa is the lack of or limited supply of water resources and sanitation (Chitonge et al. 2019). With water, sanitation and hygiene being the first ammunition to fight against the spread of the virus, this is indeed a problem that requires a holistic approach to find a long-time solution and save people's lives.

This ethnographic chapter merely focuses on the diverse adaptive measures that residents of Khayelitsha employ. It combines both theory and practice underpinnings of resilience, looking at how residents respond to water scarcity.[1] The contemporary research of resilience has some elements that have developed in different fields that, in turn, have generated definitions of the concept relevant to the context and content of the problem its addresses (Joseph 2016). Few kinds of research, however, have examined resilience in both its theory and application across the different disciplines. Additionally, Covid-19 has highlighted the challenges facing South Africa and will help fast-track the upgrading of infrastructure and the uninterrupted supply of good quality water and sanitation to all its residents.

Using a qualitative research methodology, the chapter focuses on resilience in a complex adaptive environment using Khayelitsha as a case study to demonstrate how resilience continues to shape how water is distributed, accessed and used in informal settlements. The argument presented is that residents of informal settlements, particularly shack dwellers, are consuming water close to the survival rate and change to water access can be detrimental to their health. This chapter comprises two parts. Part One provides the introduction, background and the methodology used, and establishes the problem and the contribution of the book. It further covers the topography of water and the remedial action to the crisis; it lastly summarises the historical context of Khayelitsha followed by a brief theory on resilience. Part Two includes the case study and discusses the different ways of using water and considers conversations that took place during fieldwork at the respondent's home and the communal water tap, and the conclusion. These conversations provide insight into how the water crisis affects residents' livelihoods and needs. Briefly, the chapter focuses on water scarcity, resilience theory and offers detailed descriptions and characteristics of issues of concern, as well as adaptive measures.

How, then, does adaptation relate to resilience in this chapter? According to Martin-Breen and Anderies (2011), adaptation due to climate change does not fundamentally evaluate behaviour but describes it. Behaviour may reflect short or long-term perceptions of local climate conditions. Adaptation may also be undertaken by policy makers, sectors, individuals, communities or environments. It should be noted that two other variants of 'adaptation' can be found in the literature on climate change.

First, it may be used in the same understanding of 'actions that enhance adaptive capacity with respect to climate change'. Secondly, it is occasionally used to describe what is otherwise named 'mitigation of climate change' (e.g., in Parry 2002) that is, to describe change occurred in order to minimise the magnitude of climate change or related climatic occurrences. Resilience as a concept in this chapter underscores people's awareness of the water crisis in Cape Town, including necessary adjustment in its daily consumption. Resilience also captures the activities that surround the necessity for change as a result of water scarcity. It relates to the exploration of the people's reactions to their experiences and postulations as they grapple with the reality of water scarcity. The names provided in this chapter are pseudonyms to increase the quality of the people's responses, because of the total confidentiality of all the information people have provided. Residents in Khayelitsha have been struggling with water for quite some time (see Kongo 2019; O'Brien 2014; Robins 2013a, 2013b: Taing et al. 2014).

Residents of Khayelitsha are trapped in unstructured defined residential neighbourhoods; entire unequal demographics have inherited spatially defined access to water, health, welfare, income and occupation. Such limited access has severely sparked people's mobility. While the consequences of the social hierarchy are evident in the spatial inequalities between informal settlements and suburbs, what is not immediately noticeable are the psychological effects on the individual and the community. Being compelled to live in an environment lacking water and sanitation often has negatively affected the environmental perceptions and attitudes of many shack dwellers. As Luthar and Cicchetti (2000) suggest, resilience in the study of developmental psychology is distinguished not by its focus on adaptation in general, but rather adaptation in the presence of adversity or in hazardous environment or conditions. Covid-19 marked the beginning of a new era characterised by the erection of new settlements and more intense intra-mobility, migration flows from within Khayelitsha with the population that is becoming increasingly dense and dynamic. Residents' narratives serve as a foundation through which to utilise resilience theory on the water and evaluates how their experience may inspire others who are under similar predicaments. It is with the hope that the complexity of the findings will make a significant contribution to the book and also be useful for different scholars as they are examining resilience as a relevant concept to theirs.

2. The Topography of Water in South Africa and Cape Town

Globally, it has become clear that the allocation of water resources in most areas is less a problem of physical water scarcity than a challenge of economic water scarcity (see Metha 2014). The uneven distribution of water across the planet also poses a challenge (Oyebande 2001). In Africa, the accumulation of water and ecological deficits over nearly four decades of droughts has subjected the environment to a high level of degradation and vulnerability. Drought and climate variability worsen the fragility of the continent and make water resource development a challenge (DEA 2011; WWF-SA 2016; DWS 2017). In South Africa, the insufficient levels and coverage of water services plague both rural and urban communities, creating health challenges (DEA 2011).

In comparison to other countries around the globe, South Africa has an average of 500 mm annual rainfall, and 843 m^3 water per annum. Thirty per cent of yearly rainfall runoff is mostly from surface water, with a large amount of water coming from groundwater (WWF SA 2016; DWS 2017). The World Resources Institute, South Africa, proclaimed the country a water-scarce environment[2] that is experiencing water scarcity (Reig, Shiao and Gassert 2013). Water is a source of life and essential for human necessity (Cothren 2013; Brookes and Carey 2015; WWF-SA 2016; DWS 2017). Because water is a shared resource, the increasing scarcity will directly affect South Africa's health and socio-economic development (DEA 2011). The proponents of water have argued that water facilitates social living and human life sustenance, it plays a crucial role in society and promotes social living and human life sustenance (Chitonge 2010; Chitonge et al. 2019; Johnson, South and Walters 2016). Based on the current situation, South Africa will experience a water deficit of 17% by 2030, and climate change contributes to the scarcity and drought (WWF-SA 2016; DWS 2017). South Africa faces an urgent challenge that needs immediate solutions.[3] The challenge, however, is that people tend to adapt to change only when there is a crisis. In South Africa, there is a clear imperative for continued and increased water infrastructure, which extends to those on the periphery (Rodina and Harris 2016). However, the speed and scale of population growth and urbanisation in South Africa are placing a great deal of pressure on the capacity of governments to adequately plan and meet the needs of the growing number of people in informal urban settlements (see UN Habitat 2011).

Figure 1 highlights the population growth changes in different municipalities between 2001 and 2011. The Free State, which had many districts, experienced a decrease in population.

As shown in Figure 1, Cape Town's population increased by 15% between 2001 and 2011. Cape Town obtains roughly 400 million litres of water from its dams. While service delivery remains a challenge, the migration processes exert pressure on service delivery in the economic centres in the country (PICC 2012). Cape Town's population increased from about 2.4 million in 1995 to an estimated 4.3 million in 2018. On the other hand, dam storage only increased by 15 per cent over the same period. While the Berg River Dam is one of the most critical water sources for the City (it began to store water in 2007), it has been the only significant addition to water storage infrastructure since 1995. Thus, water development is not keeping pace with population growth.

Figure 1: Map illustrating population growth in South Africa between 2001 and 2011

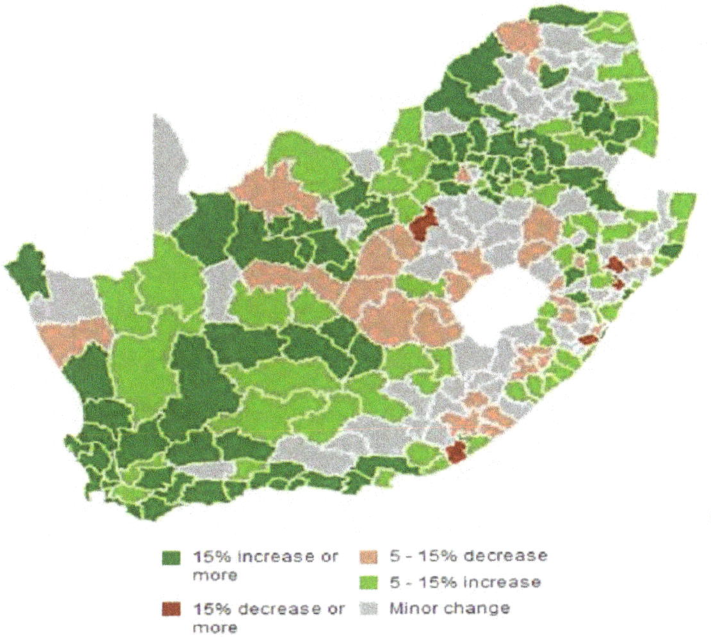

Source: Statistics South Africa, 1996. The People of South Africa Population Census, 2011 Census in brief

Table 1 shows that from 2014 to 2017, there was a gradual decrease in water levels from about 300%. There was a slight increase in water levels in 2018 at the same time, dam levels almost doubled from 2017, but they are still half of the 2014 levels. However, the data above shows that the availability of water resources in Cape Town is declining. Another key indicator is the year-to-year storage statistics. The city water storage was at 101% in 2014, 69% in 2015, 55% in 2016 and 29% in 2017, while there was a slight improvement in 2018. From 2019 to 2021 Cape Town experienced good rain, thus it can be tracked how much water has been stored in the main dams supplying the city compared to the previous years.[4]

Table 1: City of Cape Town dam water levels November 2021 Water dam storage

MAJOR DAMS	CAPACITY		%	%	%	%	%	%	%
	ML	2021	2020	2019	2018	2017	2016	2015	2014
BERGRIVER	130 010	100.2	100.7	100.1	99.3	68.2	62.0	83.5	100.9
STEENBRASS	33 517	93.6	95.0	99.4	85.7	53.3	63.3	79.7	101.2
STEENBRASS	31 767	98.7	93.1	92.7	69.8	100.8	100.3	102.5	100.6
THEEWATERSKLOOF	480 188	101.7	99.8	75.4	57.2	26.1	48.9	70.8	103.1
VOELVLEI	164 095	98.0	95.2	90.0	94.8	28.0	53.6	48.3	100.6
WEMMERSHOE	58 644	95.3	98.3	94.8	91.0	48.9	68.7	68.7	99.8
TOTAL STORED	898 221	893 456	885392	757 998	663678	338544	496 582	627 229	915 698
% STORAGE		99.5	98.6	84.4	56.9	29.3	55.3	69.8	101.9

Source: City of Cape Town, 2021

Findings depicted in Figure 2 reveal underlying trends in average water usage in a million litres per day (MLD), measured by the treated water supplied (includes losses) in Cape Town. The line graph depicts an upward trend in water usage for the period running from 1970 to the end of the 20th century. This period witnessed a gradual rise in water usage in Cape Town, from an average of slightly above 200 million litres per day (MLD) in 1970 to a daily average of above 900 million litres. It translates to more than 350% growth in water usage between 1970 to 1999. The period saw Cape Town's black population increasing more than three times faster than the whites and almost twice as fast as the coloureds (Wilkinson 2000). A series of investments were made to expand and enlarge the water supply infrastructure further away from Cape Town because the government wanted to provide water to the growing population.

This rise in water usage can, therefore, be attributed to the growth in the black population. The water losses level also rose in the same period, as inferior pipes often leaked water, thereby generating water bills far beyond what users could pay (Smith 2004; Von Schnitzler 2008). These water losses prompted protests, including refusal to pay for water and other services that were deemed inadequate, for instance, pipe leaks (Maphela and Cloete 2020).

Figure 2: Water consumption as measured by the treated water supplied (includes losses), average for each year in million litres per day (MLD)

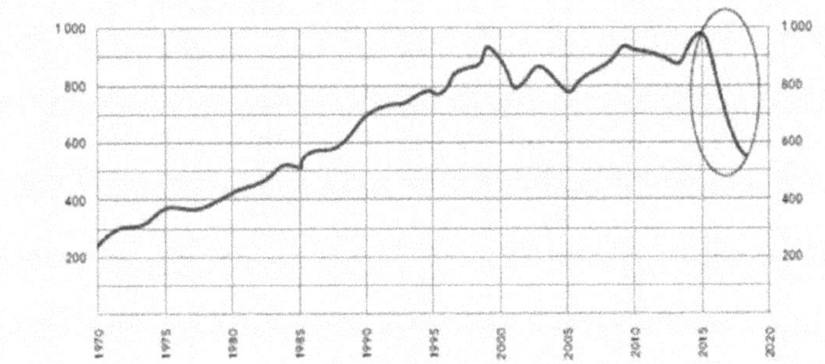

Source: City of Cape Town. Total water consumption in Cape Town Since 1970 to 2020

A sharp decline in water consumption occurred in mid-1999, crossing to the early 2000s, from above 900 litres per day on average to below 800 litres on average per day in 2005. The decrease in water losses also compounded this due to the reduction of instances of leakages. After enacting the National Water Act in 1998, the government introduced formal water conservation and demand management (Enqvist and Ziervogel 2019; Ziervogel 2019a, 2019b). The early 2000s represented a change of course for the city, both in response to the 1998 National Water Act and an increasingly constrained supply in its remote areas. The remarkable reduction in water demand was achieved by public awareness campaigns, repairing leaks, strong; and water-based commodification on market-based pricing (Brown and Magoba 2009; Smith 2004). The results were impressive, but to the detriment of the most vulnerable residents with the large part of the growing population residing in informal settlements where most residents rely on public taps and use less than a third of the water that residents in the wealthy parts of the city do (DWS 2018a; Rawlins 2017).

From 2005 to 2015, another significant rise in water consumption was attributable to negligence by the residents to stick to the standards and regulations of the 1998 National Water Act. The figure shows that during the period running from 2015 there has been a substantial decline in water losses and water usage. The period reported at least a 50% decline in average daily water usage in Cape Town. From 2015 to 2017, water use was reduced by over 40%. At the same time, both the population and the economy continued to grow. Water has also become much more expensive, which affects use (Bond 2019). The period encompasses the most recent drought where water usage got far below the average usage per person in the other South African metros (Ziervogel and Parnell 2014; Wolski 2018). During this period (2015 to current), households, businesses and institutions are investing in alternative sources of supply (such as groundwater, rainwater tanks and reuse).

Viljoen's (2016) study found that, depending on the income category, the households had varying levels of access to alternative sources of water. In the informal settlements, 8% of the participants reported using rainwater and 25% used grey water (Viljoen 2016). Almost half of the participants in low-income households (40%) had access to alternative water resources, including spring water and groundwater, in addition to rainwater and grey water, and the households using ground water consumed up to 79% less than those using other alternative water resources. Only 30% of the medium/high income households had alternative water resources, with 14% using rainwater and 13% groundwater (Viljoen, 2016).

2.1. Water Scarcity and Restriction as Remedial Action to the Crisis

There are various ways of measuring water scarcity which are all accepted measures. If water scarcity occurs in a substantial area and affects many people in the area, the city becomes a 'water-scarce' environment. However, Rijsberman (2006: 6) argues that it is challenging to define the concept, as several factors are involved in determining whether to classify an environment as a water-scarce. Ennis-McMillan's (2001) study influenced how the researcher approached his research into water scarcity by providing another characteristic of the issue. Ennis-McMillan's (2001) work on the importance of water can be beneficial in examining the consequences of water scarcity, as he studied the importance of water in Mexico City, and explored the community's daily life and the meaning they give to the drinking water. Through his examination, Ennis-McMillan (2001: 373) shows how the people's reality on uncertainty was related to disruptions in water usage. His research further exemplifies the importance of having an adequate water supply and probes the social and biological challenges if there is a lack of necessary water supplies. Ennis-McMillian's (2001) illustration is appealing to this case study because it applies the concept that water scarcity does not have a single or universal definition. In the context of South Africa, water scarcity is a result of poor governance and water policy, lack of insufficient surface and groundwater resources, and inadequate funds allocated for water exploration and service delivery projects.

In 2017, the City of Cape Town approved Level 5 water restrictions. Level 5 restrictions prohibit the use of municipal drinking water for non-essential purposes. Water restrictions for domestic usage increase pressure on household management. Level 6B restrictions came into effect on 1 February 2018, along with punitive tariffs for water consumers. Level 6B restricted citizens to reduce the usage of water from 75 litres per person further a day to 50 litres. Furthermore, the City of Cape Town unveiled its preparation for Day Zero with operational plans for 180 water collection stations. According to the city's programmes, Day Zero means 75% of the City's water taps will be turned off, excluding those in hospitals, business or industrial areas and informal settlements. The rest of the communities will access water at one of the 180 water collection stations. Besides the City of Cape Town was developing plans to access groundwater and build a desalination plant to complement its traditional water sources. There is no concrete evidence on how residents of Khayelitsha responded to the prevailing water crisis.

'Day Zero' was an expression used by the City of Cape Town municipality to refer to the anticipated date when they would turn off the water running from most of the taps (Tandwa 2018). During that period, people's behaviour changed, like their taking shorter showers and the collection and reuse of greywater (Mahr 2018; Poppick 2018). As a form of resilience to the crisis, some people purchased and installed rainwater tanks and sunk boreholes. There were also reports exposing a kind of water delinquency to which there was 'water police' to issue fines for 'water waste' such as car washes or watering lawns. Some people, particularly those in the affluent areas, opposed the city's pressures to save water. Organisations opposed the privatisation of water (Dougan 2018). These different responses reflected the difference in the lived reality for people across the city concerning the problem.

These mitigation efforts to prevent 'Day Zero' had fostered even more inequality in an already unequal society. Many residents of Khayelitsha do not have full municipal services because some of their places are unrecognised 'informal settlements'. With a significant number of the residents already frustrated with the service delivery, at the same time trying to hustle for personhood, most were not able to engage with the municipality's print campaigns that attempted to explain the implications of the crisis. As a result, a knowledge gap exists, leaving the residents, who are most affected by the water-saving campaigns, with the least knowledge and understanding of their harsh reality. They are replacing lawns and plants needing much water with substitutes needing less water, and they are also investing in water-saving devices such as low flow taps, water-saving showerheads and smaller toilet cisterns. Other behaviour and conduct, such as taking shorter showers and using shower water to flush toilets, is likely to change over time, but not to pre-drought norms. The drought has changed Cape Town's relationship with and handling of water. However, the challenge remains to reach a sustainable level of wise water use.

Khayelitsha means 'new home' (Tshehla 2002). Notoriously known for its rapid growth, Khayelitsha is one the biggest townships in South Africa after Soweto in Gauteng Province and Mdantsane in the Eastern Cape Province (Ndengwa et al. 2004: 5). The history of Khayelitsha entangles with the challenge for urban permanence of Africans in Cape Town. As Ntsebeza (2019) points out, this historical challenge exemplifies a lot of African people in the Western Cape. Khayelitsha was declared in parliament in1983, as low-cost housing and formalised shack development project to be established in an area about 25 km away from the City Centre for both 'legal' and 'illegal' black Africans, located on the south-eastern part of the metropolis in underused army training camp (Ndengwa et al. 2004:5). The area emerged as poor and overcrowded, with underdeveloped and poorly maintained essential services such as water and sanitation and lack of infrastructure. This disparity resulted in overburdened facilities and the emergence of characteristic socio-ethnic and socio-economic asymmetries. These asymmetries have created an urban morphology which places residents at the City's perimeter – often at great distances from their places of work (Ntsebeza 2019). On the other hand, the then minority white municipal areas had lesser populations to serve with much higher concentrations of economic activity and adequate infrastructure.

One of the significant challenges to water infrastructure development in Khayelitsha is the township's large population and fast growth that outstrips service delivery. Many households still use the bucket system for toilet facilities with no flush toilets. The municipality supplies water, but the absence of individual household taps forces residents to access water through communal taps (O'Brien 2014). Some residents collect water in 25-litre containers from the communal taps. Nevertheless, they manage household activities such as washing clothes, cooking, bathing children and catering with the limited water provided to them. What captivates the lack of service delivery is water leakage, broken communal taps and toilets in an undesirable condition that some had become as refuse dumpsites. There is the maintenance of toilets in some areas where some of them are proportionally assigned to five families per toilet. These shared toilets are more likely to have a level of maintenance, as families secure them with the locks. This kind of landscape is not unique to Khayelitsha but similar to other informal settlements such as Philippi, Imizamo Yethu in Hout Bay, Dunoon and Joe Slovo. In the context of the case study of Khayelitsha, scarcity is unsatisfied demand, tensions between consumers and competition for water over insufficient flows related to access to the communal tap.

2.2 Point of Fracture on Resilience

It is challenging to define resilience because it describes properties of either an isolated object or a system. Clarification is needed of what is being considered before one can ask about any property it possesses, including resilience. However, the World Resources

Institute (2008) attempted to define resilience as 'the capacity to change in the face of change'. For residents to be able to propose mitigation measures for foreseen risks, they need to better understand the critical points of resilience in the environment in which they operate to remain sustainable. In the Khayelitsha context, resilience, in this chapter, refers to the ability of residents to absorb disturbance (i.e., a risk) and still retain its essential function and structure regarding the usage of water. Managing resilience is all about understanding the social context in which Khayelitsha exists with particular attention to the drivers/risks that would cause water scarcity to cross thresholds between alternative regimes – knowing where the limits might enable residents to enhance aspects of their operation to ensure that the residents maintain their resilience. In this chapter, resilience is not about the ability of residents to bounce back but rather the residents' capacity to absorb disturbance and continue with their livelihood. Strategic resilience is not about responding to a one-time crisis. It is about having the ability to change before the case for change becomes desperately obvious.

Water provision through communal taps is becoming an integral component of local government to respond to service delivery as it is according to the local authorities the mechanism used to address uncertainties and hazards. However, in the light of global change it has become more evidential that all health risks are multifaceted and interconnected and cannot be tackled in isolation from each other. There is a greater need for an integrated and systemic approach to health risk to better prepare both the government and its residents to address increasing levels of uncertainty and intensity of risk events, their time frame, and the dynamic, probabilistic and, often, nonlinear natures of the states of all natural and constructed environments on which the system's vulnerability and resilience depends. The challenge for governments is to better understand the interconnectedness of their risk landscape by means of understanding the social and environmental system in which they operate (Gunderson et al. 2010). This will allow them to manage for resilience which will enhance the likelihood of sustaining desirable pathways for continued growth in a changing and unpredictable environment.

Proponents of resilience maintain that sustaining a system requires analysis and understanding of feedback and, more generally, the dynamics of the interrelations between the government institution and residents for the integrated understanding of humans in nature. This interrelationship is referred to what Nyamnjoh (2018) termed conviviality. Nyamnjoh (2018) shows that conviviality reassures the empowerment of individuals and groups, which involve a conciliation, and contestation of agentive forces within a community of states. Nyamnjoh (2018) provides us with a way to think of and understand people and social relations through the notion of what he calls 'conviviality relationship'. The engagement and communication between both parties can work toward a better understanding of the risks and scale of uncertainty to their operations, thereby facilitating better planning for sustainability, resilience and adaptation within Khayelitsha.

The current water management approaches have commonly viewed environmental risk in isolation from the interlinked social system in which they exist. Conviviality indicates that one cannot separate these systems and still obtain a representative view and understanding of the impact and implications of the interactions of each component as part of the broader system. Thus, the proper unit of study and action in which to address water scarcity and sustainability is the linked social-environment system approach. In this regard, the government needs to appreciate that as residents and societal institutions they are embedded in the cyclical processes of the social-environment system in which they operate.

In order for the government to be able to propose mitigation measures for foreseen risks, they need to better understand the key points of resilience in the social-ecological system in which they operate so as to remain sustainable. By understanding how and why the system as a whole is changing, residents will be better placed to build a capacity to work with change, as opposed to being a victim of it. In the context of Khayelitsha, managing resilience is all about understanding the social context in which the residents exist, with particular attention to the drivers/risks that would cause the system to cross thresholds between alternative regimes (Gunderson et al. 2010). Knowing where the thresholds might lie will enable the government to enhance aspects of its operation so as to ensure that the system maintains its resilience. As Walker et al. (2004) put it, resilience is not about the ability of a system to bounce back but rather the system's capacity to absorb disturbance and still behave in the same way. Strategic resilience is not about responding to a one-time crisis. Carpenter and Brock (2008) have described resilience as not about rebounding from a setback as a 'broad, multifaceted, and loosely organized cluster of concepts, each one related to some aspect of the interplay of transformation and persistence'. In the words of Walker et al. (2004), it is about continuously anticipating and adjusting to deep, secular trends that can permanently impair the environment of a core water supply. It is about having the capacity to change before the case for change becomes desperately obvious.

The complexity of the challenges currently facing the residents in Khayelitsha, especially in terms of fundamental uncertainty around water, requires a shift in the way water distribution and how they understand resilience. There is a need for a friendly approach in water distribution strategies which can better address complexity, dynamics and uncertainty for municipality operational and sustainability planning (Rodina and Harry 2016).

Part Two

3. Basic Needs Consumption

Residents of Khayelitsha find themselves trapped in racially defined residential neighbourhoods, and entire racial demographics have inherited a spatially defined access to water, health, welfare, income and occupation (Rodina and Harris 2016). Their struggle of how to reconcile, be recognised with local realities for many years is crucial. The interpretation of their lived realities though these narratives have taken different/many forms and challenge the debate and literature around water. The results are, however, mixed but residents still decry the distribution of water by the municipality do not satisfy and reflect if at all, their lived realities of living with a limited amount of water.

The first question in the interview was to get information about what residents considered to be their basic needs for water. Most respondents stated that drinking, bathing, cooking, laundry and washing dishes were their needs. A middle-aged woman from the 35 to 59 age group responded that her need for water is for her child. Her response demonstrated that she considered the water needs of her child as a main priority. Another woman in the same age group spoke about caring for her children and how she must have different strategies for using water. Another usual response was, 'The basic need of water is for my kidneys,' which was the response of a male pensioner aged 60 to 75.[5] Although some of them did not provide the exact amount of water usage, their responses demonstrated that their basic consumption needs are crucial in the following categories: personal hygiene, cooking, health and, lastly, drinking.

The second question sought to understand the residents' daily water usage for basic needs. This question was uncomfortable and challenging in terms of getting direct responses from the people who did not primarily understand the problem. The rephrasing of the question to how much water they felt they wasted if any, provided some clarity. Out of the 36 informants, 20 provided a percentage and a measurement in litres. On average, some stated that 80% of their total water use is for basic needs. Based on the 25-litre containers used by residents as a guide, the daily water need is perceived to be 50 litres per person per day. In the context of scarcity and adaptation, the results demonstrate that residents consume water close to the survival rate of water consumption which makes it challenging to adapt further.

Based on the interviews, the chapter reports on a difference in the unit of measurement of water usage. Respondents preferred to use buckets rather than litres as measurement. As an essential reference, the standard size of the buckets in Khayelitsha, according to respondents, can hold 25 litres of water. The analysis of data is through respondents' responses based on individual gender and age. The average estimated daily usage of water, as well as the average daily need for water, according to respondents' responses, was calculated using a 25-litre container as a measurement.

The average daily water consumption among the sample was one container of 25 litres, equating to 25 litres per person per day. One-third of the respondents indicated that they use 50 litres of water per day or less, and the rest of the group stated that they use an average of between 50 and 100 litres per person per day. However, there were three exceptional cases from three male entrepreneurs running car wash businesses. These men indicated that they could not quantify the number of litres they used per day, arguing that they probably needed more than 350 litres. When asked further about their water needs, they responded that they valued their car wash businesses because that was the only source of income.

Consequently, they were not concerned about the issue of water scarcity. Most people who were reluctant to respond to this question argued that they did not perceive water consumption as something that can be easily quantified. Omitting the outliers, the respondents could account reasonably well for their water usage, and their answers appeared accurate. Given that the constitutional right for free essential water is 25 litres per person per day (DWF 2007), this chapter shows that besides the limited amount of water, many residents of this informal settlement can fulfil their basic needs within the current water restrictions. Since some of them share a communal tap, the individual limits of using water do not apply directly to them.

Out of the nine informants in the UT section, an informant in the age group 18 to 34 estimated that their daily water usage is 50 litres a day. The remaining respondents responded using 25-litre buckets as their standard measurement. Two elderly couples aged between 60 to 75 could not estimate the amount of water consumed per day. Still, they indicated that their families used two buckets of water as well as a smaller container that they filled when necessary (excluding the water for personal hygiene). Another middle-aged female from the 35 to 59 age group indicated that she used four buckets of 25 litres a day and went to the tap only when necessary, while two females aged between 18 to 34 indicated that they collected water at different times during the day to fill up one bucket each. One of the females was unsure whether her bucket had a capacity of 15 or 25 litres. From an observation point of view, the usage of water is shallow. Therefore, it becomes challenging to emphasise on adaptation. There is an official statistic that has confirmed what the data have captured in terms of water usage (see Viljoen 2016).

4. Water Usage in Khayelitsha

Through observation, residents collect water daily, 'hanging around' the tap several times in a day. Many of them do not have showers facilities, and they use buckets when bathing. As residents' proximity to the communal water taps differs, those nearby may use one 25-litre bucket or container to collect water, while those staying further away use two buckets of the same size to avoid frequenting the tap too often. The use of water differs in many ways from saloon owner to car wash. A group of men that own car wash businesses and frequent the communal water tap to collect water often any time needed. Women selling meat and other entrepreneurs provide an understanding of the amount of water consumed in making chips (see Sive demonstration in section 4.4).

Table 2: Daily water use by age group in litres per activity

	Young aged from 18-34	Middle-aged from 35-59	Elderly aged from 60-75
Personal hygiene	50 l	50 l	25 l
Laundry	75 l	100 l	50 l
Household/cooking	75 l	75 l	50 l
Drinking	20 l	50 l	50 l

Source: Author's calculations using informants' information

Table 2 demonstrates that individuals' daily water use does vary systematically with age. The middle-aged and the young respondents consume a significant amount of water on personal hygiene compared to old respondents. In terms of household/cooking, the elderly, at 50 litres, are the ones that consume less than the other two groups. One probable explanation might be that people in the age group of 60 to 75 are less involved with household matters. In terms of drinking water, young people, aged 18 to 34, use less, which can be attributed to the youth lifestyle of drinking fizzy drinks rather than water.

Table 3: Daily water usage by gender in percentage (%)

	Personal hygiene	Laundry	Drinking	Household & cooking
Female	70 %	80 %	80 %	80 %
Male	30 %	20 %	20 %	20 %
Total	**100**	**100**	**100**	**100**

Source: Author's calculations using informants' information

The data show that age and gender influence water consumption. The data in Table 3 demonstrate that women use a significant amount more water than men in all categories investigated – personal hygiene, laundry, cooking and drinking. Women used 80% of the household water for washing, cooking and drinking compared to 20% for the men. Equally, women used 70% of water for personal hygiene compared to 30% for men. Culture and gender expectations likely influence women's usage of more water compared to men due to their resilience as pillars of the homes. Cultural concepts of beauty are likely to be a contributing factor in differential water usages observed. Thus, gender is often a critical factor in determining individuals' adaptations and daily water usage.[6]

Table 4 below, shows that individuals' daily water consumption does not differ much according to age and gender. However, use is above the average water usage per municipality.

Table 4: Number of residents interviewed per age group and daily water use per litre as reported

Age	Number of residents	Minimum Water Usage	Maximum Water Usage
18-34	13	75 l	350 l
35-59	16	50 l	200 l
60-75	7	25 l	50 l

Source: Author's calculations using informants' information

In terms of age, Table 4 shows that young residents aged between 18 and 34 years tend to use more water compared to those between 35 to 59 years. The difference is likely due to the daily activities of the latter, including running households and businesses such as hair salons, car washes and laundries. Elderly residents aged between 60 to 75 use less water than those between the ages 35 to 59 and those between 18 to 34. Nevertheless, individually or combined, the data show that the daily consumption is higher than that prescribed by municipalities during the crisis.

4.1. Awareness of the Water Crisis

Awareness itself is a function of two elements. One is the message passed on to the community by the City authorities while the other is the message among the consumers. The first question in the interview was about awareness of water scarcity in the country. This question is critical to determine whether and how the responses of the residents who are conscious about water scarcity differ from those who are not. Out of 36 informants, five responded that they were aware of water scarcity problems, saying they had heard of water scarcity problems but seldom thought about them because there had been no water cuts and 31 said they were not aware at all. One female in the age group 35 to 59, who sold food on the street near the taxi rank, refused any notion of water scarcity and stated that there is much water. Another response was from a female in the age group 60 to 75, whose son works for a landscape company, who stated that she was aware that water is scarce in this country because 'my son told me'. Another male (18 to 34 age group) explained that his sister, who travelled to Namibia, told him about her experiences. Both responses illustrate how people's occupations and travel experiences influence their perceptions of and knowledge about the development of the water crisis.

Table 5 illustrates that awareness of water scarcity is shallow. Out of 36 participants, 31 were not aware. Only five were mindful of the water crisis in Cape Town. This figure demonstrates that awareness of water scarcity is shallow, probably because of the lack of a strong awareness campaign by the municipality in Khayelitsha. It is challenging to adapt to an environment where there is no awareness. There were several contrasting perspectives presented accompanied by residents' dissatisfaction with the municipality in terms of poor service delivery and lack of communication. Some argued that Cape Town's City had introduced forced measures to curb water waste by providing a limited amount of water litres per household per day. Municipal authorities installed a device to monitor the supply to formal houses with a designated number of litres of water provided per day. The installation to curb water waste has been highly contentious as it happens mostly in low-income residential areas (Mahlanza 2014). According to the residents, when water from the formal households runs out, these residents reportedly relied on alternative methods to obtain water, the most common practice being to cross into the non-formal housing areas to collect water from communal taps. However, this gives way to a new wave of stress, including wasteful behaviour.

Table 5: Awareness of water scarcity

	Number of residents aware of water scarcity	**Number of residents not aware of water scarcity**	**Number of residents unresponsive**
Female	3	21	24
Male	2	10	12
Total	5	31	36

Source: Author's calculations using informants' information

The question about how a limit of 25 litres a day would impact on the people's lifestyle did not apply to the 11 informants who stated their present daily water use is 25 litres or less. There were mixed responses from the remaining informants. However, many people believed that they could limit water usage if they were more conscious about the water crisis and preventing water waste. One male (60 to 75 age group) explained that it is impossible to live on 25 litres a day. He claimed to be a plumber with some experience quantifying water use and estimated his primary daily water use (and need) at 40 litres. From the above responses, one gets a sense of how awareness influences their attitudes.

One young man aged between 18 and 34 years responded that, 'It will be a war.' Another middle-aged man (35 to 59) responded, saying,

'That is not possible. We are not going to pay. Government has money to maintain us. That is what we vote for, for better service. We do not see why we need to pay for water in the area we live in.' These responses are not surprising considering the socio-economic circumstances and the predicament, which caused adverse reaction and anger towards government service delivery.

There was a similarity in responses from four respondents – two residents aged between 35 to 59, and the other two middle-aged couples (35 to 59). One said that, 'It will be impossible to restrict or cut water in the informal settlement because of the marginalisation of our communities. Water cuts will further kill our people.' Others said, 'Why would we care about a government which does not care about us?' and 'Let us use the water.' These responses suggest a claim to the right to water. These extreme reactions indicate the unwillingness to save water because of the broken relationship with the government. A middle-aged female (35 to 59) stated that, 'If the government cannot provide basic services, then this is a give-and-take situation.' Another explained that the bucket system still exists saying, 'When you cannot go to the toilet at night because of crime, is that dignity? The bucket just changes colour from grey, black to white, the one we have now.' The elderly age group seems discouraged, with the middle-aged group still hoping for change. Those aged from 18 to 34 were angry about service delivery.

Sive showed his 25-litre buckets of soaked meat and chopped potatoes in the back, explaining the process of making *shisa nyama.*[7] He demonstrated his adaptation strategy by putting the meat and potatoes in different buckets three-quarters full of water. The buckets are refilled with fresh water when they become too dirty. He does this four to five times every day and argues that he needs four to five buckets of water always at hand for meat and chips. According to him, that was not a new adaptive measure but a practice even before the water crisis. His entrepreneurial skill demonstrates the disparity of one's needs based on his or her daily activities and the amount of water consumed – in this instance, in the process of making chips.

A male entrepreneur aged betwee' 35 to 59, referred to as Toto, did not provide any estimates and seemed confused by the questions. A fascinating interview was with an elderly man aged between 60 to 75, referred to as Wezo-an ANC war veteran who is in his late seventies. Wezo did not comprehend any of the questions asked. Asake, who was one of the research assistants, asked him how much water he consumes daily. He responded immediately, 'I use it when I want it,' without any further explanation. This response may be an illustration of attitude and lack of response to water restrictions.

4.2. Prioritisation of Water Usage

Prioritisation is a relative concept and it involves many factors. The question about how people prioritise water enabled us to understand how people assign their water personally. Most responses were expected, including drinking, cooking and showering. Tables 2 and 3 display the findings of the essential categories for water consumption, differentiated by gender and age. One woman mentioned '*Umgidi*',[8] Emphasising the importance of cultural traditions, and another woman responded: 'for my son'.

There was no clear evidence on adaptation because some use buckets while some use hosepipes, with no incentive for water saving to the advantage of their business. Men prioritise water for business and often use a significant amount of water in that sense. From the response above, one may assume that if there is an incentive for saving on water consumption, some may have a different attitude toward water and may initiate change.

The data indicates that women prioritise household hygiene more than men (see Table 3). Analysis of gender tends to be superficial in the water sector, as many assume that improved water access would reduce women's burdens and therefore be useful for gender equity. Furthermore, women are also managers of household water and responsible for individual and household health and well-being. As stated earlier, in most developing countries, women play an important role in household management, because they have to bear the workload of water collection. Scholars such as Strang and Linnhoff-Popien (2004) argue that water is associated with feminine power. Adaptation or no adaptation, the primary assumption during conversations with both men and women is that women's concerns are to do with collecting water and domestic use. On the other hand, men are household providers and water consumers through businesses such as car washes. These narratives reproduce themselves because of assumptions about the 'household' and the false dichotomy between domestic and productive domains – where the woman's productive activities are visible, however, not as important as men's income-generating activities.

Some responses illustrate the efficient usage of water and adaptability by women. Many argue that scarcity for them is not new, while others indicate that they have been living with limited access to water for their entire lives. However, prioritising water is their primary concern together with sanitation. Lindiwe said, 'We prefer to do our washing on Saturdays, clean the house and do other duties that require water usage.' As one informant commented, 'When you cannot go to the toilet at night because of crime, is that dignity? The bucket just changes colour from grey, black to white the one we have now.'

Linda and Monde are women activists interviewed – one working as a cleaner and the other one unemployed. Both stated that in the past, they managed water disasters such as floods, drought and water scarcity. These women argued that they are willing to work hand-in-hand with the government to conserve water during the water crisis. They claimed that they have been asking for the government's support for many years with their water-related issues with no success. As they stated, 'Although we women take part in making decisions regarding water usage in our household, we do understand and see how people misuse water, more particularly men. We close the tap when left running, but we still feel neglected, men should learn how to appreciate it.' According to Linda and Monde, the current crisis allows men to realise the importance of involving women in decision making.

Briefly, the role of women in water usage is crucial because of the use of buckets, rather than hosepipes, as measurements and are the first to close the tap when left running. Their actions may translate into the understanding of what adaptation means. However, with many people using one communal tap, it has become difficult for some of them to monitor water wastage. The significant role of women as providers and users who waste less water has seldom been invisible in institutional arrangements for the development and management of water resources (Cap-Net/WGP 2005: 11). This finding agrees with the observations of Caber (1994) and Ahmed (2007), who stated that women are visible in their caregiving role and that policies reproduce this role. The same finding relates to Arora-Jonson's (2011, 2013) observation that women's roles can be extended outside of the private family realm to include the community and the environment. Arora-Jonsson (2011, 2013) argues that women should be 'guardians of the environment' because women are better suited for environmental protection and adapt quickly to water crises.

4.3. Residents' Adaptation to the Water Crisis

Adaptation is the attempt of an individual to conform to an environment, reconciling personal tendencies and rules imposed by the environment and the search for a balance between what is possible and what is not. In the context of drought, Jones and Boyd (2011) defined adaptation in times of shocks and stress as *ex-post* and *ex-ante* coping strategies. The general meaning of adaptation is a change in either people's behaviour or the way people approach an event in terms of resolving a challenge. Adaptation to a water crisis depends on many factors. The ability to adapt to a crisis is influenced by what is called 'determinants of adaptation' (Smit et al. 2000). Maddison (2007) points out that perception and adaptation plans are two vital elements of adaptation, which means that communities need to experience a change in drought conditions and then adopt a set of coping strategies to address it.

Although it was challenging to directly ask residents whether they were adapting to the water crisis, adaptation is not just about consumption. It also includes an attitude towards water consumption. From observations looking at how water is left running without closing taps, this signals that there is no adaptation. Besides the feeling of being neglected, there were neither water cuts nor restrictions on communal taps and no visible information provided to the community regarding the water crisis. The water price offers an incentive to adapt, but the sharing of communal taps may not allow for such an incentive. The lack of environmental consciousness has not curbed the attitude of residents; instead, it has created water waste which has become a relatively fixed feature in Khayelitsha. As demonstrated earlier, if one consumes water at a survival rate, there is little that one can do and then it becomes difficult to adapt to the crisis due to lack of awareness (see residents' responses above). The underlying concern is to find the best means for the city authorities to provide adequate service (Rodina and Harry 2016).

The other aspect of adaptive ability is change: the ability portion of an adaptation to a new way of functioning. However, the terms relate to resilience through the description. There is also a question about what one should be doing to build resilience. It is not always desirable; scarcity of water is a highly resilient state. Those on the peripheric setting with a lack of service delivery may not see the current functioning sustainable. Because of limited resources, one may have to decide, for instance, whether to use water freely or promote the resilience of an environment. Studies done by Lebel et al. (2006), suggest that building the resilience of an environment requires including those who are on the periphery, promoting social justice and accountability at all levels. Resilience suggests consistency when confronted with an event that involves change, but to find a standard definition of the term opens up many questions: What is constant? Which kind of change? Over what period? The response to these questions cannot fall under one rubric; the context under which this place the resilience concept is necessary to understand water in an informal setting. There is a plethora of these contexts available; however, various concepts speak from resilience in individuals or a single object, to the system, to adaptation.

Conclusion

This chapter interpreted the main findings from the research process to make meaning of the patterns and perceptions found in the analysis of the data. These findings were then placed in the context of the broader discourse on adaptation to the water crisis. The chapter also addresses inequality in water distribution in South African townships, drawing from studies conducted in Khayelitsha Site B (Kongo 2019) Phiri in Soweto (Maphela and Cloete 2019) in the City of Johannesburg, and Dunoon (Mahlanza, Ziervogel and Scott 2016). The chapter illustrated that, although the adaptation to the water crisis provided by the study areas are worth isolating from generic discourses on adaptation to the water crisis, the level of inequality is still more pronounced when the comparisons are drawn between the wealthier suburbs of Cape Town and the informal settlements such us Khayelitsha.

The chapter examined resilience that continues to dictate the attitudes and behaviour of residents, also whether and how the water crisis is affecting the livelihoods and needs of residents in informal settlements. Several factors make this a promising exercise. These include the richness and complexity of the narrative record and, also, the extreme nature of residents in both sections. Moreover, how the access to water and its usage and imaginaries of deep time have served as a space of contestation for several direct social forces and relations. In short, all of the overdetermined, culturally interesting practices and ideas that emerge when residents from different gender and age of a given experience and tradition set out to provide their experiences with water amid a turbulent history. It discussed the different ways of water usage and reflected on conversations carried out at the communal water tap and within residential houses. In terms of gender, there are differences in water consumption with women consciously using a significant amount of water.

The narratives have demonstrated that stories are not merely a vague statement, but are often embedded with meaning, providing points to understand the lived reality. Based on the data collected from the TT section, from a purely qualitative analysis of the informants' estimations, the Free Basic Water Policy relates to the basic needs of water. The same report could not be made of the data from the UT section, because most of the informants did not provide precise daily water consumption estimates. How adaptation takes place, whether residents keep functioning or break down depends on different variables. The narrative and experience with water highlighted in this chapter demonstrate this. In this chapter, resilience refers to the ability of residents to generate different ways of operating during water scarcity.

This chapter has further demonstrated that there is nothing universal or predetermined in people's adaptations to the water crisis, the resident's basic water needs and daily consumption. Without an understanding of how the current context of water allocation and the system works, and how people perceive and adapt to water, as well as the community's consumption of water, it will be problematic to change current consumption patterns and meet the basic water needs of all South Africans. There are a large number of researches that use some aspect of the resilience concept. Given the limited space provided, the chapter presented residents' narratives and experiences only. The stories and expertise help the reader to understand how the ideas that constitute resilience theory, or possibly better, resilience concept translate into practice.

In brief, residents of the informal settlement, in particular shack dwellers, consume less water than all segments of the society (affluent domestic users, industry and agriculture). Due to lack of awareness of the water crisis by the residents, it is challenging to refer to adaptation. Residents characterised the municipality as unhelpful and negligent, as the message packaged by the City Council has hardly reached them, and emphasising the government's failure and its continued marginalisation as they consume water close to the survival rate of water consumption. A further change in water consumption is detrimental to health. Those with businesses, including men, consume a large amount of water and prioritise water for their companies as do their women counterparts who use water for household chores. Besides the difference in water usage, there is also wastage of water through the means of hosepipes to wash the cars, and members of the community do not often close communal taps or report water leaks to the municipality. The study suggests that the current government must address more than just the political consequences of apartheid and the exclusionary system. It must simultaneously confront its social and economic legacy. This challenge lies precisely in the realm of 'service delivery'. Access to water, in all the various senses of the word, is at the core of the challenge confronting the South African government.

Notes

[1] Like adaptation, unless all points are shared, with a clear vision of the future, what constitutes a positive coping strategy will be contested. Even refuting has its benefits.

[2] South Africa has less than 1,000 m^3 of fresh water available annually per person.

[3] Considering the difficulties surrounding the water crisis in Cape Town, this chapter assists policy makers to assess progress at the municipal level critically.

Therefore, the lack of adaptation to the water crisis can give authorities a sense of how residents are responding to the crisis.

[4] How does one differentiate between locating not just the study of the city's inaction during the unequal distribution of water, which later on resulted in a statement by the World Health Organization and by the IMF, and congratulating the city for doing something miraculous during the water crisis when, in fact, the City of Cape Town was ostensibly saved by the rain? What would be the thoughts on the actual argument that underpins the city's water conservation.

[5] The National Youth Policy 2009–2014 in South Africa classifies young people as those within the age group of 14 to 35 years. (See South African government /National youth policy.) This paper uses the age classification as per the South African Constitution. However, the study classified participants in three categories: A young person as any person who appeared to be under the age of 18 to 34 years old. Middle-aged is any person between 35 and 59 years, and those over 60 as elderly or pensioner.

[6] The study did not include transgender individuals.

[7] *Shisa nyama* is a Zulu expression for 'burnt meat'. It began as a way for township butcheries to dispose of offcuts. It soon became a gathering place for up-and-coming urban professionals wanting to catch up with peers and reconnect with their roots, local township residents and those who now live in the suburbs. They quickly evolved and became entrepreneurial ventures and are now much more than a place to eat braaied meat and listen to good music. The characteristic of these places is coal, smoke and flames, and its juxtapositions attract the public. Currently, *shisa nyama* is open weekdays and nights too.

[8] A South African traditional practice or Xhosa cultural event to welcome a boy returning as a man from the initiation, with no English translation.

References

Beck, T. L., Rodina, E., Luker, L. and Harris, L. (2016). Institutional and policy mapping of the water sector in South Africa, Vancouver, Canada: Program on Water Governance and University of British Columbia.

Bond, P. (2019) 'Blue Economy threats, contradictions and resistances seen from South Africa', *Journal of Political Ecology*, Vol. 26, No. 1, pp. 341–362.

Brookes, J. and Carey, C. (2015) 'Goal 6 – Rising to the challenge: Enabling access to clean and safe water globally', *The UN Chronicle: Beyond 2015*, available: https://unchronicle.un.org/article/goal-6-

rising-challenge-enabling-access-clean-and-safe-water-globally (accessed 10 April 2018).

Brown, C. and Magoba, R. (2009) Rivers and wetlands of Cape Town: Caring for our rich aquatic heritage, Cape Town, South Africa: Water Research Commission.

Carpenter, S. and Brock, W. (2008) 'Adaptive capacity and traps', *Ecology and Society*, Vol. 13, No. 2, p. 40.

Cothren, G. P. (2013) Understanding rural water supply and access in South Africa, Master's thesis. North Carolina State University, available: https://repository.lib.ncsu.edu/bitstream/handle/1840.4/8147/Cothren%20MP%20Final%202%20January%202013.pdf?sequence=1&isAllowed=y (accessed 24 September 2018).

DEA (Department of Environmental Affairs) (2011) South Africa's second national communication under the United Nations Framework Convention on Climate Change, Pretoria: Department of Environmental Affairs.

DWAF (Department of Water Affairs and Forestry) (2007) Free Basic Water, South Africa: DWAF, pp. 1–47.

DWS (Department of Water and Sanitation) (2018a) Water outlook 2018 report, Revision 24, Cape Town, South Africa: Department of Water and Sanitation.

___________ (2018b) Water Outlook 2018 Report, Revision 27, Cape Town, South Africa: Department of Water and Sanitation, retrieved from http://resource.capetown.gov.za/documentcentre/Documents/Cityresearchreportsandreview/WaterOutlook2018-Summary.pdf.

___________ (2017) Review, evaluation and optimisation of the South African Water Resources Monitoring Network: Implementation Strategy, Pretoria: Department of Water and Sanitation.

Enqvist, J. P. and Ziervogel, G. (2019) Water governance and justice in Cape Town: An overview, *Wiley Interdisciplinary Reviews: Water*, Vol. 6, No. 4, p. e1354.

Gunderson, L., Kinzig, A., Quinlan, A. and Walker, B. (2010) *Assessing the Resilience of Social-Ecological Systems: A Workbook for Practitioners. Resilience Alliance.*

Johnson, H., South, N. and Walters, R. (2016) 'The commodification and exploitation of fresh water: Property, human rights and green criminology', *International Journal of Law, Crime and Justice*, No. 44, pp. 146–162.

Jones, L. and Boyd, E. (2011) 'Exploring social barriers to adaptation: Insights from Western Nepal', G*lobal Environmental Change*, Vol. 21, No. 4, pp. 1262–1274.

Joseph, J. (2016) 'Governing through failure and denial: The new resilience agenda', *Millennium*, Vol. 44, No. 3, pp. 370–390.

Lebel, L., Anderies, J., Campbell, B., Folke, C., Hatfield-Dodds, S., Hughes, T. and Wilson, J. (2006) 'Governance and the capacity to manage resilience in regional social-ecological systems', *Ecology and Society*, Vol. 11, No. 1, p. 19.

Luthar, S. and Cicchetti, D. (2000) 'The construct of resilience: Implications for interventions and social policies', *Development and Psychopathology*, Vol. 12, No. 4, pp. 857–885.

Maddison, D. (2007). The perception of and adaptation to climate change in Africa, (Policy Research Working Paper 4308), Washington, DC: The World Bank.

Mahlanza, L. (2014) Water management devices in Cape Town: Just adaptation, or weapons of mass destruction? Master thesis. Cape Town, South Africa: Environmental and Geographical Sciences, University of Cape Town.

Mahlanza, L., Ziervogel, G. and Scott, D. (2016) 'Water, rights and poverty: An environmental justice approach to analysing water management devices in Cape Town' *Urban Forum*, Vol. 27, No. 4, pp. 363–382).

Mahr, Krista (2018) 'How Cape Town was saved from running out of water', *The Guardian*, 4 May, https://www.theguardian.com/world/2018/may/04/back-from-the-brinkhow-cape-town-cracked-its-water-crisis.

Maphela, B. and Cloete, F. (2020) 'Johannesburg's implementation of the National Water Act, 1998 in Soweto, South Africa', *Development Southern Africa*, Vol. 37, No. 4, pp. 535–552.

Martin-Breen, P. Anderies, J. M. (2011) 'Resilience: A literature review', *Bellagio Initiative*, Brighton: IDS

Mehta, L. (2014) Water and human development, *World Development*, No. 59, pp. 59–69.

Nattrass, N. and Seekings, J. (2001) 'Democracy and distribution in highly unequal economies: The case of South Africa', *The Journal of Modern African Studies*, Vol. 39, No. 03, pp. 471–498.

Ndengwa, D., Honer, D. and Falde, E. (2004) The links between migration, poverty and health: Evidence from Khayelitsha and Mitchell's Plain, Working Paper No. 73, Southern African Labour and Development Research Unit, Centre for Social Science Research, University of Cape Town.

Nyamnjoh, F. B. (2018) 'How Amos Tutuloa can inspire: (Re) situating and (re)imagining contemporary sociological knowledge within the context of South Africa', *CODESRIA Bulletin*, Vol. 2018, No. 1.

O'Brien, Megan (2014) 'The Worth of Water: A Look at the Water Scarcity Crisis and the Perceptions of the Basic Need of Water in South Africa', Senior Theses, Trinity College, Hartford, CT 2014.Trinity College Digital Repository, http://digitalrepository.trincoll.edu/theses/431.

Oyebande, L. (2001) 'Water problems in Africa: How can the sciences help?', *Hydrological Sciences Journal*, Vol. 46, No. 6, pp.947–962.

Parry, M. (2002) 'Scenarios for climate impact and adaptation assessment', *Global Environmental Change*, Vol. 12, No. 3, pp. 149–153.

PICC (Presidential Infrastructure Coordinating Commission) (2012) A summary of the South African National Infrastructure Plan, available: http://www.economic.gov.za/downloads/presidential-infrastructure-coordinating-commission/202-picc-summary-of-sa-national-infrastructure-plan/download (accessed 12 November 2017).

Poppick, Laura (2018) 'What's behind Cape Town's water woes?', Smithsonian.com. https://www.smithsonianmag.com/science-nature/day-zero-looms-cape-town-watercrisis- may-signify-new-normal-180968128/.

Rawlins (2017) 'The political economy of water reallocation: A case study of the Berg water management area, South Africa', Oxford, England: University of Oxford, https://doi.org/10.1093/oxfordhb/9780199335084.013.24.

Reig, P., Shiao, T. and Gassert, F. (2013) Aqueduct water risk framework, (WRI Working Paper), Washington, DC: World Resources Institute.

Robins, S. (2013a) 'The Toilet Wars: Politicisation of Human Waste', *Cape Times*, 27 September.

Robins, S. (2013b) 'How Poo Became a Political Issue: Sanitation is an Old Global Issue', *Cape Times*, 2 July.

Rodina, L. and Harris, L. M. (2016) 'Water services, lived citizenship, and notions of the state in marginalised urban spaces: The case of Khayelitsha, South Africa', *Water Alternatives*, Vol. 9, No. 2, pp. 336–355.

Smit, B., Burton, I., Klein, R. and Wandel, J. (2000) 'An anatomy of adaptation to climate change and variability', *Climatic Change*, Vol. 45, No. 1, pp. 223–251.

Stats SA (Statistics South Africa) (1996) The People of South Africa Population Census, 1996: Census in brief, available: www.statssa.gov.za (accessed 2 October 2017).

Strang, T. and Linnhoff-Popien, C. (2004) A context modelling survey, Workshop Proceedings, First International Workshop on Advanced Context Modelling, Reasoning and Management, 7 September,. UbiComp, Nottingham, England.

Taing, L. Vice, K. L. Schroeder, M. and Spiegel, A. (2014) 'Free basic in informal settlements: an ethnography of so-called communal toilet use & maintenance'. Report K2120/1/14 to Water Research Commission of Southern Africa, University of Cape Town.

Tandwa, Lizeka (2018) 'Drought Crisis: Three Provinces Declared National Disasters', *Mail &Guardian*, 14 February, https://mg.co.za/article/2018-02-14-drought-crisis-threeprovinces- declared-national-disasters.

Tapela, B. N. (2012) Social water scarcity and water use, WRC Report No. 1940/1/12, Gezina, KwaZulu-Natal: Water Research Commission.

Tshehla, B. (2002) 'Non-state justice in post-apartheid South Africa: A scan of Khayelitsha', *African Sociological Review*, Vol. 6, No. 2, pp. 47–70.

UN Habitat (United Nations Habitat) (2011) Urban Patterns for Sustainable Development: Towards A Green Economy, UN Habitat Draft Working Paper.

Viljoen, N. (2016) City of Cape Town Residential Water Consumption Trend Analysis 2014/2015.

Walker, B., Holling, C., Carpenter, S. and Kinzig, A. (2004) 'Resilience, adaptability and transformability in social-ecological systems', *Ecology and Society*, Vol. 9, No. 2, p. 5.

Wilkinson, P. (2000) 'City profile: Cape Town', *Cities*, No. 17, pp. 195–205, https://doi.org/10.1016/S0264-2751(99)00059-1.

Wolski, P. (2018) 'How severe is Cape Town's "Day Zero" drought?', *Significance*, Vol. 15, No. 2, pp. 24–27.

WWF-SA (World Wildlife Foundation South Africa) (2016) *Water: Facts and futures*, Cape Town: World Wildlife Foundation South Africa.

Ziervogel, G. (2019a) 'Building transformative capacity for adaptation planning and implementation that works for the urban poor: Insights from South Africa' *Ambio*, Vol. 48, No. 5, pp. 494–506.

Ziervogel, G. (2019b) Unpacking the Cape Town drought: Lessons learned, Cape Town, South Africa: Cities Support Programme and National Treasury of South Africa.

Legislation

Constitution of the Republic of South Africa, 1996, available: http://www.gov.za/DOCUMENTS/CONSTITUTION/constitution-republic-south-africa-1996-1 (accessed 24 September 2021)

Chapter 7

Resilience or Resistance: Subjectivity and Citizenship in the Context of Ugandan Mourning Rituals

Gaku Moriguchi

Introduction: Resilience in African Societies

On 10 November 2010, my friend Godfrey (of authentic Ganda lineage), who later became my research assistant, took me to Kisekka Market, an old market located in the west of the Old Taxi Park in the centre of Kampala, Uganda. It had been designated for urban redevelopment, and the rights to the land were sold without informing the stakeholders, such as stallholders and other daily users of the market. Godfrey and I went there that day because we had heard that the Kabaka (king) of Buganda, Ronald Mutebi II, was going to visit Kisekka.

In anticipation of the Kabaka's arrival, the town was bustling with activity, and the streets were more crowded than usual. As I was passing by a petrol station on Namirembe Street, which runs from the Old Taxi Park to the New Taxi Park, I saw some men playing drums by the roadside. Fascinated by the scene, I started recording a video of the men with my digital camera. Two medium-sized drums with relatively large heads and short shells (known as *embuutu* in Luganda) and one medium-sized drum with a long shell and small head (*engalabi*) were set on the ground; each drummer was playing a different rhythm. Another performer was playing a maraca, and in the middle of the performance, someone from the audience started blowing a vuvuzela.[1]

Realising that they were being recorded, someone held up a picture of the Kabaka in front of the drums. Some of the men around me, who were wearing *kanzu*, the traditional Baganda costume for men, began dancing to the rhythm. Several times, I was asked for money; however, when I informed them that I was there to record Ganda culture, they quietly withdrew. After the performance, some of the performers came forward to shake my hand.

Such interaction is quite rare on the streets of Kampala. People mainly engage in street performances of traditional music to earn money. The impromptu drum-centred performance that I recorded was done by a group of people who did not know each other. Later, Godfrey informed me that some women stallholders from the market had worked throughout the previous night to clean Kisekka Market and polish the pavements in preparation for the Kabaka's visit. On the way to the market, I saw plastic-coated prints of the Kabaka were being sold on the streets (for 10,000 UGX, equivalent to around 3.00 USD). Other items were also on sale, including visors made of bark with a totemic animal of one of the 52 major Ganda clans inscribed on them (5,000 UGX, equivalent to around 1.50 USD). People who bought and wore such visors seemed to proudly parade their clan identity while walking in the streets. People familiar with the daily life of Kampala would find it unusual to see residents spending their time the way they did that day, because they gathered to sell such goods only during election periods. Crowds that gather for an election campaign are usually given cash, or they ask for an allowance to attend gatherings; people who work for the king attend for free and are generally those who have taken on different responsibilities in the election process. In other words, the drumming performance, the cleaning of Kisekka Market and the gathering itself on the day in question did not have any political purpose; they were done only to honour the Kabaka.

Such celebratory activities for the king were also observed, nationally and internationally, during the Kabaka's wedding in Mengo, Kampala in 1999 (BBC 1999), intended to represent the strong ties between the king and his subjects in the Kingdom of Buganda. The Kabaka is a political and cultural symbol not only for the Baganda people in Kampala but also for people elsewhere. However, when I asked Godfrey and other Kampala residents about their ties with the Kabaka, they gave me a seemingly inexplicable answer: 'Many of the people are not Ganda. They claim to be Ganda people but are in fact migrants originally from another ethnic group.'

Based on this puzzling answer regarding the nature of the social ties between the Kabaka and his subjects (the people in the market), I will discuss the resilience in African societies from anthropological and social scientific perspectives, which focus on multiplicity and rituality. Before describing the ethnographic cases, however, I need to clarify the notion of resilience itself in the postmodern/

postcolonial context which is characterised by complexity and relationality.

Some of social scientists believe that resilience does not focus on a specific factor. In his book *Resilience: The Governance of Complexity* (2014), David Chandler stated that resilience is a nonlinear, dynamic and complex concept. He discusses that individuals, communities, nation-states, economies, the natural environment and any other actors are entangled together, and interact with one another in the process of building resilience, leading to contingent sequences and system dynamics. The factors involved in this process are not always predictable and thus prove difficult to disentangle. Chandler critically compared the classical and post-classical understandings of the concept of resilience:

> The etymological roots of classical understandings of resilience are framed in terms of the inner resources and capacities of the autonomous individual and therefore are implicitly linked to the classical liberal subject of modernity (Chandler 2014: 6).
>
> The etymological basis of 'post-classical' framings of resilience can be found in a much more relationally embedded understanding of the subject. ... The subject does not survive merely through its own 'inner' resources; the subject survives and thrives on the basis of its ability to adapt or dynamically relate to its socio-ecological environment (ibid: 7).

According to his argument, resilience has become an important point in international development policy discourse, especially in the last decade, leading people to form their own subjectivity in certain circumstances. Although the resilient subject is considered in opposition to the external environment characterised by disasters, poverty and conflicts, these conditions are reflectively related to the human mind. As Chandler stated in his book, 'the nature of being is complex, relational, embedded and contextual' (ibid: 50). As per post-classical understandings, the concept of resilience relates to something between our internal self and socio-ecological conditions, which can help promote national development and build resilient selves and environments.

On the other hand, 'the nature of being' in the contexts of African societies is multiply embedded inside of individuals. To analyse this aspect, I will review some Ugandan ethnographic works, focusing on the ties between the nation-state and local communities in post-colonial Africa. These works suggest the puzzling attitudes of people in the Kisekka Market and the sense of community among them, which are closely related to the sense of local and individual resilience in Uganda. The Kabaka, Baganda symbols, rites and incidental conviviality have been influencing people of Ganda and non-Ganda migrants, providing them with a feeling of belonging, even though they do not customarily belong to the Buganda kingdom and are not secure in the region. Since the 1960s, Uganda and its neighbouring countries have suffered from civil wars. Specifically in Uganda, even after Museveni took over Kampala in 1986, regional insurgencies have incidentally taken place. Considering the suffering of people and society during these insurgencies, the term 'resilience' is crucial for the people of Uganda. Recovery from wars and disasters must be redeemed carefully in an African societal context from the anthropological perspective.

Regarding resilience in Africa – that is, people's autonomy and subjectivity with regard to addressing disasters, poverty and conflicts – the meaning of 'subject' is dependent not simply on the state but mainly on each person's belonging to a particular ethnic group, which is the relational subjects in South Africa as Ferguson discussed (Ferguson 2015). To apply Chandler's ideas to the current African situation and to consider the relationship between African citizenship and resilience, it is important to examine Mahmood Mamdani's *Citizen and Subject* (1996). Mamdani discussed the dilemma of African citizenship, proposing that the public sphere in modern African nation-states has been divided into two types: one is governed by civil law and represents citizens, while the other is ruled by the customary laws of specific ethnic groups. The colonial legacy of 'divide and rule' caused the bifurcation of states in Africa, which 'contained a duality: two forms of power under a single hegemonic authority' (Mamdani 1996: 18). It has continued to cause suffering in the form of clientelism, conflicts and the so-called failed state condition.

As Mamdani discussed in his book, the subjectivity of people committed to their nation-state in post-colonial Africa can be characterised as either resilience or resistance. It means one aspect of citizens of the nation-state and another aspect of subjects of tribal/ethnic groups. In other words, People's nature toward the state power has a duality, which he described as Janus-faced, and would be named differently in each historical context. Societal autonomy and the relational subjectivity in ethnic groups function as resilience when they encounter the 'crises' of their society, like when the people of Uganda struggled against the HIV/AIDS pandemic after insurgencies and miraculously survived. Once the subject of national recovery development is established, which is an integral part of the resilience process following a natural disaster or war, the distorted relationship between the state and its citizens does not force people to subjugate themselves to the modern state. People, however, cannot be simple subjects in the development policy process; they are also the subject to corruption and civil war, which are the subjects of extraversion. People exert their power to fill their own bellies by resisting the civil law of the nation-state but subjugating themselves into relational networks of kins and tribal groups. It, in turn, is the subject of the 'politics of the belly', as theorised by Bayart (2009), and this societal network as social capital is also the source of resilience in the moment of the crisis. Resilience is not based on the nation (even though the resources come from national and international sources) but on people's autonomous and relational subject, which is based on kins in the post-colonial African nation-state.

To overcome this post-colonial divide, Museveni's regime adopted a no-party democracy (a nonpartisan system) in 1986. (This was later rejected by a national referendum in 2005). Simultaneously, the new government promoted decentralisation and the local council (LC) system to enhance the local community's ability to achieve economic development and provide social security. The LC system was called the Resistance Council (RC) system, which laid the foundation for the National Resistance Army (NRA) that waged the Ugandan Bush War against Obote's Ugandan National Liberation Army (UNLA) from 1980 to 1986. Resistance against oppressive power and a community-centred political approach (that is, a bottom-up approach) were the core ideals of the NRA (later known as the military wing of the National Resistance Movement (NRM)), which advocated for democracy in the newly reformed Uganda.

However, in the years following 1986, this community-centred and resistance ideology gradually collapsed. In the past three decades, the NRM itself has become an oppressor, and there has been rampant clientelism and corruption (Flanary and Watt 1999). During the recent protests over the 2021 general election results, demonstrators were met with police violence. In 2007, the Ugandan government proposed the Peace, Recovery and Development Programme (PRDP) to improve the conditions of the populace in

Northern Uganda following insurgencies by the Lord's Resistance Army (LRA). It was supported by the international community, which made large donations. However, donations amounting to 24.5 million USD were misused by the Prime Minister's Office (Daily Monitor 2017). Such corruption is widespread in Ugandan daily life. For example, the entire budget of a road construction project may suddenly disappear, and it may later be revealed that almost all the money was spent by the project leader on personal expenses (Author interview with a local citizen in Wakiso District, August 2015).

Corruption in Africa has been the huge issue that Chabal and Daloz described as a part of disorderly political instrument of postcolonial nation-state in Africa (Chabal and Daloz 1999). Furthermore, Hyden has argued that the corruption and clientelism comes from the economy of affection, which is based on the very social nature of African people (Hyden 2007). Additionally, Motoji Matsuda (1999), a Japanese anthropologist, quoted the discussion of James Scott's *Weapons of the Weak* and argued that, in Kenya, such cases of corruption and sabotage reflect the 'soft resistance' of the weak members of society against poverty and a difficult national situation. Thus, the subject of resilience in Africa does not promote the national public benefit; although a part of resilient and resistant life in Africa, it does not create national unity which could lead the hegemony of neo-patrimonial state (cf. Hyden 2007).

Therefore, there are two important aspects of people's relational subjectivity in Africa: one is citizens' resilience when subjugated to the government, while the other is resistance in conflicts against the state. The difference between naming it resilience or resistance depends on the context of the person who names it. On the one hand, the concept of resilience involves the notion of modern citizenship of the African nation-state in order to empower people's capacity and adaptability for the national development and recovery. On the other hand, it includes the subject of resistance under the current political environment in Africa, to disunite and break down the basis of the modern system of the nation-state.

I do not imply that African resilience and citizenship do not function to promote social coherence and strengthen the people's capacity as other contributors of this book discussed. Rather, I assert that this kind of African resilience functions in both ways – building and undermining the modern nation-state if Africa. Through such autonomy and self-reliance in African societies, which are independent of the nation-state, it is possible to explore an alternative relationship between the state and its people. To investigate this issue, I will examine three Ugandan ethnographic cases from the 1990s to the 2000s. These cases describe the independence of each analysed society from the state of Uganda after the civil war. They indicate Africans' resilience built on a network of ethnic and societal groups, such as clans and local churches, against the brutal violence brought about by the state and modernity in Africa. All cases focus on the function of each ethnic group's burial/funeral rituals, which are motivated by mourning for people who died in recent insurgencies in Uganda. The collective sense of loss and remembrance is key to social coherence in Africa; it could form a connection based on the new notion of resilience – that is, in the context of our discussion, African conviviality and citizenship – between the living and the dead. Lastly, to examine these cases, I will also consider Francis B. Nyamnjoh's discussion of conviviality and citizenship (Nyamnjoh 2015a, 2018).

2. Resilience as a Political Condition: The Case of Uganda and the NRM Regime

As mentioned in the previous section and suggested by prior studies, there has been rampant clientelism and corruption in Uganda (Wiegratz et al. 2018; Asiimwe 2018). Since 2006, after multi-party politics was restored in Uganda, Museveni and the NRM's political campaigns have become money-spinning ventures, representing a great source of patronage for the people. However, the patron–client relationship between the state and the people is inextricably linked to the precarious practice of extraversion (cf. Bayart 2009). For example, suppose politician A distributes money or necessities to the electorate in his or her district who then decide to vote for him or her. However, when politician B arrives and provides the electorate with more money and goods, then the voters switch allegiance to him or her. In the patron–client relationship in contemporary elections in African democratic politics, the patron always undergoes comparison and competition with others in terms of the amount of wealth and goods promised, so the patron's political status is never stable, though in the traditional clientelism argument, the patron–client relationship is fixed, not fluid. The client simply utilises the money or goods and services offered by the patron and then proceeds to the next patron. This lacks the stability of the symbolic capital possessed by traditional chiefs and kings, and a patron's inability to buy votes leads to the constant fear that power can be easily transferred to someone else. Thus, the politician as patron is another actor in the process of extraversion, someone who seeks an equal share of wealth and goods from higher-ranking patrons in the political party to continue to satisfy people's endless appetites and desires. The political community in Uganda thus has a vertical, downward structure. The patron–client relationship is always unstable and subject to opportunism on the part of the client, especially that provided by election campaigns and national development projects, such as PRDP in Northern Uganda (Asiimwe 2018; Branch and Yen 2018).

However, previous anthropological studies conducted in Africa by Japanese researchers have rarely reported such proactive extraversion (c.f. Matsuzono, Nawada and Ishida 2008; Nishi 2009). Rather than having a negative implication, this may represent the adaptive and creative subjectivity in African development and modernisation, which have been promoted by the repressive state power and are considered the flexible self and soft resistance (cf. Matsuda 1999; Ogawa 2011). Here, African people's subjectivities neither means 'the development subject' (Ferguson and Gupta 2002) nor refers to 'the flexible subject', which is associated with the global capital flow in a neoliberal situation (Ong 1999). Development is essential for the modernisation and industrialisation of the nation-state and to ensure support for the implementation of the telos of modernisation, regardless of the actual state of society (Ferguson 1990). This involves the settlement (even if temporary) of wage labourers (even if immigrants) within the territory of the state, the development and participation of more workers, the formation of capital based on the labour, and the construction of roads and industrial infrastructure, such as factories (cf. Escobar 1996; Ferguson and Gupta 2002). Ultimately, labour, capital and industrial infrastructures are the foundation of tax revenues and military service, which support the sovereign authority of the state. Consequently, the formation of a nation as a 'disciplined body' of citizens engaged in political discourse can take place with the advance of development and modernity. This is also referred to as 'subjection' of the self (Foucault 1991; Butler 1997). By referring to Althusser's notion of power and interpellation, Butler clarifies the process of 'subjection' as below:

> 'Subjection' signifies the process of becoming subordinated by power as well as the process of becoming a subject. Whether by interpellation, in Althusser's sense, or by discursive productivity, in Foucault's, the subject is initiated through a primary submission to power (Butler 1997: 2).

The modernity which Foucault describes is based on the pervasiveness of state power in a society achieved through a political environment focused on the advancement of development projects, welfare and the mass media. African peoples and societies have found a way to resist state power achieved through such social discourses by flexibly (and sometimes defiantly) adapting to their surroundings (Matsuda 1999; Ferguson 2006).

In recent modern history, however, African states have not been on the stable path of development and modernity because of several reasons: the global industrial recession of the 1970s that followed the oil shock, the structural adjustments of the World Bank and the IMF in the 1980s, and the numerous post-Cold War conflicts in the 1990s (Takeuchi 2009). The influence of these major global trends on African underdevelopment has been sufficiently discussed in the existing literature (cf. Moss 2011: 105–119). However, there is a lack of research on the specific aspects of African citizenship, patronage and clientelism, and the exploitation of the public for vested interests, such as extraversion, which are related to the authorised subjects of nation building (cf. Comaroff and Comaroff 1999). Paradoxically, the sense of citizenship and subjectivity, or 'soft resistance' in Matsuda's words (1999), against the background of the discourse of development and capital formation, overlaps the sense of resilience in the local community (Chandler 2014: 83). These are two sides of the same coin of nation building in post-colonial Africa.

In *Citizen and Subject*, Mamdani argued that there are two types of colonial legacies in modern African states. One is the 'citizen' as an agent of nation-state formation, as legitimised in civil society, whereas the other is the 'subject' as an agent of cultural groups of 'tribal peoples', which impedes state formation in Africa and the practice of extraversion. Mamdani asserted that the contradictory and conflicting relationship between the citizen and subject is a specific feature of the modern African state, which he referred to as a 'bifurcated state'. He stated that, through indirect colonial rule, urban areas and colonial state capitals inherited a modern legitimate civilian system that guaranteed citizenship to residents, while he described local areas as regions with customary law that include subjugated colonial subjects. According to him, this duality in the post-colonial regime bifurcated African states and led to not only conflicts by armed militia groups but also to a lack of state unity and the practice of extraversion by ethnic groups, which are the modern historical roots of colonialism. Therefore, the pervasiveness of civil wars and corruption in the form of clientelism within modern African states can be said to be due to people's search for belonging not in the state but in their ethnic group ruled by customary law.

Local subjects of customary law cannot be easily understood as developmental agents of the state, such as national citizens. They can never be included within the nation-state. They are the subjects of soft resistance against the state, and they can sometimes become overwhelmingly violent, as Mamdani (1996) described the rebels in Western Uganda in the 1960s (ibid: 197–200) and migrant workers in South Africa in the 1970s (ibid: 227–255). It can thus be difficult for them to coexist alongside resilient actors who support national development. Incidentally, the actor who supports national development could have previously been the subject of resistance against state sovereignty. Such a case has occurred in Western Uganda in recent years.

Museveni's regime has promoted cultural policy and recognised several kingdoms and kingships as responsible for the interests of the ethnic groups within the Great Lakes region of East-Central Africa. Under the NRM, five kingdoms were reinstated, including the Rwenzururu Kingdom, which was endorsed by the government in 2008. In 2009, Charles Mumbere was appointed as the king of the Bakonzo people in Western Uganda. Although aware of the active function of culture and ethnicity in politics, the NRM government has nevertheless strictly prohibited the political participation of cultural leaders, such as kings and chiefs. The government has projected the reinstatement of these kingdoms as major national reforms in Uganda (Johannessen 2006), since they assumed that kings and their subjects would be subjected under the state law of Uganda, which finally would lead them to be citizens in the modern sense.

However, on 27 November 2016, the police and army (Uganda People's Defence Force (UPDF)) of the Ugandan government raided the royal palace of the Rwenzururu kingdom and found many illegally held firearms and explosives. The resultant conflict led to the death of more than a hundred people on both sides, UPDF and the king's guard. Arrested following the clashes, Charles Mumbere remains indicted on charges of treason as of 2021. The Bakonzo people have a long history of resistance since the colonial era. In the current civil war in the Democratic Republic of Congo (DRC), they are active actors in rebel groups and are known there under the name Banande (Mamdani 1996; Prunier 2009).

Many scholars have asserted that ethnic and tribal groups are essential social actors in African politics; ethnicity as a colonial social construction has been emphasised and critically reviewed by several anthropological studies (cf. Cohen 1978; Parkin 1969). In the 2007–2008 post-election violence in Kenya, the Kikuyu people, the largest ethnic group in Kenya, who had played a significant role in the Mau Mau uprising, fought against the Luo and other ethnic groups over alleged election fraud in the presidential election. More than a thousand people died in the turmoil (Tsuda 2008; Lafargue and Katumanga 2008). This crisis suggests that African people do not support the integration of citizens into the state but are more likely to favour being subjects of ethnic groups within a nation. This citizen–subject duality has been a curse to Africa; it cannot be easily integrated into the nation-state and is an uncomfortable aspect of post-colonial Africa. Therefore, the supposed actors of resilience, whether citizens or subjects, are a significant factor (or subject) of resistance against the state. This dual aspect of resilience and resistance in African nation-states must be carefully considered.

In addition, duality and multiplicity in Africa have also been discussed as essential aspects of African citizenship. One dimension of this duality and multiplicity is people's local citizenship – that is, their belonging to multiple ethnicities – which has been suggested as one of the reasons for the colonial social construction of 'African ethnicity'. Many Ugandans, especially those living in slums in Kampala, where I conducted my research, tend to have a sense of belonging to multiple groups and shift between their identities and citizenships according to the country they live in and the language, ethnicity, associated customs and social context of the region they currently inhabit. They change their identity depending on the person they are interacting with and the place and context in which the interaction takes place. As Matsuda indicated in relation to the case of Nairobi, Kenya, notions of belonging, such as nationality, citizenship and ethnicity, which are generally implied by one's name, are likely a set of clothes that one can take off and put on at will, although the number of outfits is limited (Matsuda 1999).

Chris, a professional night watchman and the father of my host family in my research field, is one such person who can change identity at will. For example, in addition to his mother tongue, Lukonzo (the Konzo language), he speaks Luganda (the Ganda language, one of the most common languages in Kampala), Kiswahili, English, Kinyarwanda (the language of Rwandan immigrants), Acholi and some related Nilotic languages, such as Alur and Lango. In the slum in which he lives, he usually identifies as a Konzo from Western Uganda and not as a Ugandan citizen. His close friends, however, know that he is a Nande from the DRC, which is how he identifies himself to Congolese migrants. The Konzo and Nande peoples are considered to have no significant differences in terms of language, clan formation, etc.; the only difference between the two comes from the border between Uganda and the DRC. Nonetheless, anyone of African origin can freely cross the border with almost no obstacles because border polices accept the people's dual citizenship of two nations.

I met another person from the DRC while conducting my research in 2015, a 27-year-old named Henri. From December 2014 to March 2016, he lived in Chris's house, slept at night, when Chris was at his workplace, and prepared meals for him. Until the age of 11, he had lived in a village near Kasindi in the DRC. After moving to Kampala, under the patronage of his paternal uncle who worked as an accountant at a supermarket in Kisementi (a business centre in Kampala), Henri completed his secondary education (Senior 1–4). In addition to his mother tongue, Lukonzo/Lunande, he speaks French, English, Kiswahili and Luganda. Chris and Henri came from the same village, which is located between Kasindi and Bwera; however, when asked about their nationality, they admitted to holding both Ugandan and Congolese nationalities. In recent years, it has become easier to register one's nationality before an election (or more accurately, to receive a national identity card provided by the NRM government). In an interview I conducted in August 2015, Chris mentioned that 'each country gives us a card to encourage us to vote for their government'. He further added that it was also possible, in some cases, to obtain a national identity card of some other neighbouring countries, such as South Sudan and Kenya, before a national election in that country. Of course, the possibility of obtaining such a card depends on the political situation of the country in question at the time. In addition, based on his language skills and relationship, Chris believes he can obtain South Sudanese or Kenyan citizenship. He speaks Nilotic languages and, from 2014 to the present, he has been in a relationship with a South Sudanese woman belonging to a Nilotic-speaking group. Many people, at least many Congolese migrants living in slums, believe that it is possible for them to obtain citizenship. Therefore, citizenship or nationality is simply a superficial attribute to be employed opportunistically for people moving about between Uganda, the DRC and other neighbouring African countries. These people belong to multiple African ethnicities and nationalities.

3. Resilience of African Local Communities

Recently, these people lay claim to multiple belongings, especially considering the focus of immigrants on nationality and sovereignty in modern African states (cf. Geschiere 2009: 17). In the sense of multiple belonging, the nature of African citizenship is controversial in terms of defining the nation-state, although many people, such as Chris and Henri, have easily crossed ethnic and national boundaries. Belonging and citizenship are also essential to the discussion of resilience and resistance. However, the question of where to belong plagues people in nations historically shaped by colonialism and modernity (Mamdani 1996); people show allegiance not to the nation-state but to their kinship and ethnic group to feel socially secure, which is especially difficult in Africa where people are nationally secured and sometimes in vulnerable conditions in their daily lives. As seen in the previous section, people's belonging and autochthonous condition cannot be simply reduced to their nationality and ethnicity. Therefore, determining African citizenship, as well as African resilience, is an ambivalent project. The debate on resilience or citizenship in the context of Africa not only concerns the question of where people belong physically but also relates to the question of where they belong socially. Their sense of belonging not only exists in regionally defined ethnicity but also in social ties and the performativity of rituals of nationhood and autochthony. This is supported by Geschiere: in Cameroon, from the 1960s to the 1970s, private funeral rituals were complementarily utilised in building autochthony and nationhood (2009: 190).

As argued earlier in this paper, resilience especially as social autonomy of groups within the framework of modernisation – wherein the society is supposed to be a part of the integration into the nation-state – can easily lead to significant corruption in the form of misuse of aid money, which can be interpreted as 'soft resistance'. In the African context, the society that people imagine is not directly linked to the nation-state. Therefore, in this section, I will examine three ethnographic case studies, analyse the relationship between rites and societies, and consider resilience in the Ugandan context. I have chosen Uganda because of the numerous insurgencies and political disasters that have taken place in the country until now and the resilience shown by the people in their recovery process. All three cases relate to funeral rites: the burial rites of Teso society in Eastern Uganda, the Ganda's *Olumbe* in Central Uganda and the Alur's *myel agwara* in Eastern Uganda.

In *Beyond the State in Rural Uganda* (2009), the British anthropologist Ben Jones described the post-civil war reconstruction of the Teso region in Eastern Uganda. The conflict in Teso, the so-called Teso insurgencies, did not end in 1986 when Museveni took power in Kampala with the NRA/M. It continued until the early 2000s because of the actions of the LRA and other rebel groups. Jones indicated that, following the conflict, the reconstruction of the region was not necessarily undertaken by the state of Uganda; rather, local organisations, such as burial societies and church groups, in the Teso region were responsible for the reconstruction.

In his book, Jones did not use the term 'resilience'; however, the current condition of Teso society and their recovery process indicate their resilience after the war. Most people in the region experienced the loss of loved ones. The insurgencies disrupted the social order. Jones (2009) asserted that it was possible for them to maintain order by organising burial societies. The conflict overturned the age-related social order in the Nilotic ethnic groups in the region; against customary law in Teso society, many elders were killed by the young. However, the opportunity to bury their dead through funeral rituals enabled the people to overcome such moral failings or difficulties and return to everyday life.

Furthermore, Jones argued that the act of mourning functioned to share the social memory of people in Catholic, Anglican Ugandan and Born-Again churches in the region. Funds for burials were collected and managed in collaboration with local organisations and churches. Consequently, they were able to at least partly preserve their self-reliance and moral order, and rebuild society by adapting themselves to the post-conflict situation. In other words, the establishment of economic cooperation, the implementation of redistributive economic policies and the practice of burial rituals to help with grief played an important role in their recovery.

Jones also asserted that the recovery was carried out beyond the influence of the state of Uganda. In places such as the Teso region, where people distrust the current Ugandan government, societies are marginalised and not protected by the state, and this separation promotes their resilience, which comes into play when mourning begins for those who died in the conflict.

In the second ethnographic study examined here, which was conducted in Buganda in Central Uganda and its associated societies, Mikael Karlström discussed the lineage-based clan system of the Ganda people and the establishment of the ritual called *Olumbe* (Karlström 2004). The Buganda Kingdom consists of 52 clans, which are called *ebika* (sing. *ekika*) in Luganda. Each clan claims to have a common ancestor and is an exogamous group. These clans are hierarchical; the *Kasolya* is at the top, followed by the *Mutuba* and *Lunyiriri*, with a family household, *Enda*, at the bottom. People of the highest lineage occupy the top positions in the *Lukiiko*, the Parliament of the Kingdom of Buganda. *Omukulu ekika* (clan chief) is the main cabinet member, supporting the Kabaka, the king of Buganda.

Regarding *Olumbe*, Karlström described it as not simply a funeral rite but also something that serves as a nexus between the different lineages within each clan. Unlike burials in the Teso region, *Olumbe* is carried out a few years after the burial. It is considered a succession rite through which another person takes over the position in the clan left open by the death of a person. In other words, the relatives of the dead person assemble to grant the person's authority in the clan to a successor from the new generation, such as the dead person's younger brother or son, and to mourn the death. This ritual allows the kin of the dead person to reaffirm their collectiveness, sense of social belonging and group identity. Karlström emphasised that the social stratification in Buganda inspires a new morality in people and provides them with the necessary foundation for development and modernity.

He also indicated that the social stratification based on lineage and the communal nature of *Olumbe* suggests the presence of conviviality in Africa (cf. Nyamnjoh 2015a) and contributes to development that is independent of the state. This is another form of African resilience and a variant of civil society, as suggested by both Jones and Karlström. However, Karlström and Mamdani partly ignored some essential facts of Buganda. Most of its population consists of migrants: domestic ones from other Bantu ethnic groups of Ankole, Nyoro, Tooro and Soga, and international ones from Rwanda and Burundi who have migrated since the 1930s (Fortt 1954). Because the majority of the Ganda population has immigrant roots, my interlocutor, Godfrey, mentioned that, as stated in the introduction, 'many of the people are not Ganda' when talking about the people who had gathered in Kisekka Market. In addition, becoming a member of clan lineage through *Olumbe* is only possible for people in the wealthy middle class with the prestigious title of landholder.[2]

Regarding the commonalities between the two rituals – the burials by church groups in Teso and *Olumbe* in Ganda organised by clan groups – both serve the purpose of mourning the dead. Moreover, in both cases, people encounter death as a tear in the fabric of society (Hertz 2013) and their networks emerge through the emotions evoked by the death of their kin and neighbours. Social mourning functions as a compensation for the death in the society, and people feel intensely affected by the death and thus mourn for the dead. In *Divinity and Experience: The Religion of the Dinka*, which described personhood in a South Sudanese ethnic group, Godfrey Lienhardt made the following controversial statement: 'The Dinka have no conception which at all closely corresponds to our popular modern conception of the "mind" as mediating and, as it were, storing up experiences of the self' (Lienhardt 1961: 149). By this, Lienhardt did not mean that 'the Dinka people have no mind', as generally claimed by some critics (cf. Schmidt 2017); rather, he meant that the Dinka people did not have a conception of a mind that is internally made-up and coherently responsible for its own decisions, which is what the Western conception of the mind is. The 'mind' of the Dinka is somehow externalised and responds to rituals and communal religion, which surround individuals and give them personhood in society. He also stated that '[i]f the word "passions", *passiones*, were still normally current as the opposite of "actions", it would be possible to say that the Dinka [religious] Powers were the images of human *passiones* seen as the active sources of those *passiones*' (Lienhardt 1961: 151). *Passiones*, which emerge from incidents and rituals in the context of African society, are considered key to making connections among individuals and forming communal relationships of conviviality (Nyamnjoh 2015a). They also help understand African resilience as a hybrid concept involving individuals and their social environment. The presence of *passiones* and conviviality in Africa suggests that the subject and personhood are not an internalised mind of self, as European, American and Japanese are believed to keep, but are an externalised agency incidentally linked and corresponding to others' lives, societal entities and the physical environment; thus, people are impassioned about the rituals to preserve their sense of social life and continuity when they encounter death. This provides a new perspective on the sense of resilience and citizenship in the modern African context, about which many researchers seem to have reached an impasse.

Lastly, Noriko Tahara described the *myel agwara* of the Alur in Northwest Uganda, as an example of ritual citizenship in Africa (Tahara 2018). Tahara stated that the spirit of the dead, called *tipo* in Alur, plays an important role in the world of the living. *Myel agwara* is performed to communicate with and pacify the *tipo*, ensuring a smooth passage for the dead to their ancestral world. The last *myel agwara* was performed in 1987.

An important feature of *myel agwara* is that it must be performed by more than two clans in cooperation with each other. This is mainly because of the several roles involved in the ritual, including playing music and dancing, preparing a great feast and sacrificing a large number of cattle. The last ritual was performed by four clans of the Alur, namely the Pamora, Angal, Padolo and Paera. Tahara emphasised that performing the ritual together developed a sense of cooperation among the clans, leading to a sense of communality and common citizenship among the Alur. Thus, despite the division because of the border between Uganda and the DRC, ritual citizenship emerged among the Alur people.

As observed in the ethnographic studies on the Teso and Ganda, mourning and burial rituals for the dead serve an important function for the living, helping them develop a sense of communality and social identity within a larger group. As Lienhardt argued in relation to the Dinka case, *passiones* for the dead encourage people to act as engaged members of society, based on their lineage and convivial social relationships.

4. Conclusion: African Resilience and Citizenship

Ritual citizenship in three ethnic groups in Uganda, as described in the previous section, certainly does not represent the best example of African resilience when considering the influence of the power of the state of Uganda. These cases are not completely independent of state power or post-colonial conditions. For example, the Buganda Kingdom and its clan lineage system were transformed through the intervention of the British colonial administration (Hanson 2003). After independence from Britain in 1962, Edward Mutesa II, the thirty-fifth Kabaka of Buganda, was chosen as the first president of Uganda under the surveillance of the British colonial regime. Buganda and its clan lineage system developed as a quasi-state within Uganda, with the people as subjects of the Kabaka.

The burial rite of the Teso is also problematic, although it has been argued that it is independent of the state. Christianity in Uganda, including all churches – the Church of Uganda, Catholic Church, Born-Again Church and others – is deeply rooted in colonialism and the Enlightenment movement, which influenced colonial/post-colonial governance in Uganda (cf. Mudimbe 1988). The discourse of Christianity itself functions as pastoral power, the notion of which Foucault explored in his *History of Sexuality* as the people's lives are nurtured instead of being governed (1990), to control smaller religious groups in rural areas; this power is carried and exercised by bishops in Kampala, the capital of Uganda. The Anti-Homosexuality Act, which was implemented in 2014, was influenced by Christian discourses, mainly of the Born-Again Churches, reflected in the national interest and diplomatic policies of Uganda.[3] The Act identified the hidden sexual minority as an internal enemy and intended to make people disciplined subjects of the national sexual discourse (Moriguchi 2014; Bompani 2018). Furthermore, the Ugandan mourning ritual was an important issue in the NRM's campaign for the 2016 general election. Umeya (2018) argued that Museveni exploited the agency of the dead in his re-election campaign by organising the reburials of, or commemorative ceremonies for, the dead, especially of West-Nilotic origin, killed during Amin's regime in the 1970s. This re-election strategy was a success, and Museveni was able to retain support in the Eastern region, particularly Tororo District, compared to Gulu and Lira, where opposition parties won office at the local level. When considering the reasons for the NRM and Museveni's maintenance of power for more than 35 years, it is important to consider that mourning ritual attendants, and even the dead themselves as agencies, are included as the subjects of the national resistance/resilience movement. In this context, African resilience comes into play when dealing with national policy and state power. Studies such as those by Jones and Karlström naively invent the free subjects or citizens of autonomous and resilient African local societies to pursue the unique discourse of African civil society (cf. Comaroff and Comaroff 1999).[4]

Nonetheless, there still exists the possibility of finding resilient subjects or citizens who are neither dependent on the state nor defined by the national borders in the African context. People of immigrant origin gathered in Kisekka Market for the Kabaka's visit knew that they temporarily belonged to the kingdom and its ritualised figurehead, the Kabaka. Group coherence – as social resilience among individuals and ethnicities – functions as subjectivity in the kingdom in relation to the people's desire to belong. For the same reason, Chris and Henri of Konzo/Nande can freely shift their citizenship between nations. African people are aware that alternative subjectivity and citizenship in other political contexts in Africa are always available to them. They can be agents of rebellion/resistance when they detach themselves from a particular nation-state. The African hero in Tutuola's fictional world was described by Nyamnjoh as follows: 'being a hero requires being a composite – amenable to shifting bodily shapes and with the capacity for presence in simultaneous multiplicities, in familiar and unfamiliar ways' (2015b: 12). Citizens and subjects in Africa thus are a 'composite' with 'simultaneous multiplicities'. They are ritually motivated to be subjects with *passiones*, as Tahara indicated in the case of ritual citizenship. Rituals and a sense of belonging thus provide people with subjectivity and require them to adopt a particular form contributing to their multiplicity, which reveals their resilience through social activities. However, African resilience is a composite of multiplicities rather than a specific fixed form of resilient society.

Acknowledgements

This article is based on the paper which was presented in the symposium 'Resilience in Africa' at Nagasaki University on 16 November 2019. The research was financially funded by JSPS Kakenhi Grant (16H056664) and JSPS NRF joint research project, 'Human Resilience in the face of man-made and natural disaster in Japan and South Africa: Ethnographic Perspective'. I gratefully thank Tamara Enomoto, Kiyoshi Umeya, and Anthony Simpson for reviewing this paper, their fruitful advice and their generosity. I would also like to show my appreciation to all the scholars I met in South Africa who inspired me with the basic idea for this paper.

Notes

[1] https://www.youtube.com/watch?v=QBlar-NU8PYQ

[2]. Another title of the Ganda clan leaders is *Bataka*, which means the landlord in Luganda. In this regard, belonging to a clan involves belonging to the clan's land. For the historical development of the land tenure system in Buganda, see Hanson (2003).

[3] The bill, signed into law by Museveni, was considered by Christian fundamentalists and conservatives in the NRM an integral part of the political campaign for the 2016 general election; however, the Constitutional Court of Uganda subsequently reviewed the Act and ruled it invalid.

[4] See Whyte and Whyte (2004: 613–614), especially on the paper of Karlström (2004).

References

Asiimwe, G. B. (2018) 'The impact of neoliberal reforms on Uganda's socio-economic landscape', in J. Wiegratz, G. Martiniello and E. Greco (eds) *Uganda: The Dynamics of Neoliberal Transformation*, London: Zed Books, pp. 145–162.

Bayart, J-F. (2009) *The State in Africa: The Politics of Belly*, London: Polity Press.

BBC (1999), 'Uganda's "wedding of the century"', http://news.bbc.co.uk/2/hi/africa/431503.stm (accessed: 20 April 2022).

Bompani, B. (2018) 'Religious economies: Pentecostal-charismatic churches and the framing of a new moral order in neoliberal Uganda', in J. Wiegratz, G. Martiniello and E. Greco (eds), *Uganda: The Dynamics of Neoliberal Transformation*, London: Zed Books, pp. 303–317.

Branch, A. and Yen, A. (2018) 'Neoliberal discipline and violence in northern Uganda', in J. Wiegratz, G. Martiniello and E. Greco (eds) *Uganda: The Dynamics of Neoliberal Transformation*, London: Zed Books, pp. 78–94.

Butler, J. (1997) *The Psychic Life of Power: Theories in Subjection*, Redwood City: Stanford University Press.

Chabal, P. and Daloz, J-P. (1999) *Africa Works: Disorder as Political Instrument*, London: James Currey.

Chandler, D. (2014) *Resilience: The Governance of Complexity*, London: Routledge.

Cohen, R. (1978) 'Ethnicity: Problem and Focus in Anthropology', *Annual Review of Anthropology*, Vol. 7, pp. 379–403.

Comaroff, J. L. and Comaroff, J. (1999) 'Introduction', in J. L. Comaroff and J. Comaroff (eds) *Civil Society and the Political Imagination in Africa: Critical Perspective*, Chicago and London: University of Chicago Press, pp. 1–43.

Daily Monitor (2017) 'Court finds Kazinda guilty of syndicate corruption', https://www.monitor.co.ug/uganda/news/national/court-finds-kazinda-guilty-of-syndicate-corruption-1703740, 31 May (accessed: 1 May 2021).

Escobar, A. (1996) *Encountering Development: The Making and Unmaking of the Third World*, Princeton, NJ: Princeton University Press.

Ferguson, J. (1990) *Anti-politics Machine: 'Development', Depoliticizeation, and Bureaucratic Power in Lesotho*, Cambridge, UK: Cambridge University Press.

____________ (2006) *Global Shadows: Africa in the Neoliberal World Order*, Durham, NC: Duke University Press.

____________ (2015) *Give a Man a Fish: Reflections on the New Politics of Distribution*, Durham, NC: Duke University Press.

Ferguson, J. and Gupta, A. (2002) 'Spatializing states: Toward an ethnography of neoliberal governmentality, *American Ethnologist*, Vol. 29, No. 4, pp. 981–1002.

Flanary, R. and Watt, D. (1999) 'The state of corruption: A case study of Uganda', *Third World Quarterly*, Vol. 20, No. 3, pp. 515–536.

Fortt, J. M. (1954) 'The distribution of the immigrant and Ganda population within Buganda', in A. I. Richards (ed.) *Economic Development and Tribal Change*. Cambridge, UK: W. Heffer & Sons, pp.77–118.

Foucault, M. 1991(c1977), *Discipline and Punish: The Birth of the Prison*, translated from the French by Alan Sheridan, London: Penguin Books.

__________ (1990) *The History of Sexuality*, Vol. 1, translated from the French by Robert Hurley, London: Penguin Books.

Geshiere, P. (2009) *The Perils of Belonging: Autochthony, Citizenship, and Exclusion in Africa and Europe*, Chicago and London: The University of Chicago Press.

Hanson, H. E. (2003) *Landed Obligation: the Practice of Power in Buganda*, Pourtsmouth, NH: Heinemann.

Hertz, R., 2013, *Death and the Right Hand.* Translated by R. Needham and C. Needham, London: Routledge.

Hyden, G. (2007) 'The economy of affection and the moral economy in comparative perspective, *Afurika Kenkyu (Journal of African Studies)*, Vol. 70, pp. 35–50.

Johannessen, C. (2006) 'Kingship in Uganda: The role of the Buganda Kingdom in Ugandan politics', *CMI (CHR. Michelsen Institute) Working Papers*, 2006-8.

Jones, B. (2009) *Beyond the State in Rural Uganda*, Edinburgh, UK: Edinburgh University Press.

Karlström, M. (2004) 'Modernity and its aspirants: moral community and developmental eutopianism in Buganda', *Current Anthropology*, Vol. 45, No. 5, pp. 595–619.

Lafargue, J. and Katumanga, M. (2008) 'Kenya in turmoil: post-election violence and precarious pacification', *Les Cahiers d'Afrique de l'Est/The East African Review*, Vol. 38, pp. 1–14.

Lienhardt, G. (1961) *Divinity and Experience: the Religion of the Dinka*, Oxford: Oxford University Press.

Mamdani, M. (1996) *Citizen and Subject: Contemporary Africa and the Legacy of Late Colonialism*, Princeton, NJ: Princeton University Press.

Matsuda M. (1999) *Teikou-suru-toshi: Nairobi, Imin-no-sekai-kara (Resisting City: The world of migrants in Nairobi)*, Tokyo: Iwanami-shoten.

Matsuzono M., Nawada H. and Ishida S. (eds) (2008) *Afurika-no-Ningen-kaihatsu: Jissen-to-Bunkajinruigaku (Human Development in Africa: Practices and Cultural Anthropology)*, Tokyo: Akashi Shoten.

Moriguchi G. (2014) 'Han-douseiai-hou no seiritsu to "Uchinaru-teki" no soushutsu' (Anti-homosexuality bill and the invention of internal enemy), *Kokusai-kaihatsu Jaanaru (Journal of International Development)*, Vol. 691, pp. 54–55.

Moss, T. J. (2011) *African Development: Making Sense of the Issues and Actors*, Second Edition. Boulder and London: Lynne Rienner Publishers.

Mudimbe, V. Y. (1988) *The Invention of Africa: Gnosis, Philosophy, and the Order of Knowledge*, Bloomington and Indianapolis: Indiana University Press.

New Vision (2016), 'Rwenzururu palace raided, king arrested', https://www.newvision.co.ug/news/1440930/rwenzururu-kings-palace-raided, 27 November (accessed: 1 May 2021).

Nishi M. (2009) *Gendai-Afurika no Koukyousei: echiopia-shakai ni miru komyuniti, kaihatsu, seiji-jissen (Publicness in the Modern Africa: Communities, Development, and Political Practices in the Ethiopian society)*, Kyoto: Shouwa-dou.

Nyamnjoh, F. B. (2018) 'Rethinking citizenship in 21st century Africa', *Bunkajinruigaku: Japanese Journal of Cultural Anthropology*, Vol. 83, No. 2, pp. 180–191.

___________ (2015a) 'Incompleteness: frontier Africa and the currency of conviviality', *Journal of Asian and African Studies*, Vol. 52, No. 3, pp. 253–270.

___________ (2015b) 'Amos Tutuola and the elusiveness of completeness', *Stichproben. Wiener Zeitschrift für kritische Afrikastudien*, Vol. 15, pp. 1–47.

Ogawa S. (2011) *Toshi-wo-ikinukutameno kouchi: Tanzania-no reisai-shounin Machinga no minzokushi. (Cunningness for the Urban Survival: Ethnography of Machinga, Petty Traders in Tanzania)*, Kyoto: Sekai-shisou-sha.

Ong, A. (1999) *Flexible Citizenship: The Cultural Logics of Transnationality*, Durham, NC: Duke University Press.

Parkin, D. (1969) 'Tribe as fact and fiction in and East African city', in P. H. Gulliver (ed.) *Tradition and Transition in East Africa*, London: Routledge & Kegan Paul.

Prunier, G. (2009) *From Genocide to Continental War: The 'Congolese' Conflict and the Crisis of Contemporary Africa*, London: Hurst.

Schmidt, M. (2017) 'Godfrey Lienhardt as a skeptic; or, Anthropology as conceptual puzzle-solving', *Hau*, Vol. 7, No. 2, pp. 351–375.

Tahara N. (2018) 'Creation of cooperativity through mourning: ritual citizenship among the Alur people in the republic of Uganda', *Bunkajinruigaku: Japanese Journal of Cultural Anthropology*, Vol. 83, No. 2, pp. 233–255.

Takeuchi S. (2009) 'Gendai-afurika no sensou (Conflicts in the modern Africa)', *Afurika-Kenkyu* (*Journal of African Studies*), Vol. 74, pp. 51–61.

Tsuda M. (2008) '2007nen Kenia sousenkyo-go no kiki (Crisis after the general election 2007 in Kenya)', *Afurika repooto* (*Africa Report*), Vol. 47, pp. 3–8.

Umeya K. (2018) 'The agency of the dead and its effect on western Nilotites: Looking back on the 2016 Uganda general election', *Bunkajinruigaku: Japanese Journal of Cultural Anthropology*, Vol. 83, No. 2, pp. 233–255.

Whyte, S. and Whyte, M. (2004) "Comments", *Current Anthropology* Vol.45, No. 5, pp. 613–614.

Wiegratz, J., Martiniello, G. and Greco, E. 2018, Introduction: interpreting change in neoliberal Uganda, in J. Wiegratz, , G. Martiniello, and Greco, E. (eds.), *Uganda: The Dynamics of Neoliberal Transformation*, London: Zed Books, pp. 1–40.

Chapter 8

Resilience, the Massification of Grief and the COVID-19 Pandemic

Kharnita Mohamed

I[1]cannot perceive the world we are becoming. In the midst of dying and the continuing debilitation wrought by COVID-19,[2] most of the routines, if not the demands, that constituted the everyday have been suspended. Who we will be in the aftermath, if there is an aftermath, is a mystery. What we know of human history is that some will continue and worlds will be made and remade, contested and changed, relinquished and resisted. All the ways in which worlds get shaped and stumble along into futures unimagined and yet influenced by our presents, our pasts and sometimes desired futures will continue. Though whether the worlds that come into being may be worlds we wish to bequeath to those we love or would have loved were we to survive is another matter entirely. The humans who become[3] in these new worlds, no matter how capacious their endurance to withstand precarity in the face of global epidemics and climate vulnerability, do not have vulnerability distributed evenly. For most dispossessed people in the Global South, new disasters will merely be another set of debilitating conditions to endure. And that they continue in worlds that are brutal, that wilfully injures and debilitates[4] them to wrest profit or some kind of fantastical racialised security,[5] that neglects them and treats them as less than human, that they carve lives within these worlds that seek their annihilation and degradation, lives that have joy and continue to seek comfort in a multitude of ways is palely understood as resilience.[6]

Living during COVID-time[7] is to endure days that yawn and accelerate. For those of us lucky enough or structurally able to work from home, because of the type of labour[8] and ownership of technology which allowed us to retreat into our sanitised bubbles, the days blur into a mishmash of domesticated labour or belaboured domesticity. Affect is at times a force (Rosaldo 2013) that traps you in a long silent scream that has nowhere to go; between social distancing and the alienating intimacy of lives that are partially broadcast to social media publics. At other times the vicissitudes of COVID-time lulls you into a strange immobility where all you do is scroll, scroll, scroll, up and down your Facebook feed, reeling from one disaster to another. Crossing huge distances without leaving your couch, the intensity of affect (Massumi 2002), coursing through your body, holding you in stasis. Huge cataclysmic world events merging with the death that has become constant, coming at you in your work emails, WhatsApp groups, Instagram and on Facebook. Family, family friends, your friends' parents, someone you met once somewhere and never forgot, people you love who have lost people they love, students and staff at your institution. Constantly wondering when the loss will be so close that it will shatter every part of you, whether it will be your death that shatters the people who love you. And from your couch you cross time and space, barely able to hold onto the holes that have been carved into your life, into the memories of your childhood or to take a deep enough breath to convince yourself that you are not next.

You don't go to the funerals. 'Social distancing' and 'super spreader' are the words that (allow you to) create a bridge out of absence. Balancing the cruelty of your absence and the hug you cannot give and the useless words that have lost meaning from too much repetition with the cruel risk that your presence might produce more death, more debilitation. Yet if you could have gone to the funerals, you might well not have. You know that you would not have had the stamina to go to a funeral or two or three or four a day. That you could not go to homes and comfort the bereaved whose families are smaller, sometimes by two or three or more members. I almost remember there may have been families where there were more. I don't remember all that well nowadays or make notes like a good anthropologist, tallying the death toll and noting the events like I did right there in the beginning. I really don't care that I am not either. In a neoliberal society where work is supposed to be life, perhaps that is a new kind of sacrilege. Nonetheless, we are not who we were.

You write out your tired condolences on a Facebook wall, on WhatsApp. They intersperse the day. 'So sorry for your loss', you write, over and over and over. Social media as a graveyard. Except all the mourners are words that at some point the bereaved may return to, to like or heart or care, or cry or be angry about. Sometimes the bereaved dies. Once you type hastily and agonise over misspelling 'sorry'. That day worrying takes a lot of time. You forget to go back and edit and never forget the error. It is not all bleak though. You laugh. A lot. At silly posts, at Donald Trump, at cat videos and try not to think. You reminisce and laugh. Sometimes you feel like it is life asserting itself in the face of death, sometimes your laughter carries a jagged edge of desperation. You laugh anyway.

You are supposed to be writing about grief,[9] violence, impairment, debility, disability and precarity. Your heart cannot bear it and your psyche does not know how to hold onto so much death and violence and to make something meaningful with it, something writerly. Bearing witness to ordinary and routinised structural violence was brutal before a pandemic. No-one had ever prepared you for how your heart would break or how sorrowsome losing your belief in the intrinsic goodness of the world would be. And how angry you would be. Even though you knew that feminist rage moves worlds, brings new dreams to life and is often grounded in feminist love and hope (see Ahmed 2004). But this witnessing of unstoppable death, arrived at in the mysteries of hospitals you cannot visit, this witnessing of COVID's relentless onslaught, mapped onto the midst and aftermath of the devastation wrought by enslavement, colonialism, apartheid and postapartheid abandonments feels like it is destroying parts of you.

You owe a book chapter on grief and disability and something that holds some kind of hope by virtue of the biosociality you observed in your research on disability. There needs to be something about resilience. This chapter. You ignore it for months. You are not the kind of writer for whom writing is to process. You prefer writing in the aftermath. You learned to cope with trauma by not relinquishing control, you are not very good at it. That fictive control is how you save yourself from drowning. You remember vaguely, that there was a time when you had some kind of intellectual understanding of what resilience might be. The evidence is somewhere in emails and on a folder that had just the texts you needed and some of the preliminary writing. You cannot make sense of the words that you read. They bleed into each other and blur on the page and find no purchase in the narrow, narrow intellectual world that COVID locks you into. One in which hungry Black[10] people are beaten when they beg the city for food.[11] A man is killed in his own backyard for drinking a beer.[12] For six weeks, homeless people are put into a fifty-eight million Rand concentration camp with four marquee tents and mattresses on the floor and not enough food or sanitation or medical assistance, in Strandfontein[13] on the sandy Cape Flats close to the Indian Ocean, where an apartheid government once forcibly relocated Black people. A naked man is ripped from his shack and forced to watch as the pre-pandemic exercise of rendering Black people homeless resumes.[14] There are long queues for food all over the country with few masks in sight. White people fight to exercise[15] and to surf.[16]

A maskless white man tells me COVID is for defectives and he is not defective. A white woman tells me COVID is a hoax and the blood of Jesus will protect her. I tell these stories over and over and laugh. Because if I don't, the despair at how long we have to live with white supremacy tears me apart. Black people too will assert versions of these discourses and yet, when it comes from white people, it rankles. There is something in the tone, in the disbelief about the virus, the insouciance, that makes you realise that it is still a world where some are imagined as beloved of God and some as defective. This eugenic discourse renders people like me, who for centuries were made vulnerable to disease by the rapaciousness of white supremacy, culpable for COVID's rampaging through our midst. For not being beloved of God, for being defective, for being Black.

And yes, there are incredible initiatives across race, wealth and creed to feed people, provide masks, to step in where the state could not or would not reach. And amidst all that you try, over and over, for the dry prose you are reading to leave you with something other than a slight feeling of absurdity at the unaffected temerity of that dry, dry prose from very good anthropologists, very good published scholars. Nothing sticks. There is only room for the rage and the sorrow and the messy loves and the day-to-day detonations coming at you on all the screens you own. There are weeks which become months of nothing sticking. When you cannot work, you feel like a failure.

The machinification of academic labour demands humans work as if they were machines, as if their purpose is work. In the world of the academy to be a faculty member who is overcome with the devastation of your world and who needs care, is to fail. To be a person with human sentiments, human needs, is to be a failure. It does not matter that you know this is neoliberal subjectification, that there is a history to labouring sensibilities and institutional demands. To understand your historical becoming, is not necessarily to transcend your history. The pandemic intensifies the demands for unending capacities to care: for your students, your institution, the new technologies you must learn, your research and the indices that mark a successful career. The academy does not care that those indices don't mark a joyful life, a generous life, a life grounded in the world around you. The absence of these would not be personal failings. Failing to produce, to make your days and labour into a product, this is to fail. And so, you fail, and fail, and fail.

You fail. The country fails. People die. And at some point, the hunger stops feeling like an emergency. The COVID numbers are like all those incalculable numbers this country loves. Matric results that don't tell us anything about education, except that you should worry about the future and wonder how failure can be celebrated so very publicly. Crime statistics that don't tell us anything about well-being or care about whose lives are devastated. Some of the most respected journalists and public intellectuals repeat the COVID statistics day after day: how many infected based on those who could get a test, how many deaths and, at some point, they start enumerating the recoveries of a disease whose trajectory is poorly understood. A disease where some people have begun talking about Long COVID, month upon month of debilitation. A future where chronic illness, impairment and debilitation may well be widespread. You worry about this. After all this is a country that will use a water cannon on the temporarily disabled when they are forced into a packed queue in the street after the state discontinues life-giving funds.[17] Who will shoot a disabled boy during a pandemic.[18] Who couldn't provide adequate transport and schools and training for people with disabilities before COVID. Your research on people with disabilities has shown you just how unprepared we are for the scale of impairment that COVID will leave behind. And so, you worry.

We do not know who all those COVID numbers represented, lumped together, the dearly departed. Even though a meme begins to circulate stating that the numbers of the dead are now people as the scale of death intensifies. It was always people, always close somewhere to someone. We do not know how much devastation was left in death's wake. Which child can no longer go to school? Which lover will no longer have a wedding? What do those empty beds feel like? Did they scream in their socially distanced houses when they heard? Except you do know. The infected and the affected. You have few words except that stupid, stupid, stupid sentence: 'So sorry for your loss.' So sorry for the nights you will wail or maybe your grief will not allow tears or sound, and will make you so deeply quiet, that nothing will ever penetrate your stoicism until of course, something does, something improbable and utterly ordinary. Life does that, takes you by surprise even in the aftermath of grief. Or will your grief, like Rosaldo's (2013) headhunters, lead to rage and breaking the bodies of others.

You know too many people whose deaths have foreclosed futures of people you love, people you know. You remember the smell of their homes, how it felt in their presence and how very long it has been since you saw them, and you wonder how long before you will see their affected, those who remain after the dearly beloved has departed. How long before you can hold them, reach out a tender hand to stroke away a tear or offer a tissue. Feel the wetness of their tears in your hair or have them hold you as you sob and sob. Someday perhaps you will smile tremulously through the tears, be there when the softer things that make life sweet reasserts itself.

You can't imagine what touch will mean then in that distant future. Sometimes you are beset with envy at the people touching on one insipid Netflix series after another. Sometimes incomprehension, anxiety, unbearable unbearable loss. Another world, another time. The affective forces of COVID-time remaking your body. Remaking what warning and alarm and danger feels like on the surface of your skin. You are not so accustomed to feel the often glacially slow work of subjectification change you so rapidly. You think you are alone in your alarm until others in your virtual world express it better than you could. A generation whose sensitivity to touch has shifted, for whom the imaginary of touch is speeding along into another time. You think of the research that will emerge on COVID and the remaking of subjectivity, remaking of temporality and you are already tired of the decades and decades of work that COVID will produce. You tell a friend. You both laugh, you know the kind that hits your belly. You can barely stop laughing, as you imagine the titles of papers and books that you will be reading, supervising, writing. You realise, in time, your exhaustion told you before you understood intellectually that you will never be free of COVID. The academy is always a place of sticky time, sticky space. In the time of the university, COVID will be thought of from every possible angle and will be hooked into every intellectual fashion for decades to come. People will continue to die. Perhaps not of COVID, but whatever those continuities of power are – racism, sexism, capitalism, ableism, heterosexism, nationalism and on and on – that allow the massification of vulnerability and marginalised people to die in a crisis, whether due to poverty, HIV-AIDS or COVID or xenophobia or climate crises or land theft and on and on. And you and others like you in the academy whose normalised vulnerability exposed you to persistent, continuous death and debilitation will have to live with trauma and pretend that you are resilient and can spring back like the timber from which the concept of resilience first emerged (O'Dougherty Wright and Masten, 2015).

You cry as you write this. Foregoing the cool rationality you never aspired to anyway and the kind of anthropology that prefers alienation in that maxim we like to teach as epistemic relation: make the strange familiar and the familiar strange. It feels like the first proper expression of grief. You never could have been that kind of scholar anyway. No native anthropologist can truly be. Even if the texts they shape attempt to conform to disciplinary conventions and are dry. The outrage and tenderness always bleeds through even in the driest of prose, and so too does the falsity of outrage of those good anthropologists with their vicarious suffering on behalf of others who they can always escape when they need to. There are stakes for us, native anthropologists, for our bodily integrity, for our hearts, the shapes of our lives. Even when we are not good anthropologists. Political, ethical, ontological, methodological and epistemic stakes. And so we choose to be vulnerable in our mode of representation (Behar 1996), so as to assert the emotional force that experiencing (Rosaldo 2013) being there is. When your work is on the ways in which settler colonial violence through apartheid and the postapartheid and its continuities break the bodies and psyches of people who look like you, people who you love(d) to maintain inequality, and then attempt to write in the midst of an epidemic whilst watching the horror of how that unequal distribution of vulnerability will decimate your community, then the idea of alienated writing is macabre anyway.

You never want to be that resilient. And anyone who expects that kind of resilience from you, does not see you as human or feel humanely disposed to you. The institutions in which we work that demand continuity, at all costs, do not rely on our resilience, rather it is a new mode of oppression. You are reminded that on slaveholding plantations, plantation owners would whip the enslaved, mutilate their bodies, injure their psyches, destroy their families and send them back to work, bleeding and bruised. As long as you labour, how you feel, what damage you work with, does not matter. You try not to think too much about what continuity entails or what kinds of pretty concepts will be used in the months and decades ahead to understand this time to mask endurance despite a grief we can barely comprehend yet, continuity despite the world falling apart around you. You begin to perceive anew how instrumental reasoning works in managing worlds and the constraints of agency.

Work never ceases. It as if there is no epidemic, and because there is an epidemic there is so much more work. Sometimes having to work saves you, gives your days a shape. At times it is the raft you didn't think you would need again. Sometimes having to work is all that holds you together when you have no resources left. When you are grieving and you, the wordsmith, cannot articulate what you are witnessing. There are no words, no memes. Working breaks you into pieces you don't think you will even remember to find if the epidemic is ever over. You send lots of stickers on WhatsApp: fun, frivolous, floral. There are no words. Sometimes that little dinosaur with hearts pouring out of it makes you feel like love sticks. Sometimes everyone is too far away and it doesn't matter, the pixelated image closes the conversation and it is okay.

If someone were to look at you in those moments when you are laughing at some small time-consuming frippery online where most of your life happens now, they might think you are resilient. Or watch you watch those hours and hours of Netflix, so little of which you remember, phone in hand, just waiting for the message that will shatter the semblance of calm. Or if they were to collate and analyse the tasteless, silly jokes you are making and being playful because some days that is all you have. They might think you are bouncing back and making a life by celebrating small pleasures. That you are exhibiting resistance. Resilience. Despite never stopping to worry. Despite that feeling of betrayal, you know the one, that slimy, oily one that makes you feel like you should not be feeling anything except mourning. That struggling to cope is the betrayal. Even if your laughter has an edge and places you at the precipice of a wailing that were it to start, you are terrified, might never stop. Despite your dead being more present than they have ever been, some of whom have departed years, decades ago. You wish they were here to help you and glad that they don't have to feel these feelings you are struggling to live with.

And those you love, all those deep and full loves who sometimes have vexed you in the mess of pre-COVID life, you love them in COVID-time where nothing is sure and time is precious. You worry about their breath. You worry about masks and sanitiser and who they are allowing to breathe the air around them. You make plans and cancel them, you see each other at a distance. It has been a long time since you touched each other. Love is not touching now. Your eyes learn a new language, to replace the curve of your smile and your muffled words underneath your mask. You relearn how to talk on the phone for hours. You learn how to talk about your wills and prepare for each other's deaths and there is something painful in it and infinitely gentle and patient as you make plans for the worst and in so doing affirm love. The old secrets and antagonisms no longer matter. You talk about your beloved dead and you remember the worlds that brought you to this moment, the entangled griefs and joys you have been reshaped by.

You know in the conversations of wills and reminiscing about your dearly departed that the world will continue without you, without them. Whoever remains will be battered and bruised but the world will continue, in new form, but continue it will. You witness this continuity every day, you are part of it. Continuity is not to live a full life, though. Continuity is not necessarily the capacity to make worlds that heal. You have seen many who have chosen to break the world around them to reflect the parts of them that had been broken. But you also know there will be love, joy, all the beauty the world can offer to match whoever remains' capacity to receive it. Perhaps this is what we mean by resilience except we have seen far too many societies repress their collective anger, fear, pain and trauma, to chase those feelings that make you think all is right with the world and move on to annihilate other people's who were different from them. The destruction of so many worlds in the Global South by former serfs, feudal peoples who were broken by monstrous, acquisitive monarchies that those same serfs tried to recreate through stolen labour, stolen land and pompous stupid hierarchies in the colonies. People who butchered and guillotined people in the pursuit of freedom and exported their violences to their colonies to feel safe in their republics. And when they left, even if just in name while continuing to bleed those places through the tribute they extracted, they left behind populaces who rarely did the work of mourning and healing in the aftermath with the fullness required. Resilient colonialism (Nyamnjoh 2016) may rest in the shadows that are ignored in the aftermath of incalculable devastation.

You miss hugging the children who own parts of you where a hopeful resilience might reside. You worry about them and yearn for a future that does not require them to endure hardship that will be reframed as resilience. You are angry about the world that they are in now, the one where inequality is so normalised that when a pandemic rages, there will be a constant stream of people at their door looking for help, for food. For them to be the line between life and starvation. If they are to be the kind of adults to nurture a better world, they will answer. You worry about what love and intimacy will be like for them. It hurts you when they peep from behind their masks. It terrifies you to see their maskless faces out and about. It hurts even more when you have to stop them and yourself from holding each other tight. And every now and then you risk it and don't sleep for days until you are all sure that your need for them and theirs for you has not had fatal consequences. And still, they make you happy. 'They are resilient,' people say, you say when you talk about it. You imagine everyone nodding as the platitude circulates, comforted by the children's resilience. The children are also bored and tired of being trapped at home away from their friends. Their comforting resilience allows us to go on anyways, tread into the everyday and plan despite radical uncertainty.

You have new conversations. Too many have lost jobs, too many who were already living on the margins. You learn to talk about money and food security and the things that bodies need to be sustained; who needs, who can help, and everyone is stretched and it is okay. There are many who are not okay though and that is not okay. People who are hungry, who are desperate. You cannot help everyone and you ignore the guilt. Somedays you manage to and on others your already erratic eating habits become even stranger. Binge, starve, yo-yo between that treat that will kill you and that healthy nutritious meal that tastes of love and it all tastes like expensive guilt. You know rationally what you should do. You just cannot make your body do it and so much of the stuff you have read about agency and resistance are just stuff you have read. If there is a later, you promise yourself, you can find a way to live in a rational body that will submit to some kind of discipline and not feel like the armour between you and all the feelings you are suppressing. That future you hope the children are resilient enough to survive. As long as you are taking all the vitamins that now have a place on your kitchen counter, and without which you cannot start a day, you too may just come out of this. Those pills are your prayer and your fetish. An invisible army in your body you have to trust to ward off the virus, even if they don't complete the alphabet: B, C, D, E for Echinaforce and jump over everything else to Z for Zinc. It is expensive and you don't want to think what little armies are at work in the bodies of those who don't even have food to get their vitamins from.

You are angry that most Black people do not have what they need to stop the virus from circulating, not enough room in their tiny homes,[19] not enough water to wash their hands, not enough money for soap and sanitiser or food. Angry that without a pandemic and lockdowns, they were already living precariously, beset by debilitating conditions.

Already disproportionately debilitated, disproportionately living with injury as a normal consequence of inequality. Every now and then you remember that the mines have not stopped operating. But then your research has told you to not be surprised that the mines are putting more Black men and now women too in harm's way and you know that they will be discarded when they become ill (Ledwaba and Sadiki 2017). That many Black people, some of the fortunate few who are able to work, will usually be the workers that are in harm's way breaks your heart. They are and will be the lubricant that allows society to keep moving, the go-betweens our privileged private, sanitary lives and the threatening public awash with the virus. You know they will travel in full buses and taxis and when the trains are running, that the trains will be far too full for social distancing to have any meaning. Some of them will be your friends, your relatives. You don't know what to do with that. They know it is dangerous, they have no choice. They tell you how dangerous it is, when you ask. Sometimes they laugh when they tell you about the full taxis where no-one wants to open the window. All the things you know about pandemics, about disability, about structural violence, about debility, cannot do a damn thing about it. They will go back to neighbourhoods with houses that are too small, and not many people are wearing masks. Men will continue to run around outside with guns and weapons sowing unrelenting terror and trap them in their too small homes in gang wars that even lockdowns can't stop.[20] You could not do a damn thing about it before and you cannot do a damn thing now. Someday, someone at a conference somewhere will again expect you to listen as they 'theorise' the stuff of your nightmares, because it is interesting to think about just so they can show people they don't really care about how well they can play with the newest intellectual fad. They are usually wrong.

You will see people who look like you in the back of stores, outside in parking lots, out of the view of most customers, without their masks. Relieved to be breathing fresh air and talking to their colleagues with whom they have had to face death every day. Whatever it is that happens to your body that winds you up tightly into inescapable dread when you are out there in your infrequent forays from your private, controlled sanctuary, hits you as you sit in your car outside your home. For those few minutes between inside and outside, you are immobilised and cannot make your body move, shake off what you have seen, and felt. All that you know about affect does not loosen your shoulders or the screaming recriminations and worries that you don't allow yourself to voice. They know. Those people sitting outside talking to their friends, their colleagues know. They are the people who have to wear a mask all day, dealing with anxious people just like me and it is their hands that are peeling from constant sanitising. After all, most of the dying is happening in their worlds,[21] most of the illness, most of the long, long waits at hospitals that have always been underprovisioned. Maybe that is resilience to sit and continue old friendships and rivalries over a cigarette during your break without a mask while a pandemic rages. It is also people who look like you who are standing outside hospitals, praying for the families that they cannot visit, standing vigil at windows, waving up to their loved ones. Muslims in fezzes and scarves, standing metres apart, praying in Arabic. Christians: Catholics, Apostolics, Calvinists and every denomination and none of the differences matter. The videos circulate on WhatsApp, on Facebook. You know some of the people who are standing there, going from hospital to hospital. Maybe that is resilience, to be able to plead to a God and maintain belief in a God when you are bargaining for life, relinquishing life to an afterworld.

Some days you think that if you were truly a good anthropologist, you would be out there with them. Instead, you are content to follow their movements through one of your Facebook friends who is organising the visits and carefully documenting this moment, doing and documenting. He does not need you to document and dryly analyse something about the role of religion in coping with COVID or standing and bargaining or whatever stupid clever anthropological thing you are interested in exploring. And then you wonder, for what possible reason would you want to report it anyway to an audience of anthropologists; to do what exactly with? For what possible reason would you want to objectify these people who are trying to wrest life from death for an audience who have read many, many such texts spanning decades, centuries. Why? So they can cogitate over these new forms of resilience with their peers at expensive conferences? When few of them would ever fully understand or care what it feels like to live with so many possible ways of dying, possible ways of living. And for all their knowing, your knowing, so little of the dying has stopped. Across centuries. And what is more, you know some of them who merely by reading a text about the deaths and maiming of people just like you will feel entitled to tell you what this experience truly means, school you about it. They have no idea how foolish they sound or how impertinent their expression. Or how disfigured their thinking when they begin to drown these responses to calamity in words that have no meaning when your people are pleading at the borders of life and death, at a window where your loved one is surrounded by machines, or waving at you from a hospital window, close enough for your eyes to kiss but so, so far away.

And you, are oh so very tired. Of the smugness. The rank stupidity that has absolutely no power to wrest life from death. To make the dying livable in the aftermath. What of method? What of epistemology you wonder? Day after day when your thoughts manage to stick, to hold on to these ideas that mean so much and yet nothing at all when all you are is longing to hold the people you love. Thinking about thinking does matter, it matters who thinks, who writes, how, for what purpose. It matters. It matters that we can grieve and feel and break under the loss too and when we reanimate our dead in thought, that we remember that not everyone survives and that worlds break and we break and it can never ever be undone even if we find new ways to love, to live with loss. There is no springing back like timber, no way back to an equilibrium that has not existed for centuries anyway. And a world where positive adaptation to so much overwhelming death is expected, resilience as a concept, is just another feature of the death-dealing that coloniality has bequeathed us.

Notes

[1] A note on style: the essay attempts a mode of affected writing in which affect is not only a descriptive mode of rendering experience but also makes an ethical demand on the reader. Stewart (2007) in *Ordinary Affect*, uses 'she' to show that the self who is writing is not the experiencing self and thus demonstrates the distance of the self who writes an affected account that approximates but cannot fully describe an epochal condition. Unlike her, I have used 'I' and 'you' to enter into a conversation with the reader. Like Behar (1996), I agree that anthropology has always been conducted by an 'I' who is somehow more complex than those others they describe, and that the fantasy of alienation as epistemology is just that, a fantasy. As is well-accepted now, we are always imbricated in ethico-political relationships even if our epistemologies attempt to transfigure these relations in textual form. Whilst Stewart's temporal tactics to displace the presentness of the I, with the pastness of a 'she' is productive, for my purposes in this essay it does not feel appropriate. The affective at the moment of writing is immanent and not representative of a past and not so much located in events of grief, given the collapse of grieving events due to their ubiquity, as in a grieving sensibility where questions of existence are ongoing and feel amorphous.

[2] In response to COVID-19, South Africa declared a national lockdown on 26 March to 15 April. The lockdown started at Lockdown level five which had severe restrictions of movement and has since moved between varying levels of lockdown in response to threat assessments; which at times privileged disease prevention and others privileged economic measures. At the time of writing, South Africa was in Lockdown level three. See South Africa's COVID-19 Risk Adjusted Strategy with the varying lockdown levels at https://sacoronavirus.co.za/covid-19-risk-adjusted-strategy/.

[3] Biehl and Locke (2017); whilst not inspired per se by Biehl and Locke or their genealogical investment in Deleuze, my formulation of life-making as immanent and emergent (Fischer 2018) bears a resemblance to becoming as formulated in their introductory chapter, as well as in accordance with many of the authors in their edited volume *Unfinished: an anthropology of becoming.* Like Nyamnjoh (2015a, 2015b) who has long argued that incompleteness as an epistemology, ontology, politics, methodology and thus ethical relation, grounded in his readings of Amos Tutuola, is the only way to engage a world in which difference and fragmented belongings can be ordinary, the authors too in this volume refuse over-determining modes of interpreting subjects. They make room for shifts and changes in becoming for individuals in relation to concrete events and circumstances. Akin with my understanding of the capacity to endure extreme violence, Biehl and Locke (2017) do not romanticise endurance of structural violence, or foreclose the possibilities for joyful living or generate notions of agency that are without creativity and/or limits.

[4] On debility, I am drawing on Livingston (2005) and more notably on Puar's (2017: xvii–viii) argument in *The Right to Maim* which shows how disability as a liberal category crucially ignores how racial capitalism depends on the right to debilitate and debility's normalisation is a form of massification of injury that is

'endemic rather than epidemic and exceptional'. For the ways in which disability and thus debility are disproportionately experienced by the Global South, see Meekosha (2011).

[5] Written from and thinking with South Africa, I am operating with the sensibility that South Africa is a racist, heteropatriarchal, capitalist, ableist settler colonial society in which security is configured as a racist masculinist endeavour that depends on the use of violence to secure a perceived vulnerable and fragile white, middle-class and wealthy elite, including Black elites. Perceived Black criminality is engaged through the logic of coloniality. Despite a democratic postapartheid Black majority government, the majority of Black South Africans live in endemic and debilitating poverty. The state and its proxies, which historically existed to secure white settler colonial rule, achieved domination through multiple and layered violences and treated as normative, extrajudicial forms of punishment, and the suppression of the Black majority. Structural violence and Black suffering is treated as negligible and justifiable. This entails fewer forms of security against vulnerability for the Black majority. The majority of Black people do not enjoy ownership of land and decent housing with amenities such as water, electricity, sewerage control, access to efficient and dignified healthcare, excellent education and access to higher education and livelihoods that allow flourishing lives. Gender-based violence across all racialised demographics is rampant and forms of social control rely on patriarchal modes of violence such as a militarised police force. Within neoliberal postapartheid South Africa, the market has been used to continue segregation for the Black majority. Whilst a few Black elites have political power and attained social mobility this has not redressed structural violence for the Black majority. This is not to say that many, many people do not attempt to create worlds that contain care, joy, love and beauty. They have, across centuries, in spite of the dehumanising structural forces arrayed against them. There are testaments all around us in small acts of care, public kindnesses and mercies. Not everyone survived though, and for some joy came at the expense of others.

[6] Resilience is a concept derived from the physical sciences in regard to a systems' capacity to recover from a stressor and return to equilibrium (Barrios 2014) and was first used in 1818 in the scholarly literature by Thomas Tredgold to describe timber's capacity to bounce back (O'Dougherty Wright and Masten 2015). One of the primary definitions of resilience is the capacity to adapt positively to change though the concept has been fluid and changed over time (O'Dougherty Wright and Masten 2015). For Panter-Brick (2014: 432), resilience is the 'process of harnessing key resources to sustain well-being'. She also states that resilience is entangled with risk and that slippages occur with both concepts' usage. Risk often collapses statistical probability and generalises vulnerability to populations and changes risk probabilities or the capacity for resilience into individual or community traits. So, for example, she shows how a risk of vulnerability to violence, becomes violent people or violent communities, rather than communities with high levels of violence that do not affect everybody equally or entail the same consequences. McCubbin and Moniz (2015) also warn that ethical researchers should be mindful that the expectation of oppressed groups to be resilient, rather than changing the unequal distribution of vulnerability, may enforce oppressed people to respond with resilience. I was struck forcibly by this possibility when I

read Nancy Scheper-Hughes's (2008) attempt to move from a psychological trauma model in conditions of structural violence to one of resilience where loss is normalised and narrativised to give meaning to loss and responded to with humour and multiple other techniques or, as she puts it, 'talents for life'. I was reminded of the young men in Elaine Salo's (2018) ethnography in Manenberg, South Africa, who to show strength or *sterk bene* would endure beatings as part of becoming men or the South African men in Reihling's (2020) study who refigured traumatic events to produce a sense of invulnerable masculinities. Whilst these may be thought of as resilience and adaptations to injurious worlds where violence is endemic, these are not worlds that we should bequeath a future. Well-being should not be invulnerability and performing imperviousness to loss. Rather, we should be figuring out how to remake these worlds so that people do not have to find strategies to endure persistent and overwhelming loss.

[7] This is an early attempt at exploring the sensibilities of COVID-time which offers an avenue for further research. As routines fall apart, the limits on mobility and thus the collapse of spatial (re)figurations within smaller physical circuits and concomitant enlarged virtual modes of sociality take hold, the collapse of work and home, the different ways in which leisure and consumption are practised, whether to adhere to social distancing and COVID sanitary practices or in rebellion to these reconfigurations of space, there is an attendant qualitative difference to the movement of time during the COVID-19 pandemic. Shifts in temporal sensibilities are, of course, intersected by race, gender and other vectors of being and becoming. To provide some examples, many women have had increased burdens of child care and domestic labour during lockdowns to the detriment of their careers (see Mosomi, Thornton and Branson 2020). The multiplicity of roles that co-existed in the domestic sphere created time deficits for many women who mothered. Many in the middle-class who had access to internet infrastructure were able to lockdown at home and engage in an intensified global news media and also the very many and very quickly overwhelming amount of work-related and entertainment events that shifted online. This changed the reach of some events which would not have been made available online previously but also entailed significant investments of time. See also Peckham's (2020) brief exploration of the chronopolitics of Covid-time. Exploring the sense of living in an event, he notes the shift into forms of slow time where constituent features of the contemporary such as 'fast food' and mobilities have been curtailed and of course, for those with access, the intensification of virtual worlds. Of particular interest too, is the way metaphors of war, as with other diseases, have become a feature of COVID-time.

[8] I have been struck by how not only how most manual labourers are not able to be physically distant but also how tied to class and gender it is. See Mosomi, Thornton and Branson (2020).

[9] Most theories of grief focus on the individual, are based on Northern ontologies of subjectivity and treat grief as a response to singular losses rather than a response to multiple and continuous traumatic events (McLea and Mayers 2017). For Butler (2004) how grief is constituted, understood and circulates in the social imaginary and which subjects are grievable is ineffably tied to whose 'lives count as lives' (p. 20). Further, she asserts that rather than grief privatising suffering, it can also produce new forms of the political, new forms of community by constituting

new forms of dependency and ethical subjectivity. Butler (2004) avers that 'grief contains the possibility of apprehending a mode of dispossession that is fundamental to who I am' (p. 24). Within many Black, impoverished communities in the Western Cape this dispossession may be continuous because of persistent loss and unrelenting violence and is rarely considered grievable. How grief is understood and responded to within communities that are persistently dispossessed, cannot be assumed. Rather than seek to eviscerate the traumatic from everyday forms of relatedness, they may instead integrate and accommodate trauma (Ralph 2015). Wolseth (2007: 332), writing about the persistence of grief among young men in Honduras, states that persistent grief is not necessarily debilitating, particularly when the conditions causing bereavement endure and it is impossible to resolve the event that has caused grief. What he shows through looking at how young men use violence to grieve loss, is how they make grief part of the everyday. Rosaldo (2013) shows that grief for young Ilongot men was more persistent than for older men. The rage of grief had previously been ameliorated by headhunting. New sociopolitical arrangements made headhunting impossible and enforced a transition to Christianity as a site through which to deal with the rage of grief. Not always successfully. How grief is experienced and perceived is thus socio-historical, integrally connected to identity and entangled with gender, race, geopolitics, able-bodiedness, age and other vectors of the sociopolitical. On thinking about the silence around grief despite the overwhelming amount of bereavement in post-conflict and violent societies, Ross Parsons (2005) invited researchers to sit with the suffering of others. In her study on care and emergent socialities during the massification of death and illness caused by HIV-AIDS in rural Kwazulu-Natal, South Africa, Patricia Henderson (2011) shows that witnessing grief requires more than sitting with the grief of another. What is also required is careful listening and being alert when one's attention may be too much for the aggrieved or afflicted to bear. She found that sometimes focusing on one individual's suffering, may cause a researcher to miss the suffering of those who are caring for them. She also shows that during the height of the AIDS crisis where families were being decimated by death and burdened by caring for the ill, new socialities and modes of care emerge. In unremarked and largely unnoticed ways, people in a place commit to and sustain care. Care also fails and can be blocked. Grief and mourning are not just for the dead but also the loss of self that occurs when people become alienated from their bodies and former selves as a consequence of illness. Thinking with HIV-AIDS is a reminder that COVID is not the first event of mass death. I wonder about all the unresolved, unacknowledged grief we have learnt to live with in this place.

[10] Also note, that the use of racial categories is indicative of historical conditions rather than a belief that race is biological. I am using Black in a Black Consciousness sense that includes people who were oppressed in South Africa under the separate classifications of African, Coloured and Indian. What is more, my assertion of Black as a mode of identifying and recognising apartheid oppression, is not an attempt to ignore postapartheid tensions, self-identifications and new revivalist movements. Rather, by using Black, I seek commonality and express a hope that the formerly oppressed in South Africa will secure a form of peace that affords every person in South Africa the opportunity to flourish and be liberated from racist heteropatriarchal capitalist ableist settler colonial logics and practices.

[11] Hendricks, A. (2020) 'Covid-19: Roads blocked, rocks thrown during food protest in Cape Town: "We're not going to die from the coronavirus, but we will die of hunger"'. *GroundUp*, South Africa, 14 April.

[12] Makinana, A. (2020) 'Collins Khosa murder: Military Ombud finds that soldiers acted improperly', *Sunday Times*, South Africa, 19 August.

[13] Rountree, M. (2020) 'Homeless in Cape Town: Councillor blind to facts and irony of what he is defending', *News24*, South Africa, 29 May; please note that the costs of the camp varies in many of the reports and opinion pieces. In some it is thirty-two million Rand, others fifty-three million Rand and in this one fifty-eight million Rand. R32 million rand was approximately USD2,155,000 in October, 2021.

[14] Evans, J. and Gibbings, A. (2020) 'Khayelitsha man dragged naked from shack lays criminal complaint, claims torture', *News24*, South Africa, 2 July.

[15] Gerber, J. (2020) 'Level 4 lockdown: exercise regulations lack common sense, says Winde', *News24*, South Africa, 01 May.

[16] Grobler, R. (2020) 'Lockdown: Western Cape surfer claims surfing is "essential activity", in cut-and-paste of US petition', *News24*, South Africa, 15 April.

[17] Nathan, M. (2021) 'SASSA beneficiaries water blasted while Lindiwe Sisulu watches from Casspir comfort', *BizNews,* South Africa, 18 January.

[18] Shooting of Nathaniel Julies (2021) *Wikipedia.*

[19] Given the precarity of housing in South Africa for Black people, this is a loose term. There was a housing backlog of 2.3 million in 2013 (Turok and Borel-Salodin 2016).

[20] https://www.dailymaverick.co.za/article/2021-01-04-covid-19-lockdown-means-nothing-to-warring-cape-town-gangsters-and-the-bodies-are-stacking-up/.

[21] It is my world too.

References

Ahmed, S. (2004) *The Cultural Politics of Emotion*, Edinburgh: Edinburgh University Press.

Barrios, R. E. (2014) 'Here, I'm not at ease': anthropological perspectives on community resilience', *Disasters*, Vol. 38, No. 2, pp. 329–350.

Behar, R. (1996) *The Vulnerable Observer: Anthropology That Breaks Your Heart*, Beacon Press.

Biehl, J. and Locke, P. (2017) 'The anthropology of becoming', in J. Biehl and P. Locke (eds) *Unfinished: The Anthropology of Becoming*, Durham and London: Duke University Press, pp. 41–89.

Biehl, J. Locke, P. (eds). (2017) *Unfinished: The Anthropology of Becoming*, Durham and London: Duke University Press.

Butler, J. (2004). *Precarious Life: The Powers of Mourning and Violence*, London: Verso Press.

Evans, J. and Gibbings, A. (2020) 'Khayelitsha man dragged naked from shack lays criminal complaint, claims torture', *News24*, South Africa, 2 July, available at https://www.news24.com/news24/southafrica/news/khayelitsha-man-dragged-naked-from-shack-lays-criminal-complaint-claims-torture-20200702 (accessed: 28 January 2021)

Fischer, M. J. (2018) *Anthropology in the Meantime: Experimental Ethnography, Theory and Method for the Twenty-first Century*, Durham and London: Duke University Press.

Gerber, J. (2020) 'Level 4 lockdown: exercise regulations lack common sense, says Winde', *News24*, South Africa, 01 May, available at https://www.news24.com/news24/SouthAfrica/News/level-4-lockdown-exercise-regulations-lack-common-sense-says-winde-20200501 (accessed: 28 January 2021).

Grobler, R. (2020) 'Lockdown: Western Cape surfer claims surfing is "essential activity", in cut-and-paste of US petition', *News24*, South Africa, 15 April, available at https://www.news24.com/news24/southafrica/news/lockdown-western-cape-surfer-claims-surfing-is-essential-activity-in-cut-and-paste-of-us-petition-20200415 (accessed: 28 January 2021).

Henderson, P. (2011) *AIDS, Intimacy and Care in Rural Kwazulu-Natal: A Kinship of Bones*, Amsterdam: Amsterdam University Press.

Hendricks, A. (2020) 'Covid-19: Roads blocked, rocks thrown during food protest in Cape Town: "We're not going to die from the coronavirus, but we will die of hunger"'. *GroundUp*, South Africa, 14 April, available at https://www.groundup.org.za/article/covid-19-roads-blocked-rocks-thrown-during-food-protest-cape-town/ (accessed: 20 January 2021).

Ledwaba, L. and Sadiki, L. (2017) *Broke and Broken: The Shameful Legacy of Gold Mining in South Africa*, Johannesburg: Blackbird Books.

Livingston, J. (2005) *Debility and the Moral Imagination in Botswana*, Bloomington and Indianapolis: Indiana University Press.

Makinana, A. (2020) 'Collins Khosa murder: Military Ombud finds that soldiers acted improperly', *Sunday Times*, South Africa, 19 August, available at https://www.timeslive.co.za/politics/2020-08-19-collins-khosa-murder-military-ombud-finds-that-soldiers-acted-improperly/ (accessed: 25 January 2021).

Massumi, B. (2002) *Parables for the Virtual: Movement, Affect, Sensation*, Durham and London: Duke University Press.

McCubbin, L. D. and Moniz, J. (2015) 'Ethical principles in resilience research: Respect, relevance, reciprocity and responsibility', in L. Theron, L. Liebenberg and M. Ungar (eds) *Youth Resilience and Culture*, Dordrecht, Heidelberg, New York and London: Springer, pp. 217–229.

McLea, H. and Mayers, P. (2017) 'The grief and trauma project: a group work approach to restoring emotional and spiritual health to women in bereaved and traumatised indigent communities in the Western Cape, South Africa', *Social Work/Maatskaplike Werk*, Vol. 53, No. 4(1), pp. 423–444.

Meekosha, H. (2011) 'Decolonising disability: thinking and acting globally', *Disability and Society*, Vol. 26, No. 6, 667–682.

Mosomi, J., Thornton, A. and Branson, N. (2020) 'Unpacking the potential implications of Covid-19 for gender inequality in the SA labour market', Cape Town: SALDRU, UCT. (SALDRU Working Paper No. 269).

Nathan, M. (2021) 'SASSA beneficiaries water blasted while Lindiwe Sisulu watches from Casspir comfort', *BizNews,* South Africa, 18 January, available at https://www.biznews.com/global-citizen/2021/01/18/sassa-lindiwe-zulu-chaos (accessed: 28 January 2021).

Nyamnjoh, F. B. (2015a) 'Incompleteness: Frontier Africa and the currency of conviviality', *Journal of Asian and African Studies*, DOI 0021909615580867.

__________ (2015b) 'Amos Tutuola and the elusiveness of completeness', *Stichproben Wiener Zeitschrift für kritische Afrikastudien*, No. 29, 1–47.

__________ (2016) '*# RhodesMustFall: Nibbling at resilient colonialism in South Africa*', Cameroon: Langaa RPCIG.

O' Dougherty Wright, M. O. D. and Masten, A. S. (2015) 'Pathways to resilience in context', in L. Theron, L. Liebenberg and M. Ungar (eds) *Youth Resilience and Culture*, Dordrecht, Heidelberg, New York and London: Springer, pp. 3–22.

Panter-Brick, C. (2014) 'Health, risk, and resilience: Interdisciplinary concepts and applications', *Annual Review of Anthropology*, No. 43, pp. 431–448.

Parsons, R. (2005) 'Grief-stricken: Zimbabwean children in everyday extremity and the ethics of research', *Anthropology Southern Africa*, Vol. 28, No. 3-4, pp. 73–77.

Peckham, R. (2020) 'The chronopolitics of COVID-19', *American Literature*, Vol. 92, No. 4, pp. 767–779.

Puar, J. K. (2017) *The Right to Maim: Debility, Capacity, Disability*, Durham and London: Duke University Press.

Ralph, L. (2015) 'Becoming aggrieved: an alternative framework of care in Black Chicago', *RSF: The Russell Sage Foundation Journal of the Social Sciences*, Vol. 1, No. 2, pp. 31–41.

Reihling, H. (2020) *Affective Health and Masculinities in South Africa: An Ethnography of (In)vulnerability*, London and New York: Routledge.

Rosaldo, R. (2013) *The Day of Shelly's Death: The Poetry and Ethnography of Grief*, Durham and London: Duke University Press.

Rountree, M. (2020) 'Homeless in Cape Town: Councillor blind to facts and irony of what he is defending', *News24*, South Africa, 29 May, available at https://www.news24.com/news24/Columnists/GuestColumn/opinion-homeless-in-cape-town-councillor-blind-to-facts-and-the-irony-of-what-hes-defending-20200529 (accessed: 28 January 2021).

Salo, E. R. (2018) *Respectable Mothers, Tough Men and Good Daughters: Producing Persons in Manenberg Township South Africa*, Cameroon: Langaa RPCIG.

Scheper-Hughes, N. (2008) 'A talent for life: Reflections on human vulnerability and resilience', *Ethnos*, Vol. 73, No. 1, pp. 25–56.

Shooting of Nathaniel Julies. (2021) *Wikipedia*, available at https://en.wikipedia.org/wiki/Shooting_of_Nathaniel_Julies (accessed: 28 January 2021).

Stewart, K. (2007) *Ordinary Affects*, Durham and London: Duke University Press.

Turok, I. and Borel-Saladin, J. (2016) 'Backyard shacks, informality and the urban housing crisis in South Africa: stopgap or prototype solution?', *Housing Studies*, Vol. 31, No. 4, pp. 384–409, DOI: 10.1080/02673037.2015.1091921.

Wolseth, J. (2008) 'Everyday violence and the persistence of grief: wandering and loss among Honduran youths', *The Journal of Latin American and Caribbean Anthropology*, Vol. 13, No. 2, pp. 311–335.

Chapter 9

"After the Ash: Witnessing, Holding, Building..."

Photographic series

Berni Searle

21 April 2021

30 April 2021

Witnessing

Holding

Building

21 April 2021

1 May 2021

Part 4

Resilience through Art, Ritual, Agency, Resistance

Chapter 10

'Fletselites': Resilience as Problem and Possibility in Struggles for Justice in South African Schools

Marlon Swai

Introduction

This chapter is anchored in a description of an incident of racism at a private school in Cape Town that moved a group of artists and activists (or artivists as I will call them) to write, produce, record, perform and distribute the song 'Fletselites.' After briefly situating this racist incident in the larger context of several other similar occurrences across the country and the protests that followed, the chapter lays out its conceptual framework for thinking about resilience. Finally, I present an analysis of the song 'Fletselites,' showcasing historical snapshots that both help to decode the song and support the central argument for reappropriating the term 'resilience' from its hegemonic usages in order to recoup it as part of a growing set of tools for decolonising education. In particular, the chapter provides a look back at one of the central aspects of the anti-apartheid movement's struggle for equal education, in People's Education and demonstrates the extent to which 'Fletselites' rearticulates some of its tenets for the contemporary struggle.

From 2019 to 2022 the wave of incidences of racism at high schools across South Africa seemed to intensify with several gaining notoriety through media exposure and represented yet another stark reminder (as if we needed one more) of just how far behind we are lagging with regards to transforming our educational institutions out of places permeated by trauma and violence and into spaces that promote wellness-centered learning and critical thinking for the 21st century.

These incidents demonstrate the ways in which harmful forms of thinking and practice in the context of the South African school system have persisted far beyond the 'colonial period',[1] proving themselves to be stubbornly persistent, hence the amplification of calls for the decolonisation of education in recent years.[2] This chapter's characterisation of racist practices and ideas as resilient is a purposeful subversion of the discourse that commonly surrounds this term, often used in a way that patronises the most socio-economically vulnerable and demands a double wage of those already exposed to unjust systemic imbalances. As other chapters in this volume demonstrate, studying racism, classism and sexism, for example, as resilient is a useful tool with which to approach the decolonisation conundrum because these forms of discrimination seem to withstand wave upon wave of critique and resistance. After all, the post-apartheid era can in some ways be considered as a period in which we have had to come to terms with the extent to which harmful ideologies and practices have a way of surviving even as large-scale progressive change has ostensibly taken place. In the case of the incidents highlighted in this chapter and the dire state of the education system in general, there is an additional dimension when one considers that a resilience of a particular kind is being demanded of generations of youth. The South African state's lack-luster track-record of transforming this system is seeming to suggest (at best) an over-reliance on the idea that young people can bounce back from the impact of several overlapping failures of governance, ranging from infrastructural inadequacies to calamitous lags in teacher training, to threats to learners' physical safety by the rampant spread of gang influence in and around so many schools. Focusing on the incident at a private international school in Cape Town, the chapter connects the specificity of this case study to its broader socio-political and historical implications.

Why a Private School?

One might ask why focus on a private school when there is so much work to do with regards to schools that represent the experience of the majority of the South African student population? The central reason for this focus in this chapter is that these elite schools, like their tertiary counterparts, are so often positioned as the standard to which all others must aspire. Exposing the mismatch between the elite school's aspirational positioning as the pinnacle of education excellence and the reality of the everyday presence of forms of violence, especially epistemic violence, serves as a critically important point of departure for (re)calibrating what exactly decolonising education means in our context and what a high standard of education, in fact, entails. It is this mismatch that the artivists who wrote 'Fletselites' were aiming to expose when they embedded a counter-curriculum in the song that aims to put a spotlight on the systemic processes that enabled the situation in the first place, but also aims to bolster students' defences so that if they were forced to encounter such violence, that they be adequately 'armed' with a knowledge of history and a knowledge of self to mitigate, if not 'deflect,' its impact. The mixed metaphors invoked here risk playing into concepts of resilience that I am hoping to critique, so suffice it to say that this linguistic slippage foreshadows a conversation staged in the next section which clarifies the chapter's key terms and conceptual framework. The conceptual framework forms the backbone to a textual analysis of the song that makes use of literary strategies such as translation of culturally and historically specific references and linguistic nuances. The chapter also unpacks the song's references to people whose contributions to a broader definition of the idea of a "quality education," have been, and continue to be downplayed or erased, highlighting the song's dedication to the kinds of everyday struggles and quotidian heroes to which often only modes of knowledge production such as oral history or poetry can do justice.

Disclaimers

There are three important disclaimers to make at this point. First, I am one of the artists featured on the song 'Fletselites.' Second, our daughter attended second grade at one of the schools in question before we disenrolled her after concluding that the administration lacked the political will to create a safe and nurturing environment for students of colour. My personal investment in the subject matter will therefore certainly permeate the analysis throughout this paper. Lastly, the identity of the school in the central case study is abstracted due to pending legal action.

Background to the Incident

Between 2019 and 2022 a flurry of stories broke in the national news of occurrences of race-based discrimination at numerous elite schools across the country. One reporter referred to 2020 especially as 'the year of reckoning for elitist schools' (Xaso, 2021). While

NGOs like SECTION27, Sonke Gender Justice, Tshisimani Centre for Activist Education, Social Justice Coalition and Equal Education have long forced an acknowledgement of the South African government's culpability in the neglect of and dismal conditions at public schools, these incidents began to bring renewed scrutiny to some of the country's historically advantaged and disproportionately well-resourced educational institutions. For instance, in January 2019 Laerskool Schweizer-Reneke in the North West region came into the news after the Department of Basic Education launched an investigation into the circumstances surrounding a photo that went viral depicting a large group of white pupils at a long table and four black students at a different table at the back of a classroom suggesting explicit racial discrimination by the teacher in charge. (Busby, 2019) In June 2020, parents at St. Mary's DSG in Pretoria protested at the school amidst allegations of racism with placards that read statements like: 'I cannot pay for my child to be oppressed.' (Xaso, 2021) In the very next month the entire matriculating class at Bishops Diocesan College in Cape Town submitted a petition calling out 'systemic oppression' (Tembo & Geach 2020). In June 2021, Singo Ravele, a pupil at Cornwall Hill College in Pretoria shared a harrowing testimony at the Gauteng education MEC of the racism she experienced at the school since the time she was in fourth grade (Shange, 2021). In February 2022, at Hoërskool Jan Viljoen in Gauteng, the South African Human Rights Commission was called in to investigate several cases brought forth in light of a protest that arose around a group of white students threatening black students with gun violence. (Mohamed, 2022) The scourge became so rampant that media outlets could not avoid hosting urgent discussions on the topic. In one example on June 10th, 2020, leading talk radio station Cape Talk hosted a panel chaired by journalist Refilwe Moloto titled 'Where to from here? Dismantling racism at South Africa's Elite schools' (King, 2020). The panel highlighted the work of a Twitter account called YouSilenceWeAmplify that by that time had gathered close to ten thousand followers and amassed over 250 posts in which students and alumni shared stories of the trauma they experienced because of racism at the hand of staff and students.

This is but a handful of examples to highlight the depths to which the rot extends. These disturbing, though unfortunately not surprising revelations, underscore several key points I want to expand on in this chapter. The first is to emphasise the idea of the resilience of racism at the country's supposedly top schools. I want to argue that one of the major factors contributing to this resilience is the extent to which these schools have participated in the misnomer of what high quality education entails. Formally whites-only schools like Bishops, Jan Viljoen and Schweizer-Reneke enjoy advantages over previously blacks-only schools on many levels including infrastructure, teacher training, materials budgets and socio-cultural and physical environment surrounding the schools. Relatedly, another major factor is that many of the elite schools' student and teacher populations remain majority white while most of the formally black schools continue to be just that. The socio-economic factors affecting the families and communities of both school-type populations align with the racial inequities of South African society and so those elite schools become aspirational benchmarks for thousands, of whom only a tiny percentage will ever experience their so-called benefits. Because of that aspirational dimension, many of the racist practices that are now being called out, a moment informed by Black Lives Matter and other anti-racist movements, were masked by a host of norms and values inculcated in the culture of the school and meted out as language policy or dress code, disguised as formality but, in practice, operated as assimilationist ideology that amounted to a sustained and systemic discrimination against black students.

The second point that these examples help to highlight is the question of what we define as quality education. The National Policy on Whole School Evaluation (2001) is one document that the ministry of education has crafted for guiding its thinking about the multilayered approach necessary to get to grips with how to come to a set of criteria to evaluate educational institutions in a context with such a tumultuous history. Without going into too much detail about its criteria, suffice it to say here that the policy is aimed at 'improving the overall quality of education in South African schools …' by ensuring '… that all our children are given an equal opportunity to make the best use of their capabilities'. This is clearly an almost impossible task given the sheer unevenness of the socio-economic terrain, which is precisely another reason why the inequities between historically advantaged and disadvantaged schools remain so stubbornly in place. In the South African context, receiving an excellent education is inexplicably linked to access to resources, networks of upward mobility and the school's reputation with regards to academic merit. The aforementioned schools therefore continue to be feeder schools for the top universities and yet the question remains whether what graduates of those schools are receiving is a quality education or an elite education and to what degree these are two different things? Is it an education that equips students for the complexities of life in the contemporary moment, that demands they understand the clarion call for the decolonisation of education and how they fit into that equation or simply one that provides access to resources? Worse still, is it an education that renders the minority of black students who obtain it, resilient for having weathered an onslaught of micro and macro aggressions levelled at their very blackness or Africanness? The chapter aims to show that the political climate we currently face, informed as it is by movements such as Black Lives Matter, #RMF and #FMF etc. is laying bare the necessity for rethinking how we evaluate what constitutes a 'good education'. I go on to argue that the song 'Fletselites' intervenes into the debate by making clear the critical utility of the principles of 'People's Education' in this work of reimagining, but also how the song potentially offers a set of tools with which the students in question might defend themselves against the epistemic violence discussed here.

The Incident and Its Implications

In March 2021, in a life orientation class at a prominent international school situated snuggly on the slopes of the mountain known as Table Mountain in Cape Town, the teacher in charge of a demographically diverse group of eleventh graders, told the class that according to a scientific study, children of colour, even when exposed to opportunities such as gaining access to elite schools, were still prone to failure because of a lack of positive role models in their home environments. The teacher, who it is relevant to mention is white, went on to draw from the 'study' to elaborate on what she meant with lack of role models. According to this 'study', black and coloured children continued to experience failure academically because their brothers were predominantly gang involved, sold drugs and incarcerated, and their mothers involved in prostitution. The teacher did not produce the study (and never did even after the explosion of protest and inquiry in the following weeks). The students in the class were horrified and launched a complaint which eventually reached the Transformation, Diversity and Inclusion

(TDI) committee. The teacher was suspended after some pressure from particular parents within the TDI. However, to the complete dismay of the students, the teacher appeared again, just a few weeks later, back in the same classroom. This, the offence of allowing the teacher back in front of the same class she traumatised without a proper process along with a long series of bumbles to follow, diminished any sense of trust and confidence the affected students and parents might have had in the school leadership to ensure a safe, welcoming and equitable learning environment for their children. It was only after parents took the decision to picket outside of the school, drawing national media attention, that the teacher finally left the school. It is still not clear whether an agreement was reached between with the teacher and management or if she was fired, but since the incident, a cascade of testimonies going back decades started to surface of unchecked micro and macro aggressions toward students of colour that emphatically underscore the lack of will in the school's management to bring about any kind of thorough and lasting transformation.

By the end of 2021 the South African Human Rights Commission made an inquiry into the allegations and the principal was forced to make several commitments to transformation at the school, including hiring a permanent member of staff to head a long-term transformation vision. This process is ongoing, and this is where I would like to depart from the school for now, in order to zoom into the original incident and briefly contemplate what the teacher was communicating to her students in that life orientation class. To begin, it might be helpful to understand what 'life orientation' is in the first place. The Department of Basic Education defines the subject of life orientation as follows:

> Life Orientation is the study of the self in relation to others and to society. It addresses skills, knowledge, and values about the self, the environment, responsible citizenship, a healthy and productive life, social engagement, recreation and physical activity, careers and career choices. These include opportunities to engage in the development and practice of a variety of life skills to solve problems, to make informed decisions and choices and to take appropriate actions to live meaningfully and successfully in a rapidly changing society. It not only focuses on knowledge, but also emphasises the importance of the application of skills and values in real-life situations, participation in

physical activity, community organisations and initiatives. (Department of Basic Education, 2011. P.8)

Taking into account the noble intention in the aims of this National Curriculum subject, it begs several questions. Towards which destination was the teacher orienting those students? What do her actions in that moment reveal about her conception of 'responsible citizenship' and how are the students supposed to conceive of a 'healthy productive life'? What kinds of gaps in our education have occurred that such a drastic untruth like "students of colour have no positive role models" could be uttered in a class with the aforementioned mandate? One has to, firstly, conclude that a mind-numbingly myopic misrepresentation of history has occurred. Secondly, a set of blinders must be in place with regards to what even constitutes a role model. Then there is a disconcerting confidence on the part of the teacher that such a brazen falsity would not be met with immediate institutional consequences. While the students did raise the alarm and a series of botched conflict resolution processes on the part of the school management did result in protest action that went viral catching the attention of national news networks, the controversy importantly raises yet more questions about what kind of impact this had on the students. It raises questions around the teacher's competence. And it also raises concerns about what processes and competencies the school possesses for dealing adequately with conflict and injustices that occur under its watch, especially with regards to how to support a group of students, who in deciding to protest, could be seen to have pursued the learning objective of the life orientation class by grasping the 'opportunity to engage in the development and practice of a variety of life skills to solve problems, to make informed decisions and choices and to take appropriate actions to live meaningfully and successfully in a rapidly changing society'. I would argue that the very combination of, on the hand such a flagrant act of epistemic violence on the part of the teacher, and the lack of adequate processes at the school to deal with such an incident are integral components of what makes racism and discrimination so resilient at these institutions. Given the hundreds of testimonies spanning decades in which students tried to ask for processes of restorative justice, the 'lack of adequate processes' translate into a willful ignorance by the leadership – a key aspect of systemic racism.

Artivist Response

When I heard about this incident and reflected on it with my communities, several of which happen to be communities of colour, I reflected on my time as an eleventh grader. And so, it is now perhaps relevant to date myself a little bit by declaring that I was an eleventh grader during a decade characterised by a state of emergency in the last decade before apartheid came to its knees in which the regime lashed out in extremely violent ways. Why did the incident affect me and others, who have no affiliation with the school, so deeply that we immediately felt the need to control a counter narrative to what this teacher's claim suggests? One might easily assume that people like myself and others in my community, felt defensive and felt the need to fight back. However, it is more complicated than that. What we heard when this idea of 'no role models' was reported in the news, was beyond an insult. It was a direct attack and reproduction of a violence that we spent our lifetimes combatting. And so, for me it became an invitation to respond in a twofold manner. One, as artist invested in art as resistance, and, secondly, as a scholar, equally invested in scholarship as activism. As scholarship is also part of my art, I take the liberty to put this work into conversation with others who have historically found the need to frame responses to crises in this way. I therefore choose to use the terms artivist and artivism in this paper to mark the overlap of these kinds of responses. A portmanteau combining 'art' and 'activism', the usage of the term artivist was derived specifically out of collaborations in the late 1990s between Chicano artists from East Los Angeles and the Zapatistas in Chiapas, Mexico.[3] This tradition of employing art in social justice struggles is particularly apt in its application in this paper given the overlaps between anti-colonial struggles in all three contexts.

Working with artivist Quintin 'Jitsvinger' Goliath, we wrote and recorded a tribute to the struggle these and so many other students were undergoing called 'Fletselites'. 'Fletselites' featured on Jitsvinger's second full studio album *Jitsanova Volume 1: Compos Mentis* released in December 2021. The album title, *Compos Mentis*, signals an intention to reflect on what it means to be of sound mind in a context so inundated with onslaughts on our psycho-social wellbeing. The title of the song is a neologism that combines the words 'Cape Flats'[4] and 'satellites' and aims to draw attention to how we orient ourselves toward one another and in relation to our socio-political and spatial environments. Additionally, the title signposts the aim to equip the affected students with the knowledge that they come from communities rich with people who have made (and continue to make) major contributions to struggles for a more just society. While the song was initially penned in direct response to the international school incident, it was also immediately clear that it was also informed by a spirit of outrage against the surge of racist events at schools across the country. Having collaborated with Jitsvinger for a number of years around questions of justice in education and linguistic activism around the language of Afrikaaps, this moment seemed like a prime opportunity to present a reminder of the unfulfilled vision of educational justice that emerged during the anti-apartheid struggle, a vision that has so inspired our work and has served as an endless resource for thinking about how to prepare youth in the present moment to flourish intellectually in spite of the dysfunctional education system and socio-economic barriers they're expected to endure. This vision was captured by the moniker People's Education – which stood in contrast to Bantu Education. People's Education sought to reorient a generation of minds away from the notion that they were born to exist on the margins of civilisation which is what Bantu Education was designed to inculcate in black people. In the next section I showcase lyrics from the song with the aim of demonstrating how it was written for the students in that life orientation class, as a reminder that we are still dealing with the specters of Bantu Education and a reinforcement of the notion that People's Education is still critically relevant and necessary. After presenting the opening verse from 'Fletselites,' translated from Afrikaaps,[5] I lay out the conceptual framework for analysing it, which includes my definition of epistemic violence and resilience and a brief overview of People's Education. The paper then finally comes back to the song to offer some analytical reflection on how it speaks to the incident and how it embodies the spirit of People's Education.

Looooo Op
Dwars deur jou dak,
Met jou hart
Uit jou tuff skedel uit
Loooooo op
innie naghemel
elke Vonkel van
Senegal, Belville
Bengal, Melville
Nyanga, Eldos
Elke blok n parallel sterrestelsel
Soe dies vir elke drie sisters
Wat sukkel om te breathe tussen
Ou Ryan se belt en sy elbow

'Cos versprei ver en wyd
skutterende bakens
herrinder jou hoe vast en
ancient is space
vol Maan tot vol Maan
Tot jou nomme ront slaan
Is net n mette van ruimte en tyt
Selfsie plennets
ennie stere ennie berge en os helde't
lywe geskyf
net om te kan ontstaan

Anton Fransch,
larrie poppe Dans
Bontas tot Mars.
Skollies en politicians
Kry vir Coline Williams,
of naar of skaam
Skotsdene, Venus tot daa op FransHoek
Ashley Kriel se naam't oek
mass Flats appeal
Dies hannie verhal
Vannie volk ennie shepherd
As Dulcie September
Hop op oppressors
met die force van n' leopard
En Bessie Head se pen hulle geskok en lat dread't
Satima Benjamin
Blaas os naam innie heavens in
Robbie Jansen
Se stem is te grof en te handsome
Vir pop Rocket engines
met emblems van Amazon Branson
Die Schilder sisters en broese
Gie OS verbeelding bliksem en boosters

Gastrodamus, Piet en ou stoffel?
Dais os freedom hawkers
Aunty Gaairo, Ouma Grootjie,?
Dais os visionary order
En dais net n handvol sandkorrels
uit ontelbaare strande
Waar Ray en Stevie nog Wonne
Oor meteorites en isotopes
Ko analyse met Bible quotes en microscopes
Hoe temples en empires rise en flop
Terwyl os net lekkertjies vlieg innie orbit
Dies karma Virrie comma
wat al laaaankal hie moet gekommet
Soe catch a light acolytes,
Act alive when you stand and site
die ongelooflike,
die skouspelagtige,
die ontsagwekkende
flight vannie Fletselites

Looooook Up
straight through your roof
with your heart
out your tough skull
looooook up
into the night sky
every twinkle from
Senegal, Belville
Bengal, Melville
Nyanga, Eldos
Every block a parallel universe
So this is for every 3 sisters
Struggling to breath between
Ol' Ryan's belt and his elbow

'Cos scattered far and wide
Glimmering beacons
Remind you of how vast and
Ancient is space
Full moon 'till full moon
'till your number comes around
It's just a matter of space and time
Even the planets
And the stars and the mountains and our heroes
Had to hustle
Just to exist

Anton Fransch
Raised hell
Bontas to Mars
Thugs and Politicians
when facing Coline Williams
ashamed or envious
Skotsdene, Venus to Franshoek
Ashley Kriel's name also
Has mass Flats appeal
Ain't this the tale
of the Folk and the shepherd
When Dulcie September
Hops on oppressors
With the force of a leopard
And Bessie Head's pen shocks them with dread
Satima Benjamin
Blasts our names in the heavens
Robbie Jansen's voice
Is too rough and too handsome
For pop rocket engines
With emblems of Amazon Branson
The Schilder brothers and sisters,
Give our imaginations thunder and boosters

Gastrodamus, Piet and Stoffel?
Those are our freedom hawkers
Aunty Gaairo, Greatgrandma?
They're our visionary order
And that's just a handful of grains of sand
Out of countless beaches
Where Ray and Stevie still Wonder
About meteorites and isotopes
Some analyze with Bible quotes and microscopes
How temples and empires rise and flop
While we just fly in the orbit
This is karma for the comma
That should have come long ago
So catch a light acolytes,
Act alive when you stand and site
The unbelievable,
The spectacular,
The awesome
flight of the Fletselites

Conceptual Framework

The fallout of occurrences of racism at elite schools over the last three years is clearly only the tip of the iceberg. The entire school system requires a radical recalibration in line with calls for education for the people that emanate from the earliest anti-colonial education movements and the anti-racist education movements that continued that trajectory during the apartheid era and beyond. Since, at core, this chapter revolves around a set of questions about what do we want to retain from our past as a country and what needs to transform, this section clarifies how I conceive of the notion of resilience and what I mean with epistemic violence with the view to conceptualise the continuities between what was called People's Education and what is required in the current moment. To this end, this section goes on to provide a description of the historical context that gave rise to the notion of People's Education as the component of the anti-apartheid liberation struggle that sought to bring out about justice in education, outlining its aims and the philosophical predecessors, major theorists, activists and artivists involved in its co-creation.

Resilience

In this volume, Enomoto surveys the broad shifts that the resilience concept has undergone in the 21st century, particularly with regards to the manner in which it has been deployed in and in relation to the global South, with large power brokers and policy engines demonstrating the tendency to seek to either pacify populations struggling against the tide of neo-colonial conditions or avoiding to address the material and wider structural and political causes of suffering by placing the onus on the individual. Borrowing from disciplinary traditions such as applied physics, cognitive and behavioural science, psychology, sociology and, especially ecology, a major trend in these approaches has tended to conceptualise resilience as a form of bouncing back from adversity (Margolis & Stoltz, 2010; Galli & Vealey, 2008). Enomoto's chapter illustrates the push-back from subjects previously tethered to the margins by the misuses of this very discourse. The Black Lives Matter (BLM) movement, for example, has had a powerful impact on resilience discourse around the world by opening the space to critique the normalisation of some of its core assumptions. BLM has especially helped to put pressure on institutions to reckon with the stubbornness of racism in their midst. Additionally, movements such as BLM have also challenged the very terms and frameworks with which many institutions have operated. My usage of 'resilience' in this chapter aligns with these critiques articulated by the likes of Ramon Vasquez (2022), who detailed the ways in which the demands on marginalised communities to be more resilient constitutes a form of 'gaslighting'[6] and othering. Another theorist, Angela Bruce-Raeburn, working in the development aid sector and deeply informed by BLM, critiques the hegemonic usage of resilience, especially when referring to people who daily have to deal with precarity. She argues that terms like 'resilient' and 'resilience' 'serve to perpetuate inequalities while telling vulnerable people how strong they are—and therefore changing absolutely nothing in their lives' (Bruce-Raeburn 2020). On the other hand, other scholars have also argued for recouping the possibilities of the resilience concept in light of the contemporary resurgence in focus on the crisis of racism. Sims-Schouten and Gilbert (2022) for instance, point to the ample examples of grassroots work being done to enhance the ability of pressured communities to not only beat the odds but to change the odds. It is important to keep this in mind as this kind of resistance work is also still referred to as resilience. In this chapter, I make the conscious decision to distinguish the kind of work showcased by 'Fletselites' as interventions that attempt to assist communities to change the odds rather than simply beating them – an objective distinctly prevalent in the People's Education movement.

Epistemic Violence

Violence becomes a focus of public contestation when people are forced to use violence to point out that they are subjected to violence, particularly when that violence is invisibilised. The various anti-racist movements of the last decade have served to remind us that black bodies are subjected to sub-human conditions and treatment every day, and that that subjection is normalised, and that that normalisation is unacceptable. It is necessary to point this out in this chapter because the international school in question was able to continue to operate for decades while such pernicious discriminatory practices persisted within the institution precisely because those practices have been disguised as normal and not recognised as violence and abuse when that is precisely what they are.

My conceptualization of epistemic violence draws on scholarship by James Lindsay (2020) who establishes generative connections between the work of scholars such as Gayatri Chakravorty Spivak and Kristie Dotson. In Spivak's (1988) landmark essay, 'Can the Subaltern Speak?', the silencing that is visited upon the subaltern is a form of epistemic violence. For her, colonisation brought with it the (attempted) annihilation of the subaltern's voice, which included destroying knowledge systems, delegitimising traditions and beliefs, and devaluing their language. Thus, the subaltern is imprisoned by and in its own oppression. Feminist philosopher, Kristie Dotson (2011), develops this idea further by characterising epistemic violence as a type of malicious ignorance that takes place when those in a position of social dominance refuse to accommodate marginalised speakers on what Lindsay (2020) called "the epistemic terrain" between them. Dotson refers to this as 'reliable ignorance' – a type of ignorance you can expect to occur – or to be mobilised. According to Dotson, this kind of ignorance does harm by amplifying the power differential between actors in the transaction. This is the kind of violence that occurred in the life orientation class in 2021, and this is the nature of the violence that People's Education and 'Fletselites' aims to address. By claiming that youth of colour have no positive role models, the teacher reproduced the act of silencing and enacted the reliable ignorance of the traditions and the deep well of cultural and historical resources that belong to those students. According to the progenitors of People's Education, it is the task of the educator, the artist and the activist, or artivist, to prepare learners and audiences on how to access these resources, not just networks of upward mobility that require them to accept the annihilation of their own history. The very fact that 'Fleselites' is written in a counter-hegemonic language which encodes much of its resistive material in such a way as to include the students and exclude the teacher who does not speak it, constitutes a major component of its strategy to undo silencing. 'Fletselites' thereby exposes the teacher's "reliable ignorance" while challenging her and the school to rise to the occasion of learning and respecting the language and traditions of their students.

I now turn to a brief overview of People's Education to underscore the injustices it aimed to address at the height of the anti-apartheid struggle with the hopes of revealing the continuities between that struggle and the present stage of the crisis and the role of artivists as educators within it. This will provide the necessary scaffolding for the final return to an analysis of 'Fletselites.'

People's Education vs Bantu Education

The momentum of the Soweto protests of 1976 took the liberation struggle into the 1980s and the uprising intensified so much that the apartheid government declared a state of emergency. During the early 1980s, domestic and international outrage forced the Afrikaner National Party to publicly address social issues, among them education. In 1980, the year I was born, and also four years after the Soweto massacre, in the midst of school boycotts throughout the country, the state appointed the Human Sciences Research Council Commission to carry out an inquiry into education, which became known as the De Lange Report.[7] Although the report was presumably set up to address inequalities in education, it ultimately reflected the government's reaffirmed commitment to the policy of separate education departments. Because it was a move to assuage the masses, the report caused heated disagreements within the ruling white elite regarding the future of South Africa's education system. These tensions were indicative of an impending economic crisis. The discourse of 'skills shortage' dominated the national fiscal debates and the unprecedented expansion of technical and vocational education between 1977 and 1982 represented the extent of the state's intervention into a racialised political economy. (Chisholm, 1983) Education reform during this time was part of a strategy to incorporate a limited number of blacks into the white mainstream – a sign of compromises to come.

In the face of such last-ditch attempts by the apartheid state, which was now staring down the barrel of its own imminent demise, the 1980s up to the early 1990s saw the concept of People's Education capture the imagination of many South Africans (Vally, 2007). In contrast to the apartheid education system, People's Education, which built upon the successes of the Black Consciousness Movement (BCM), promised a liberation and transformation from a dictatorial and lopsided education system to one that would offer an alternative that could accommodate a more democratic vision of citizenship. The specific organisation of the liberation movement in the late 1970s and especially in the 1980s as a grassroots movement anchored in groups and projects in the 'community' brought with it an exceptional sensitivity regarding democratic principles. This sensitivity, reinforced by Paulo Freire's conceptions of pedagogy, became integral to the practice of People's Education.[7]

The idea of 'Peoples Education' was articulated in a concrete manner, after the decline of BCM, when the South African National Student's Congress (SANSCO) became a driving force behind it. SANSCO had been established near Soweto during the late 1970s, and now initiated collective actions around a range of educational grievances. SANSCO was the first national organisation to endorse opposition to the government's constitutional proposals in January 1983. People's Education was thought of, by many, to be a vehicle for conscientisation, that stimulated critical thinking and analysis and promoted the concept of 'alternative governance structures in education' (Motala and Vally, 2002). Motala and Vally argue that critical thinking, in this sense, must not be confused with what is conventionally simply thought of as 'problem-solving skills.' This conceptualisation of 'critical thinking', Motala and Vally contend, serves a post-Fordist agenda. 'Critical', in the light of the People's Education movement, infers being able to understand, analyse and, most importantly, effect the sociopolitical and economic realities that shape our lives. The emphasis on democratic governance was expressed in the call for the establishment of student representative councils and parent-teacher-student associations (PTSA). The concepts of democracy, access and equity emerged in the call for a unitary anti-racist and anti-sexist schooling system, an end to sexual harassment and corporal punishment, better resource provisioning, a different curriculum and free compulsory education. From the mid-1980s, supporters of People's Education were not only concerned with the transformation of schools; they also provided the impetus for the formation of hundreds of non-governmental education organisations, and actively challenged academics and the academy around three key areas. These were (1) accountability within the university and communities around them; (2) implementing People's Education in the universities themselves; and (3) support for developing People's Education in schools through the production of alternative courses and teaching methods (Motala and Vally, 2002). In a 1986 keynote address at the establishment of the National Education Crisis Committee (NECC), Zwelakhe Sisulu of the iconic Sisulu family, said of the movement:

> We are no longer demanding the same education as Whites, since this is education for domination. People's Education means education at the service of the people as a whole, education that liberates, education that puts the people in command of their lives. (Sisulu, 1986, pp.26)

Enter the Artivist

When musicians decided to get involved in an organised way in the anti-apartheid movement in the 1980s, some of them joined the United Democratic Front (UDF). One of the projects to emerge was Music Action for People's Power (MAPP), which sought to instill people with more autonomy (Martin, 2013). Maths teacher and trumpeter, Duke Ngcukana, who became the coordinator of the MAPP music school in 1989, recounted that when MAPP started out it was an affiliate of the UDF. They sought to use music as a vehicle for liberation and, as he put it, 'also to subvert the government through music, for instance, meetings were banned, but concerts were not banned, so through concerts you could have these rallies without the authorities knowing' (Martin, 2013).

The idea for MAPP came about at a concert at the Rocklands Civic Centre in Mitchells Plain, at which sound engineer and cultural activist, Steve Gordon, and Cape Jazz legend, Basil 'Manenberg' Coetzee, discussed the need for a structure within which to accommodate musicians and artists committed to democratic movements in Cape Town. The late historian and jazz pianist, Vince Kolbe, noted that the presence of jazz musicians at UDF rallies and gatherings underscored the rise of 'Cape jazz', a specific type of jazz that came out of Cape Town in the 1980s. While it has since become a commercial tag, musicians such as Colin Miller argue, "cultural activism became an important platform for resistance and ensured that Cape Jazz became a key vehicle of expression for the anti-apartheid movement" (Martin 2008, pp.244). Vince Kolbe concurs and adds that songs such as 'Die Struggle', composed by Mac McKenzie and Hilton Schilder amidst the municipal workers' strike of 1985, drew on the Ghoema beat and might be considered the 'birth certificate' of Cape jazz. It joined with Ibrahim's 'Manenberg' in sonically capturing the spirit of the Cape and gave way to the sound of township culture. The UDF was imbricated in this culture which was taken up by youth 'under the influence of Black Consciousness

Ideas'. The archive of sonic resources these artivists set in motion would even eventually, years later, be the very archive that artists of the hip hop generation drew on to build on and continue a legacy of resistance. In fact, the production for 'Fletselites' is built on a sample of a hauntingly beautiful excerpt from a piano piece by Hilton Schilder's late older brother, Chris Schilder.

MAPP took part in many kinds of political events and facilitated workshops with community organiations, youth groups and trade unions. It also operated as a booking agent and started a school. The school was to have four streams: a full-time music course, which branched off into a jazz section, that prepared youth to either enter the University of Cape Town or to follow a professional career, a choral programme and a music therapy course. When the school opened in 1989 it changed its name to Music Action for People's Progress. It organised outreach to many marginalised areas including Khayelitsha, Langa, Gugulethu, Athlone and Manenberg. They trained teachers and many musicians who are now part of the Cape jazz scene. They were able to expand to the extent they did by securing funding from the Swedish National Organization for Non-Profit Cultural Associations. However, when South Africa democratised, foreign aid donors no longer saw the need to contribute to the activities of former apartheid era organisations – supposedly because their activities were now no longer needed or because now economic and political control was in supposedly majority hands. They pulled funding in 1994 and, as the new government did not support them either, they were forced to cease all operations (Martin, 2008). Sadly, this was the fate of a great many organisations and social initiatives built up during the anti-apartheid struggle. This set of machinations set the country on course for the deepening of inequality in all spheres, not least in education which greatly contributed to the context described at the outset of this chapter.

Problems and Possibilities

A towering figure in the liberation movement, especially for his commitment to justice in education and an advocate for the continued relevance of People's Education, Neville Alexander, asked the following during his address at the tenth anniversary celebration of the Foundation for Human Rights in Pretoria in November 2006:

> Why is it that in spite of a constitution that was arrived at in a 20th century model of democratic bargaining and consensus building and in which are enshrined some of the noblest sentiments and insights concerning human rights, we are living in a situation where very few of those rights appear to be realized, or even realizable, in practice? (p. 41)

In spite of the Constitution's discourse around human rights and development-for-all, South Africa exacerbated a drive toward capitalist ideals when it fully integrated into the global market economy after 1994. Prior to 1994, South Africa's participation in the global market economy was limited because the international anti-apartheid boycott resulted in many nations around the world refusing to do business with South Africa. The country's sudden adoption of, and immersion into, neoliberal economic policies compromised the principles and practices established by the anti-apartheid movement of the 1970s and 1980s. Principles such as free quality education for all, education with production, participatory democracy in education, critical thinking for political action and access to higher education for the poor were reduced to the rhetoric of a hopeful, 'naïve' and jubilant moment of mass euphoria. In an invaluable (1992) collection of speeches titled *Education and the Struggle for National liberation in South Africa*, Alexander documents how the collective demand for alternative education was never appeased by the 1994 elections, but rather gained urgency and momentum in the 'new social movements.' Rather than attempting to fix a broken system, Alexander invoked the spirit of People's Education as a key tool with which to address the dilemma as he saw it, stating that "almost every black student and teacher and many a black parent sees the realization of this deal as the answer to the crisis in education.' However, Alexander also felt that it was naïve to think that alternative education stood a chance under the apartheid system.

The post-apartheid trajectory saw an emphasis on more formal hierarchical forms of knowledge, exclusionary stratification, competitive individualism, and the idea of bettering knowledge acquisition through rationalized learning outcomes replaced traditions of worker education that had been based on collectivist learning. Salim Vally (2007) addresses Alexander's question by grappling with the ways in which the struggle for equal education revealed a class dimension that was as important as race, and how class prerogatives played into the capitalist state. Vally pointed out that, while the radical education praxis has been weakened, it still exists, and its center of gravity has shifted to the new social movements post-1994'. The work of Jitsvinger in recentering the devalued knowledge systems associated with languages such as Afrikaaps is one small aspect of the shape that these new social movements have taken and 'Fletselites' attempts to index that shift to some extent.

Alexander argued that the root of the education system's problems stemmed from the country's struggle with the crisis of capitalism. He called for development-oriented organisations to cultivate and implement 'fundamental interventions that spring from fearless analysis of the structure and dynamics of a rapidly changing South Africa' (Alexander, 2013). He suggested initiatives such as cooperative rural development schemes, language projects, labour and community education projects, preschool programmes, literacy programmes and distance education programmes. He imagined that all of these programmes would work in tandem with a vision of a 'democratic socialist Azania'.

It is now nearly three decades since the end of legislative apartheid, and Alexander's fears have materialised spectacularly. A plethora of organizations, events, eruptions, sustained protest campaigns, artistic and cultural explosions make up the New Social Movements alluded to by Alexander and Vally. Rhodes Must Fall and Fees Must Fall erupted between 2015 and 2017 as direct indictments of the post-apartheid era governments' failure to heed these warnings. The socio-economic disparities painfully evident in larger South African society are transposed directly onto the education system and, indeed, are reproduced by that system as well. The call for free and decolonial education that culminated in FMF magnify the extent to which People's Education has not yet been achieved and implemented at a country-wide level and yet continues to be critically needed. Amidst all of this, schools such as the ones in question continue to reproduce a class system that is still delineated by race. The concluding section takes a closer look at key lyrical moments in 'Fletselites' to understand how the song, as a mere spec in the upswell of resistance to the resilience of oppression, mounts a critique and hopes to contribute to a toolbox that the students in question may access to stand up to the epistemic violence that marks the current crisis.

Fletselites: Resilience and Resistance in the Here and Now

When Zwelakhe Sisulu said "We are no longer demanding the same education as Whites, since this is education for domination," it echoes precisely what is at stake when one pits the education represented by the teacher in the life orientation class against the counter arguments presented by 'Fletselites' – education for domination versus education at the service of the people. Let's begin with the title. By creating a portmanteau that combines the terms Cape Flats and satellites, the writers signaled an interest in commenting on the tension that exists between the notion of a centre and a periphery. This tension is amplified by the choice to write the song in a contested language such as Afrikaaps which effectually excludes the teacher, in this case the perpetrator, from fully grasping its meaning, Jitsvinger's exploration of futurity in the album, which includes examining imagining alternative futures, inspired the opening motif of the song, which has the listener "staring" up into the night sky and seeing blinking lights. Multiplying several layers of meaning into this notion of peering up, the title is also inspired by the geo-political reality that students of colour face when attending elite schools by invoking the idea of the satellite as a feature of the periphery. Every black student in South Africa who has attended a former white school or university can attest to the arduous physical effort it takes to make the journey to school every day. Even if they are lucky enough to live in residences or have a family home in the suburbs close to the school, the relationship to the outskirts of the city, to their rural homes are never far behind. For the majority of students attending the school in question, showing up for school at 8 am in the morning and competing with counterparts who might just stroll to school or enjoy a coffee at a café on the way to class is a major factor in defining the school-going experience. The idea of coming from the margins is not just a philosophical or ideological one but inscribed in the body. What is more, is that it would be undignified to complain about that very obvious and very visceral competitive (dis)advantage and so, for the most part, such struggles have been invisablised for the longest time. For all these reasons, the added indignity of having one's history and the achievements of one's ancestors silenced in the way that it was during the life orientation class is a double insult. Therefore, the title and thesis statement of the song 'Fletselites' cuts to the heart of an attempt to reconfigure what is centre and what is periphery. If one only scans the names mentioned in the song, Ashley Kriel, Anton Fransch, Bessie Head, Dulcie September, etc., one begins to contemplate the massive archive of contributions these people have made to intellectual and cultural production, to our understandings of and our ability to access human rights. The very title of the song therefore beckons the students in that life orientation class to seriously reflect on what they are being asked to orientate themselves toward? Who in fact are the kinds of role models the teacher was envisioning? Who are her role models and what have they contributed to the country and the world? The portmanteau, in the Freirian spirit of dialogue over monologue, invites playfulness and inquiry and harkens back to the definition of 'critical thinking' as intended by the People's Education movement, inviting listeners to analyse and, most importantly, effect the sociopolitical and economic realities that shape our lives. In one community-based workshop, Jitsvinger invited youth participants to co-create a definition for 'Fletselites' and an array of fluid and thought-provoking offerings came back at him including for instance "Fletselites give out important information, it's the light of the place'.[8] The opening verse goes on to elaborate on (re)orientation, the centre/periphery dynamic and the notion of illumination:

Looooo op Dwars deur jou dak, Met jou hart Uit jou tuff skedel uit Loooooo op innie naghemel	Loooooook up straight through your roof, with your heart out your tough skull loooooooook up into the night sky
elke vonkel van Senegal, Belville, Bengal, Melville, Nyanga, Eldos Elke blok n parallelsterrestelsel	every twinkle from Senegal, Belville, Bengal, Melville, Nyanga, Eldos Every block a parallel universe

The listener is compelled by the writer to reflect. At first it seems as though one is simply being asked to look up into the sky, but very quickly you are positioned inside a structure with a roof between you and the sky and so the reflection required is both external and internal – a gesture toward re-orientation. It goes on to encourage a reflection on the connection between disparate yet deeply connected places – Senegal, Bellville, Bengal, Melville, Nyanga, Eldos[9] – disparate because they are so distinct, connected because they are all in the global South; disparate because they comprise hundreds, if not thousands of languages and nationalities, yet connected because they have all been indelibly touched by colonialism; disparate by virtue of their physical distance from each other but proximal in the way they function as satellite localities to some centre or the other – centres of commercial enterprise, centres of economic opportunity and political power. The end of the stanza positions them as parallel universes in much the same way that 'the ghetto', wherever it is located, whatever the particularities of its local context, seems to share likenesses. The gesture toward the parallel relationship between communities in these locations points to the critical consciousness that People's Education was so intent on fostering. It is an invitation to think about the ways in which African and Asian diaspora living in impoverished conditions in locations such as these force us to see each other as competition rather than understanding the historical and systemic causes of our marginality. The next stanza expands on the specificities of what connects us in our marginality by pointing to one of the most devastating ills that arise as a symptom of the post-colonial dilemma, femicide.

Soe dies vir elke drie sisters	So this is for every 3 sisters
Wat sukkel om te breathe tussen	Struggling to breath between
Ou Ryan se belt en sy elbow	Ol' Ryan's belt and his elbow

While this chapter and the case studies presented here highlight the racial aspect of the toxicity in school environments, race, class and gender are tightly imbricated components of the crisis and many of the testimonies that have emerged also implicate the schools in terms of their failures to adequately transform with regards to gender in their curricula. The lyrics however, turn the focus inward toward marginalised communities to demand a self-reflectivity in terms of how gender-based violence is reproduced internally. Recalling Motala and Vally's reading of how critical thinking operated as a core learning objective in People's Education, this verse signals the artivists' interest in cultivating processes of learning and reflection that enable listeners to 'understand, analyze and, most importantly, affect the sociopolitical and economic realities that shape our lives.' This was really the job of the life orientation teacher. Moving from an acknowledgement of the complexities involved internalised oppression, the verse moves on to ask the listener to participate in effecting change by understanding the beacons of hope that emanate far and wide – the contributions of people who put their lives on the line in order to present alternatives life paths for generations to follow.

'Cos versprei ver en wyd skutterende bakens herrinder jou hoe vast en ancient is space Selfsie plennets ennie stere ennie berge en os helde't lywe geskyf net om te kan ontstaan Anton Fransch, larrie poppe dans Bontas tot Mars	'Cos scattered far and wide Glimmering beacons Remind you of how vast and Ancient is space Even the planets and the stars and the mountains and our heroes Had to hustle just to exist Anton Fransch Raised hell Bontas to Mars

Aligning with the mandate in the People's Education movement to propagate curricula that function as 'vehicles for conscientization,' the verse now goes on to introduce a short list of people, role models *par excellence*, who committed their lives to doing just that. What's more is that a crucial part of the 'pernicious ignorance' committed by the teacher in question is that the contributions of militant youth political activists, Anton Fransch, Coline Williams, Ashely Kriel and Dulcie September, or the wealth of intellectual work by radically conscious writers like Bessie Head or the deep archives left to us by liberationist musicians such as Robbie Jansen, Satima Benjamin or the Schilder brothers and sisters are not front and centre in the national curriculum. It is my contention that had the students in the life orientation class owned with conviction that people like the short list in the song hailed from their very own communities the impact of the teacher's act of epistemic violence might have landed very differently. The intention behind the rest of the opening verse in 'Fletselites' is to draw the listener into finding out more about the likes of Anton Fransch, a youth commander in Umkhonto we Sizwe[10] who was killed on 17 November 1989 in Cape Town by police and South African defence forces for his anti-apartheid activities. 'Fletselites' hopes to equip those students with the confidence that people like Coline Williams, a drama student at the Joseph Stone Institution in Athlone, Cape Town, also made a major contribution to the freedoms we now all enjoy after giving her life as a Umkhonto we Sizwe operative.

After listing several (unsung) struggle heroes, the verse eventually culminates in a smaller group of people that it seems to posit as the pinnacle of this list.

Gastrodamus, Piet en ou stoffel? Dais os freedom hawkers Aunty Gaairo, Ouma Grootjie? Dais os visionary order	Gastrodamus, Piet and ol' Stoffel? Those are our freedom hawkers Aunty Gaairo, Greatgrandma? They're our visionary order

In suggesting that the students in that class have no positive role models, only "prostitutes" and "drug dealers," the teacher was robotically playing into the kinds of colonial discourses that Spivak sought to upturn, when she conceptualised colonisation as an attempted annihilation of the subaltern's voice which included destroying their knowledge systems, delegitimising their traditions and beliefs, and devaluing their language. Leading up to the above excerpt, the role models 'Fletselites' offers those students are in fact even marginalised within the margins, being as they are figures that have been obscured from what have become preferred and celebrated hegemonic struggle icon narratives. This final excerpt, however, goes a step further to elevate two 'unknown' but widely familiar maternal figures Aunty Gaairo and Ouma Grootjie as the apex of this list of heroes with which the students might arm themselves against the teacher's act of silencing and erasure. Elevating an aunty and a great-grandmother as the figures representing 'our visionary order' emphasises the commitment with which 'Fletselites' pledges to reorient those students' perspectives as to the sources of 'high quality education' that can be found on their very own doorsteps. By suggesting that what can be learned from our mothers, aunties, grandmothers and great-grandmothers might, in fact, be a pinnacle in our intellectual achievements drives home the point I started to make at the outset of this chapter. The resilience of racism and other forms of toxic discriminatory practices in educational institutions has a great deal to do with the way in which they have participated in exceptionalising their own positions as the centre of the project of learning, rather one aspect of a broader and more expansive vision of education. 'Fletselites' was only released in 2021 and so it is at the beginning stages of the work that its authors hope it can do. One must also state that its limitations are clear. It can only contribute to the processes imagined in this paper. These processes, the vision that People's Education set forth, require multifaceted and layered approaches from all stake holders. For the artivists who created 'Fletselites,' and for the students for whom it was written, the real work lies ahead.

Conclusion

This chapter has examined resilience in the context of current and historical educational justice struggles in South Africa. Showcasing artist responses to incidents of epistemic violence in schools, the chapter has argued that the song 'Fletselites' complicates hegemonic conceptualisations of resilience. From the perspective of the students, the fact that such manifestations of epistemic violence could take place in what is supposed to be a post-apartheid South Africa is one of the most urgent problems they/we face. On the other hand, from the perspective of the artists who created the song, so many of the solutions they offer the students revolve around a knowledge of people, ideas and practices of resistance conversant with historical struggles. Resilience therefore became a necessary heuristic device in this chapter, because coming to grips with the complexities of the South African education crisis demands both a reckoning with the staying power of unjust practices while, simultaneously, reappraising the continued utility of strategies of resistance against injustice adapted from past struggles. 'Fletselites' was therefore analysed against the backdrop of several historical precedents that demonstrate the ways in which artists/ activists/ artivists and educators/entertainers/edutainers have committed themselves to working with the country's most vulnerable student populations to make sense of (and transform) their circumstances. 'Fletselites' extends aspects of the vision put forth in the People's Education movement and therefore celebrates forms of resistance to epistemic violence, whose adaptability and durability are rooted in what I have suggested to be a far more robust set of propositions than other more normative deployments of the resilience concept.

Notes

[1] I use this periodisation with the due amount of caution given the neo-colonialism/post-colonial debate

[2] Protests against injustice in education have been continuous throughout the post-apartheid era, but they have intensified in the last ten years. The formation of organisations such as Equal Education who run campaigns to highlight the plight

of infrastructural inadequacies and a host of other aspects of the crisis coincides with the efflorescence of #RMF (Rhodes Must Fall), #FMF (Fees Must Fall), #StopRacismAtPretoriaGirlsHigh, #PhillipiHigh and other related movements which gained a global presence between 2015 and 2019.

[3] See Gonzalez, A. R. (2015); Gonzalez, A. R. (2021); Sandoval, C., & Latorre, G. (2008).

[4] The Cape Flats is a geopolitical location in the Western Cape, comprising peri-urban townships designated by the Group Areas Act of 1950 for black, coloured and Indian people as they were categorized under apartheid. Many of the students affected by the incidents highlighted in this paper come from this area.

[5] Afrikaaps is a term coined by Quintin 'Jitsvinger' Goliath that has circulated widely as a resonant counter-hegemonic rethinking of the language of Afrikaans. Jitsvinger conceptualized this term while collaborating with several artivists on the Hip Hop theatre production and 2010 documentary of the same name. The term signifies an attempt to wrest ownership of the language away from white Afrikaner nationalism and address the erasure of the black/African/indigenous contributions to the language's genesis. See Alim, H. S., Williams, Q. E., Haupt, A., & Jansen, E. (2021))

[6] Gaslighting is a colloquial term that refers to a form of psychological manipulation that makes someone doubt their experience and perspective on a situation, often resulting in questioning their sanity or sense of reality. The term is derived from a 1944 film of the same name and became popular in the 2010s. It has been a particularly useful concept in identifying forms of racism or at least strategies for maintaining oppressive behaviour and disguising micro-aggressions. See DiGiulio, Sarah. "What is gaslighting? And how do you know if it's happening to you?". NBC News. Retrieved 13 July 2018.

[7] This is the third major report on education to appear in South Africa.

[8] See Paulo Freire's (1973). *Education for Critical Consciousness.* Bloomsbury Publishing

[9] A sample of this conversation appears on the album recording.

[10] This segment of the verse primarily takes advantage of the rhyme possibilities of putting these locations together, yet when juxtaposed, other socio-political intersections present themselves. Senegal refers to the West African country; Bellville is a suburb in the Western Cape and major transport nexus; Bengal refers to the geopolitical region in South Asia, specifically the Indian subcontinent at the apex of the Bay of Bengal;, Melville is one of the oldest suburbs in Johannesburg, Gauteng – seen as a once bohemian cultural hub, is also a Pan African hub; Nyanga meaning Moon in isiXhosa is both a township in the Western Cape and a town in Zimbabwe; Eldos is short for Eldorado Park, a township of Johannesburg Soweto.

[11] Meaning 'Spear of the Nation' – the military wing of the liberation struggle.

References

Alexander, N. (2013). *Education and the Struggle for National Liberation in South Africa*, Essays and Speeches by Neville Alexander (1985–1989), Cape Town, South Africa: Skotaville Publishers.

Alim, H. S., Williams, Q. E., Haupt, A., & Jansen, E. (2021). "Kom Khoi San, kry trug jou land": Disrupting White Settler Colonial Logics of Language, Race, and Land with Afrikaaps. *Journal of Linguistic Anthropology*, *31*(2), 194-217.

Bruce-Raeburn, A. (2020). 'Opinion: the hustle—white saviors and hashtag activism', *Devex*, 12 June 2020 [online], available: < https://www.devex.com/news/opinion-the-hustle-white-saviors-and-hashtag-activism-97463> (accessed June 2022)

Busby, Eleanor. (2019). 'Demonstration outside South African School accused of separating black and white pupils' https://www.independent.co.uk/news/world/africa/south-africa-school-segregation-black-white-racism-teacher-pupils-laerskool-schweize-reneke-a8721111.html.

Chisholm, Linda (1983). 'Redefining skills: Black education in South Africa in the 1980s', *Comparative Education Review*, Vol. 19, No. 3, pp. 357–371.

Department of Basic Education (2011) Curriculum and Policy Statement. Life Orientation, pp. 8. www.education.gov.za/portals/

DiGiulio, Sarah. (2018). "What is gaslighting? And how do you know if it's happening to you?". NBC News. Retrieved January 2022.

Dotson, Kristie (2011). 'Tracking Epistemic Violence, Tracking Practices of Silencing'. *Hypatia*, 26 (2), 2011: 236–257, pp. 236–237.

Fataar, Aslam (1997) 'Access to schooling in a post-apartheid South Africa: Linking concepts to context', *International Review of Education/Internationale Zeitschrift für Erziehungswissenschaft/Revue Internationale de l'Education*, Vol. 43, No. 4, pp. 331– 48.

Freire, P. (1973). *Education for Critical Consciousness.* Bloomsbury Publishing

Galli, Nick and Vealey, Robin S. (2008). '"Bouncing back" from adversity: Athletes' experiences of resilience', *The Sport Psychologist,* 22 (3): 316–335.

Goliath, Q.(Jitsvinger), Davids, R. (Robert Black), Swai, M. (Caco). (2021). 'Fletselites' on *Jitsanova Volume 1: Compos Mentis.* Track 4. SAMRO

Gonzalez, A. R. (2015). *Another City is Possible: Mujeres de Maiz, Radical Indigenous Mestizaje and Activist Scholarship.* University of California, Santa Barbara.

__________ (2021). *Autonomy road: the cultural politics of Chicana/o autonomous organizing in Los Angeles, California* (Doctoral dissertation).

Government Gazette Vol. 433, No. 22512 of July 2001, Pretoria. pp.1.

King, Sara-Jayne. (2020). 'Where to from here? Dismantling systemic racism in South Africa's elite schools' https://www.capetalk.co.za/articles/386399/where-to-from-here-dismantling-systemic-racism-in-south-africa-s-elite-schools

Lindsay, James. (2020). 'Epistemic Violence' www.newdiscourses.com

Margolis, J. D., & Stoltz, P. G. (2010). How to Bounce Back from Adversity-People who survive setbacks have one thing in common: Resilience. Here's how you can strengthen yours. *Harvard Business Review, 20*, 86.

Martin, D. C. (2013). 'Sounding the Cape music,identity and politics in South Africa', *African Minds.*

Mohamed, Shiraaz. (2022). 'Gauteng Education MEC Panyaza Lesufi visits Hoërskool Jan Viljoen after racial incident' https://www.dailymaverick.co.za/article/2022-02-15-gauteng-education-mec-panyaza-lesufi-visits-hoerskool-jan-viljoen-after-racial-incident/

Motala, S. and Vally, S. (2002) 'People's Education: From People's Power to Tirisano', in Peter Kallaway (ed.) *The History of Education under Apartheid, 1948-1994: The Doors of Learning and Culture Shall Be Opened*, Cape Town: Pearson, p. 183.

Sandoval, C., & Latorre, G. (2008). *Chicana/o artivism: Judy Baca's digital work with youth of color.* MacArthur Foundation Digital Media and Learning Initiative.

Shange, Naledi. (2021). 'Cornwall Hill College has become the stuff of nightmares, says black pupil' https://www.timeslive.co.za/news/south-africa/2021-05-31-cornwall-hill-college-has-become-the-stuff-of-nightmares-says-black-pupil/

Sims-Schouten, W., & Gilbert, P. (2022). Revisiting 'resilience' in light of racism, 'othering' and resistance. Race & Class, 64(1), 84–94. https://doi.org/10.1177/03063968221093882

Sisulu, Z. (1987). People's education for people's power. *Issue: A journal of opinion*, *15*, 18-29.

Spivak, Gayatri Chakravorty (1988). Can the Subaltern Speak? _Die Philosophin_ 14 (27):42-58.

Tembo, Theolin; Geach, Chelsea. (2020). 'Bishops Matric class calls out systemic racism' https://www.iol.co.za/news/south-africa/western-cape/watch-bishops-matric-class-calls-out-systemic-oppression-racism-49085271

Vally, Salim (2007) 'From People's Education to neo-liberalism in South Africa', *Review of African Political Economy*, Vol. 34, No. 111, pp. 39–56.

Vasquez, R. (2022). You just need more resilience: Racial gaslighting as "Othering". *Journal of Critical Thought and Praxis*, *11*(3).

Xaso, Lwando. (2021) 'Institutional-racism: The-real-price of admission to white schools too high for black kids' https://www.dailymaverick.co.za/opinionista/2021-06-05

Chapter 11

Japanese Folk Performing Arts as Community Resilience

Maho Araki

1. Introduction – Application of Community Resilience to Folk Performing Arts Study

Continuity and succession are major topics in traditional music and the performing arts. Many traditional music and performing arts around the world continue to pass on their traditions, adapting to different circumstances, backgrounds and reasons. There are many ways to achieve this, both at global and local levels. This also applies to Japanese folk performing arts. There are so many different folk performing arts that it is impossible to define them in one word, but here we define folk performing arts as 'performing arts which are inherited from previous generations, especially in the life of local communities, in terms of time, place, and performers, except for professional performing arts which are mainly performed on the stage' (Hyoki 2010). The performers of folk performing arts and the people involved are not professional musicians or performers, but farmers, fishermen or businesspeople working in the area where the performance takes place. Therefore, a folk performing arts community is more like a community of people living in a particular village or area than a community of dance lovers or peers.[1] Folk performing arts are performed by the people of the community and passed on from one generation to another within that community.[2]

There are two main reasons why the institutions and environment surrounding the folk performing arts have changed. One is the change in rituals and religious meanings with the modernisation of Japan. For example, in Japan, folk performing arts, with beating drums and dancing, are used to pray for rain. However, in the modern age of infrastructure, people rarely do so. Thus, performers are sometimes unsure of what they are performing in terms of folk beliefs. Performers often give passive reasons for folk performing arts such as 'because it is an ancestral art' or 'because it is a routine annual event in this area'. We often hear of people who continue to do it for social reasons, such as 'it is a folk performing art with a long history and tradition, so my generation cannot discontinue it (because it would damage community relationships)'. This is partly due to the problems of the Japanese system in protecting their cultural heritage through the designation of cultural properties, which is the second reason. When a folk performing art is designated as a cultural asset, in a rather extreme sense it is labelled as having historical value and must be preserved as a cultural property in the ideal form of cultural property administration, or the folk performing arts are utilised as a tourist resource and appear in various events so that they are constantly exposed to the outside world.

Folk performing arts continue to be influenced by external political pressures, such as the imposition of historical and economic values. In addition, what is given by outsiders, especially by cultural property administrations, is often a system and money. For example, outsiders designate folk performing arts as cultural assets and invest money in their communities, or use them as tourist resources. However, are the people involved in the folk performing arts buried in capitalist economic thinking, and are they only at the mercy of this external pressure? No matter how many reasons performers give for their passivity, it is inconceivable that many folk performing arts are continued and passed on by the community of performers to this day.

Helping us advance this discussion of folk performing arts is the concept of resilience. Resilience is often observed in the humanities and social sciences, generally in the context of how well a community responds to external shocks (Beel et al. 2017: 460). The term has since been adapted to a variety of subjects, including the environment, individuals, social systems and communities, thereby producing a variety of definitions. Therefore, the definition and use of the concept of resilience as such remain debatable (Pink and Lewis 2014: 700). Community resilience is usually discussed in the context of resilience to climate change and natural disasters (Skerratt 2013). Japanese folk performing arts have often been discussed in terms of their potential to contribute to the resilience of affected communities after an earthquake (especially the Great East Japan Earthquake in 2011) (Hayashi 2018: 6). However, these debates promote or redress this logic by placing the onus on communities to adapt to the impacts of capitalism, associated tourism, climate change and natural disasters

(MacKinnon and Derickson 2012: 266). The passive or dominant stance of local people and their communities has been questioned, and in reaction, there has recently been a focus on the positive actions of local people and communities (Magis 2010: 405; Kirmayer et al. 2011; Skerratt 2013: 36).

The active work of these local people and their communities is never a 'stability-shock-stability' structure that reacts only during external shocks (Skerratt 2013: 45). The proactivity of their actions continues to vary regardless of the presence or absence of external shocks. In other words, fixating in the discussion of resilience solely on the dominant narrative of shock-related reactive definitions risks unnecessarily limiting the analysis, because it clearly avoids proactive processes and broader adaptive outcomes (Skerratt 2013: 45). We must also consider the possibility that, in the event of an external shock, the community will not only recover to its previous state, but that the shock will also generate new developments within the community. It has already been said that the culture a community possesses in the first place is an active one that creates meaning, identity and form through a historical process (Turner 1997).

It is important to indicate that when we think about the agency of communities, we should not take a monolithic view but also consider their diversity. This shows that there is an asymmetrical network of human decision making and behaviour (Leslie and McCabe 2013: 115). Case studies that examine proactive behaviour and change in terms of resilience tend to analyse the general trends and behaviours of groups or communities (e.g., commercial fishermen). However, these studies do not explicitly focus on variations within these entities in terms of how people respond to challenges and changing circumstances. While behavioural variation is acknowledged, it is seen as transitory, and the consequences of its existence are not considered, partly because it requires long periods of observation and partly because it is difficult to generalise causality within complex systems in the context of historical contingency and path dependence (Leslie and McCabe 2013: 115). However, looking at proactive movements within communities and their changes, it appears that communities tend not to break down existing class distinctions (unequal power relations), but rather strengthen them. In communities, diversity also has multiple scales (individual, family and regional) (Skerratt 2013: 36), and the diversity of responses on one scale may act synergistically or contradictorily with the effects of diversity on the other. Therefore, it is important to focus on the diversity of scales, unequal relationships in the community and gradation of decision making and actions related to it (Leslie and McCabe 2013: 114). Subsequently, it is necessary that referring to resilience within the community is useful in considering the proactive dynamics of the folk performing arts community.

In this regard, we first describe the general impact of the cultural property protection system on the continuation and succession of the Japanese folk performing arts. Second, we consider Iou Jima's *Taiko Odori* and Kesennuma's *Uchibayashi* as concrete examples to investigate the detailed dynamics of the community of folk performing arts, centring on performers and focusing on community resilience, such as diversity of scales, unequal relationships in the community, gradation of decision making and actions related to it. This study does not elaborate on the concept of resilience in the humanities and sociology but rather attempts to reveal new aspects of Japanese folk performing arts practice with some evidence of resilience discussed so far.

2. Protection and Utilisation of Cultural Assets in Japan

In the environment surrounding folk performing arts, there are two external influences: cultural assets and tourism resources (Hashimoto 2016: 123). Regarding cultural assets, the position of preserving folk performing arts in their 'original' form is assumed. On the other hand, tourism resources are a way to oppose this position and make folk performing arts correspond to modern society, to promote tourism and commercialisation for the promotion of local products, and to utilise them (Kawamura 2015: 114). This legal system of 'preservation' through cultural property designation, and 'utilisation' as a tourist resource appeared alternatively in post-war Japan. The law for the Protection of Cultural Property, which gave rise to the present designation of folk cultural property, was passed in 1950, and thereafter, the 'preservation' of folk performing arts became a reality in 1975. Subsequently, in the legal system, folk performing arts have been interpreted as 'intangible', protected by certain groups, and regarded as a property to be preserved by the public (Kawamura 2015: 114).[3]

In 1992, a law stipulating the active use of folk performing arts as a tourism resource was passed. It is commonly known as *Omatsuri*

Ho, or festival law. Many local governments have started to use local festivals and folk performing arts as cultural resources to revitalise their communities. Furthermore, in 2001, *Furusato Bunka Rekishi Jigyo*, promoted by the Agency for Cultural Affairs in Japan, allocated hundreds of millions of dollars to each prefecture to promote the use of folk cultural property for local development. The aim was to revive folk events, especially traditional festivals and folk performing arts, as unique local cultural assets and to revitalise the region (Iwamoto 2003: 174). In some areas, according to this *Omatsuri Ho*, folk performing arts were treated as symbols of a specific region. In 2003, the Convention for the Safeguarding of Intangible Cultural Heritage was adopted at the United Nations Educational, Scientific and Cultural Organization (UNESCO) General Conference, and Japanese folk cultural properties and performing arts were confronted with the global situation of cultural protection. In this way, through the historical changes of the legal system, Japanese folk performing arts have repeatedly been involved in the superficial conflict of 'preservation' and 'utilisation', and under the contemporary legal system, they are at the mercy of the contradictory policy directions of 'preservation' and 'utilisation'. Folk performing arts have been brought into the global negotiation of intangible cultural heritage.

However, it has been argued that folk performing arts are not at the mercy of such laws and are required to change within them. Rather, they respond to the laws and reinterpret and use them in their own positive ways. In modern Japanese society, people's occupations and lifestyles have changed, as have the communities where folk performing arts are held and the meaning of folk performing arts. For example, people dance or sing to pray for a good harvest in areas where agriculture used to be prosperous, but because of urban development, agriculture is no longer practised in the area, and the belief of praying for a good harvest has changed. Performers of such folk performing arts have accepted that they have become tourist resources through the designation of cultural property and *Omatsuri Ho*, and they seek a way for their folk performing arts to survive by utilising them as a tourist attraction (Thornbury 1994). Alternatively, folk performing arts, designated as national intangible folk cultural properties, are protected by a system backed by the essentialist discourse of folk cultural property and accept the meanings given to them by others, but performer's practices do not conform to the meanings expected by others. Performers practise based on their own interpretations and continue to develop new ones. This is because, after the period of high economic growth in Japan of the 1970s, folk performing arts were re-contextualised in new social relations, and the practitioners themselves were looking for new meaning in their performing arts. In addition, many communities of folk performing arts say that to continue, they sometimes emphasise belief as a strategy to make the value of their performing arts recognised by outsiders, such as cultural property administration, researchers and the media (Hyoki 1997). UNESCO's intangible cultural heritage has also been reported to impact folk culture. It has been reported that the form of performance has changed in part because a folk culture was inscribed on the representative list of intangible cultural heritage in 2009. And the people involved felt more confident about continuing folk culture, which encouraged them to continue (Foster 2011: 90). In other cases, community members can seek self-representation on the internet while cleverly appropriating messages from the mass media (Kawamura 2001: 687).

The passive or dominant stance of the local people and their communities has been questioned, and recently, the focus has been on the positive actions of local people and communities.[4] This has also been reported in previous studies of folk performing arts. However, these reports are in the context of cultural property and tourism resources versus community people, and the people of the folk performing arts community are viewed as making only one decision or action within a single community, in a monolithic manner. However, in reality, there are several levels of decision making. As indicated in the discussion on resilience, the community of performers is diverse, with multiple scales, such as individuals, specific generations and newcomers, and the importance of capturing different scales of movement within the community has been proposed. Nevertheless, especially in the last 20 years, the number of performers has been decreasing worldwide owing to an aging population, a declining birth rate and young people moving to urban areas.

Thus, recently, the practice of folk performing arts has become more concerned with the actions of the individual rather than the group. Furthermore, in terms of resilience, the social context in which folk performing arts are practised continues to change, as indicated previously. It is assumed that the folk performing arts community is changing because of various factors, both inside and outside the community. When we consider this community, we should not focus on the impact of only one shock or disaster; we must consider the factors that have affected the community diachronically and synchronically. The following section examines specific case studies.

3. Case Studies

3.1. Taiko Odori in Iou Jima

First, employment on Iou Jima relates to the practice of performing arts.[5] Iou Jima is a small island with approximately 120 residents located in Kagoshima Prefecture, southern Japan. At the height of its population, there were approximately 600 people, but when the island's mines closed, there was no longer any employment for the islanders, who then left in search of jobs. Since then, the population has fallen drastically, and today only a few people live on the island. Currently, thanks to the government's efforts to attract newcomers from all over Japan, the ratio of newcomers to those born and raised on islands has increased. However, in Kagoshima Prefecture, which has 26 inhabited islands, Iou Jima is one of the smallest in terms of population and area and is, therefore, not well known or recognised even within the prefecture. The basic means of transport to Iou Jima is ferry. The ferry brings people and goods from mainland Japan four days per week, and it takes approximately four hours to travel from the port in the city of Kagoshima to Iou Jima. However, on windy days, when the sea is choppy and the ferry is cancelled, Iou Jima is often cut off from both the mainland and the rest of the islands.

Work on Iou Jima is essential to the livelihood of islanders, who all engage in their share of activities. Many of the essential jobs are not done by contractors from outside the island and who come to live on the island, but by islanders who share their jobs with workers from the town hall. Only a few are involved in animal husbandry, work individually in the field or fish for their own consumption. Because of the small island population, everyone knows each other, and one islander says that they are like 'one family', sharing the good and the bad. They also keep a close eye on the working attitudes of others to ensure that they contribute equally. They clean roads on the island several times a year by themselves. It is a rule that all islanders must participate and those who do not are seen as not being supportive. This is due to the isolation of the island and the limited number of people who must protect it.

In the summer,[6] islanders organise two days of folk performing art called *Taiko Odori* (a drumming dance), which is performed by ten men. *Taiko Odori* was said to have originated approximately 420 years ago when a war broke out, and three islanders saved the feudal lord and won the war. As a result, the feudal lord gave them this dance to celebrate their triumph. The performance consists of one person who plays a gong and sings a song (*Kaneuchi*), and ten people who each wear a drum on their abdomen and beat it with both hands (*Odoriko*). The drummers form a circle around *Kaneuchi*. *Kaneuchi* is the leader of the group, and the ten *Odoriko* listen to the sound of the gong and the song while they dance and beat drums simultaneously. The dance is very bold and the drummers wear decorated bamboo on their backs, which they twist while they shout at the same time. These performers dance in front of a shrine on the island for about two hours each day, starting at about 5 p.m. On the second day, after the dance, the performers go around the island in a line beating the gongs and drums. During *Taiko Odori*, there are also masked gods called *Mendon*, who wear striking masks unlike those usually seen in Japan, obscuring who they actually are and making them appear like gods from another world. When performers sing and dance, *Mendon* runs around, hitting the heads and bodies of the spectators with branches. At the end of the second day, when the performers finish dancing in front of the shrine, *Mendon* and performers line up and walk around the island, beating their gongs and drums as they go from house to house. The purpose of this is to collect all the bad luck on the island with the branches carried by *Mendon*. Finally, they go to the beach, where the performers walk toward the sea beating their gongs and drums, and *Mendon* shakes the branches furiously, sweeping all bad luck away from the island.

Taiko Odori was designated as an intangible folk cultural property in Kagoshima Prefecture in 1989. *Mendon* was inscribed on the list of UNESCO intangible cultural heritage in 2018 as part of *Raiho-Shin*, ritual visits of deities in masks and costumes. In particular, since the inscription of *Mendon* on this list, the performing arts of this small island have attracted attention both inside and outside. *Taiko Odori* and *Mendon* were grouped together and introduced to the outside world. However, since only *Mendon* has been included in intangible cultural heritage, it has gained attention and increased recognition. The performing arts day is one of the busiest tourism days on the island, with TV stations and journalists coming from outside the island to see the 'strange festival', in which *Mendon* appears. Many sightseeing tourists join the islanders to watch *Taiko Odori* and *Mendon* (*Mendon* is the main attraction). As there are few other tourist attractions in Iou Jima, the government began to promote *Mendon* as an island's signature resource. In particular, the government has treated *Mendon* as if it were representing the image of the island and has moved away from its character as *Raiho-Shin*. Since *Mendon* became a UNESCO intangible cultural heritage site, it has been invited to many events outside the island. As a result, *Taiko Odori* and *Mendon* have been increasingly performed outside the island's religious context.

However, in reality, the islanders have not been distracted by these developments but rather reacted to them with their own interpretations and logic. On the day of the performance, the islanders explained to the tourists and journalists who came to the island about *Taiko Odori* and the shrines related to *Mendon* until the time of the performance. The explanations include the significance of *Mendon* (to ward off bad luck), the origin of the drum dance, the dedication and belief of *Mendon* masks at the shrine, and taboos, such as not crossing in front of the shrine or entering the shrine during the performance. In addition, islanders introduced the history, culture, and geography of the island by showing its monuments. At the beginning of the tourist performance, islanders announce through a loudspeaker, 'We are going to perform (*Taiko Odori*). Please clap your hands to support us.' Afterwards, the islanders and tourists sit on the same rush mat and watch *Taiko Odori* while drinking and eating together. *Mendon* runs around, hitting all spectators with branches, regardless of whether they are islanders, tourists or media members. The islanders are not just using performing arts as a tourist resource to meet the expectations of people from outside the island, but they also introduce the island's geography, history and culture in a strategic way to make the various aspects of the island better known and raise its profile. In reality, the emphasis placed on explaining the origin and beliefs of the arts to people outside the island is not only to make the arts more accessible to them but also to reaffirm the meaning of these arts for the islanders themselves. Since *Taiko Odori* and *Mendon* were designated as cultural assets and intangible cultural heritage, they have tended to be seen by the outside world as more of a 'strange festival.' However, when the festival is held annually on the island, unlike events held off the island, islanders are more concerned with religious aspects. The masks of *Mendon* are purified at a shrine before the performance begins; those playing *Mendon* appear as gods, and performers bathe in seawater and drink sake to purify their bodies before singing and dancing. *Mendon* and performers eventually gather all the bad luck on the island and drive it away. As islanders are required to perform at events outside the island, the meaning of the performance could easily be forgotten, and by explaining the religious aspects of the performance with tourists and other visitors, the performers themselves can reaffirm the value of their beliefs and the meaning of their performance.

The above shows that the islanders have expanded their interpretation in response to external stimuli, such as cultural heritage and the influence of tourism, and developed their own performing arts. However, at another level, Iou Jima's performing arts practices are driven by very different community logic. In *Taiko Odori*, only men over the age of 12 years are eligible to participate. Nevertheless, only ten men who qualified were able to dance. The ten men tend to be chosen with a preference for those who are natives of the island and have watched and learned *Taiko Odori* from a young age, but they are chosen for more than just their dancing ability. Iou Jima is a small island with only a handful of inhabitants who live together as 'one family', sharing the island's work and helping each other. This means that daily cooperation between islanders is essential. As the island is often hit by typhoons, islanders clean up after the typhoons and share food when a ferry is unavailable. Therefore, it is unfavorable to have uncooperative islanders when such events occur. It may have taken only one such instance to make them unpopular. If a person is left alone, the relationship between him and other islanders deteriorates. However, this would mean that the island would also lose valuable community members; therefore, the dilemma is that the person should not be left alone. Therefore, key people, such as the community head, try to compensate for the lack of cooperation by daring islanders to participate in *Taiko Odori*. Islanders who choose to perform are generally not afraid to say no. They dance with other islanders to practise *Taiko Odori*, and on the day of the event, they dance together to try to repair their relationship.

In some cases, newcomers are recommended to become performers. Of course, they have little or no experience with *Taiko Odori* and may not dance well. They may only have partial relationships with islanders, and recently, newcomers have increasingly worked with people from outside, for example, online, rather than doing essential work on the island, so they may not be involved in many things on the island and may be seen as contributing very little. However, these newcomers are important workers on the island and other islanders want to build good relationships with them. Therefore, by performing *Taiko Odori* in front of the islanders, who see them as spectators, they demonstrate their participation in island events, which helps them become accepted as islanders. As their numbers increase, newcomers must cooperate and work with islanders in everyday life. However, these newcomers often receive the most attention and preferential treatment from outside the island, and the people born there have a strong desire to be respected as among the few original island residents. As islanders have been watching and performing *Taiko Odori* since childhood, they have more experience and skill than newcomers. For this reason, islanders are given priority as performers of *Taiko Odori*, and stand out from the crowd. In this way, they try to maintain the honour and prestige of being islanders. Furthermore, *Mendon* attracts more attention externally than the performers of *Taiko Odori*, but if one looks at the order of the performers and *Mendon* on the island, one will see that after the 10 performers have been chosen, the people who were not chosen would be given the roles of *Mendon*. In fact, on the island, performers of *Taiko Odori* are more important than those of *Mendon* in the selection of roles. On the day of the event, only performers are given preferential treatment such as being offered food. Therefore, being chosen as a performer is considered a greater honour than being chosen as a *Mendon*. This is another aspect of the logic of the community on the island that differs from the perceptions of people outside the island.

Thus, in Iou Jima, the emphasis on the historical and religious significance of *Taiko Odori* is not only to meet the expectations of tourists and the media and to raise the profile of the island by becoming a cultural and intangible heritage site but also to reaffirm the meaning of the dances for the community itself. While the Iou Jima community has been able to take advantage of the power and economy outside the island, it has also worked to improve and repair individual relationships in everyday life so that they can live better in their own society.

The island is a society and a community. Regarding the diversity within it, we need to focus on constant changes in some communities. The location of the next case study is Kesennuma City, which was affected by the Great East Japan earthquake in 2011. The recovery of folk performing arts communities in the affected areas and their ability to resume performing arts have been noted and seen as 'resilience'. However, we discovered that it was not because of the external shock of the disaster that they were able to cope, and that the performing arts changed. Looking at the medium- and long-term situation before and after the disaster, folk performing arts and their communities had already responded to and changed before the disaster.

3.2 *Uchibayashi* in Kesennuma

Kesennuma is a city located in the northeastern corner of Miyagi Prefecture in the Tohoku region of Japan. As of December 12, 2020, the population of Kesennuma was 61,520.[7] Kesennuma's core industry is fishing, which has long been a base for pelagic and offshore fishing, attracting boats from all over the country. In Kesennuma, many communities play music called *Uchibayashi*.[8] *Uchibayashi* community includes people living in each village of the city. In other words, communities in villages are divided into administrative divisions. *Uchibayashi* is performed at festivals and celebratory community events, mainly to pray for the safety of fishing boats, a good catch, a good harvest, mountain gods, rain and other forms of good fortune. The music is mainly played on drums and Japanese bamboo flutes. In some villages, music is associated with tiger dance (an art form in which two people play the role of a tiger wearing a tiger's head and cape) and the Seven Deities of Good Luck. It is thus considered a form of good luck. Historically, the origins of *Uchibayashi* are unknown, but it has been said to have existed in some villages since the 1700s and in others since the 1900s. In the 1940s, a major change occurred during and after the Second World War, when many *Uchibayashi* communities were suspended or forced to close down. Many communities were revived during the 1970s and the 1980s. However, there was a long period before the revival, and some communities lost their ability to play *Uchibayashi*, in which case communities in neighbouring villages taught their own *Uchibayashi*.

Currently, approximately 40 communities in Kesennuma have their own *Uchibayashi*. Most communities have music similar to *Uchibayashi*. However, these common tunes were played slightly differently in each community, with each community adding its own twist to the base music, drum rhythm, tempo and flute melody. Each community prides itself on having a different twist to the common music, and until recently it was not easily taught to people outside the community. Today, there are two main types of *Uchibayashi* community: Traditional *Taiko* and Creative *Taiko*. Traditional *Taiko* is a community-based form of *Taiko* (drum) that is based in a single village and associated with the beliefs of its inhabitants. Performance teaching has been conducted for generations in that community. In some Traditional *Taiko* communities, there are strict restrictions on who can perform, such as being related only to family lineage or being the eldest son in the community. Some Traditional *Taiko* have been designated as cultural property by Miyagi Prefecture and Kesennuma City and are attracting attention as historic and prestigious musical performances from both inside and outside the city. Creative *Taiko* is not based on a particular village, but is created by *Taiko* enthusiasts from across villages. Unlike Traditional *Taiko*, which is associated with religious beliefs, creative drumming is more performative and technical, with more upbeat drumming techniques that have been created in recent years by relatively young people who have descended from traditional drummers. Occasionally, Creative *Taiko* performers try to hone their skills by taking lessons from professional drummers outside Kesennuma. As Creative *Taiko* is not based in a village, it has been performed at newly organised events in Kesennuma and beyond; thus, the drumming itself is not linked to any religious beliefs, such as praying for safe voyages or fishing. Creative *Taiko* was based on the arrangement of traditional *Taiko* music and its original composition. However, it was generally taboo for Traditional *Taiko* performers to participate in Creative *Taiko*. The reverse was also true. It was unthinkable for a member of a Traditional *Taiko* to join another Traditional *Taiko* community. The 2000s witnessed the emergence of a derivative community in Middle *Taiko* (a name given for convenience by the author). These were originally Traditional *Taiko* communities; however, as generations passed within the community, the younger generation adopted the elements of a more performative style of Creative *Taiko*. The Middle

Taiko community is based in a particular village, but its performance style is influenced by Creative *Taiko*.

Although the Traditional, Creative and Middle *Taiko* communities are usually compartmentalised, there is one occasion a year when they all come together, *Minato Matsuri* festival. This two-day festival, held in August, attracts many people from all over Kesennuma. The festival was initially started to revitalise the community during post-war reconstruction and is not based on any religious beliefs, but is more of an event that is now part of the tourism policy to promote Kesennuma to the outside world. *Uchibayashi* was held on the second day of the festival with approximately 20 communities participating each year (27 communities in 2019). All *Uchibayashi* communities lined up along the harbour road and simultaneously played the same music. They formed a line approximately 300 m long, and the sight of them beating their drums in unison was overwhelming. The participating communities included traditional, creative and middle drummers, and all communities were allowed to play in their own style as long as they played at the same speed. Some communities may slightly alter their original playing styles to match their speed. However, some players of Traditional *Taiko*, which is designated as a cultural property, refuse to play together with Creative *Taiko* and do not take part in the festival. Since 2008, they have had practice sessions open to the whole community: Traditional, Creative and Middle drummers. The aim of these sessions, which occurred regularly throughout the year, was to improve drumming skills during the run-up to the festival. By that stage, the Traditional *Taiko* community had been affected by the declining birth rate and aging population, which has become a serious problem throughout Japan. Some Traditional *Taiko* communities have made the difficult decision to expand their membership outside the village and have included people from other communities as performers. Thus, the *Uchibayashi* community has changed at multiple levels. Simultaneously, however, there was still division between these communities within the festival. At the festival, before *Uchibayashi*'s joint performance, there was time to introduce Traditional *Taiko* in 2008, Creative *Taiko* in 2009 and Middle *Taiko* in 2010. In addition, the arrangement of each community's performance at the festival was decided so that Traditional *Taiko*, with the longest history, would be the most prominent in the centre of the line, while Creative *Taiko* and Middle *Taiko* would be at the ends of the line.

Approximately six months later, on 11 March 2011, the Great East Japan Earthquake occurred, and Kesennuma was hit by the tsunami. These natural disasters were reported as shocking natural disasters not only in Japan but also globally. Many people were affected by the tsunami, including the members of the *Uchibayashi* community. The tsunami also swept away houses, forcing residents to move to other villages with temporary housing or outside Kesennuma. In sea-facing communities, musical instruments, tools, and costumes were washed away by the tsunami. Consequently, *Uchibayashi* community activities and the festival were cancelled, and some *Uchibayashi* communities were forced to disband. However, it should be noted that some of the disbanded communities, particularly Traditional *Taiko* communities, had been short of players before the disaster because of low birth rates and an aging population, which made it even more difficult for them to get together. The festival resumed in 2013; since the revival of the festival, there has been a new movement in the *Uchibayashi* community. For example, some performers in the disbanded Traditional *Taiko* group reunited to form a new Creative *Taiko* community. One of the oldest Traditional *Taiko* communities had previously been open only to village residents; however, after the earthquake, they welcomed people who had moved to the area, including the village, to work or volunteer in the aftermath of the disaster. The Middle *Taiko* community also welcomed members who stayed temporarily in the area for work related to the earthquake, and technical trainees from Indonesia.

This has helped blur the lines between Traditional, Creative and Middle *Taiko*. The festival also saw people who were forced to move out of Kesennuma because of the disaster and returned to Kesennuma on festival days to perform in these communities. The need to separate communities before the disaster is less important. As the number of performers continues to change, the Middle *Taiko* community gradually grows. Furthermore, Traditional *Taiko* performers joined the Creative *Taiko* community in ways previously considered taboo.

4. Folk Performing Arts as Community Resilience

We examined two case studies. We will now return to the resilience debate and discuss the findings of these studies. The first point is that in both cases, folk performing arts communities not only respond passively to shocks and pressures from outside the community but also actively work to transform them into the logic of the community. In Iou Jima, *Taiko Odori* was designated as an intangible folk cultural asset by Kagoshima Prefecture, and *Mendon* was inscribed in the UNESCO intangible cultural heritage list, attracting the attention of the wider world and demands from outside the island for performances of these 'strange festivals'. In addition, the island is trying to use *Mendon* as a resource to the extent that a tour company organises a sightseeing tour on the day a performance is held. However, islanders are also keen to promote Iou Jima to people outside the island by introducing them to the island's history, geography, landmarks and performing arts. However, the islanders themselves, by repeatedly explaining the historical origins and beliefs of the performance to tourists and the media, have been able to change their perceptions of their own performance. The islanders also attempted to reaffirm the significance of this performance. In addition, participating (or being able to participate) in the performing arts is a way for the islanders, who all work together as a community on one island, to improve and repair their individual relationships in their daily lives and to visualise and reconfirm their current social relationships through the act of choosing and being chosen as performers. This is also an opportunity for islanders to improve their lives in island societies. This is thus a survival strategy for the islanders, one not directly linked to external factors but to proactive community logic.

In Kesennuma, some Traditional *Taiko* were designated as cultural property and were differentiated from Creative *Taiko* both within and outside the community. However, some Traditional *Taiko* communities have become Middle *Taiko*, with younger generations taking on the musical elements of Creative *Taiko* rather than a fixed set of properties in terms of membership and performance style. In addition, due to a shortage of performers caused by the declining birth rate and aging population, people from outside the village who were previously not eligible to participate were invited to join as Traditional *Taiko* performers. They were no longer confined to their own communities but also joined the Creative *Taiko* community to perform. In the case of the joint performances of *Uchibayashi* at *Minato Matsuri* festival, there was a demand from outside the community to attract audiences to a joint performance by many communities with the single purpose of revitalising Kesennuma through the festival, away from the context of religious beliefs. While Traditional, Creative and Middle *Taiko* communities all participated in joint performances, the boundaries between these three communities were very clear. Some of these communities chose not to participate in joint performances to differentiate themselves. In the aftermath of the earthquake and tsunami, the communities of Traditional, Creative and Middle *Taiko* decided that they did not wish to return to normal but rather chose to blur the boundaries between themselves so that they could continue to perform, rather than being forced to remain separate. Furthermore, in the festival, the Traditional, Creative and Middle *Taiko* communities began to welcome and perform for people who had been forced to move out of Kesennuma during the disaster, as well as for those who were temporarily staying in the city, making the *Uchibayashi* community more accessible and becoming a receptacle for a wider audience.

Second, the community was not monolithic in its proactive movement but was diverse. In Iou Jima *Taiko Odori*, this is well illustrated by the selection of performers. The selection of dancers by community leaders was based on relationships between people in their daily lives on the island. For example, people who had not previously participated in the clean-up and events of the island and had not been very supportive of the island were chosen as dancers to give them an opportunity to redeem themselves as islanders and not leave out valuable community members. The intention was to provide an environment in which people could easily become part of the island by being selected. The selection of performers was also intended to maintain the pride of the islanders by prioritising those who had been dancing since childhood as the main dancers. Performers were chosen by a number of community members who also wanted them to be selected in a way that would make them more involved and present in the community. Before the performers were chosen, there were glimpses of a mixture of islanders' different intentions in the rehearsals. Accordingly, even when everyone performs the same dance, performer selection is not a monolithic process.

In Kesennuma's *Uchibayashi* community, there has been community reconstruction during the post-war period, the emergence of a community of Creative *Taiko*, a shortage of performers, the recruitment of performers from outside the

Traditional *Taiko* community, a shift in musicality from Traditional *Taiko* to Middle *Taiko* as the younger generation of Traditional *Taiko* takes over, and regular joint training between Traditional *Taiko*, Creative *Taiko* and Middle *Taiko* at the festival. Since the earthquake, communities have changed at several levels. The community did not return to its pre-earthquake state, and the shock of the disaster blurred the boundaries between Traditional *Taiko*, Creative *Taiko* and Middle *Taiko* communities. The changes in the community were not limited to the growing presence of Middle *Taiko*, Traditional *Taiko* members joining the Creative *Taiko* community and people from outside Kesennuma temporarily being accepted into the community to play together at the festival. These are just some of the ways communities interact. These were not monolithic changes, but rather changes at various levels, as communities interacted with each other and as individuals and generations within a community changed. These results also show that change involves unexpected and contingent factors owing to the intersection of people.

Third, the community does not have a 'stability–shock–stability' structure, where the community changes only in response to the stimulus of external elements but changes continuously with or without such stimulus. In the case of Iou Jima, the changes were not only that *Mendon* became a UNESCO intangible cultural heritage and that the island's survival strategy was to make the whole island more externally appealing in addition to its performing arts. The logic of the community was that an annual performance, even before it became an intangible cultural heritage, was an opportunity to improve and enhance the social relations of islanders. Alternatively, since the 2000s, as the number of newcomers has increased, there has been an opportunity to reaffirm or reinforce relationships within the island community, preserving the pride of islanders. External stimuli are not the only source of change in the community; members of the community also make active and regular changes.

In the case of *Uchibayashi* in Kesennuma, the response to a major external shock, the Great East Japan Earthquake, was noteworthy. This is because many folk performing arts were restarted about six months or one year later, and it is very rare worldwide that local culture, especially folk performing arts, is highlighted quickly after a disaster. Folk performing arts are said to have performed as an essential item for the village to be established as a region, which was a turning point in reviewing the Japanese folk performing arts. It is true that, in the case of *Uchibayashi*, the community seems to have changed its form after the earthquake and continued to respond flexibly to the external shock of the disaster. However, as we can see from previous studies, discussions of the themes of earthquake and folk performing arts tend to focus on the post-earthquake period. The case study of Kesennuma shows that the *Uchibayashi* community not only changed in response to the post-disaster shock but also that there was a continuous change from before to after the disaster. These changes have already been discussed under the first two headings, but the changes in the *Uchibayashi* community had already occurred at multiple levels before the earthquake owing to internal and external factors, and the disaster occurred in the midst of these changes. The disaster undoubtedly had a significant impact on the *Uchibayashi* community, but it was not the only external shock and could be seen as an external stimulus over a longer period. The resumption of folk performing arts after the disaster has been described as reconstruction, a change back to its original form, but in fact, the disaster was a shock that led to the new development of the community.

5. Toward a New Situation of Folk Performing Arts

There has already been a focus on how folk performing arts communities respond to or change in response to external influences, such as designation as cultural property, inscription on the list of representatives of intangible cultural heritage, social phenomena such as declining birth rates and aging populations, and natural phenomena such as earthquakes. This study draws on the debate on resilience – in particular, the debate on community resilience – to provide a deeper and clearer picture of community change. In terms of Iou Jima's *Taiko Odori* and Kesennuma's *Uchibayashi* communities, we can see that they are not only responding to external influences and being played by them, but also that community members reinterpret them and perform folk performing arts independently, or actively perform folk performing arts according to their own logic, regardless of external stimuli. The factors of change in the community are both external and internal, and they cause continuous changes in the community. To date, folk performing arts have tended to be described in terms of a single factor, but by examining various factors that are continuous over time, we can understand the changes in a more three-dimensional manner. In addition, the community, which has been regarded as monolithic, is changing at several levels, such as the diverse intentions of people in the community, unbalanced relationships, differences between generations and interactions between communities. These points can provide clues regarding the future succession of folk performing arts. We did not examine the concept of resilience itself, but by examining folk performing arts communities and their practices from the viewpoint of resilience, we believe that we can highlight the possibility of examining cultural resilience in the future.[9]

Nowadays, folk performing arts are often cancelled or postponed owing to COVID-19. Opportunities for community members to gather are lost, and successors cannot be fostered because of lack of practice. It is said that the continuation and succession of the performing arts is in jeopardy. In addition, even if the performances could be held, the community would have to give a new meaning to 'driving away COVID-19', reinterpreting the art and emphasising this as a belief. Based on this discussion, COVID-19 can be viewed as an external shock. However, when we think about the practice of folk performing arts, we should not only look at the big impact of COVID-19 but also other factors, continuous changes and the diversity of people in the community, as discussed in this paper. In this regard, we trust that this paper will be meaningful and suggestive of the current situation and future succession of the folk performing arts.

Notes

[1] Some folk performing arts are called folk performing arts even if they are performed professionally, and many folk performing arts are performed under different conditions, mainly due to the recent decrease in the number of children and the aging population in rural areas. For details of the types of folk performing arts available in English, see Lancashire (2013).

[2] 'Community' is such an important term that it has become a major topic in the humanities and sociology, so much so that there is a debate over the definition of 'community'. However, a discussion of community here would be outside the theme of this article and will therefore be left to another article. As indicated in the text, we define a community as basically a group of people living in a particular area, such as a village.

[3] In Japan, there are separate designations for cultural property at the municipal, prefectural and national levels.

[4] In some ethnographic and ethnomusicological disciplines, traditional music of indigenous peoples is judged by outsiders with mixed cultural and economic values, and ownership disputes may arise. This is considered an example of resilience (Titon 2016; Klisala 2019). The similarities with previous studies of folk performing arts are visible in the fact that the practitioners are affected (strategically) to continue against various external pressures. However, these tend to be written as activist proposals rather than the practices of the people concerned.

[5] The study period on Iwo Jima was from 31 July to 2 November 2020.

[6] The festival is held every year on 1 and 2 August in the lunar calendar, which is different every year now that the new solar calendar is in use.

[7] Research in Kesennuma has been carried out intermittently since 2017.

[8] The statements regarding *Uchibayashi* before the disaster are based on Aizawa et al. (2013), Tsuchitori et al. (2015) and Tsuchitori et al. (2016).

[9] Cultural resilience has not been in focus of as much discussion as social or ecological resilience (Bollig 2014: 276). It is said cultural resilience could be defined as a "set of contextually relative attributes (thoughts, behaviors, knowledges, resources) that intersect across different social networks, scales and institutions within lifetimes, across generations and through historical time" (Bollig 2014: 276). This paper could have presented a set of such attributes.

References

Aizawa, T., Saito, R., Tsuchitori, T. and Umeya, K. (2013) 'Research Note of Intangible Folk Cultural Properties in Kesennuma City (1)', *Study and Education of Regional Design*, No. 4, pp. 22–40 (in Japanese).

Beel, E. D., Wallace D. C., Webster G, Nguyen H, Tait, Elizabeth., Macleod M. and Mellish C. (2017) 'Cultural resilience: The production of rural community heritage, digital archives and the role of volunteers', *Journal of Rural Studies*, No. 54, pp. 459–468.

Bollig, M. (2014) 'Resilience: Analytical tool, bridging concept or development goal? Anthropological perspectives on the use of a border object', *Zeitschrift für Ethnologie*, No. 139, pp. 253–279.

Foster, M. (2011) 'The UNESCO effect: Confidence, defamiliarization, and a new element in the discourse on a Japanese island', *Journal of Folklore Research*, Vol. 48, No. 1, pp. 63–107.

Hashimoto, H. (2016) 'The sociality of intangible folk cultural properties: The location of folk performing arts in contemporary Japan', *Bulletin of the Faculty of Regional Development Studies, Otemon Gakuin University*, No. 1, pp. 121–131 (in Japanese).

Hayashi, I. (2018) 'Disaster research after the Great East Japan Earthquake: Toward collaboration between anthropology and other studies', *Minpaku Tsushin*, No. 161, pp. 4–9 (in Japanese).

Hyoki, S. (1997) 'Effects of government policies for the preservation of folk performing arts: A case study from Bitchu Kagura', *Studies on Folkloric Performing Arts*, No. 25, pp. 42–63 (in Japanese).

Hyoki, S. (2010) *Shinji to Geino no Genzai* [Shinto Ritual and Performing Arts in Present], in Kanda Yoriko and Hyoki Satoru (eds), *Minzoku Shojiten Shinji to Geino* [Folk Encyclopedia of Shinto Ritual and Performing Arts] Tokyo: Yoshikawa Kobunkan (in Japanese).

Iwamoto, M. (2003) 'Folklorism and cultural nationalism: Modern Japanese cultural policy and the desire for continuity', *Bulletin of the Folklore Society of Japan*, No. 236, pp. 172–188 (in Japanese).

Kawamura, K. (2001) 'Representation of "Folkway" on television and reception by represented people', *Bulletin of the National Museum of Japanese History*, No. 91, pp. 673–691 (in Japanese with English abstract).

Kawamura, K. (2015) 'Changes in the "preservation" and "utilization" of folk culture: A case study of festivals and folk performing arts', *Bulletin of the National Museum of Japanese History*, No. 193, pp. 113–152 (in Japanese with English abstract).

Kirmayer, L. J., Dandeneau, S., Marshall, E., Phillips. M. K. and Williamson, K. J. (2011) 'Rethinking resilience from indigenous perspective's', *Canadian Journal of Psychiatry*, Vol. 56, No. 2, pp. 84–91.

Klisala, H. (2019) 'Sustainability and indigenous aesthetics: Musical resilience in Sámi and Indigenous Canadian Theatre', *Yearbook for Traditional Music*, No. 51, pp. 17–48.

Lancashire, T. (2013) 'What's in a Word? Classifications and Conundrums in Japanese Folk Performing Arts' *Asian Music*, Vol.44, No.1, pp.33–70.

Leslie, P. and McCabe, T. J. (2013) 'Response diversity and resilience in social-ecological systems', *Current Anthropology*, Vol. 54, No. 2, pp. 114–144.

MacKinnon, D. and Derickson, D. K. (2012) 'From resilience to resourcefulness: A critique of resilience policy and activism', *Progress in Human Geography*, Vol. 37, No. 2, pp. 253–270.

Magis, K. (2010) 'Community resilience: An indicator of social sustainability', *Society & Natural Resources*, Vol. 23, No. 5, pp. 401–416.

Mishima Village Editing Committee (ed.) (1992) *Mishima-Sonshi* [Mishima Village History], Kagoshima: Asahi-Insatsu (in Japanese).

Pink, S. and Lewis, T. (2014) 'Making resilience: Everyday affect and global affiliation in Australian slow cities', *Cultural Geographies*, Vol. 21, No. 4, pp. 695–710.

Skerratt, S. (2013) 'Enhancing the analysis of rural community resilience: Evidence from community land ownership', *Journal of Rural Studies*, No. 31, pp. 36–46.

Thornbury, B. (1994) 'The Cultural Properties Protection Law and Japan's folk performing arts', *Asian Folklore Studies*, Vol. 53, No. 2, pp. 211–225.

Titon, J. T. (2016) 'Orality, commonality, commons, sustainability, and resilience', *The Journal of American Folklore*, Vol. 129, No. 514, pp. 486–497.

Tsuchitori, T., Aizawa, T. and Umeya, K. (2015) 'Research note of intangible folk cultural properties in Kesennuma City (2)', *Study and Education of Regional Design*, No. 6, pp. 52–62 (in Japanese).

Tsuchitori, T., Aizawa, T., Umeya, K. and Shoji, Y. (2016) 'Research note of intangible folk cultural properties in Kesennuma City (3)', *Study and Education of Regional Design*, No. 7, pp. 75–83 (in Japanese).

Turner, T. (1997) 'Human Rights, Human Difference: Anthropology's Contribution to an Emancipatory Cultural Politics', *Journal of Anthropological Research*, Vol.53, No.3, pp.273–291.

Websites

'Mishima Village Overview and Tourism' http://mishimamura.com/gaiyoukankou/ (accessed: 9 January 2021).

'Kesennuma City: Population and Number of Households'https://www.kesennuma.miyagi.jp/sec/s021/010/020/H28-9/20161014163117.html (accessed: 28 June 2020)

Chapter 12

Resilience to Village Depopulation: A Case Study of the S Village Festival in Sado City of Niigata Prefecture, Japan

Toshiki Tsuchitori

Introduction

In general, the concept of resilience is often used in the context of recovery and response, regarding sudden shocks (e.g., natural disasters). Particularly, in Japan in recent years, much active research has linked the reconstruction efforts after the 2011 Great East Japan Earthquake, with resilience.[1] However, the concept of resilience has been used in a wide range of areas which will be discussed later. This concept can be used in the context of short-term events (e.g., natural disasters) or long-term conditions.

This chapter focuses on resilience in long-term conditions. In particular, we consider the relationship between resilience and the ongoing phenomenon of depopulation in Japanese village societies. Village depopulation creates a long-term shock within the system. Our research site, S Village in Sado City, Niigata Prefecture, Japan (as discussed in this chapter), has suffered from several typical depopulation effects, and is in a marginal village state (a detailed explanation follows). If the current situation of S Village is anything to go by, it is highly possible that this village will disappear in the future. However, the people of S Village have begun to utilise new performing arts methods at the S festival. This addition was not made to attract tourists or migrants. This change was introduced by some residents and was not a planned or expected one. Thus, we may ask: 'Why did the people of S Village decide to make this seemingly pointless change?'

This chapter considers the concept of resilience with regard to depopulation by using the case of the S Festival in the S village of Sado Island, Niigata Prefecture, Japan.

Resilience Concepts

There is no uniform definition for resilience (Shiozaki and Kato 2012: 645). Holling (1973) introduced the concept of resilience as a characteristic for ecosystems against environmental changes (Shiozaki and Kato 2012: 643).[2]

Holling clarifies the concept of resilience by comparing it to 'stability' (Hagiwara 2016: 26). Stability refers to that 'which represents the ability of a system to return to an equilibrium state after a temporary disturbance; the more rapidly it returns and the less it fluctuates, the more stable it would be' (Holling 1973: 14). On the other hand, resilience also refers to 'a measure of the persistence of systems and of their ability to absorb charge and disturbance and still maintain the same relationships between populations or state variables' (Holling 1973: 14).

Holling later redefined stability as the engineering of resilience and further elucidated on resilience as an ecological resilience (Shiozaki and Kato 2012: 645). Engineering resilience refers to a system's ability to return to its original state when subjected to certain disturbances. It is measured based on the time taken by a system to return to its original state (Kume, Yamamoto and Shimizu 2016: I_302; Shiozaki and Kato 2012: 644). Ecological resilience refers to a system's ability to absorb environmental changes and maintain its primary properties. This is measured based on the amount of environmental change that the relevant system can tolerate (Kume, Yamamoto and Shimizu 2016: I_302; Shiozaki and Kato 2012: 644).

These resilience concepts assume that a given system's behaviour changes according to environmental changes (Shiozaki and Kato 2012: 643). De Brujin (2005) states that a system in equilibrium exhibits the following four behaviours with respect to environmental changes:

1. The system does not react at all;
2. The system reacts but returns to the equilibrium situation;
3. The system reacts and turns into another stable situation;
4. The system does not return to any stable situation (De Brujin 2005: 21).

Resilience refers to the ability to work within one or two of these above-mentioned behavioural states. According to Holling's (1973) two definitions stated above, engineering resilience refers to resilience that emerges in behaviour 2. Ecological resilience is resilience that works in both behaviours 1 and 2 (Shiozaki and Kato 2012: 644; De Brujin 2005: 22). In short, resilience can be summarised as a given system's ability to absorb shock or its ability to maintain its original function and structure even after receiving a shock (Kume, Yamamoto and Shimizu 2016: I_302). Resilience is considered non-functional if the system becomes unstable after a change in the environment, or if the system is stable but changes to something completely different. Resilience thus also refers to the original system and its ability to maintain its key elements.

Since Holling's (1973) definitions were published, the concept of resilience has been used in ecosystems but has since been applied to socio-ecosystems and social systems as well (Shiozaki and Kato 2012: 643). In this chapter, according to these definitions, resilience is used to refer to the ability to maintain the system itself and the key elements of the system, after it has received a shock.

Village Depopulation in Japan

The term 'depopulation' first began to appear in government documents when Japan achieved high economic growth in the 1960s (Odagiri 2009: 3). It was originally used as an administrative term (Yamashita 2012: 23). The first depopulation measure law, Depopulation Area Emergency Measures Act, was enacted in 1970. Ever since this development, a new depopulation measure law has been coming into force every 10 years (Yamashita 2012: 23–24). An estimated 50 years have passed since depopulation was first regarded as a problem in Japanese villages.

The nature of the depopulation phenomenon occurring in Japanese villages has changed over time. There are two patterns of population decline: 'social decline', which is caused by social factors (e.g., the outflow of young people into the city) and 'natural decline', which is caused by the occurrence of more deaths compared to births.

In Japan, village-level depopulation that occurred from the end of the 1960s till late into the 1970s was predominantly caused by a social decline in the population outflow from villages into cities (Yamashita 2012: 24). Thus, a problem emerged regarding the population gap between cities, which served as inflow destinations for the population, and rural areas, where the population outflow had become severe. However, the 'social decline'-related depopulation problem was temporarily alleviated in the late 1970s. This is because the baby boom generation (*dankai-no-sedai* in Japanese) began to return to their home villages, and thereafter a second baby boom occurred, which alleviated the population decline in depopulated areas (Yamashita 2012: 24).

The depopulation issue in local villages was thus seemingly resolved by reducing depopulation in the latter half of the 1970s. However, in the 1990s, in addition to the conventional 'social decline', depopulation began to occur because of 'natural decline'. This new depopulation phenomenon, which began in the 1990s, was called *shin-kaso* (a new depopulation) (Yamashita 2012: 24). *Shin-kaso* was caused by the aging population left behind in the villages after the youth left for cities and began families in urban areas instead. This phenomenon of depopulation caused by 'natural decline', such as *shin-kaso*, is gradually expanding, unlike the 'social decline' that subsided during the 1990s. This is one of the main factors affecting the current depopulation in Japanese villages (Odagiri 2009: 3–4).

The Marginal Village (*Genkai Shuraku*) and Its Problems

Against this background, the concept of a marginal village (known as *Genkai Shuraku* in Japanese) was advocated by Akira Ohno (2005) in the 1990s. Ohno (2005) explored the current situation of mountain-living villagers and the conservation of natural environments surrounding mountain villages as a research subject. To understand the actual conditions of these mountainous villages, the villagers' living environments were classified into four groups: continuous, semi-marginal, marginal and extinct villages.

A continuous village is one where the percentage of the population under 55 years exceeds 50% and where villagers are reproduced by securing a successor (Ohno 2005: 22). A semi-marginal village is one where the percentage of the population aged over 55 exceeds 50% and one where – although the people living in the village may have been currently secured – securing future successors is becoming difficult (Ohno 2005: 22). A marginal village is one where the number of elderly people aged over 65 exceeds 50% of the total population, and the number of elderly households living alone has increased. Consequently, the function of community activities in the village have weakened, and it is difficult to maintain a communal social life (Ohno 2005: 22–23). An extinct village is one that has literally disappeared because its population and number of houses declined to zero (Ohno 2005: 23). The term 'marginal village' refers to a village that is facing the impending disappearance of its people; hence, it is in a 'marginal' state of existence.

The concept of a 'marginal village' has become widespread in Japan and has been applied to issues beyond mountainous villages.[3] Research has been mainly conducted to grasp the actual conditions of such marginal villages and to recommend the necessary types of measures that should be taken. Thus far, research on marginal villages has proposed mainly two measures. These are the rehabilitation of the village and realistic treatment of the village.

Research advocating the rehabilitation of villages is mainstream in marginal village research. For example, Ohno (2008), a proponent of the concept of marginal villages, said that the marginalisation of mountainous villages would lead to the decline of traditional performing arts and culture, the loss of the original scenery of mountainous villages and poverty in terms of the natural environment. He asserted that 'joint watershed management' is important for the revitalisation of mountainous villages. Specifically, in the upstream, middle and downstream basin social circles, residents of the downstream regions may consider problems of other basins as their own (e.g., the devastation of mountains in the upstream region). Furthermore, it provides multifaceted support to the upstream region and jointly manages the river basin environment and its residents (Ohno 2008: 118). Odagiri (2009) stated that the community forms a particularly important target for rehabilitation measures in rural areas. Odagiri (2009) appealed for the necessity for formation of a 'handmade autonomous district', which is a new community where local residents can have a sense of ownership and work together with local colleagues (Odagiri 2009: 28). These studies have attempted to improve the situation of marginal villages by regenerating and activating them.

New emerging research has explained the importance of dealing realistically with marginal villages in a manner that is different from the rehabilitation of other villages. Hatamoto (2010) suggested enhancing community welfare to maintain the current living conditions of people from marginal villages. Furthermore, Sakuno (2010) advocated *mura-osame*, which provides social and regional care to a village that is expected to disappear, throughout the period from the expected time of functional disappearance to the actual physical disappearance of the village (Sakuno 2010: 16). In such research, it is important to maintain and support the lives of village residents by using measures that match the actual conditions of the marginal villages instead of forcibly regenerating such villages.

In the above-mentioned studies on marginal villages, there were certain differences in the direction and content of the measures; however, it should be noted that here, many of these studies have both grasped the actual situation of the marginal villages and proposed measures for the marginal villages. Ohno, who advocated the concept of marginal villages, also discussed how to grasp its actual conditions and countermeasures. In short, research on marginal villages has been considered village depopulation as a problem – that should be solved through the countermeasures discussed – from the very beginning of its concept.

The concept of marginal villages raises four major criticisms. First, among the two definitions of marginal villages (quantitative and qualitative), only quantitative rules tend to be emphasised. According to Ohno (2008), the definition of the four village divisions – including marginal villages – includes a quantitative regulation based on the age composition of the population and a qualitative regulation on whether the social communal living in the village is maintained (Ohno 2008: 22). For example, in the definition of marginal villages, there is a quantitative rule that the number of elderly people aged over 65 should exceed 50% of the total population and a qualitative rule that the function of community activities in the village must be deteriorated, thus making it difficult to maintain a social communal life (Ohno 2005: 22–23). A village is classified as a marginal village only if both these definitions are met.

However, Yoshioka (2010) and Yamamoto (2014) indicate that they rarely considered both rules when defining marginal villages, often using rules based only on quantitative guidelines that are easy to grasp when conducting village surveys. Ohno (2008), who is the proponent of the concept of marginal village, often uses a quantitative regulation to make a statistical evaluation, because the qualitative regulation of a village can only be grasped through a fact-finding survey. Therefore, when a quantitative grasping of the number of marginal villages is attempted, it is generally performed according to quantitative regulations (Ohno 2008: 22). Hence, the qualitative rule is ignored and the statistical rule that grasps the marginal village by using the quantitative rule is allowed. This tendency has been found to be particularly strong in government surveys.

Second, some local people feel odd about the term 'marginal village'. While it has seen widespread use, many people have expressed the opinion that people can feel uncomfortable about being labelled in this way. This is because the use of the term 'marginal village' may discourage living residents in a village with a declining birthrate and an aging population (Yamamoto 2014). Therefore, certain local governments now use new names to replace the term 'marginal villages'. For example, Yamaguchi Prefecture uses the term 'Small and Aging Villages'. The Nagano Prefecture Ina Regional Office uses the term 'Lifelong Active Villages'. Finally, in Ayabe City of Kyoto Prefecture, the term 'Water source villages' is used (Odagiri 2009: 46). However, this relabelling of marginal villages is not a solution to the problem, and may even obscure it. Therefore, use of the term of 'marginal village' has a certain significance (Odagiri 2009; Yamamoto 2014).

Third, there is no clear basis for emphasising the aging rate when discussing whether the continuation of the village is the limit. According to Yamashita (2012), a 65-year-old may not have any physical disability when he reaches the age of 66. Furthermore, as the average life expectancy has increased, the number of healthy elderly people has also increased. Even at the age of 70, many people may still be engaged in agriculture, forestry and fisheries, and this is not uncommon. Yamashita (2012) states that we must be cautious about the high aging rate and determine whether it is a problem (Yamashita 2012: 28).

In short, he questions the marginal village theory, which posits that, when a higher proportion of villagers is aged over 65, the settlement draws closer to its limit. Yamashita (2012) suggests that a declining birthrate is more important as a factor, than a high aging rate in considering the marginalisation of villages. He believes that it should be regarded as a problem of regional succession between generations (Yamashita 2012: 28). However, because declining birthrates are closely related to aging rates – with a strong negative correlation – it is important to focus on the aging rate as the most convenient index when grasping the phenomenon of depopulation in villages (Yamashita 2012: 28).

Yamamoto (2014) argues that quantitative provisions only are discussed in the definition of marginal villages and that the proponent, Ohno, accepts them. Yamamoto (2014) expresses scepticism about whether the quantitative and qualitative provisions of marginal villages are really connected (Yamamoto 2014: 119); if the number of people aged over 65 exceeds half the population, is it difficult to maintain a social communal life? According to Yamamoto (2014), Ohno's paper provides no such data for exploration. It is difficult to conduct a social survey to confirm this correlation. Ohno submits only correlation between the four village categories and the rate of population change to show that the four categories of villages, including marginal villages, are a meaningful concept. Therefore, the quantitative and qualitative regulations of marginal villages are not correlated (Yamamoto 2014: 119–121).

Fourth, the process of transforming from a marginal village into an extinct village is questionable. According to Ohno's (2005) definition, if the aging rate in a given marginal village continues to increase, it will eventually become an extinct village, and its people will disappear. However, Yoshioka (2010), Yamamoto (2014) and Yamashita (2012) criticised this idea after examining village surveys conducted by the Ministry of Land, Infrastructure, Transport and Tourism in 1999 and 2006. The 1999 surveys suggested that 419 villages would be extinguished within 10 years, but only 61 had actually disappeared by the time of the 2006 survey. In contrast, among villages that were not expected to disappear, approximately 130 villages did (Yoshioka 2010: 18). Based on this, Yoshioka (2010) expressed some uncertainty regarding the criteria for determining marginality because certain villages do survive even if their disappearance has been predicted, while others do not survive even if they did not appear to be limited (Yoshioka 2010: 18).

Moreover, Yamashita (2012) stated that there are no villages that have undergone all the processes of rising aging populations, village marginalisation and their disappearance (Yamashita 2012: 43). According to a survey conducted by the Ministry of Land, Infrastructure, Transport and Tourism in 2006, 191 settlements disappeared in sparsely populated areas in the past seven years. According to Yamashita (2012), the reasons for these disappearances include relocation because of dam and road constructions, group relocation projects and natural disasters. It should be noted that not all villages have disappeared due to communal living to be hindered by aging populations. In contrast, Yamashita (2012) argues that none of the villages said to have disappeared, because of aging, were ever confirmed through investigations (Yamashita 2012: 43). Yamashita (2012) also discussed cases where people had moved out of entire villages before and after the 1960s, and there were certainly villages that disappeared naturally. However, he stated that he could not confirm if the relevant village had disappeared because of an aging population, which occurred thereafter. Thus, the village could not be maintained, and it is doubtful that the marginal village changed into an extinct village (Yamashita 2012: 43).

Based on these marginal village concepts and their criticisms, the following can be said about the marginal village concept. First, the concept of a marginal village is not always precise. As mentioned previously, there are certain quantitative and qualitative rules for applying the marginal village concept. However, a marginal village is often defined based only on certain quantitative rules, and the concept's proponent, Ohno himself, accepts this fact. This means that the marginal village concept is rarely used based on its original meaning. Furthermore, the qualitative provisions necessary for defining the original marginal villages concept differ from the quantitative provisions. As there is no clear definition of this concept, the definition of a marginal village may differ from person to person.

Second, the marginal village concept was created in to emphasise how an aging population can become a social issue. Therefore, the use of the term 'marginal village' should mean that depopulation and aging are considered social problems. However, ever since it spread to the general public, this term has come to be used not only as an analytical concept but also as a real-life concept. Therefore, in fact, it should be noted that the use of the term 'marginal village' does not necessarily mean that depopulation and aging are considered social problems.

An Overview of Sado Island

Thus far, the author has summarised previous studies on resilience and depopulation in Japan. In this section, the author presents data based on field surveys. Sado Island, the survey site, is located in the western part of the Niigata Prefecture, about 67 kilometres from the port of Niigata. It is the second largest island in Japan (after the main island of Okinawa), with an area of 857.21 square kilometres (Mizoo

2007: 59). Sado Island is a combination of two islands. The northern part of the island is called the *oh-sado* and the southern part is called the *ko-sado*. The area between the *oh-sado* and *ko-sado* consists of a flat land called the Kuninaka Plain (Mizoo 2007: 59). As of 30 November 2020, the population of Sado was 53,148 people.[4] There is only one municipality on Sado Island: Sado City. Ten municipalities (Ryotsu City, Aikawa Town, Sawada Town, Kanai Town, Niibo Village, Hatano Town, Mano Town, Ogi Town, Hamochi Town and Akadomari Village) that had been located on Sado Island were merged into Sado City on 1 March 2004 (Sado City Planning Information Section 2005: 2–3).

S Village is located in the northern part of Sado Island. Although it faces the sea, there are two mountains immediately behind the village. Traditionally, the villagers' livelihoods included semi-agricultural and semi-fishing activities utilising scarce land and resources (rice and vegetable cultivation, *isonegi*,[5] fishing with nets, making and selling charcoal [later replaced by working away from home because the charcoal is no longer selling], etc.). Currently, some people make a living through guesthouse accommodation, food catering and working at the city hall.

As of October 2019, there were 28 houses in S Village and approximately 56 residents. According to tradition, S Village is said to have been formed by Honma Shirozaemon (known as *oh-ya*), who moved there from Sawada with his brother Ando Magozaemon.[6] Thereafter, 11 people joined him (Iwamoto and Takoshima 1986: 1035). These 13 ancient houses are called *ju-sannin* and *omodachi*. Their rights and characteristics include having common land (currently used as a campsite, ranch and antenna base for a telephone company) and the enshrinement of gods in each household. In 1986, there were 43 houses in S Village (Iwamoto and Takoshima 1986: 1035) and, thereafter, the number of vacant houses increased because of population outflow. Houses were demolished, and the current number has declined to 28 houses.

The S Festival

The S Festival, the autumn festival of S Village, takes place on 15 September of the old calendar. The festival's main attraction is the playing of a drum at the entrance of each village house (known as the *kado-duke* in Japanese). The festival did not originally have any performing arts, but since 2008, participants have begun to play the drums each year. In 2017, when this survey was conducted, the festival was held on 3 November.

The festival was organised as follows. First, people practised playing drums for about a month prior to the festival. The practice location was the N-shrine. Even currently, the practice is held twice a week (Friday and Saturday) for about an hour. Anyone can participate, but participants from distant areas usually only participate in the practice session held the day before the event.

The day before the festival, people raise a flag on the N-shrine early in the morning. In 2017, its flag was renewed for approximately 400,000 yen. It copied the letters written on the previous flag. Previously, both flags had different wordings, but now they are the same (the decision to make this change was taken at a village meeting). Drum training was performed at the N-shrine on the same day of the flag's hoist, some time before nightfall. Thereafter, a banquet was held in the guesthouse.

On the day of the festival, which was held at the N-shrine starting around 8:00 hours, the patriarchs of each house in the village and people who beat the drums at the festival became participants. A priest is not usually stationed at the N-Shrine (he serves as priest at 21 shrines, including the shrine in S Village). However, at the time of the festival, a priest came to this village. Since the flag was renewed in 2017, it has also been dedicated to God. After the festival, a small banquet was held at the shrine, and *omiki* (sacred sake), beer and confectionery were served to the participants.

After a small banquet, the priest purified the performing arts participants. Thereafter they beat the drums in front of the N-shrine. During the beginning and end of the performing arts programme, all the participants played drums at the N-shrine.

The drums were played by two people: one oversaw the main melody and the other the accompaniment. There are two performances: the 'Drum of S' (S is the name of this village) and 'Nota'. These were invented by M (male), who teaches drumming for the S festival (M's main occupation is iron factory management, but he is also the representative of the non-profit organisation and the director of the drum performance group known as *Kodo*). The 'Drum of S' was created first and 'Nota' was created 4–5 years later. At the festival, 'Drum of S' is played first by several people, followed by 'Nota'. The person in charge of the main melody repeats the song three times. After that, the next person has a turn. The person in charge of the drum accompaniment will be replaced by another person after a certain amount of time.

The village residents (predominantly children below the age of 20 and some people in their 30s and 40s) played the drums at the festival; other participants included children and youth from outside the village and other areas. The participants were free to leave at any point they wished. In 2017, 11 people from the village, three people born in the village, but usually residing in other areas, and 15 people residing in other areas played the drums at the N-shrine.

Thereafter, they visited each house and the sake brewing company of the village. They started the drum playing at the ward mayor's house and then go around the S Village houses in a counterclockwise direction. A few people from the group played the taiko at each house. Usually, three people play the 'Drum of S' and another three play 'Nota' per house. However, in 2017, there were many participants and sometimes six or more players. After the drum was beaten, each house provided the village with money or the participants with gifts (e.g., sake, food and sweets). In some cases, some houses provided both money and gifts.

After visiting all the village houses, everyone at the N-shrine finally played the drum, and the festival ended. It was expected to end between 16:00 and 17:00 hours; however, in 2017, the festival ended around 18:15 hours. Thereafter, the drums were packed away, and souvenirs were distributed to the children. Usually, the flag is taken down in the early hours of the following day; however, in 2017, the following day's weather was forecast as unfavourable, so it was taken down immediately after the festival. After the festival was completed, the participants freely visited each house to participate in the banquet.

How Drumming was Added to the S Festival

As mentioned earlier, the S Festival was originally a festival without any performing arts. However, the playing of the drum was added to the celebrations in 2008. C (male, aged approximately 50), who runs a guesthouse in S Village, first forwarded the idea of playing the drum. C left Sado after completing high school and became a chef in Tokyo after graduating from university. Later, he also worked as a chef at a restaurant in Taiwan but was asked to return home after his parents built a new inn in Sado. He thus returned to S Village in 1994. He took over the guesthouse and has been making a living by specialising in guesthouse accommodation since then.

C wanted to play the drum at the festival, because he did not like the previous celebration activities of the festival. Back then, the S Festival was held only on celebration days, and special food was served at night. Adults could enjoy drinking sake, but children could not. As a child, C did not know when the festival was held, and he did not understand the meaning of being part of the village community. C had always felt that people never returned to their village, because they felt no attachment to it. He hoped that the festival would encourage the village children to remain in Sado.

C said that he initially experienced much opposition toward his idea of playing the drum at the village festival. The villagers were concerned about how this practice would continue despite depopulation and how to acquire the money to buy the drums. They used a lottery grant to finance the purchase of a drum set. Regarding continuance of the drum playing in depopulated areas, they encouraged everyone to play during the festival, which made it easier for those who had left the village and other visitors to play and thus participate. Hence, by opening up the festival to everyone, it became easier to secure participants and continue the practice in the future. For example, people in T Village, a village close to S Village, also participate in the performing arts of the T Village festival by playing drums. However, people who usually live outside the village and return to the village the day before the festival cannot play the drums at T Village festival because they tend to lack practice. C stated that, to continue the festival in Sado, where the population has been declining year by year, other methods should be considered (e.g., calling in people from other areas or collaborating with universities).

Rather than creating a completely new festival, C added drum performances to the original shrine festival. He thought it more natural to build onto something that was already rooted in the land instead of creating a new festival. He said that he wanted to utilise the original village festival because holding a festival, which is a Shinto ritual, means thanking the land of S Village. C said that, in the future, the population of S Village will decrease steadily, and sooner or later, it would become impossible to visit its graves. After that, even if people disappear from S village, people related to S village may remember that the 15th of September on the lunar calendar is S festival day. And on the day of the S Festival, they may just gather in the land where the S village was and hit the drums stored in the N-shrine. C said the possibility of the above happening is a hope for the future in a depopulated village.

Currently, C does not focus on festival management. Because the lottery foundation they applied for to buy the drum aided for the public hall, so the public hall director (who has a two-year term) oversees the festival's drum-related activities. C says that now his job is to crisis-manage and attend to things when they go wrong.

Owing to the abovementioned circumstances, performing arts are now performed at the S Festival. It has been over a decade since people in S Village started playing drums at their festivals, but some people did not think that it would last. H (male, 45 years old), who lives in S Village, has been participating in the festival since the introduction of the performing arts. When he first heard that a drum was going to be played at the festival, he was sceptical about its continuance and thought that perhaps, in 10 years, there would be no festival participants. However, H thought that it would be advantageous if he had an enjoyable time and participated in the performing arts. As he continued to participate, he found that most people did not want to lose this performing art. And since this festival was designed with the help of people living outside S Village, H realised that the festivities could continue even after the children left S Village.

H feels that the autumn festival and harvest festival in Japanese villages are not familiar to the younger generation, but the S Festival, where people can hit the drums, can be enjoyed by the younger generation as well. He said that the festival would not last unless it was fun, and that the S Festival is a 'means of survival for the community'. In short, in a modern rural society that is prone to depopulation, aging and people-outflows, festivals that involve people from other areas, people who have left the village and people within the region can contribute to the survival of the community.

Resilience toward Village Depopulation

What were the findings of this research on the association of village depopulation with resilience from the S Festival example?

In this section, the author links marginal village research, which has stipulated guidelines for depopulated villages, with resilience toward depopulation. The two directions of marginal village research (reconstruction of villages and realistic treatment of villages) assume resilience toward depopulation – that is, the ability to restore depopulated villages to their original state and the ability to maintain important elements within the villages. However, this is premised on the extinction of an upcoming village – that is, a large-scale transformation of the system. It can be said that the S Festival case belongs to the latter of the two directions of marginal village research. In terms of resilience classification, this applies to ecological resilience and specified resilience. C, who played a central role in creating the performing arts for the S Festival, did not seek a dramatic reconstruction of the village, but neither did he want the village to disappear completely. It can be said that he aimed to facilitate a highly feasible recovery that was also appropriate for regional development.

How does the S Festival attempt to strengthen and maintain the village system? At the S Festival, the villagers and those who reside outside the village, beat the drum together. They also eat food and drink alcohol at the banquet. Even people who were born in the village, but currently reside outside the village, come with their children to participate in the S Festival. Hence, the S Festival builds or maintains a connection between the depopulated village, its people, those outside the village and those who have left the village. The addition of the performing art of drumming to the festival can thus be considered a change that strengthened the effect of the festival.

What is important here is not merely a connection between people but, rather, a connection centred on the grounds of S Village. Instead of creating a new festival, a performing art was added to the existing autumn festival of the area. This indicates that it may not be sufficient or necessary to simply create a new event; instead, it made greater sense to connect the event to an existing traditional festival in the area. It can be thus said that the S Festival is a performing art festival that connects people with the land of the S Village.

As mentioned earlier, C stated that his dream is that the S Festival should continue even if all the people leave the village. The future image of the S Festival, as described by C, shows that, even if the village disappears, the connection between people and the community, and between people around the area will be maintained. From a resilience perspective, this seems to be oriented toward large-scale transformations of the system, a situation where resilience does not work, but this is not the case for S Village. C believes that maintaining people's connections with the land is important for the continuance of the village. This relationship could thus be an important factor in the village system. Thus, the S Festival can be said to enhance resilience ability by maintaining important elements of the system, even after the village disappears. In short, the S Festival maintains the community of a depopulated village by building or maintaining its local connections with people outside the village.

In the case of the S Festival, a possible future of the depopulated village is predicted: even if there are no people living in the village (even if it becomes an extinct village), the village community may still exist. This is a type of virtual village based on the land of an empty village and the people who have a relationship with it. In the future, an increasing number of people living in cities may have connections to such virtual villages at the same time – that is, they may live in virtual villages. The case of the S Festival suggests the possibility that village societies that have disappeared materially can continue to exist conceptually.

In this way, by considering the case of S Village and using the concept of resilience, it is possible to determine the resilience of the village social community to depopulation. Resilience to depopulation is not always about trying to increase the population or restoring the community to its original state. Resilience to depopulation also seeks to maintain important elements of the community such as the land-centric connections between people.

Conclusion

In this chapter, we used the example of the S Festival to show how resilience toward depopulation can be maintained by promoting connections within a region, and by including those outside the village in such promotions, as depopulation progresses. Consequently, this current research showed that, in resilience to depopulation, it is important to not only revitalise the village society but also to maintain the land-centred connections between people, which may survive the community even after the village disappears. Other resilience factors for depopulation may be considered in the future. Furthermore, there are many aspects that have not yet been discussed regarding the concept of virtual villages, mentioned above.

Therefore, the author would like to investigate this concept in the future and deepen this discussion.

Acknowledgements

This work was supported by the Sasakawa Scientific Research Grant from The Japan Science Society and JSPS KAKENHI Grant Number JP21J13290 (Grant-in-Aid for JSPS Fellows).

Notes

[1] For example, see Nakazawa (2013), Yagasaki (2017).

[2] The two resilience types proposed by Holling (1973) (engineering resilience and ecological resilience) have not been actively discussed in the Resilience Alliance, which is an international multidisciplinary research organisation that was established in 1999. The Resilience Alliance uses general resilience and specified resilience instead of the two definitions proposed by Holling (Kume, Yamamoto and Shimizu 2016: I_302). General resilience refers to a system's ability to recover from various disturbances, including unexpected ones (Kume, Yamamoto and Shimizu 2016: I_302). Specified resilience is the ability to recover a specific part of the system from a specific disturbance (Kume, Yamamoto and Shimizu 2016: I_302). General resilience can be replaced with post-adaptation measures against unexpected disturbances, and specified resilience can be replaced with prior mitigation measures against unexpected disturbances (Kume, Yamamoto and Shimizu 2016: I_303).

[3] A marginal village is a uniquely Japanese concept, but similar situations do exist in other countries. Tsuchitori (2015) discusses how marginal villages compare to South Korea's situation.

[4] Sado City (2020). Website of Sado City, Niigata (online), available at: https://www.city.sado.niigata.jp/ (accessed 27 December 2020).

[5] *Isonegi* is a traditional fishing method in Sado. One or two people get into a small boat, look into the sea with box glasses (known as *kagami* or *guras*) and fish with piercing and hooking tools (known as *yasu*, *kama*) attached to a rod (Ogawa 1964: 403–404). People catch shellfish and seaweed during the day and fish and octopus at night (Ogawa 1964: 403).

[6] Another version of the tradition is told in S Village. According to this version, the person who came from Sawada with Honma Shirozaemon was Ishii Jirobee.

References

De Brujin, K. (2005) *Resilience and Flood Risk Management: A System Approach Applied to Lowland Rivers*, Delft: DUP Science.

Hagiwara, Y. (2016) 'Resilience of community and its necessary conditions: With a focus on the views of sociology', *The Journal of Social Science*, No. 82, pp. 25–45 (in Japanese).

Hatamoto, Y. (2010) 'Critical study on marginal village Theory: from local area promotion to local community-based welfare (focus on a survey on the aged life at Tokuji in Yamaguchi city)', *Bulletin of the Faculty of Human and Social Services, Yamanashi Prefectural University*, No. 5, pp. 1–15 (in Japanese).

Holling, C. S. (1973) 'Resilience and stability of ecological system', *Annu. Rev. Ecol. Syst.*, No. 4, pp. 1–23.

Iwamoto, M. and Takoshima, S. (1986) 'Faith and life in Seki Village', in: Aikawa Town History Compilation Committee (ed.), *History of Aikawa Town, Sado: Document Collection Vol. 8 Folklore in Aikawa No. 1*, Niigata: Aikawa Town Sado District, pp. 1033–1059 (in Japanese).

Kume, T., Yamamoto, T. and Shimizu, K. (2016) 'Resilience of coastal agricultural fields to natural disasters: Toward application of resilience concept to agricultural structure improvement projects', *Transactions of the Japanese Society of Irrigation, Drainage and Rural Engineering*, Vol. 84, No. 3, pp. I_301– I_306 (in Japanese).

Mizoo, Y. (2007) Tourism Town Planning: Report from the Field of Niiharu Village, Sado City, Kotohira Town and Kawagoe City, Tokyo: Hara Shobo (in Japanese).

Nakazawa, H. (2013) 'Resilience and social care two years after the Great East Japan Earthquake: Based on a case study of temporary housing in Kesennuma', *The Annual Review of Sociology*, No. 26, pp. 17–27 (in Japanese).

Odagiri, T. (2009) *Revitalization of Agricultural and Mountain Villages: Beyond the 'Marginal Village' Problem*, Tokyo: Iwanami Shoten (in Japanese).

Ogawa, H. (1964) 'Fishery skills and customs', in 9 Society Association Sado Investigation Committee (ed.), Sado: Nature, Culture and Society, Tokyo: Heibonsha, pp. 402–411 (in Japanese).

Ohno, A. (2005) *An Introduction to Environmental Sociology of Mountain Villages: Contemporary Mountain Villages Becoming Marginal Villages and Cooperative Watershed Management*, Tokyo: Rural Culture Association Japan (in Japanese).

Ohno, A. (2008) *Marginal Village and Regional Regeneration*, Shizuoka: The Shizuoka Shimbun (in Japanese).

Sado City Planning Information Section (2005) The Birth of Sado City and Realization of One City on One Island, Niigata: Sado City Planning Information Section (in Japanese).

Sakuno, H. (2010) 'A note on how to capture "marginal village" and "mura-osame"', *The Journal of Shimane Association of Geographers*, No. 44, pp. 15–27 (in Japanese).

Shiozaki, Y. and Kato, T. (2012) 'Definitions of resilience and vulnerability in natural disaster research and related fields', *Seisan kenkyu*, Vol. 64, No. 4, pp. 643–646 (in Japanese).

Tsuchitori, T. (2015) 'A sketch of certain genkai shuraku in Japan: As compared with studies of depopulated villages in Korea', *The Journal of Next-Generation Humanities and Social Sciences*, No. 11, pp. 153–171 (in Japanese).

Yagasaki, T. (2017) 'The resilience of local communities: The Great East Japan Earthquake and a relocation project in the Moune District of Kesennuma City, Miyagi Prefecture', *Journal of Geography (Chigaku Zasshi)*, Vol. 126, No. 5, pp. 533–556 (in Japanese).

Yamamoto, T. (2014) 'Critical assessment of genkai-syuraku (marginal hamlets) Theory', *Journal of the Faculty of Management and Information Systems, Prefectural University of Hiroshima*, No. 6, pp. 113–123 (in Japanese).

Yamashita, Y. (2012) *The Truth of Marginal Village: Can Depopulated Villages Eliminate?*, Tokyo: Chikuma Shobo (in Japanese).

Yoshioka, M. (2010) 'What is the "margin" of the marginal villages?', Annual report of the Institute of Cultural Science, Risshō University, No. 48, pp. 17–30 (in Japanese).

Part 5

Researching Alternative Understandings of Resilience

Chapter 13

Resilience through the Socio-Musical Significance, Cultural Symbolism and Material Agency of Labrosones (Horns and Trumpets)

Kolawole Gbolahan

Introduction

The term 'resilience', within the parameters of this chapter refers to the material strength and deeper layers of meaning that are associated with Labrosones,[1] their sounds, and how these associations have continuously contributed to their relevance unto the present. 'Resilience' is a term that has been adopted within this chapter as a 'heuristic device' (Chandler 2013: 278).[2] In other words, it is an interpretive concept through which theories of socio-musical significance, cultural symbolism and the material agency of labrosones can be investigated and creatively presented. This chapter presents how these theories intersect and help to unpack and categorise factors that have contributed to the resilient nature of labrosones despite years of cultural alienation and Western hegemony, exercised through early armchair anthropologists and comparative musicology.[3] These approaches contribute to current academic works on discourses around resilience, and present the myriad of ways the term has been conceived of and applied in diverse fields of study (i.e., psychology, engineering, ecology and sociology).

Resilience – 'it's everywhere' states Duffield (2013: 55), from the natural to the physical and social environment, and from popular media to social policy and political discourse, 'resilience now operates as a *lingua franca* of preparedness, adaptability and survivability across a variety of fields'. On one hand, this variation widens the applicability of the term, while on the other, can often breed ambiguity, and in the words of Chandler (2013: 276) 'disillusionment with its understanding'. For example, the idea that resilience is a virtue to be given to peoples of a certain economic class by liberal global elites and loaded with expectations of them being resilient.

Masten and Powell (2003: 4) and Duffield (2011: 8) articulate two interpretations of what resilience is and is not. The former put forward resilience as a 'normative or ideal concept, a goal rather than a final state of being and therefore can only be measured or calculated as a comparative or relative quality'. The latter argues that resilience should not be 'conceived as a fixed capacity held by individuals or communities but as a relational process specific to the problem or crisis and the social interactions set in play by this'. Considering these scholarly interpretations, resilience not only encompasses the ways in which an organism or material object survives, adapts and bounces back from shock, but also its interpretive powers used to understand the human condition and its relational response to crisis. This wide applicability suggests that, like Duffield (2013) stated, resilience is everywhere.

So, why resilience? For a book based on resilience, one would expect at the very least, one of its chapters would attempt to answer this question. However, this chapter does not attempt to answer such a question. Rather, it acknowledges the depth and concerns on resilience brought forth by these scholars and adopts resilience as a heuristic device in order to draw attention to factors that have contributed to the resilient nature of labrosones and specific cultural practices. It also seeks to demonstrate how labrosones become socio-musically significant, culturally symbolic and gain agentive power through the symbiotic relationship formed through continuous adoption of them.

The term 'resilience', within the parameters of this chapter, is equally applied in order to unpack the material strength of labrosones. This relates to their ability to withstand unfavorable weather conditions and their resistance to decomposition. The chapter presents the deeper layers of meaning that are associated with labrosones and the sounds produced through them as a form of resilience and reflects on ideas around their meaning making and power relations.

Many musicians often understand their instruments as an extended voice that produces in time, their intentions and affect, which is then projected onto the listener in a performance context.[4] Such capacities have made these instruments worthy objects of inquiry within fields of academia, such as ethnomusicology and anthropology. Consequently, within these fields a plethora of scholarship abounds, various meanings have been adopted, and a continuous string of theories continue to be applied. From the critically acclaimed work of Bennett (2010) to Bates (2012), musical instruments have been interpreted through multiple lenses: the former explores the material agency and latent potential of a material object (i.e., labrosones), while the latter outlines and argues for us to study the social life of musical instruments. Earlier works (Kartomi 1990) also suggest that musical instruments are objects made of varied materials that are often symbolic of cultural traditions unique to a group of people: their sounds carry subjective meanings interpreted through an internal logic peculiar to members of these cultural traditions (Geertz 1973). Additional insights from Doubleday (2008: 3) assert that 'instruments are significant cultural artifacts invested with a wide range of meanings and powers; to possess or play one is to wield power'. Through their presence and through the sounds they produce, they have a special ability to transform consciousness, to embody metaphors and to mediate their player's affect. This unique capacity and complex association with sound producing instruments (i.e., labrosones) as it were, captures the resilient and adaptable nature of these instruments and their sound. Their ability to be multi-functional and yet retain significance in diverse contexts is a factor this chapter argues has made them resilient up to this present day.

This discourse continues further with a chronological layout of the chapter, opening with an overture presented in the form of a poetic and creative literary style, reminiscent of Fela Kuti's extended instrumental exposition before his lyrical delivery often shaped by critical analysis of Nigeria's state of affairs (political and cultural). The intention here is to creatively capture the historical journey of labrosones and explore diverse ideas associated with them in different cultural traditions. This proceeds into the body of the chapter, which provides context, analysis and relevant examples to better clarify ideas embodied by the three main theories: socio-musical significance, cultural symbolism and the material agency of labrosones. The chapter then arrives at its conclusion, which again retains a lyrical/metaphoric approach reminiscent of the literary works of African authors like Chimamanda Ngozi Adichie, Wole Soyinka and Chinua Achebe.

Poem: The Horn

Clarion calls: a call to war, a call to warn, and a call to mourn.
Proclaimed for victory, signaled for battle, symbolic of cultures, played to worship, and herald
to praise.
Blasted in the fields, blared in the
festivals, blown in the synagogues, and synonymous to the courts.
Sacred to the rituals, symbolically known to carnivals,
Gendered by men, bellowed for royals,
and adopted for signals. Constructed with shells, made from vegetables, gutted from the sables, and hunted from the cattle.
It is the sound played through the
Horn.

Countless are the tales, endless are the histories, numerous are the events known to define and unveil the mysteries, the metaphors, the sacredness, the symbolism and diverse utilities acknowledged with horns and trumpets. Due to a long historical documentation, a variety of indigenous names and functions have also been associated with these horns, likewise their construction materials have seen many changes based on ecological availability and cultural preferences. With each nation, society, community and fields of study presenting its own scholarship, claiming its own legends and significance of the horn, it is no doubt that the multilayered meanings and importance attached to the horn from peoples around the globe has made it an instrument worthy of enquiry. To some anthropologists, it is perhaps a material culture; to some ethnomusicologists, perhaps a sound-producing instrument culturally symbolic of traditions; and to the musicologist, it is classified under a generic name – labrosones; to the hunter – a tool; to the king – part of his regalia and a symbol of authority; to religious fraternities – it is documented in their sacred books[4] as an old relic used to conquer battles, to blow the sound of judgment, to relay messages, and as containers for all manner of liquids (i.e., oil/alcohol). In ritual performances, it represents the sound of diverse spirits; in the military its sound is used to signal the call to war and to retreat; and to the musicians, it is one of the many musical instruments revered for its dominating and defining sound. Clearly through the millennia, horns and trumpets have garnered currents of meanings, scholarship and cultural history.

In order to appreciate the resilience of these instruments and their sound, it is crucial to draw upon the physical evidence revealed by archaeological excavations. These have shown horns and trumpets to be arguably among the oldest wind instruments to define historical events and cultural practices; further rendering them integral to world history. The practical use and cultural significance of horns and trumpets at the centre of this study vary dramatically on the African continent and across the globe: from the trumpets excavated from the tomb of Pharaoh Tutankhamun (Fig. 1) of the 18th dynasty, used to summon soldiers to war (Montagu 2014: 71; Kirby 1947: 33), to the *amakondere* royal horns (Fig. 2) used among the Baganda and Banyoro people of Uganda to celebrate wedding festivities and coronations of their kings (Nannyonga-Tamusuza and Solomon 2012: 35).

Fig. 1 Tutankhamon's Trumpets. (Montagu, J. In World Archeology, Taylor & Francis- 1981

Fig. 2 *Amakondere*, side-blown gourd trumpet (Trowell & Watchman

Horns and trumpets playing within these cultural communities have assumed different roles – and the ethos that was attached to them – and were vital to their social development. Playing these instruments was more than just a musical activity, it was a special responsibility given to elite elders and carefully selected men, seldom women, within these cultural communities. Though some trumpets and horns had comparative similarities within these communities such as the Asantes of Ghana and the Himbas of Namibia, the primary differences varied from their indigenous names, sizes and bore construction. These examples buttress the resilient nature of labrosones, further embedding how they have developed through unique stages of transformation in terms of performance practice, social ideology and function, status and symbolism, gender norms, and bore construction. Hence, this chapter brings to light how they have contributed to the cultural, political and musical landscape that has shaped, informed and catalysed communities continentally.

Introducing and Establishing the Intersections of a Theoretical Triplet for Labrosones: Socio-Musical Significance, Cultural Symbolism and Material Agency

In contrast to the historical manifestation of labrosones stated above, the playing of horns and trumpets during the 21st century has often been regarded solely as a musical activity. Its earlier and more diverse roles within early civilisations of African, Asian and European societies have not been prioritised, nor well understood in labrosone pedagogy at tertiary level. This limitation with regards to labrosone pedagogy in the 21st century can be attributed to the mechanical and decontextualised approach in the musical instrument classification scheme of Von Hornbostel and Sachs (1914). The research sub-field that has traditionally dealt with the systematic study and classification of musical instruments is called 'Organology' (Magnusson 2017). Von Hornbostel and Sachs's (1914) 'Classification of Musical Instruments' is arguably the most revered and widely adopted scholarly work within academic fields and beyond, and has served as the foundation for later classification systems (Elschek 1969; Knight system 2010; MIMO 2011). The value in this work pertains to its ability to systematically classify and accommodate a variety of instruments across the globe within its scheme – a factor lacking in its predecessor's scheme (Mahillon 1880). However, despite the value of Von Hornbostel and Sachs's (1914) attempt, it holds an inability to give context to the diversity of instruments classified within it. Its rational and systematic approach narrowly highlights the instrument's physical features (i.e., material, sound texture) and ignores their social-historical contexts (i.e., gendered nature, cultural symbolism).

Central to this chapter's objective is to investigate and present these historical and varied manifestations of these labrosones; unpack the cultural practices that have kept them significant till this present despite efforts made by earlier works in Western academic disciplines to commodify them; lastly, present analysis of the theoretical triplet and adopt the above perspectives as factors that have contributed to the resilient nature and relevance of labrosones up to this present day. During my undergraduate studies, I focused primarily on trumpet-teaching techniques and music making with the trumpet, and attention to its historical background and its other complex historical roles fell outside of my academic scope. With hindsight, this lacuna has ripened my will to contribute this chapter as a thematic continuum that unpacks ideas around the term 'resilience' through diverse historical and cultural manifestations of labrosones. Hence, the following paragraphs seek to introduce and establish the intersection of this theoretical triplet and how they thicken ideas of resilience with regards to labrosones, the sound produced through them and cultural practices in which they have been significant.

The Socio-Musical Significance of Labrosones

Dawe (2012) defines musical instruments (i.e., horns and trumpets) in a way that simply could not be put more clearly, as:

> A musical instrument is much more than the sum of its parts. It can be measured and weighed, its acoustic properties investigated, the ecology of its wood documented, its metals sourced, the site of its sound activation identified, and its sound spectrum plotted. However, made to be played, whether one person's noise or another person's music, when musical instruments sound out they are invariably made to make meaning (changing soundscapes, affecting emotions, moving bodies, demarcating identities, mobilizing ideas, demonstrating beliefs, motioning values), which in turn, makes them potent social and cultural phenomena. As sites of meaning construction, musical instruments are embodiments of culturally based belief and value systems, an artistic and scientific legacy, a part of the political economy attuned by, or the outcome of, a range of associated ideas, concepts and practical skills: they are one way in which cultural and social identity (a sense of self in relation to others, making sense of one's place in the order of things) is constructed and maintained (p. 1).

Insights such as Dawe's align with a chain of scholars whose work has focused on the study of musical instruments through an ethnographic lens and, when read together, broaden the ideas of these instruments beyond simple sound objects. Further, they are encouraging their readership to be aware of the broader perspective and the deeper layers of meaning and identity embodied by these instruments. Factors, such as their acoustic and material properties, associated cultural practices and beliefs and their economic and political value, are also brought to light through these engagements. In other words, beyond their sound, I argue, that the range of complex relations associated with labrosones thus holds the ability to transform consciousness, a power which has ultimately made them a site of meaning construction. This strand of thought amplifies dominant conceptual ideas of music and instruments peculiar to diverse cultural communities. Insights from the two oldest systems of instrument classification – the Chinese *Pa Yin* and the Hindu *Natyasastra* scheme[5]– exemplify Dawe's conclusion. The former links instruments to weather seasons, magic, ritual practices and political power (Needham and Robinson 1962), while the latter links instruments such as the *vina*[6] (Fig. 3) to the parts of various indigenous gods and the divinity of human beings.

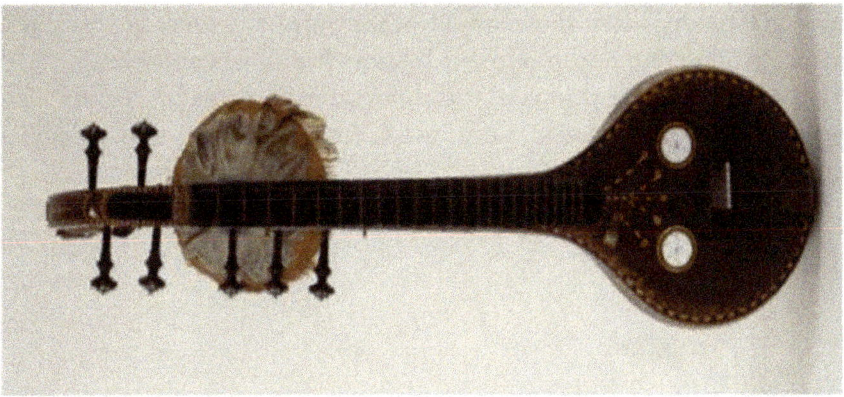

Fig. 3 Sarasvati *vina* (MIMO)

Considering insights from such scholars thus far, this chapter argues that meanings vested in these sound-producing objects do not arrive in isolation from their ecological provisions, societal traditions, ethos and functions of music. Rather, these factors align to influence the cognitive processes through which meanings are given to these instruments and thus give relevance to the theory of 'Socio-Musical Significance'. To strengthen this argument, presented in the next paragraphs are contextual examples of labrosones that outline their indigenous names and meanings that have been attributed as a direct result of their socio-musical significance.

Across the entire subcontinent of India,[7] the continuous use of conch shell trumpets for several millennia has been attributed to its religious significance (primarily to the practice of Hinduism and Buddhism) and dates back to at least between 600 AD.[8] The *Bhagavat-Gita* and other Hindu scriptures describe how avatars on earth during these sacred times significantly used different types/species of conch; an association that has also contributed to some of these conches being named after their famous avatars. Of these conch shell species/type, the *Turbinella Pyrum* (Fig. 4) called *chank* in India (also known as the classic *chank* of the Vedas) was the most important of them all; believed to have been used by Vishnu and of his avatar Krishna (Hornell 1914: 119). In the *Vedas,* the conch is a war trumpet and its sound is attributed to the creation of the world. It is also believed that on the last day on earth, when the world was in flames, Shiva, one of the three major deities revered in Hinduism, will sound the conch (Sachs 1940). Though the use of the *chank* in the subcontinent of India seems more popular within sacred contexts, there are records that have stated other purposes such as signaling, magic, healing and entertainment by non-Buddhists and Hindus.

In addition, inscriptions of the *chank* on early coins in Ceylon[9] also reveal how these shells were used for economic and political purposes (Montagu 2018).

Fig. 4 End-blown Turbinella Pyrum conchshell trumpet Locally referred to as Chank in India (Montagu 2018: 67)

In the north and southwest of China there are accounts of various shapes and colours of shells used for sound production; (1) *Charonia Tritons* (Fig. 5), is a shell found on pacific coastlines used for signalling by infantry soldiers and fishermen in both regions; (2) *Turbinella Pyrum* is from India and used by Buddhist sects in the north called (*Ying Fo*) and by the *Nanman* aboriginal peoples of south-west China for Buddhist music. The conch shell trumpets in this region are mostly end-blown and are often accompanied by cymbals. Here we observe how the conch can also be used within the context of an instrumental ensemble; and (3) *Hemifusus Colosseus* (Fig. 6), referred to locally as *Hailuo*, is a gastropod[10] known to flourish widely in Chinese waters and is culturally preferred for making conch shell trumpets in China. Here the horns are all end-blown and are used by boatmen in

Chekiang and Shanghai. Among the Naxis peoples in the western region of China, the conch shell trumpet, *Hailuo*, is also a sacred instrument believed to embody supernatural powers. This belief has attracted strict rules that determine when they may be played and which particular individuals (i.e., *dongba,* a male indigenous *Naxis* priest) may play or touch the instrument (Helen 2011: 56). A careful overview of the multifunctional possibilities of the conch shell and other sacred ethos associated with this horn in the subcontinent of India, likewise in the north and southwest of China, can perhaps help in strengthening Dawe's (2012: 1) epiphany on musical instruments. The significance of the conch is not only limited to its acoustic properties; further to this is a range of associated ideas embodied by its sound, and the gender roles that equally determine access to touching or playing the conch.

Fig. 5 Side-blown Coronia Triton conch shell trumpet (Montagu 2018: 119)

Fig.6 Hemifusus Colosseus Conch shell, locally referred to as hailuo in China. (has not yet been made into a trumpet) (Montagu 2018: 87)

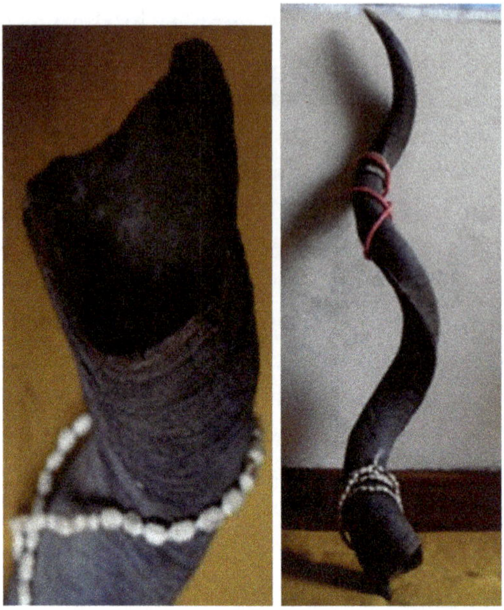

Fig. 7 Side-blown and curved (kudu horn. B) Length: 1m.27cm. Bell diameter: 9.3cm. Photos by author in author's personal collection

The kudu horn (Fig. 7) is a significant sound-producing instrument with a long historical trajectory peculiar and symbolic of the cultural traditions of people known to occupy the eastern and southern regions of Africa. Its significance has been linked to how the sound of the *kudu* horn is traditionally woven into the social fabrics of these regions. Evidently, it has adopted diverse indigenous names, aesthetic preference and technical craftsmanship as it travels through each ethnic group within this region that has harnessed its multifunctional nature. Amongst the Venda people, it is indigenously referred to as *phalaphala.* It is a very important instrument played only by men for official purposes and for all kinds of ceremonial uses, and it is also a social (rather than individual) property collectively belonging to a kraal. In earlier times, a chief often had an official signaller or envoy designated to summon his subjects to work for him on occasions when co-operative work was necessary, so also to call dancers from surrounding kraals to the chief's, in order to execute a national dance known as *tshikona.* An important Venda practice also associated with the horn is to announce when the star (*Sirius*) appeared in early winter mornings. This signalled the commencement of harvesting, and the first man to notice it climbed on a high hill and blew the *phalaphala* horn in order to spread the news; this act came with a reward of a cow, which was presented to the player by the chief. Other uses include sounding the call to arms, which on hearing it, warriors would seize their weapons and report at the chief's kraal.

It is imperative to state for possible linguistic variation and, perhaps for semantics consideration, that the name 'kudu' refers biologically to one of other animals (sable antelopes, Oryx) that belong to the family of *Bovidae* and from which the specimen (horn) is gutted. Furthermore, animals within this family are generically referred to as *kwatha* by the indigenous peoples of the southern region of Africa, with each ethnic group having its own indigenous names given to the animals' horn when made into a labrosone. Though there are instances where a particular animal horn within this family is preferred to make a labrosone, however, due to the extinction of the preferred animal, other animals within the same family are commonly used whilst their indigenous name and technicalities (side-blown) still stays the same. For example, the Venda's *phalaphala* and the Chwana's *lepapata* were labrosones preferably made from the horns of sable antelopes in earlier times. However, as hunting of these animals became difficult over time due to their extinction and perhaps protection of game animals, the kudu's horn has been used as a replacement without a change to its indigenous name, *phalaphala* (Kirby 2013). This is also the case with communities in Eastern Africa.

For example, the Abaluhya community of Western Kenya, *olwika* is the indigenous name used in referring to horns made from any antelope, cow or buffalo, and it is used for sending messages and for ritual purposes (Odwar 2006: 89). Another example is the *baragumu* (Fig. 8), the indigenous name used in Tanzania to refer to hunting horns made from any antelope. Antelope hunters often play it during the ritual held before their departure to the next hunt (Beede Gallery of the National Music Museum).

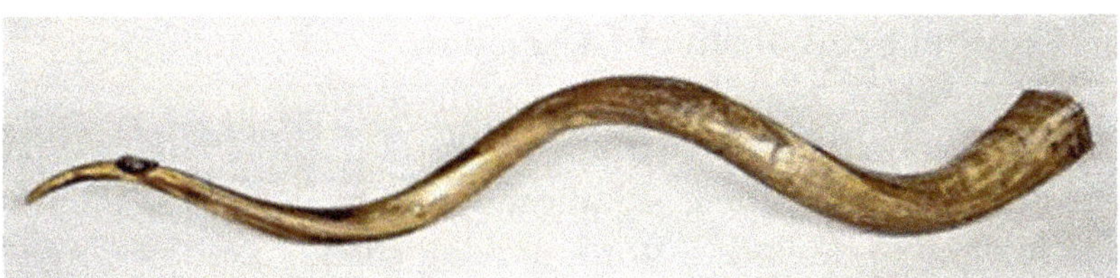

Fig.8 *Baragamu* (Beede Gallery)

These paragraphs have chronicled labrosones and their sound, like avatars from Hindu mythology (i.e., Krishna, Shiva), they embody, represent and testify to the diverse meanings, ethos, cultural and social identity associated with labrosones that arise from their socio-musical significance. Despite countless attempts to decontextualise the significance of these sound-producing cultural objects, and alienation of the indigeneous peoples who constitute these communities from practices that have defined them for centuries. The deeper layers of meaning of these labrosones have seen them survive and retain significance till this present day. Like hemp plants, the multifunctional quality of labrosones has seen them woven into social fabrics and cultural traditions by the communities cited above through to the present day. Despite invasions of new technologies and proliferation of new cities ushered in by modernisation, the 'embodiment of culturally based belief and value-based systems' (Dawe 2012) of labrosones has evidently sustained and allowed them to be adopted into new and constantly changing social contexts.

These qualities stated above evidently reflect the resilient nature of these labrosones taking into consideration their capacity to sustain traditions known to define these cultural communities. To illustrate this, the ritual chants from Tibetan monasteries and the Hindu and Buddhist communities beyond Asia are not complete without the playing of the conch. Boatmen in Chekiang, Shanghai and other coastal communities in China run the risk of colliding into each other's boat without the use of the conch as foghorns. This also applies to the kudu horn and the Venda chiefs and kings; their regalia are incomplete without the blast of the kudu horn that heralds their coming and signify the extent of their might. Beyond objects carved out of the shells of marine animals or horns of *bovidae* mammals, the socio-musical significance of these labrosones is a factor that has allowed them to manifest in diverse ways, attributed many meanings, and as a result has made them resilient.

The Cultural Symbolism of Labrosones

Tangible objects (i.e., instruments) used in these cultural spaces (i.e., monasteries) become significant over an historical period by being integral to traditions. Without them such traditions would not manifest as they have. For example, the *shofar* (Fig. 9) and the sound produced through it are both essential to the religious practice of

Judaism in the Jewish community (i.e., call to the synagogue, a call to repentance). Another similar example is the conch shell trumpet *hora/horagai* (Fig. 10), a ritual instrument symbolic of and significant to the religious practice of esoteric Buddhism in Japan. According to Fukui (1994), it is believed that playing the instrument has the potential to make a man wise. Its sound is played to accompany sutra chanting, rituals such as the *omizutori* (water drawing) portion of the Shuni-e rites at the Todai-ji in Nara, to send forth departed souls, used to give signals in the military and instructions on Shugendo.[11] The Buddhist scriptures (Hokekyo, Ko-on-kyo, Shugen-shuyo-hiketsu) further liken the sound of the *hora* to the roar of a lion which will suppress the evil mind.[12] Here, we observe the significant association between a material object (i.e., *shofar/hora*) and how its acoustic properties function as crucial elements of religious practices (i.e., Judaism and Buddhism) that have defined these cultural communities up to this present day.

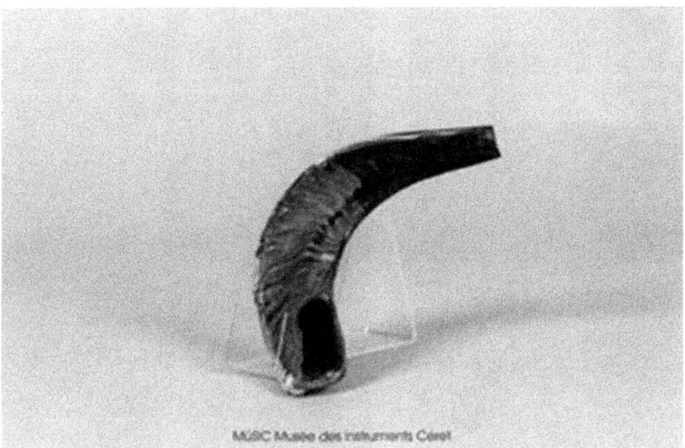

Fig. 9 *Shofar* (MIMO)

Considering how significant these horns are in enhancing the sacredness of these practices, in relaying crucial messages and embodying ideas that are symbolic of religious practices known to these cultural communities, I argue that labrosones, as material objects with this cultural capacity and their long history of functional use are likely to be implicated in a physical/emotional attachment with their users. This in turn gives the object a peculiar potential; the ability to be a symbolic representation of a religious practice or other cultural traditions. In other words, tangible objects such as this can be summed up under the term 'Material Culture', as they symbolise ideas and identities recognisable or interpreted by a cultural group. This argument can be thickened by drawing insights from other relative fields of study that have strengthened the theoretical paradigm of cultural symbolism, innate to material culture (i.e., labrosones).

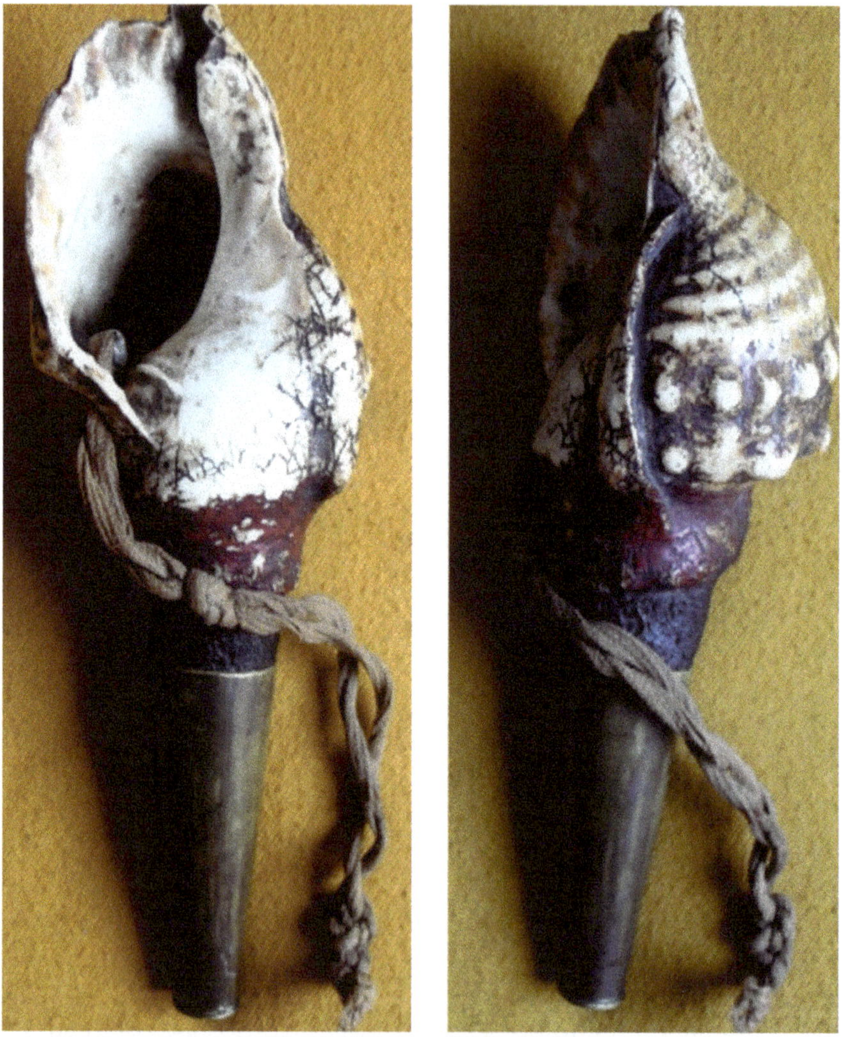

Fig. 10 End-blown with mouthpiece (Charonia Tritonis conchshell trumpet) Locally referred to as the *Hora/ Horagai* in Japan. Photos by author of author's personal collection

The early American anthropologists, Clifford Geertz and his colleagues at the University of Chicago, and Victor Turner at Cornell, pioneered the movement of 'Symbolic Anthropology' that was prominent at the beginning of the 1960s. Although this movement had two major variants,[13] one thing they achieved, despite their differences, was to put the understanding of symbols as a key aspect within the interpretation of both culture and its society. Geertz further argued that 'culture is not something locked inside peoples' heads but rather embodied in public symbols, symbols through which the members of a society communicate values and ethos passed on through traditions to future generations' (Geertz 1973 in Ortner 1984: 129). With this established, it is imperative to state that, just as folklores are vectors that help carry spatial history and legends, material culture can be argued as vectors of the theory, 'cultural symbolism'. Material culture refers to how specific categories of objects and places come to symbolise ideas and highlight social values over a period of being socially significant to a collective of people. An essay titled 'Material Culture and Archaeology', by Patnaik (1995) reflects on how the study of culture has been a central concern to the disciplines of archeology and anthropology. The variety of approaches[14] adopted in scholarship within these two fields has been vital, analytically and methodologically efficient in helping to unpack traditions that define peoples and their cultural practices.

As written by Patnaik (1995: 59), 'material culture is the finished or unfinished product carved out of the contextually situated materials and resources. It is a corpus of a conscious collective and an embodiment of the mentally perceived design'. Thus, material culture has the potential to reveal the level of technology attained and symbolise ideas and values embraced in a socio-historical space at a specific time. This further aligns with Herskovits's (1955: 305) definition of material culture as the human-made part of the environment. Binford (1972: 20) takes this analysis further, stating that material culture can and does arguably represent the structure of the total cultural system, further synthesising three major functional sub-classes of material culture: 'sociotechnic, ideotechnic and technomic'.

Using insights from these scholars, we can acknowledge these labrosones beyond the material scope of a sea animal's skeleton or horns gutted from the heads of *Bovidae* mammals. Rather, we can understand them as a sound-producing material culture capable of symbolising ideas, values and traditions that define a collective of people. Using insights from Patnaik (1995) and Binford (1972), the next paragraphs seek to present elements of these labrosones that justify their classification under these subclasses of material culture. Furthermore, it will reveal how each subclass symbolises such phenomena as tradition, ideas and values known to define cultural communities.

Sociotechnic

Sociotechnic material culture refers to material objects that function in the social subsystem of the total cultural structure (Binford 1972). These subsystems engage with tangible objects that embody social ethos and possess the cultural capacity to symbolise unspoken references to either an individual or a collective. Examples of such material objects that fall within this category are: a king's crown, a warrior's coup stick and a magician's wand. In the same way that Binford's example of this class of material culture demonstrates the social ability of an object to communicate references to people who share cultural traditions, there are also labrosones that possess such abilities. Examples from Trowell and Waschman's (1953: 353–359) ethnographic accounts on the material culture of diverse ethnic groups in Uganda cite the use of several labrosones beyond producing sound. Of these are: the *obute,* a side-blown trumpet and the *olwet* an end-blown trumpet. The *obute* (Fig. 11) is popular amongst the Acoli ethnic group and it functions specifically as an alarm to call people on special occasions, for example, announcing the death of an important person, to send warnings at the approach of a dangerous animal or to summon soldiers to battle. While the *olwet* (Fig. 12) is fairly common across Uganda and it is known for how it allows the player to establish individual musical motifs that make the player identifiable over long distances. In addition to this, when members of these ethnic groups hear such calls from far away, they can easily identify which individual or clan's horn is sounding.

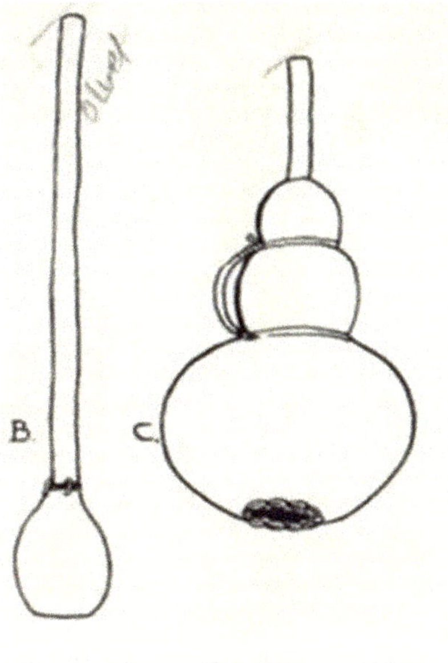

Fig. 11 C: Obute of the Acoli ethnic group **Fig.12** B: Ugandan Olwet. (Trowell & Watchsmann 1953: 363)

Ideotechnic

This subclass highlights elements of a material culture that place their primary functional context on the ideological component of the social system. Objects that fall under this class of material culture are imperative to signify, imply and symbolise the ideological rationalisation for the social system and provide the symbolic milieu in which individuals are acculturated. Items such as figures of deities, clan symbols and symbols of natural agencies (Binford 1972) fall within this subclass. A relevant example is a short end-blown horn, symbolic of the Jewish temples and cultural community. According to Montagu (2014: 49–55), "the *shofar* today, in the Western or Ashkenazi tradition is used mainly for ritual purposes, principally on Rosh Hashanah, the Jewish new year (also known as *Yom t'ruah*, a day of trumpeting)". It is blown five times in the morning service to call Jews to repent for their sins over the next ten days. The ethos associated with the *shofar* and its capacity to communicate ideas at the same time attributes a religious and ritual ideology to the horn. A second example is the *amakondere* trumpet; these are side-blown gourd trumpets symbolic of the royal court's coronation in Bantu Uganda and beyond the border in Tanzania. They are played in sets of five and accompanied by the royal drums. Only high-ranking musicians play these trumpets as they are generally regarded as a symbol of royalty and prestige primarily due to the fact that they form part of the chief's and king's regalia (Trowell and Waschman1953: 354; Montagu 2014: 7).

Technomic

According to Patnaik (1995: 60): 'technomic material culture signifies those artifacts having their primary functional context in adapting to demands of the natural environment'. For coastal communities, the ocean is central to their geographical advantage. It is an environmental feature of great economic value and thus becomes culturally vital to the social fabric of these communities. Fishing often becomes their main source of income and the use of conches thus becomes embedded into multiple activities. Conches have functioned as signalling tools, like foghorns, to both fishermen and sailors whose practices are a defining character of the cultural and economic traditions known to these communities. In other words, the shells of these sea animals represent a vital material culture beyond their sound capabilities and thus their significance is multi-layered.

The conch shell trumpet can be viewed as a technological achievement that has made it a sound material culture and, simultaneously, a functional tool key to adapting to the environmental demands. Thus, we can assert that this technological achievement and its functionality justify the classification of the conch shell trumpet as technomic material culture. A similar example from a different animal and ecological context is the trumpet *onjembe erose*, an end-blown conical trumpet known to the Himba tribesmen in Namibia. The trumpet is made from the horn of a gemsbok with a resonating chamber made of beeswax bulb. Men of this cultural community use this trumpet to herd their cattle by chanting and trumpeting; the chanting is a form of praise for the cattle and the sound played through the trumpet is for leading the cattle (Gibson 1962: 258).

These examples of labrosones holding the capacity to culturally symbolise traditions (both sacred and secular) that define a collective of people are only a fraction of the variety that exists globally. Even so, in the presence of this omission, we can establish that the function of these labrosones goes far beyond the musical and, in many instances, their playing (the music-making) is secondary to the symbolic function of the music, instrument or events (Johnson 1995: 264). Due to the historical evidence of their involvement in enhancing traditions that belong to a collective of people, labrosones can thus become vectors of cultural ideas and likewise be viewed as culturally symbolic of a tradition. If we once again adopt Dawe's (2012: 1) insight on musical instruments and substantiate it with practical evidence of the manifestations of labrosones stated so far, we can appreciate that, however they were intended to be played, 'whether one person's music or another's noise', both the materials used in making these labrosones and the sounds produced through them embody the capacity to 'symbolise culturally based belief and value systems'. This chapter thus acknowledges the symbolic capacity of these labrosones as an inevitable factor that has significantly empowered and culturally contributed to the resilient nature of labrosones until this present day.

The Material Agency of Labrosones

Conches of marine animals have been put forward as some of the oldest labrosones (Montagu 1981, 2014, 2017, 2018; Fukui 1994). They have been documented as functional in navigating ecological demands and sustaining cultural traditions. Horns gutted from other animals and trumpets made out of other materials have also been documented as integral to cultural practices for millennia. Central to this chapter is to corroborate insights thus far with an exploration of the material agency of labrosones in order to further establish the intersection of the theoretical triplet. In other words, this section highlights how the socio-musical significance and cultural symbolism of labrosones entangles these sound-producing objects in webs of complex relationships, which equip them with potential to hold a significant degree of power for action and intervention.

Eliot Bates (2012: 371), in his article 'The Social Life of Musical Instruments' argued for a 'paradigm that encompasses the full range of possible human-object-divine relations, as exemplified in instrument making, performance, musical healing, and numerous other domains'. A paradigm such as Bates's positions the material object as a central subject of study and allows the unpacking of ideas such as: (1) how human intention is exerted onto material objects (i.e., labrosones) in order to initiate action and project emotion; (2) the performative and integrative capacity of material objects in diverse contexts; and (3) how a material object's significance and symbolic capacity align in making it revered and valued beyond its material properties. Unpacking these ideas, readers can begin to imagine labrosones and other material objects as helping to sustain a tradition beyond being incidental to but rather constitutive of a social structure. The ingenuity and relevance of Bates's work is further characterised by the summation of insights originating from Science and Technology Studies (STS)[15] and recent anthropological and political science work on material culture.[16] In the words of Bates (2012: 372):

> What ties together the approaches/insight from these studies (STS, recent anthropological and political science work on material culture) is a shared concern with examining the performative and integrative capacity of things to help make what we call society (Pels, Hetherington and Vandenberghe 2002: 2), and theorizing the social to include people, animals, material objects, spaces and ideas/concepts. Importantly, these studies help create awareness of the equally significant power inherent in other elements (e.g., ecological conditions), aside from humans to constitute the 'social'. Furthermore, themes at the nucleus of STS, anthropological, and political science approaches to material culture are: (1) analysing the relations between humans, nonhumans and more-than-human (Haraway 1984); (2) ethnographic examination of the process of production (of the actor)[17] and its ability to adapt to and negotiate the social-cultural structures that constitute its environment; and (3) the transfer of agentive power onto inanimate objects through human intention.

For clarity we must establish that objects do not independently assume this power. What becomes apparent is how ideas of what humans think an object can do is married to the inherent capacity in the object itself in order to achieve a personal or collective purpose. For example, though a *shofar* or the *hora* holds inherent capacity to produce sound, it cannot achieve this on its own. Only with the will and intention of a player can its acoustic potential be realised. It is not to say that humans do not hold a high degree of agency (i.e., the ability to cognitively initiate an action), but we must acknowledge that without the availability of the significant object, the human intention is unlikely to fulfil the needed act. Thus, both humans and material objects relative to the sustenance of cultural practices or general survival within a social space are actors that collaborate in order to garner agentive power; a symbiotic relation that constitutes vital materiality of the 'social' and ideas of material agency.

I draw insights from Gell (1998) and Cooke (1996) to highlight the theoretical relevance of material agency in relation to prior theories (socio-musical significance and cultural symbolism). This scholarship unpacks additional factors that have contributed to the resilient nature of labrosone.

Gell's work, *Art and Agency*, explains the 'reciprocal process that provides images with agency'. They do so by referencing the attention of a viewer (i.e., an hindu worshipper), who is focused on the eye of a god that is symbolised by a carved material object (i.e., figurine). In this context, 'the god looks at the viewer just as the worshipper looks at the god, the viewer imagines he is being looked at as he sees himself reflected in the gaze of the god' (1998: 120). Of course, a meticulous breakdown of the cognitive and spiritual process involved here is far more complex. However, we can establish that this 'reciprocal process' provides significant evidence of how agentive power is shared or transferred between two actors.

The ethnographic accounts of Cooke's (1996) *Music in a Ugandan Court* reveals how kings and high-ranking chiefs in the Baganda kingdom traditionally use sound-producing material objects (i.e., *amakondere*, royal drums) to assert authority and parade their wealth. This is achieved by employing the services of carefully selected instrumentalists (most often men), who play as an ensemble in order to dignify the public affairs of the king, in and beyond his palace. An insight also drawn from Cooke's account is the significance of the role given to the *Amakondere* within the royal ensemble. In this ensemble, the trumpet gives an impressive blast of sound that heralds the king's presence or signifies his departure. This significance further gives this trumpet and its player a revered status amongst other instruments and instrumentalists, even beyond the palace.[18]

The transfer of agentive power from human intention onto a material object in this context is exemplified in what constitutes a material world of agency: the *amokondere* trumpet, the trumpeter and the king. Thus, the cultural practice of heralding the king's presence and the trumpet player's intention to dignify the king's public affairs are tied to the acoustic capacity inherent in the material object. This material world of agency operates symbiotically to achieve a collective purpose (i.e., sustaining a revered cultural tradition).

According to Bennett (2010: 9), 'the curious ability of inanimate things to animate, to act, to produce effects, either dramatic or subtle, can be termed thing-power'. Bennett broadens the idea describing it as 'agency beyond an inherent capacity only held by humans, but rather something seen as differentially distributed across a wide range of ontological types'. In other words, any material object, within any network can be seen as having equal capacity for action. Just as much as we ascribe much power, mystique and allure to human intentions, any significant material object crucial to the sustainability of human survival or cultural traditions also has the capacity for action, and thus holds a significant degree of agency. Hence, both the labrosone and its player become implicated in a symbiotic network; one where each constituent part has to cohere in order to be significant. For example, the ecological conditions have to be favourable for the availability of the specimens (i.e., conches and horns) gutted from the marine animals and *bovidae* mammals in order to make the desired labrosone. This example highlights how integral each actor within the network is to the other. What becomes apparent from the examples cited is a degree of agency that is arguably held by both the significant objects and the humans that adapt them to sustain their traditions and navigate their society.

The objective of this section is to corroborate material agency with theories previously explored in this chapter (social-musical significance and cultural symbolism). It seeks to do this in order to, firstly, establish their theoretical intersections and, secondly, acknowledge the agency of sound-producing objects as an important factor that has contributed to the resilient nature of these labrosones. Hence, I argue that labrosones that become socio-musically significant to unique traditions known to a cultural community inevitably become a material culture with the potential to symbolise ideas and communicate meanings. This implication allows for the transfer of agentive power onto the labrosone; it gives the sound-producing object a significant degree of material agency, enabling the continuous practice of a revered cultural tradition. Furthermore, the adoption of the theoretical triplet within this chapter has allowed for the categorisation of factors that, I argue, have contributed to the resilient nature of labrosones.

Conclusion

The ideological continuum used within this chapter, like branches, gives balance to a deeply rooted tree and, like the aerial view of a great river, visualises the multiplicity of theories that thicken the term 'resilience' and shows us how it has been applied across disciplines. With these ideas around resilience acknowledged, the chapter adopted the term to refer to the material strength, the deeper layers of meaning associated with labrosones and their sounds, and how these associations have become contributing factors to their resilient nature. The idea of resilience as a heuristic device through which we can unpack the socio-musical significance, cultural symbolism and the material agency of labrosones was investigated and creatively presented (Chandler 2013). The chapter used the intersection of the theoretical triplet as a resource to unpack and categorise factors that have contributed to the resilient nature of labrosones, despite years of cultural alienation and Western hegemony exercised through early armchair anthropologists and comparative musicology.

Analysis of and practical examples from the theoretical triplet were put forward to highlight the following significant dimensions: (1) the deeper layers of meaning; (2) the capacity of a sound-producing material to project culturally based beliefs and value systems; (3) the inherent and imposed agentive power of culturally significant objects; and (4) how all these manifestations of labrosones have rendered them resilient across a long historical period. Focus has been given to admonishing the readership to conceive of labrosones beyond the contours of their materiality or objects gutted from animals and crafted with other materials. Another intention of the chapter was also to present labrosones as a culturally symbolic, sound-producing material culture with significant capacity to project their player's intention, to embody the identity of a cultural community and hold a degree of agency. As has been shown, the sounds blown through the Jewish *shofar* or the Indian *chank* relay a deeper meaning to members of the cultural community and those who embrace the religious ethos and symbolism associated with these labrosones. This potential is mirrored in the sound of the kudu horn, *amakondere* trumpet and other labrosones blown in different social contexts across the African continent. 'Resilience Through the Socio-Musical Significance, Cultural Symbolism and Material Agency of Labrosones' is an ongoing study with broader aims and objectives that seek to contribute to scholarship (within academia and beyond) on 'Resilience' and 'Labrosones.

Notes

[1] A generic term for lip-vibrated wind instruments, i.e., horns and trumpets. The former are made from animal horns, such as kudus/other cattle, rarely from human bones, and the latter, from materials such as conch shells, vegetables, brass, plastic, etc. These wind instruments can either be blown from the side or the tip end. Hence, they are technically referred to as 'end-blown or side blown horns' (Musical Instruments Museum Online 2011)

[2] Chandler attempts to unpack the nature of discourses around resilience and its problematic and disillusioned understanding with liberal internationalists. The author presents resilience as a heuristic device in order to draw attention to this disillusionment, the ineffectiveness of the 'quick fix' approach by liberal institutions in state building and empowering communities to cope with risks and stresses.

[3] Fields of study with early works argued to have been intentionally carried out in order to decontextualisze cultural practices of the peoples and communities studied; equally these early works contributed ideologically to the colonisation of these communities.

[4] For example, ritual gatherings (e.g., offerings to indigenous gods/healing/ warding off evil spirits), entertainment platforms (e.g., concerts/festivals, ceremonies/coronations/rites of passage/burials) (Montagu 2014; 2018; Fukui 1994; Odwar 2006).

[5] For example, in the Bible (Joshua 6: 4; Judges 7: 20; I Samuel 16: 13. (King James Version)), in the Bhagavad Gita (1: 13–19) and in the Qur'an (18: 99, 27: 87). The variations also range from the *ojembo erose* (Fig. 3), a straight conical trumpet unique to the Himba people in Namibia that is used to herd cattle (Gibson 1962: 258), to the *aluut* (Fig. 4) of the Karamoja region in Uganda. The *aluut* is a side-blown animal horn used by herd boys to frighten away hyenas or predators that might harm their cattle while grazing in the field (Trowell and Waschman1953: 353). Amongst the Asante people of Ghana, the *akan* ivory trumpet (Fig. 5) made from the tusk of an elephant was used for ceremonial purposes (Kaminski 2012: 21). A final example is the *hora/horagai* (Fig. 6), an end-blown trumpet made from the shellfish, *Charonia Tritonis*, and which is a ritual instrument symbolic of and religiously significant to the practice of esoteric Buddhism[6] in Japan (Fukui 1994). Also known as secret Buddhism, has a special tradition in the belief that the most profound doctrines of Buddhism are to be kept secret, although the origins of this school can be traced back to the second century in India, the teachings of this school tell that all things in the phenomenal world have their basis in Daimnichi Nyorai and arise from him (Fukui 1994: 48).

[6] The Hindu-Indian scheme – *Natyasastra* – is approximately two millennia old. Both are still relevant to date (Kartomi 1990).

[7] The Vina's parts are analogous to the various gods. The instrument symbolises the divinity of human beings. It has numerological significance and is considered

to be the most complete of instruments, because it has the fundamental drone within itself (Subramanian 1985: 15). It is perhaps the most revered instrument in India and Sri Lanka. The Chinese instrument classification system (*Pa Yin* scheme) may date back to the third millennium B.C.E and the Hindu-Indian scheme Natyasastra which is approximately two millennia old; both still relevant till date (Kartomi 1990).

[8] Afghanistan, Pakistan, India, Bangladesh and Sri Lanka.

[9] According to Montagu (2014: 29) and Yuan and Mao (1986: 83), the earliest use of conch shell trumpets has been documented between 150 BC and 600 AD

[10] A region popularly referred to as Buddhist Island in Sri Lanka.

[11] Invertebrates that walk using their stomach as a foot while carrying their helical shells on their back (Brusca and Brusca 2003).

[12] An ancient pre-Buddhist worship of certain mountains as holy ground. In the course of the Nara era (A.D. 710–794) Shugendo, combining elements of other traditional and imported religious orders (i.e., Shintoism, Confucianism, Taosm, Buddhism, esoteric Buddhism), emerged as a coherent religious group towards the end of the 12th century (Fukui 1994: 48).

[13] These cultural attributions of the *hora* are also informed by personal interactions with academics and everyday people during my last visit in July 2019.

[14] (1) The operations of culture and (2) the operations of society, which were independently invented (Ortner 1984).

[15] I.e., categorising ideas and tangible objects that define a cultural community into material and non-material dimensions.

[16] A fieldwork-based ethnographic discipline with works focusing on invention and technological adoption (see Bijker 1995) and the practices of laboratory work (see Latour and Woolgar 1979). Other STS works have also explored musical technologies, including failed innovations in European classical instrument design (Bijsterveld and Schulp 2004), the shift in manufacturing of audio recording technologies (Théberge 1997) and the invention of the Moog synthesiser (Pinch and Trocco 2002; Pinch 2008).

[17] Much of these works examine visual arts and material artifacts in everyday life (Gell 1998; Miller 1998; Vannini 2009).

[18] In the context of this chapter the term 'actor' is adopted based on the definition presented through the Actor-Network Theory, which presents an actor as neither a subject nor object. Rather as a source of action 'something that acts or to which activity is granted by others, it implies no special motivation of human individual actors, nor humans in general' (Latour 1996)

[19] The king's *amakondere* players were respected officials who in earlier times carried their trumpets in a pouch wherever they went and were immune from punishment for any misdeeds they committed (Cooke 1996: 447).

References

Adichie, C. N. (2009) 'The Danger of a Single Story' https://www.ted.com/talks/chimamanda_ngozi_adichie_the_danger_of_a_single_story /transcript (accessed: 21 April 2020).

Bates, E. (2012) 'The social life of musical instrument', *Ethnomusicology*, Vol. 56, No. 3, pp. 363–395, doi:10.5406/ethnomusicology.56.3.0363.

Bennett, J. (2010) *Vibrant Matter: A Political Ecology of Thing*, Durham, NC: Duke University Press.

Berliner, P. (1993) *Soul of the Mbira: Music and Traditions of the People of Zimbabwe*, Chicago: University of Chicago Press.

___________ (1976) 'The poetic song texts accompanying the mbira dzavadzimu', *Ethnomusicology*, Vol. 20, No. 3, pp. 451–482, doi:10.2307/851045.

Bijker, W. E. (1995) *Of Bicycles, Bakelite and Bulbs: Toward a Theory of Sociotechnical Change*, Cambridge, MA: MIT Press.

Bijsterveld, K. and Marten, S. (2004) 'Breaking into a world of perfection: Innovation in today's classical musical instruments', *Social Studies of Science*, Vol. 34, No. 5: 649–674.

Binford, L. R. (1972) *Model Building—Paradigms, and the Current State of Paleolithic Research. An Archaeological perspective*, New York: Seminar Press.

Brusca, R. C. and Brusca, G. J. (2003) *Phylum Mollusca. Invertebrates*, Sunderland: Sinauer Associates, Inc.

Chandler, D. (2013) 'International state building and the ideology of resilience', *Politics*, Vol. 33, No. 4, pp. 276–286.

Cooke, P. (1996) 'Music in a Ugandan court', *Early Music*, Vol. 24, No. 3, pp. 439-452, www.jstor.org/stable/3128260 (accessed: 12 May 2020).

Dawe, K. (2001). 'People, objects, meaning: Recent work on the study and collection of musical instruments', *The Galpin Society Journal*, No. 54, pp. 219–232.

___________ (2005) 'Symbolic and social transformation in the lute cultures of Crete: Music, technology and the body in a Mediterranean society, *Yearbook for Traditional Music*, No. 37, pp. 58–68, doi:10.2307/S074015580001122X.

___________ (2012) 'The Cultural Study of Musical Instruments', in *The Cultural Study of Music*, Routledge, pp. 217–227.

__________ (2015) 'Materials matter: Towards a political ecology of musical instrument making', in *Current Directions in Ecomusicology*, Routledge, pp. 117–129.

Doubleday, V. (2008, June). 'Sounds of Power: An Overview of Musical Instruments and Gender', *Ethnomusicology Forum*, Vol. 17, No. 1, pp. 3–39.

Duffield, M. (2011). Total war as environmental terror: Linking liberalism, resilience, and the bunker. *South Atlantic Quarterly*, *110*(3), 757-769.

Duffield, M. (2013) How did we become unprepared? Emergency and resilience in an uncertain world.

Elschek, O. (1969). *System of graphical and symbolic signs for the typology of the aerphones*. Vyd. SAV v Malotirážnom stredisku, t. Stat. tisk., Praha.

Fukui, H. (1994)'The hora (conch trumpet) of Japan', *The Galpin Society Journal*, No. 47, pp. 47–62, doi:10.2307/842662.

Gibson, G. D. (1962). The Himba Trumpet. *Man*, *62*(11), 160-163.

Gell, A. (1998) *Art and Agency*, London: Clarendon Press.

Geertz, C. (1973). Chapter 1/Thick Description: Toward an interpretive theory of culture. *The Interpretation of Cultures: Selected Essays, New York, Basic Books.*

Haraway, D. J. (1984). Primatology is politics by other means. In *PSA: Proceedings of the Biennial Meeting of the Philosophy of Science Association* (Vol. 1984, No. 2, pp. 488-524). Cambridge University Press.

Helen, R. (2011) *Echoes of History: Naxi Music in Modern China*, New York: OUP.

Herskovits, M. J. (1955) *Cultural anthropology*, in Knopf (text ed.), American Pychological Association.

Hornell, J. (1914) 'The sacred chank of India', *Fisheries Bureau Bulletin*, No. 7, Madras.

Johnson, H. M. (1995). An ethnomusicology of musical instruments: Form, function, and meaning. *Journal of the Anthropological Society of Oxford*, *26*(3), 257-269. Kaminski, J. S. (2012). *Asante Ivory Trumpet Music in Ghana: Culture Tradition and Sound Barrage*. Ashgate Publishing, Ltd.

Kartomi, M. (1990) *On Concepts and Classifications of Musical Instruments*, Chicago and London: The University of Chicago Press,

__________ (2001) 'The classification of musical instruments: Changing trends in research from the late nineteenth century with special reference to the 1990s, *Ethnomusicology*, Vol. 45, No. (2), p. 283.

__________ (2005) 'On metaphor and analogy in the concepts and classification of musical instruments in Aceh', *Yearbook for Traditional Music*, No. 37, pp. 25–57.

Kirby, P. R. (1947). The Trumpets of Tut-ankh-amen and their Successors. *The Journal of the Royal Anthropological Institute of Great Britain and Ireland*, *77*(1), 33-45.

Kirby, P. (2013). *The musical instruments of the indigenous people of South Africa.* NYU Press.

Knight, R. C. (2015). The knight revision of Hornbostel-Sachs: a new look at musical instrument classification. *Oberlin College Conservatory of Music.*

Latour, B. (1996) 'On Actor-Network Theory: A Few Clarifications', *Soziale Welt*, Vol. 47, No. 4, pp. 369–81.

__________ (2005) *Reassembling the social: An introduction to actor-network theory*, Oxford: Oxford University Press.

Latour, B. and Steve, W. (1979) *Laboratory Life: The Social Construction of Scientific Fact.*, Beverley Hills: Sage.

Magnusson, T. (2017). Musical organics: a heterarchical approach to digital organology. *Journal of New Music Research*, *46*(3), 286-303.

Mahillon, V. C. (1880). *Catalogue descriptif et analytique du musée instrumental du Conservatoire royal de Bruxelles, précédé d'un Essai de classification méthodique de tous les instruments anciens et modernes, par Victor Charles Mahillon,...* C. Annoot-Braeckman.

Masten, A. S., & Powell, L. (2003). A Resilience framework for research, policy. *Resilience and vulnerability: Adaptation in the context of childhood adversities, 1.*

Miller, D. (ed.) (1998) *Material Cultures: Why Some Things Matter*, Chicago: University of Chicago Press.

MIMO Consortium. (2011). Revision of the Hornbostel-Sachs classification of musical instruments by the MIMO Consortium. *Available in: < http://network. icom. museum/cimcim/resources/classification-of-musical-instruments.*

Montagu. J. (1976) 'One of Tutankhamon's trumpets', *The Galpin Society Journal*, pp. 115–117.

__________ (1981) 'The conch in prehistory: Pottery, stone and natural, *World Archaeology*, Vol. 12, No. 3, pp. 273–279, http://www.jstor.org.ezproxy.uct.ac.za/stable/124238.(accessed 12 May 2020)

___________ (1992). *The Sounds of Oceania: An Illustrated Catalogue of the Sound Producing Instruments of Oceania*, Auckland: Auckland Institute and Museum.

___________ (1996) 'Instruments', *Early Music*?, Vol. 24, No. 3, pp. 529–534.

___________ (2014) *Horns and Trumpets of the World: An illustrated Guide*, Lanham, Maryland: Rowman & Littlefeld.

___________ (2017). How music and instruments began: A brief overview of the origin and entire development of music, from its earliest stages. *Frontiers in Sociology*, *2*, 8.

___________ (2018) *The Conch Horn: Shell Trumpets of the World from PreHistory to Today*, Hataf Segol Publications.

Musical Instrument Museums Online Consortium. (2011). Revision of the Hornbostel-Sachs Classification of Musical Instruments, the MIMO Consortium.

Nannyonga-Tamusuza, S. A. and Solomon, T. (2012) The International Symposium on Ethnomusicology in Uganda, *Ethnomusicology in East Africa: Perspectives from Uganda and Beyond*, Kampala, Uganda: Fountain Publishers.

Needham, J. and Kenneth, R. (1962) 'Sound (acoustic)', *Science and civilization in China*, Vol. 4, *Physics*, Cambridge: Cambridge University Press, pp. 126–228.

Odwar, H. A. (2006). *Traditional Music Instruments of Kenya: A Resource Book for Teachers and Learners*, Maseno, Kenya: Hato Publishers and Research.

Ortner. S. B (1984) 'Theory in anthropology since the sixties', *Comparative Studies of Society and History*, Vol. 26, No. 1, pp. 126–166.

Patnaik, S. (1995) 'Material culture and archaeology', *Indian Anthropologist*, Vol. 25, No. 2, pp. 59–64, http://www.jstor.org/stable/41919780. (accessed 12 May 2020)

Pels, D., Hetherington, K. and Vandenberghe, F. (2002) 'The status of the object', *Theory, Culture & Society*, Vol. 19, No. 5-6, pp. 1–21.

Pinch, T. (2008) 'Technology and institutions: Living in a material world', *Theory and Society*, Vol. 37, No. 5, pp. 461– 83.

Pinch, T. and Frank, T. (2002) *Analog Days: The Invention and Impact of the Moog Synthesizer*, Cambridge, MA: Harvard University Press.

Sachs, C. (1940) *History of Musical Instruments*, New York: Norton.

Subramanian, K. S. (1985) 'An introduction to the Vina', *Asian Music*, Vol. 16, No. 2, pp. 7–82.

Théberge, Paul (1997) *Any Sound You Can Imagine: Making Music/Consuming Technology*, Hanover: Wesleyan University Press.

Trowell. M, and Waschman. K. P. (1953) *The Tribal Craft of Uganda*, Geoffrey Cumberlege: Oxford University Press.

Vannini, Phillip (ed.) (2009) *Material Culture and Technology in Everyday Life: Ethnographic Approaches*, New York: Peter Lang.

Von Hornbostel, E. M., & Sachs, C. (1961). Classification of musical instruments: Translated from the original german by anthony baines and klaus p. wachsmann. *The Galpin Society Journal*, 3-29.

Yuan, B. and Mao, J. (eds) (1986) *Zhongguo shaoshu minzu yueqi zhi* (Musical instruments of China's ethnic minorities), Beijing: Xin shijie chubanshe.

Chapter 14

The Resilience of Apartheid and Xenophobia: A Glimpse into Ethnicity and Citizenship in Uber Business in South Africa

Kiyoshi Umeya

1. Introduction

Cape Town, the 'Mother City' of South Africa, is a beautiful city with several tourist attractions. While Uber is an extremely convenient mode of transportation for tourists, most Uber drivers are part of illegal businesses that do not have a permit from the Western Cape. Drivers of minibuses are occasionally arrested, and their vehicles are seized due to lack of permits. There is a sense of tension that one may be caught someday while engaging in business.

In this crime-filled region, there is a chronic sense of tension with 'others', which is similar to wariness. Although apartheid based on 'race' was officially abolished in South Africa, cultural others, especially foreign workers, tend to continue living in the same communities. Due to economic factors, such as the gap between the rich and poor, foreign residents often live in socially and spatially separated categories.

This created an ethnoscape with well-defined boundaries. Zimbabweans comprise more than 80% of Uber drivers. Such stereotypical ethnoscapes offer limited opportunities to come into contact with others and form categories for mutual understanding that transcend ethnicity and nationality.

Such categories tend to function as walls for people on both sides and, if a negative image develops, create an atmosphere ripe for conflict and violence. This caused a number of riots in South Africa.

In September 2019, a xenophobic riot occurred in Johannesburg, targeting both foreign people and South Africans. This is the case for past riots. This is evidence that the category comprising the confrontation unit has become an empty template.

In such a situation, it is known that social media tend to have a negative effect, often leading to intentional instigation. Some South

African politicians utilise a technique called xenophobic populism to ensure votes. Although this approach wins elections against the background of voters who claim vested interest and privilege as South African citizens, it justifies xenophobia, which may lead to the withdrawal of foreign capital and businesspeople from South Africa.

The stereotype of 'foreign criminals' who were hostile in election campaigns was prominent in South Africa. However, the focus switched from criminals to foreigners, making them the target of conflict and violence.

Economic poverty is superficially part of the reason why people turn to xenophobic violence; however, South African economy faces a critical situation due to xenophobic violence.

2. Uber in Cape Town

'This isn't Uber! Please make sure to get the story straight. This isn't Uber!'

At the entrance to the Waterfront, the vehicle in front was stopped by the police, and a white man who seemed to be a tourist got out. It appeared that our vehicle would also be stopped.

'Hey, how much did you pay for this Uber?' the police officer asked me, seeming not to know much about the Uber system. Most Uber charges are made using credit cards and paid after exiting the vehicle; therefore, no transactions are concluded at that stage. 'No, I'm just taking a friend. I'm not an Uber driver,' said the driver. However, the police officer did not give up easily, saying, 'Show me your smartphone!'

I was a little surprised, wondering if the police have the authority to inspect personal belongings. At the same time, the vehicle in front was taken by the police.

I immediately called the Zimbabwean by his nickname and tried to create an image of the friend who was picking me up. I responded to the police officer's request to take out my smartphone by saying, 'I forgot it at home.' However, it seemed as if they were about to perform a pat-down.

Fortunately, the driver seemed to have two smartphones, and he managed to get out of the situation by hiding the smartphone with the Uber app and showing the one without it to the police officers. However, although I actually had a smartphone, I had forgotten my passport; therefore, I may have been in a precarious situation. In

South Africa, carrying an identity card is compulsory for every traveler. I would not have been able to complain if I were also rounded up.

This could have been a big problem; however, the police officer seemed to not want to make it a big problem. A few days earlier at Sea Point, police officers conducted forced inspections of personal belongings and confiscated items, leading to increased criticism of abuse of authority. There were even videos of the incident on YouTube.[1]

The police eventually gave up and we were released. It was on a weekend in May 2019.

South Africa, including Cape Town, which had a happy image as a tourist spot with beautiful blue skies and two oceans, had moments when I felt somewhat suffocated. There was a tense feeling of playing Russian roulette that somehow, someday, a bullet would come out. It was far from 'tolerance', and a feeling of being trapped sometimes arose.

According to one statistic, 57 people were killed every day in South Africa.[2] Most of these were late-night crimes occurring in cities and townships, which meant that the risk of walking outside in the city increased at night. If one was targeted, it was probably over. Momentum and security became more severe. Most compounds were behind high voltage electric fences. After getting dark, by the late evening, the police patrolled; however, at midnight, patrols stopped, causing people to avoid going outside.

I heard that the owner of a shop on Long Street closed his shop for some months, as there were many robberies during winter. Most South Africans seemed to feel trapped in such a tense lifestyle.

3. Mysterious Businesses that Operate Illegally

Uber, a very convenient mode of transportation for tourists in Cape Town, seemed to be mostly operated illegally.[3] Police officers could arrest Uber drivers, if desired. It is similar to the Hanshin Expressway, where everyone drives approximately 100 km/h, although the speed limit is 60 km/h. If the police wanted to, they could easily round up the offenders.[4]

Similarly, police officers occasionally set up traps near the Waterfront and cracked down on drivers, usually on weekends. Their vehicles, being used for business without a permit, were seized and could not be regained without first paying a fine of R10,500 (Fig. 1, Fig. 2). This was not usually the amount that people involved in such a business could obtain in a few days.

I heard that even if a person raised the funds and could pay the fine, there were long lines at the window and processing took time. Therefore, the person could only reclaim the vehicle after two or three days. While this was only a rumour, it was said that these fines provided financial resources for the police; however, it is unlikely that this was the original design. Some among the Osaka Prefectural Police Force secretly asserted that such a situation is plausible. Even if true, this was unlikely to be intentional, as that would indicate true corruption and would necessitate examination of the issue at a different level than in the present paper.[5]

Uber drivers heading to the Waterfront communicated with each other to check if the police set up checkpoints.

I heard that some people once applied for a permit. However, applicants were no longer reported, and it was said that, even if a permit was granted, it took two to five years. 'It is ridiculous to wait a few years in order to start working with Uber,' said one Zimbabwean driver. Certainly, the appeal of the Uber business model is that one can start working immediately without any preparation.[6] 'Who knows if I will still be in the Uber business in five years,' said another driver.

If my conversations with drivers are anything to go by, it would appear that the Uber office was aware of this structure and seemingly gave up on obtaining permits.

Uber's advertisements were quite appealing, claiming that one could start a business by simply installing an application. Even if one did not own a vehicle, it was possible to rent one. Referrals could also be received. Uber claimed that there were almost no initial expenses, although, according to some informants, it was quite expensive. Global citizenship was Uber's slogan, with a statement that there was no discrimination.

It was a great opportunity for immigrants to easily enter the business without a large amount of capital. Many of the drivers in my conversations and interviews rented vehicles for approximately R10,000 per month to start the business. If one worked hard in such conditions for two years, it was reportedly not impossible to be able to purchase a secondhand or used vehicle of one's own and become a business owner. Some of the drivers I spoke with of Zimbabwean nationality not only purchased vehicles within a few years but purchased multiple vehicles and lived comfortably by renting them to other drivers.

Training was provided in the office for drivers, and corporate efforts were being made to supply quality drivers.[7]

It was a threat to existing taxi drivers, who felt that their territory was encroached upon. In fact, the government intervened through labour unions. There were also some violent incidents regarding parking spaces, such as taxi drivers collectively stealing Uber drivers' vehicle keys.[8]

4. Zimbabwean Drivers

In order to leave Rondebosch, where the University of Cape Town is located, it was necessary to catch a HiAce screaming 'Kaapstad' [ˈkɑːpstat] (meaning Cape Town in Afrikaans). It cost R10 to get to the bus stop behind the station. As Uber is a door-to-door service, the quality of service differed and it was difficult to make a simple comparison; however, the price was roughly one-tenth the cost. A regular taxi was 50%–100% more expensive than Uber. Moreover, as taxis often did not have GPS, they tended to become lost, causing irritation. On the other hand, Uber drivers almost never got lost. Through the matching system, a customer could hail from anywhere and at any time. This was an extremely convenient service for customers. In my experience, there were only a few times that I had to wait for more than five minutes.

While no accurate statistics were available, according to the data that I have gathered, more than 80% of drivers were from Zimbabwe, followed by DRC Congo, Malawi, Rwanda, Somalia and Tanzania. This was, in a sense, a microcosm of neighbouring migrants who came to South Africa. However, there was a significant imbalance, seemingly due to several factors. First, the high proportion of Zimbabweans may reflect the hyperinflation and economic collapse that occurred in their home country.

In addition, the key to becoming a driver in South Africa, especially in Cape Town, where there are many tourists, was being able to speak English, more so than Afrikaans. This is in stark contrast to the market for shared minibus taxis, the mode of transportation of residents, with many Afrikaans speakers as drivers and conductors.

Zimbabwe is strong with respect to English due in part to President Mugabe's policy of granting education. On the one hand, these policies contributed to the serious economic crisis symbolised by hyperinflation. On the other hand, as a result, Zimbabwe boasted an English literacy rate of over 90%, one of the highest on the continent (the literacy rate for Malawi, for example, was in the 70% range).[9] Malawians who can use English confidently tended to be elite, whereas even the poorest Zimbabweans received a high degree of English education. A large percentage of the population in Zimbabwe can speak English comfortably. South Africa boasted an overall literacy rate of 94%; however, this included Afrikaans. In addition, leading to an overwhelming disadvantage for international business, the low literacy rate in some regions continued to cause challenges.[10] Highly educated people in Zimbabwe participated in the Uber business. In the past, these migrants lived in the suburbs of Maitland and Parow and formed residential areas. However, land prices in these residential areas skyrocketed and newcomers appeared to be living closer to townships near the airport.

Naturally, there were also incentives related to international relations, such as the special exception permit called the Zimbabwean Exemption Permit (ZEP), which allowed Zimbabweans who were already in South Africa to stay until 2021. It was the successor of the Zimbabwean Special Dispensation Permit (ZSP), which expired in 2017. This permit eliminated the risk of deportation and allowed them to obtain a South African driver's licence, which was welcomed by Uber. The Department of Home Affairs did not reveal how many Zimbabweans were working in the country under this status; however, if the status was not renewed in 2021, they would immediately face illegal status in the country.[11]

In South Africa, anyone seeking to work must have a work visa. However, many documents are required to apply for a working visa. Some required documents appear impossible to obtain.

In particular, a police report from the home country is required from all people 18 years of age or older and having resided in the country for a year or longer. While it was often difficult to obtain such a certificate from the police in most African countries, officials in Zimbabwe were extremely supportive in this regard.

Citizens of Zimbabwe seemed to obtain certificates without problems. The existence of the ZSP and ZEP frameworks, while tentative, suggested that Zimbabwe attached great importance to

South Africa as a place of work and a place of residence, and that South Africa accepted this as a mechanism. However, the future is uncertain at this point.

5. Stereotyping Ethnicity

Some stereotypes were propagated in South Africa, some of which were based to some extent in fact. For instance, apart from Uber, Zimbabweans mostly work in the hospitality sector. When asked about the origin of people who are serving customers at restaurants, 'Zimbabwe' is the common response. In contrast, many kitchen staff who do not serve customers were reportedly from Malawi. Stereotypes suggest that Malawians are good at housework and never steal. Congolese people were stereotyped as conversational.

If such stereotypes are circulated without specific data or concrete cases, categorising and popularising may occur, and reality may be ignored. Thus, the blank template is only a category of people different from us, and it stops people from being a gathering of living human beings and stops them from being identified by citizenship, race or ethnicity and serves only as the basis of the conflict. Stereotypes may create violent conflict and discrimination.

Taking a close look at the lessons of the past, while being cautious of 'race' categories, there may be conflicts between genders that consider gender as crossing ethnicity and race and believing this to be better than apartheid.

At a demonstration (#nene) following the murder of a female student at the University of Cape Town, hundreds of women were dressed in black and surrounded the Houses of Parliament. While initially, the goals were clear, the content gradually changed and there was risk of the situation transforming into hostility against men.

Trauma in violent cases, especially related to apartheid, seems to have caused the public's sensitivity.[12] South Africa may have a background that could inadvertently lead to aggression, cruelty or violence toward persons in another category.

6. 2019 Johannesburg Riots

Xenophobic incidents that occurred in the vicinity of the central business district (CBD) of Johannesburg in early September 2019 did not directly target Uber drivers.[13] The fact that the death of the taxi driver was the direct trigger, and what happened in sync with the strike that demanded the exclusion of foreigners from working as truck drivers became synchronised with the topic and could be observed in the Uber business. The Human Rights Watch announced that more than 200 foreign truck drivers were killed in South Africa since March 2018.[14]

The riots reportedly started on 1 September 2019, when a taxi driver who tried to quit being a drug dealer died. This resulted in riots and looting of foreigner-owned stores in Jeppestown and the CBD of Johannesburg. By 5 September, 497 people were arrested, during which time looting spread to the town of Alexandra. A mosque in St Georges Mall was attacked, and all the stores in the mall were looted. The rioters were shot and killed by the shop owners. Many shopkeepers were arrested.

A Zimbabwean was set on fire and killed after being assaulted by a South African mob. His child was burnt to death at the same time.[15]

The riots were reignited in Johannesburg on 8 September 2019. The mob marched on the CBD, repeatedly looting shops while criticising foreigners. Mangosuthu Buthelezi, a Zulu leader who viewed the situation seriously, called for a return to peace and made a public speech to call for the end of violence.[16]

The riots coincided with a nationwide strike protesting the hiring of foreign truck drivers from outside South Africa. In KwaZulu-Natal, many cargo trucks were burned, and foreign truck drivers were attacked.[17] According to the police, more than 680 people were arrested on suspicion of being involved in the riots.

In response to these riots, the Football Association of Zambia (FAZ) cancelled an international football match with South Africa in Zambia due to 'security concerns in South Africa'. The Zambian Pick n Pay (supermarket chain) was targeted by looters, which was also seen as retaliation.

In Nigeria, all stores and service centres operated by the South African telecommunications company MTN were temporarily closed following retaliatory attacks in response to the South African riots. Multichoice and Shoprite were closed, causing other South African companies to temporarily cease operations.[18]

Following the riots, Nigerian President, Muhammadu Buhari, summoned the South African High Commissioner and raised concerns about the case with South African President, Cyril Ramaphosa. The Nigerian government cancelled participation in the

African Economic Forum in Cape Town in retaliation for the riots and closed the South African embassy due to security concerns.[19] All Progressives Congress, the Nigerian ruling party, claimed to confiscate and nationalise South African companies in Nigeria in retaliation for attacks on Nigerian citizens.[20]

In September 2019, more than 640 Nigerians registered for a free flight to Nigeria in response to the attacks on foreigners.[21] The free flight was provided by a private donation from Allen Onyema, the CEO of Air Peace, whose hub is in Lagos.

By the end of October, approximately 300 people who were seeking refugee status from organisations such as UNHCR due to the riots in Johannesburg engaged in a sit-down at St George's Mall, Waldorf Arcade in front of the UNHCR office in Cape Town. Human rights activist, Papy Skami, one of the central figures of the left-wing extremist group Kongolese Freedom Fighters (KFF), which was formed under the influence of the South African left-wing political party Economic Free Fighters (EFF), was involved in the instigation.[22] Publicly, they sought safe refuge outside the country. On 30 October, the police set out to expel them, clashing with the crowd and making more than 100 arrests.[23] An NGO provided food; however, the authorities requested to cease this provision.[24] Although it was intended to eliminate this sit-in completely, using the Methodist Church as a base, protest activities continued from 27 January 2020.

7. Hotbeds of Xenophobia

South African celebrities, such as Manaka Ranaka, Cassper Nyovest and Nadia Nakai, publicly criticised xenophobia and the resulting riots.[25]

However, behind such a seemingly common-sense declaration, the government issued a controversial official statement. In 2015, the South African Minister of Small Business Development, Lindiwe Zulu, urged foreign business owners to disclose their trade secrets and warned that peaceful co-existence with local business owners could not be expected without this.[26]

According to Zulu, isolation under apartheid created disadvantages for South African entrepreneurs, leaving foreign entrepreneurs with an advantage. While Zulu's views faced widespread criticism, they had the explanatory power to make struggling South African entrepreneurs want to comply.[27] As long as the economy was favourable, it could be regarded as a personal opinion. There was an atmosphere in South Africa that allowed ministers to make such statements.

A study by the Competition Commission, the national antitrust regulatory authority, found that foreigners were more successful than citizens in business performance. The results of a survey of competition dynamics revealed concerns that the advancement of foreign entrepreneurs would be linked to such riots, as they were regarded as blocking the growth of small businesses in South Africa.[28]

Gastrow discovered that in Johannesburg, a centre for African immigration, small-scale retailers from Somalia were successful as a result of business efforts, such as low-margin sales, long opening hours in busy areas and offering a wide range of products, calling the phenomenon 'Somalinomics'.[29] Merely looking at statistical results as success of 'foreign' managers did not reveal such efforts.

According to a Zimbabwean Uber driver, 'We work on Saturdays and Sundays, and I do not think that we will quit working in the evening from sundown. Having satisfied the difficult police report requirement, we have come to work here. A taxi driver who only speaks Afrikaans and is complaining may be the one who becomes involved in a murder case related to drugs in the vicinity of Cape Flat. And they always try to take off from work from Friday afternoon "because family is important", right?'

However, this is merely an assumption and an example of a stereotype reflected from the opposite side.

Some social media researchers indicated that fake news stories were circulating, causing panic among South Africans.[30] Negative comments were repeatedly made to foreign workers through social media for months before the riot. This is similar to the case of 'Radio Télévision Libre des Mille Collines' (RTLM) during the Rwandan genocide.

Nigeria closed its diplomatic missions, and countries announced their absence at the planned summit to be held in Cape Town. The president gave a speech to calm the situation.

According to the 2011 statistics, South Africa, which accepted more than 2,200,000 immigrants, has had intermittent xenophobic events (the total population as of November 2019 was 58,828,043).[31] Following the May 2008 riots, xenophobic riots occurred repeatedly in 2015 for various reasons. In 2008, 62 people were killed (of these,

21 were South Africans). In 2015, riots also occurred in Johannesburg and Durban.

South African human rights NGOs, such as Right2Know, asserted that the riots were a result of 'xenophobic populism' supported by South African politicians, such as Goodwill Zwelithini kaBhekuzulu, the reigning King of the Zulu, Herman Mashaba, the Mayor of Johannesburg, and President Ramaphosa.[32]

On 25 March 2019, approximately 100 people attacked foreign-owned companies in Durban. Approximately 50 people were running for help to local police stations and mosques, and three people died. In his speech regarding the ruling African National Congress (ANC) election manifesto in the 2019 South African general election, President Cyril Ramaphosa promised to crack down on foreigners involved in criminal activity. In other words, he could win the election by boosting xenophobia.

The utilisation of xenophobia in this election was severely criticised; however, the rule of thumb was that the election could be won by encouraging xenophobia.[33]

The Human Sciences Research Council reported the causes of the 2008 riots as:

1) relative deprivation, especially intensifying competition for jobs, products and housing;
2) tThe process of grouping using a narrow nationalistic psychological classification;
3) a sense of privilege that South African citizens should be treated exceptionally, or the sense of superiority of South Africans over other Africans; and
4) a form of exclusive citizenship or nationalism that seeks to exclude others.[34]

This was likely the same for the 2019 riots.

The group/grid theory of Douglas, inherited from Burstein, is relevant here (Douglas 1970, 1978; Spickard 1989), where the group and grid are high among the narrow groups. It is theoretically assumed that the boundaries and the pressure of roles expected from each group were high. It can be said that this was inevitable. Moreover, the economy of the country also suffered a great crisis due to these riots. Bad economic situations give momentum to xenophobic stories, creating a downward spiral.

In October, minibus drivers held a series of protests in Cape Town. They did not simply refuse to drive. Particularly on Friday, the 18th, 23 minibuses blocked the N2 highway. While it was not possible to view the full picture, they used taxis to block the traffic of essential positions of the CBD and the Waterfront, creating a major disruption.[35] The drivers, whose vehicles were confiscated by the police due to a lack of permits, reportedly protested the abuse of power.

In addition, even in clashes with the police mentioned above, people merely said, 'Come on, come on' via WhatsApp voice messaging. Some in the crowds initially gathered with little understanding of the situation. WhatsApp groups were connected for a variety of purposes, making it possible to send information to a wide range of people regardless of the leaders' intentions.[36] Twitter accounts such as #LeavingSA, #DRCongo and #CapeTown were also used.

On Africa Day in May 2019, Francis B. Nyamnjoh made an appeal for 'Ubuntuism' at the University of the Free State.[37] He understood the structure of xenophobia through 'insiders and outsiders', advocating openness and return to tolerance during the tense situation of obstruction complicated by hostility.

8. Insiders and Outsiders

Modern states regulate the mobility of outsiders through the legal system with the aim of preserving the existing interests and structure of the state. As such, the procedures from request to approval of necessary documents for a work visa and the mechanism by which a state or city manages specific labour can be observed. These legal systems and procedures show a strong tendency to protect insiders and citizens, and outsiders usually face some difficulty in obtaining citizenship. While foreign workers are encouraged to work, the issuance of work visas and regulations regarding the entry of businesses are ambiguous and simultaneously strict and lax. While it is very difficult to meet all legal requirements, it is possible to operate a business in practice.

There are conflicting messages here. One is the public message that people may come and work here if they are beneficial to the country, while the other is, 'We can always send you back at any time.' This suggests that foreign workers are carefully maintained as outsiders who do not have complete citizenship and do not threaten the interests of insiders.[38] Furthermore, there should be sufficient agency to protect insiders, at least for institutional design.

However, for insiders, this remains insufficient. However, even if the number of immigrants is reduced, the frustration of residents will not end if their economic situation does not improve. Under a neoliberal, neoclassical, neo-Keynesian, or Trumpian philosophy, where maximising self-interest is good and rational, one's success is the result of one's efforts. However, such philosophies perceive the cause of one's plight as being due to 'others' trying to take a share of the pie, believing foreigners to be the problem.[39]

However, while xenophobic populism may lead to winning elections, it causes trouble for the national economy. This should be clear simply by considering the loss South Africa suffered from responses to xenophobia by countries such as Nigeria. The economy visibly cooled down, as there are no more investors or tourists, let alone leaders, making visits.

On November 1, 2019, Moody's Investors Service barely maintained South Africa's investment rating at Baa3. Baa3 is the lowest rank in the intermediate grade, just above what is considered junk. The outlook changed from negative to stable.[40]

9. Stereotypes and the Uber Business as Templates

Due to the factors discussed above, a market consisting mainly of Zimbabweans emerged for the Uber business in Cape Town.

Therefore, the visual distinction between ethnicity and skin colour was preserved in the cityscape. As such, even after the end of political apartheid, social apartheid subdivisions could be observed.

For instance, only white people who drove luxury vehicles could be seen in restaurants and bars in Sea Point or Kalk Bay at night. On the other hand, those standing outside in the cold wind, perhaps with little money, smoking cigarettes and marijuana, tend to be 'colored people' and 'black people'. Black people usually watch parked vehicles to earn a meagre income. In fact, the 'white people' may not even be South Africans. However, stereotypical images of a 'luxury white residential area' may cause these perceptions to recede into the background, creating apartheid in urban spaces. There are, of course, living spaces where various ethnicities mix due to work or university studies.

The ethnoscape, which does not betray such stereotypes, results in an empty template as there are no expectations of mutual negotiation across spaces. Such a cognitive framework merely provides categories of separation from others. While this does not provide hints for understanding others, it creates the appearance of understanding others, which becomes the embodiment of stereotypes. Such embodied stereotypes are extremely vulnerable to externally injected images, whether intentionally or otherwise. First, if the stereotypes comprising the first key were rewritten based on actual experience as a way of understanding others, spatial separation would prevent this.

It is easy to imagine what happens when an image with a certain degree of explanatory power is injected into a place that relies on stereotypes, as reality is not well understood. Many of the images tend to be simplistic and far removed from the actual situation. Initially, it would be easy for a 'foreigner who is a criminal' to be simplified to just 'foreigner', or for a 'man who rapes a woman' to be simplified to just a 'man'.[41]

Perhaps due to the effects of xenophobia, Uber drivers tend to hide all information about their birthplaces, which was mostly filled in from April 2019. In addition, there were problems related to this in terms of business. An Uber driver said, 'There were many customers who cancelled after finding out that the driver was from Zimbabwe or DRC Congo'. Therefore, drivers stopped writing their birthplace on their profiles.

I argue that this is an increasingly dangerous situation. It is likely to create many people in the 'people unlike us' category, who are of unknown origin and identity. It appears that self-defence measures created more dangerous conditions.

Many victims of riots were victims of accidental explosions. As such, it is easy to imagine how such riots were carried out based on irrational motivations, and how target selection was not well planned.

The key may be lack of secondary, more elaborate categories advocated by Kamau and Rutland for classifying people of different nations to minimise bias.[42] They are caught between both the insider and outsider world, such as the Kalanga Elite of Botswana who are *makwerekwere* and faced ambiguities regarding citizenship.[43] Originally, this was a xenophobic discriminatory term for foreign elements; however, it was reinterpreted by Nyamnjoh as being an extremely dynamic factor. Such an ambiguous position is highly precarious;

however, such intermediaries activate matters from their surroundings.

10. Conclusions

Regardless of how deceptive the concept of race is in terms of sociology and anthropology, it is a method that classifies people by their immediate appearance and exerts strong classification power. Regardless of actual reality, it is possible to visualise which ethnicity is dominant in the business based on impression.

As such, the story of apartheid is arguably one of the most unfortunate experiences in human history.

Furthermore, as Trumpian philosophy spread around the world, the expansion of self-interest, in combination with exclusionism and privilegism based on citizenship, became prevalent. The HSRC analysis is sufficient to examine these factors.

Violent cases of xenophobia, which reignited this year, could be regarded as the resilience of xenophobia against the background of the resilience of apartheid. In that sense, while Uber's rhetoric of global citizenship may seem appealing, the Uber business itself, which is prosperous, may also act as a detonator of the powder keg.

It is unsurprising that minibus drivers and even Uber drivers from South Africa do not have permits, as even South African citizens cannot easily obtain them. However, even if insiders and outsiders are equally burdened, is this fact accurately recognised? Most Zimbabweans and people from other countries may consider this to be discrimination against foreigners without realising that it is equally difficult for South Africans. It is easier and more advantageous to engage in self-defence in the face of such a difficult situation.

Japan is also full of inconsistencies, such as a highly deceptive foreign trainee system. Japan is faced with the same predicament of xenophobia. There is an unfortunate memory that people were once disadvantaged due to the ascriptive aspect of 'race', although the concept of 'race' itself is a creation of the Victorian era. However, this concept may be easily revived when some incident occurs, as xenophobia tends to be resilient.

However, we should improve inconsistent situations one by one and regain the Ubuntuism and tolerance advocated by Nyamnjoh. It is unknown when and where *makwerekwere*-like activity that, in a sense, symbolises the potential of Africa may appear. As such, I feel that South Africa's citizenship itself must be made more open. These are some of my personal opinions while looking at the pile of documents required for a work visa that will likely not be granted.[44]

Notes

[1] Police officers arrest a woman in Sea Point without clear cause - YouTube https://www.youtube.com/watch?v=a4mcCebR7IM (retrieved 10 November 2019).

[2] https://www.afpbb.com/articles/-/3189269 (retrieved 10 November 2019).

[3] Applying for a public operating licence | Western Cape Government https://www.westerncape.gov.za/service/applying-public-operating-licence (retrieved 10 November 2019).

[4] Hanshin Expressway is a highway in Japan between Osaka and Kobe with a speed limit of 60km/h. The usual speed limit of highways in Japan is 80km/h.

[5] However, while this is only a rumour, it was said that pressure from the mafia was involved in adjusting the number of minibuses and controlling the number of issuances of operating permits.

[6] About Uber – Our Story – Vision for Our Future https://www.uber.com/za/en/about/ (retrieved 10 November 2019).

[7] Although it happened only once, I became the third customer. The driver drove dangerously, such as going in the wrong direction. Furthermore, the driver could not speak English well.

[8] Taxi drivers drive fear into the hearts of Uber drivers | News24 https://www.news24.com/SouthAfrica/News/taxi-drivers-drive-fear-into-the-hearts-of-uber-drivers-20191003 (retrieved 10 November 2019).

[9] Zimbabwe | UNESCO UIS http://uis.unesco.org/en/country/zw?theme=education-and-literacy (retrieved 10 November 2019).

[10] Poor literacy levels still a concern in SA | Daily News https://www.iol.co.za/dailynews/poor-literacy-levels-still-a-concern-in-sa-14601496 (retrieved 10 November 2019).

[11] ZEP Permits for Zimbabweans in South Africa: What you should know https://www.intergate-immigration.com/blog/zep-permits-zimbabweans-south-africa/ (retrieved 10 November 2019).

[12] Simplistic thinking should be avoided, as negative impressions of others may cause extreme violence. Such situations have embodied storylines leading to violence in the past, highlighting that the situation should be treated seriously.

[13] Johannesburg chaos: Alleged 'xenophobic' violence erupts again [video] https://www.thesouthafrican.com/news/xenophobic-violence-south-africa-latest-news-8-september/ (retrieved 10 November 2019).

[14] South Africa: Deadly Attacks on Foreign Truck Drivers | Human Rights Watch https://www.hrw.org/news/2019/08/26/south-africa-deadly-attacks-foreign-truck-drivers (retrieved 10 November 2019).

[15] 'Zimbabwean woman recounts how husband was beaten, burnt to death in Katlehong', Saturday Star, https://www.iol.co.za/saturday-star/news/zimbabwean-woman-recounts-how-husband-was-beaten-burnt-to-death-in-katlehong-32498218 (retrieved 10 November 2019).'Zim woman recounts how husband was beaten, burnt to death in SA', Nehanda Radio, https://nehandaradio.com/2019/09/07/zim-woman-recounts-how-husband-was-beaten-burnt-to-death-in-sa/ (retrieved 10 November 2019).

[16] 'IN FULL: Mangosuthu Buthelezi's message against xenophobia' https://www.timeslive.co.za/politics/2019-09-08-in-full-mangosuthu-buthelezis-message-against-xenophobia/ (retrieved 10 November 2019).

[17] 'Scores arrested in looting, xenophobic protests' | News | National | M&G https://mg.co.za/article/2019-09-03-scores-arrested-in-looting-xenophobic-protests/ (retrieved 10 November 2019).

[18] MTN, MultiChoice shut branches in Nigeria amid protests over SA attacks | Fin24 https://www.fin24.com/Companies/ICT/mtn-multichoice-shut-branches-in-nigeria-amid-protests-over-sa-attacks-20190904 (retrieved 10 November 2019).

[19] Nigeria pulls out of South Africa summit after deadly riots | South Africa News | Al Jazeera https://www.aljazeera.com/news/2019/09/nigeria-pulls-south-africa-summit-deadly-riots-190904171823632.html (retrieved 10 November 2019).South African embassy in Nigeria closed after retaliatory attacks | News24 https://m.news24.com/SouthAfrica/News/south-african-embassy-in-nigeria-closed-after-retaliatory-attacks-20190905 (retrieved 10 November 2019).

[20] Nigerian ruling party demands takeover of SA firms | Fin24 https://www.fin24.com/Economy/nigerian-ruling-party-demands-takeover-of-sa-firms-20190908 (retrieved 10 November 2019).

[21] Hundreds of Nigerians to take free evacuation from South Africa - Reuters https://www.reuters.com/article/us-nigeria-safrica-idUSKCN1VV0ZD (retrieved 10 November 2019).

[22] Kongolese Freedom Fighters https://www.kongolesefreedomfighters.net/ (retrieved 10 November 2019).

[23] Chaos in Cape Town as refugees evicted from city centre protest | GroundUp https://www.groundup.org.za/article/unhcr-refugees-evicted/ (retrieved 10 November 2019).

[24] Refugees order Gift of the Givers out of Methodist Church in Cape Town | News24 https://www.news24.com/SouthAfrica/News/refugees-order-gift-of-the-givers-out-of-methodist-church-in-cape-town-20191107 (retrieved 10 November 2019).

[25] Manaka Ranaka on xenophobic attacks: 'It makes me ashamed to be South African' https://www.timeslive.co.za/tshisa-live/tshisa-live/2019-09-03-manaka-ranaka-on-xenophobic-attacks-it-makes-me-ashamed-to-be-south-african/ (retrieved 10 November 2019).

[26] Reveal trade secrets, minister tells foreigners https://www.businesslive.co.za/archive/2015-01-28-reveal-trade-secrets-minister-tells-foreigners/ (retrieved 10 November 2019).

[27] Mind your own business, minister | Business | M&G https://mg.co.za/article/2015-01-29-mind-your-own-business-minister (retrieved 10 November 2019).

'Foreign business owners are not the enemy' - DA | News | National | M&G https://mg.co.za/article/2015-02-02-00-foreign-business-owners-are-not-the-enemy-da (retrieved 10 November 2019). Small business minister wants spaza-shop trade secrets – The Daily Vox http://www.thedailyvox.co.za/small-business-minister-wants-spaza-shop-trade-secrets/ (retrieved 10 November 2019).

[28] Small foreign-owned retailers in South Africa are more competitive than local rivals – Quartz Africa https://qz.com/africa/431733/small-foreign-owned-retailers-in-south-africa-are-more-competitive-than-local-rivals/ (retrieved 10 November 2019).

[29] (PDF) Somalinomics: A case study on the economics of Somali informal trade in Cape Town | Vanya Gastrow、 Roni Amit – Academia.edu https://www.academia.edu/6827880/Somalinomics_A_case_study_on_the_economics_of_Somali_informal_trade_in_Cape_Town (retrieved 10 November 2019).

[30] YouTube https://www.youtube.com/watch?v=8SZj4RHhzos (retrieved 10 November 2019).

[31] New York Times & others STILL wrong on number of immigrants in South Africa | Africa Check https://africacheck.org/reports/new-york-times-use-plagiarised-article-to-back-up-sa-immigrant-number/ (retrieved 10 November 2019). South Africa Population (2019) – Psychology Worldometers https://www.worldometers.info/world-population/south-africa-population/ (retrieved 10 November 2019).

[32] Right2Know blames Mashaba, Ramaphosa, Zwelithini for attacks on foreigners | IOL News https://www.iol.co.za/news/politics/right2know-blames-mashaba-ramaphosa-zwelithini-for-attacks-on-foreigners-31739481 (retrieved 10 November 2019).

State Is Complicit In Xenophobic Violence Undermining The Rule Of Law – Right2Know Campaign https://www.r2k.org.za/2019/09/02/state-is-complicit-in-xenophobic-violence-undermining-the-rule-of-law/ (retrieved 10 November 2019).

[33] Xenophobic attacks spark South African response – BBC News https://www.bbc.com/news/world-africa-47765863 (retrieved 10 November 2019). Electioneering must be free from xenophobia and respect all | Cape Times https://www.iol.co.za/capetimes/opinion/electioneering-must-be-free-from-xenophobia-and-respect-all-20098851 (retrieved 10 November 2019).

[34] 'Violence and xenophobia in South Africa: Developing consensus, moving to action', Human Science Research Council. Wayback Machine

https://web.archive.org/web/20091124132407/http://www.hsrc.ac.za/Document-2994.phtml (retrieved 10 November 2019).

[35] Taxi protest: Cape Town commuters warned of strike action on Tuesday https://www.thesouthafrican.com/news/cape-town-taxi-protest-updates-when-tuesday-22-october-2019/ (retrieved 10 November 2019).

[36] Social media on Cape Town protests & 'police brutality': 'This is horrifying' https://www.timeslive.co.za/news/south-africa/2019-10-31-social-media-on-cape-town-protests-police-brutality-this-is-horrifying/ (retrieved 10 November 2019).

[37] https://www.ufs.ac.za/docs/default-source/web-story-documents/nyamnjoh_ubuntuism-lecture_20192105_final-version.pdf?sfvrsn=6d2d8921_2 (retrieved 10 November 2019).

[38] Nyamnjoh (2016: 16). Nyamnjoh rejects these modern diplomatic functions as too rigid and as an example of the intolerance of citizenship boundaries.

[39] Nyamnjoh (2016).

[40] Moody's keeps South Africa above junk for now – with a negative outlook https://businesstech.co.za/news/finance/350787/moodys-keeps-south-africa-above-junk-for-now-with-a-negative-outlook/ (retrieved 10 November 2019).

Moody's leaves South Africa teetering on brink of 'junk' - Moneyweb https://www.moneyweb.co.za/news/south-africa/moodys-changes-sas-outlook-to-negative-from-stable/ (retrieved 10 November 2019).This is what awaits South Africa if Moody's cuts its rating to junk – Moneyweb https://www.moneyweb.co.za/news/south-africa/this-is-what-awaits-south-africa-if-moodys-cuts-its-rating-to-junk/ (retrieved 10 November 2019).

[41] The embodiment of stories of violence tends to cause desperation.

[42] Kamau and Rutland (2008: 183–208).

[43] Nyamnjoh (2016: 93), for Kalanga elites, originally migrated from Zimbabwe, see Werbner (2004).

[44] If Nyamnjoh indicated the flaws of citizenship for the 'complete gentleman', he would likely advocate 'flexible citizenship' (Nyamnjoh 2016: 239–241). In that sense, the peculiar 'Westernness' of South Africa may in part hinder the development of African potential.

References

Kamau, C. and Rutland, A. (2008) 'A quasi-experiment on the effects of superordinate categorization on liking of people from other nations.' *Psychology and Developing Societies*, 20(2), 183 -208.

Nyamnjoh, F. B. (2016) *Insiders and Outsiders: Citizenship and Xenophobia in Contemporary Southern Africa*, London: Zed Books.

Werbner, R. (2004) *Reasonable Radicals and Citizenship in Botswana: The Public Anthropology of Kalanga Elites*, Bloomington: Indiana University Press.

Chapter 15

Resilience of Face-to-Face Identity among East African Pastoralists

Hazama Itsuhiro

I East African Pastoral Society and Ethnicity

When considering the relationship between ecology and ethnicity in the field of East African pastoral societies, the fluidity of group boundaries as one of the key factors in surviving natural disasters cannot be overlooked. The natural environment is undergoing severe climate change, and fertile pasture and water areas vary greatly by year and season and shift irregularly. Under these circumstances, the exclusive occupation of a particular place by a particular population is ineffective as a survival strategy. For a population that resides in the arid savanna, it is easier to live in a manner such that multiple groups are loosely connected and allow each other to move and use resources. For example, according to Sobania's historical study, the 19th-century East African pastoral society was comprehensively integrated such that mutual border crossings between ethnic groups were allowed. The savanna migrants could take advantage of their mutual ties to escape the frequent droughts and plagues and quickly recover from the loss of livestock herds (Sobania 2011). The old East African herders moved as individuals, families and larger groups in times of disaster, and the communities into which they settled embraced them as peers in their daily lives.

The subsistence mode of life in the arid savanna enables a symbiotic coexistence with outside groups as a characteristic of ethnic identity in pastoral societies, providing transformative freedom wherein individuals can freely enter and leave the 'us'. Researchers of East African pastoral societies have widely shared this theory of an interrelationship between culture and nature. Due to the necessities of life that demand shifting ecological resources (water and grassland), the contours of the imagined whole continually implode and renew. This phenomenon inevitably creates social groups that conceal within them the question of the homogeneity of the 'us'. In other words, the most radical ethnic characteristic that East African pastoralists perceive and within which they conduct their interactions is the structural order, wherein there is a single homogenous ethnic group in the upper hierarchy and wherein the 'us' is categorised, segmented and stratified into ranks of classification, and is a tentative thing. Thus, their feeling toward life, based on the natural environment, includes a catabolic mechanism that always illuminates such a self-evident fiction. The topic is covered more specifically below.

The model of traumatic memories constructed among those living in the affluent first world assumes the transience of crucial difficulties, as straightforwardly systematised in the clinical model of post-traumatic stress. However, for people living in protracted crisis situations and exposed to recurring trauma, the emergency of real catastrophic hardship is not a state of exception, but a place of everyday life. One question being raised in this paper concerns what is required to survive and even to thrive where existential threats are ordinary and usual events. What are the sources of resilience and relative invulnerability that I have been hinting at? Human resilience in the context of pastoralist life involves a certain amount of manipulation verging on ethnicity and face-to-face interaction.

In East African pastoral societies, the same clans and subclans exist and are spread over ethnic groups that have different languages, histories and customs. Therefore, individuals can belong to multiple ethnic groups. Based on the clan principle, an individual can choose from various ethnic identities the one that best suits their situation. This mobility and flexibility of identity runs through the principle of the group in pastoral societies (Matsuda 1998; Schlee 1989). Even when individuals are in the midst of ethnic conflicts, where there is mutual suspicion and hatred between groups, they can use their nonethnic identity (clan identity) to find common grounds and defend their livelihood. The relationship between the upper (ethnicity) and lower (clan) taxa can be reversed. In East African pastoral society, there is no absolute structure with ethnicity at its peak; instead, the structure incorporates a view of groups in which the lower groups constantly aim for higher positions in the structure.

However, research into this trend of the reversal of the hierarchical relationships of order has receded into the background of mainstream East African pastoral research since 2010. Much of the recent research into ethnicity has highlighted the real problem: a homogenous population constructed from ideologies of a common origin and common birthplace that embodies the world as an ever-shrinking circle of inclusion (Schlee 2013; Korf et al. 2015; Galaty 2016). For example, according to G. Schlee, entering into the late 1990s and 2000s, ethnic territories were demarcated in northern Kenya, and the politics became increasingly ethnicised. Simultaneously, ideas of national rights and cultural defence were spreading worldwide. As a result, there has been a rapid spread in movements that tolerate and encourage violence against and the elimination of minority groups (Schlee 2013).

Ethnicity is a controversial topic. Its importance is immeasurable in contemporary African pastoral research. Absolute loyalty, a homogenous, hard sense of belonging upon which those individuals in the territory relied, formed a pillar not only for the ethnogenesis of the African pastoral peoples but also for modern European nation building, and it supported the ruling system. Ethnicities, as nations and nepotistic machines, create formal ethnic identities that enter into war and destruction against outsiders.

Considering the ethnicity of African pastoral peoples is equivalent to considering the mode of rule in the modern world. However, this paper does not conduct analyses to formally redefine ethnicity. By contrast, this paper focuses on identities that are face-to-face that transcend formal ethnicities and bind together different cultural communities in a context in which armed groups attack outsiders. The goal of this paper is to focus on life-threatening interactions between the members of mutually heterogeneous social groups, namely, showing mercy in collective combat, to investigate the micro negotiations that occur when individuals suddenly break through the obviousness of formal ethnic identities and to determine the reality of the subjects' experience when in contact with the 'other,' who then appears to them in a fundamentally different manner than before negotiations began.

In this case, 'showing mercy' refers to the intentional act of saving the life of an enemy, more specifically, a member of an external group, in the midst of a lethal collective attack. On the battlefield, an individual's belonging to and empathy toward their social group are sharply questioned and evidenced by the killing of the enemy. Saving the lives of members of an outside group casts doubt on an individual's sense of community and belonging to their social group. This paper captures the moments in which the organisational behaviours of groups are destabilised by the open, impromptu attitude that emerges when the modern East African pastoral peoples' loyalty conflicts with their prosocial attitudes toward life. In other words, this paper aims to describe and analyse the aggressive force that subsumes the 'I' into the concept of the 'we' and the force that antagonises it, specifically, an interaction in which multiple sources of 'I' resonate.

The research was conducted among the Karimojong, Dodoth and Turkana. The analysis focuses on materials obtained among the Dodoth, but supplementary research materials from the Turkana are also used.

II The Meaning of Death in Combat

The East Sudanese and East Nile language-speaking groups are composed mainly of herders in Tanzania, Uganda, Kenya, Sudan and Ethiopia. They raise livestock, such as cattle, goats, sheep and camels, and their diet is highly dependent on their products. Anthropologists have identified a subordinate group of East Nile herders that constitutes a cluster of linguistic and cultural similarities (Murdock 1959). According to this list, the Karimojong, Dodoth, Jie and Turkana, covered in this paper, in addition to the Test, Toposa, Nyangatom and Jiiye, comprise the Karimojong cluster.

They reside on the borders of Uganda, Kenya, South Sudan and Ethiopia but were originally a single group (Gulliver 1955; Dyson-Hudson 1966; Lamphear 1992; Gray 2000). Because of the groups' migration from the highlands of Moru-apolon in northwestern Kenya approximately 200 years ago and the raiding of livestock within the cluster, they gradually differentiated into distinct groups (ethnicities) (Lamphear 1992). Despite this phenomenon, the raids continued, and the conflicts and alliances among the ethnic groups continually changed. In the second half of the 20th century, modern firearms, such as the Afromat Kalashnikov and the G3, were developed and manufactured in the north and spread throughout the plains. These evenly matched battles continue to this day wherein individuals use these firearms, and these individuals have killed many people (Hazama 2019).

Even in a society with prolonged low-intensity conflict, coming to terms with the death of others is difficult. I began to realise this when I started my 14th research expedition (since 2002) to the Dodoth in

December 2018. As usual, I set up a tent in the *ekrul* (a living space for mothers and their children) of a lady named Lomus within the *ere* (homestead), where I conducted a live-in survey. I eventually began calling her 'mother'. Lomus's second son, Popo, was killed in a raid in 2010.

Popo was killed by raiders. Following the central government's domiciliation policy accompanying forced disarmament starting in 2006, disorderly livestock management laws were implemented. The military specified times and routes for daily grazing. Livestock had to be housed in camps adjacent to the army garrison and in accordance with military orders. Livestock owned by Popo's father, Lonya, were also housed under military surveillance in a livestock camp in Kurao, approximately 10 kilometers northwest of the settlement. One day, at midnight, in March 2010, the Jie were attacked by raiders. The army was unable to protect the livestock, and all of the herds were stolen from the pens.

Upon learning of the attack, Popo, who was in the village, began to pursue the enemy east along the river that crosses the village to the south and runs from east to west. If an individual travels southeast along the escarpment that forms the border between Kenya and Uganda, they will find an area of shrubland called Naburaii. Upon being ambushed, the raiders opened fire on the individuals who had followed them. Popo was killed, along with six others. The government had already confiscated all the guns from the inhabitants of the *ere*, and all of the individuals killed were unarmed. Popo's younger brothers, Naunya and Louru, returned from the scene and informed their mother, Lomus, of his murder.

In the Dodoth society, the emotions of a mother who has lost her child cause her to want to commit suicide. How would Lomus deal with her loss of will to continue living? I wanted to listen to what she had to say so that I could understand. I recorded Lomus's story (more precisely, her story in her words) and then that of Lomus's eldest son with the help of my research assistant, Lopech. Finally, I translated her account from the Dodoth language into Japanese. What follows is an excerpt:

> Conversation 'Old words …'
>
> Lomus: Death had come. Of course, that's what had happened. Popo was dead. When my children (indicated toward Naunya and Louru, sitting next to one another) returned from where he had died,

everyone from all the clans came. They tried speaking to me, but I was in pain. It was very painful. That's right. I cried and I cried. And then, I forgot. I just stayed quiet. Oh! When the *etau* (heart) strikes suddenly, it is natural to review again and again in your mind what caused it. I remember it in my heart.

Lopech: What did people say when they spoke to you?

Lomus: They said, 'Please forget it, because we will all die someday.'

Yes! That's right.

Death is something that's always been there.

Lopech: Did you listen to [understand] them?

Lomus: I heard everything that they said. I spoke. When I remembered, I said, 'Why?' Humans die, of course. And it's something that we forget. I said, 'Everyone will forget him.' I hold on to old words. I still remember in my heart. Even now, my heart remembers. I recall it over and over again and want to resist it. I remember when we were all talking together. Those who have lost someone to death remember the forgetting. People even forget death when they have a lone child taken from them (she extended all the fingers on her right hand and turned them upward and wrapping her other hand around the root of the middle finger, she yanked it).

The phrase 'to have a lone child taken' is a reference to the symbolic idea that a person who is with others dies and disappears. Lomus describes Popo as a dead person 'taken' from his fellow living relatives, spouse and friends. Lomus's impression is that she is filled with pain at the irreplaceability of others and at the strangeness of the everyday world.

Due to Popo's death and from the tear that had emerged from having been torn suddenly from the physical self to which she had clung, Lomus attempted to remain out of reach of her companions. She did not eat, sleep or talk, and attempted suicide. What is the meaning of 'I hold on to old words (*ngakiro kolong ekerumete nguna*)?' When I asked Lopech, who helped me transcribe the conversation, he took hold of my arm while sitting on a chair to my left. His right hand wrapped around my bicep. 'A person who wants to die will try to travel far away on their own, so this is how you catch them (*akirum*)' – this gesture of *akirum* reminds the other of the fact that one's companions are 'here' and, in one word, conveys the unique social phase in which survivors find themselves. Lomus experienced such melancholy and grief that all of the *ere* worried about her *edeke* (as though a pathology), but she was saved each time by forgetting the death of her beloved other, something that had been spoken of by her fellow women and co-wives, who had also experienced the loss of a child or grandchild in the same manner. Additionally, she realised that she was still alive (those who have lost someone to death remember the forgetting). I observed these 'healing song' scenes (Hazama 2016). There, she attempted to blend her experiences from the past into the present and bring to life, with the others, past lively interactions that she had had with the deceased while he was alive, such as walking, eating, working, laughing and talking. She could share her grief with these gentle companions, stepping back through time and back again; this 'held on to her' and enabled her to eventually return to the world with her companions.

The disposition of 'being there for someone as a companion' has been established as an inter-physical aspect of reality that precedes individual interactions, and Kazuyoshi Sugawara indicates that its origin can be said to have taken form from the accumulation of expansive mutual exchanges (Sugawara 2002: 298). In the Karimojong cluster, every time a community member is killed because of raiding, the constant activities in the living area accumulate from the disappointment and desperation, and serve as sources of a joint illusion of ethnicity to help members return to normal life. The deaths of herders who reside in such areas of low-intensity conflict are the basis for a generation of ethnic identities and their origins.

III Interaction on the Battlefield

The modern significance of fieldwork on East African pastoral society, which anthropologists have described as an acephalous society, is the exploration of how society can survive without a hierarchical order and the control of power at the top, and this inquiry posits that it is possible to present an observable model based on the vivid physiognomy of the people. In this paper, based on the narratives of individual human beings, I describe and analyse the act of sparing a life during collective warfare to preserve observability as much as possible.

At the Dodoth and Turkana survey sites, some school-educated and employed young individuals can speak English and Swahili, but they mostly reside near the towns. The residents of the villages that I lived in during my research do not use writing in their daily lives. With regard to education, few that live there have attended elementary school (Dodoth: 4 out of 221 people; Turkana: 1 out of 17 people). Based on the accounts I was able to gather in a survey in the Dodoth and Turkana, I found 14 cases in which lives were spared. All the individuals who spoke of these episodes did not speak any language other than their ethnic language with which they were born and raised, and they could neither read nor write.

An Integrated Circuit (IC) recorder was used for the digital audio recording of the episodes of lifesaving referenced in the analysis, with one exception, and the transcriptions were saved. After recording the stories, I played the IC recorder and asked a family member (research assistant) with whom I was residing to repeat what they had said so that I could write it in my field notes. After listening to the stories in their entirety, I translated them into Japanese. For the parts that I did not understand, using my limited knowledge, I communicated in a broken form of the local language and used gestures with the family with whom I was residing to create a Japanese translation. The Turkana vocabulary created by Itaru Ohta, a researcher in Turkana since 1978, was essential to this process (Ohta 1989). Only the episode 'Help me to leave this place', which I discuss later, was transcribed and translated literally on the spot in a notebook. The woman speaker had visited my tent and began speaking without a warning. I thought the account would not feel natural if I stopped her to prepare the recorder, so I did not record this particular interview. The cases in which a life was spared depended on cultural norms that determined who should be helped, and they could be put into the categories of 'sparing the life of the loser', 'sparing the life of a prisoner of war' and 'sparing the life of the weak'. The life-sparing episodes are presented below as synopses and sorted by category; thus, please refer to the excerpts as necessary. In what follows, square brackets ( ) at the beginning of each case indicate a case title, and hexagonal brackets 〔 〕 indicate the year in which the life-sparing episode occurred.

1 Sparing the life of the Loser

P. Roscoe, who is reexamining low combat mortality rate among the members of New Guinea's slash-and-burn farming society, the Dani (Dugum Dani), who constitute one of the most famous examples of ritual-intensive forms of warfare, indicates that they tend to allow the individuals they have injured to flee (Roscoe 2011). The Dani avoid pursuing the enemies they have injured. Roscoe explained that pursuing an enemy in a flooded terrain poses a substantial risk to the attacker. However, the herders of the Karimojong cluster spare the life of enemies whose lives were threatened even when there was no danger in hunting them. The following episode was narrated by Elamach (estimated to be 65 years old), the paternal grandmother of Awoton, a young Turkana man, who spent exactly one month residing with me as my research assistant during my live-in survey in the Turkana in the August of 2018. Elamach's father participated in the battle in the episode and told Elamach of the event.

> (We had finished) [1975] The Karimojong travelled to Moruangikiryoko to raid the Turkana. Before the attack, the Karimojong men were climbing a mountain to scout for their position. A Turkana goat herder recognised the shadow as the enemy while he was grazing his goats. The Turkana men, who received a report from the herder, a boy, rushed to seize the mountain and attacked the Karimojong for seven days. The Karimojong were killed one after another, leaving only a few isolated survivors on the mountain. They raised white feathers on branches, waving them, and shouting, 'Hey! There's none of us left! Everyone is dead!' and 'Hey, leave us alone! We are done for.' The Turkana told them to leave, and the Karimojong left.

In this case, their request to have their lives spared was conveyed by gesturing with objects understood by both cultures. The white feathers (i.e., the feathers that stand vertically on the heads of ostriches) are the men's hair ornaments. The individuals who did not have white feathers shook *ekari* branches instead, a type of linden. When individuals encounter an enemy on the plains, shaking an *ekari* branch indicates that they have no intention to fight. *Ekari* branches and white feathers play the role of the white flag stipulated by law during war in that they signal surrender or that the individuals have no will to fight. This phenomenon is consistent with B. Straight's particular insights into cases in which the sparing of lives occurs, wherein she examined scattered anecdotes in the literature with a strong tendency to focus on killing rather than on the sparing of life. She posited that the act of raising a white flag was an expressive gesture shared across cultural boundaries. The urgency of this gesture has a grammar-like quality through which individuals can appeal for mercy on the battlefield (Straight 2017). However, caution must be used in such situations. The 'voices' of the Karimojong cluster, the losers of the battle, were not blank spaces of information transmission for which they used 'gestures' as a 'shared code'. Elamach said, 'Hey! Leave this place. We are done here!' mimicking the words that had been spoken by the Karimojong.

Hearing the words of the Karimojong people, the Turkana people did not kill their remaining members – perhaps 10 – and left, sparing the enemy. Or how many were they? I don't know. We told them to leave. Nobody was telling them to stay. We said leave, and they left.

The Karimojong temporarily revealed through gestures their common code, appealed to their enemy that they had no means remaining with to fight and commanded, 'Hey, leave us alone.' The Karimojong did not merely wait silently for the mercy of their opponent, the Turkana, to materialise. The Turkana believed what the Karimojong had communicated (i.e., that they were done for), stopped the massacre and released their opponents while telling them to 'leave this place'.

In this narrative world (episode), the cries of the Karimojong and the Turkana were clear interactions and continually regularised and systematised as requests for their lives to be spared and the acceptance of their lives being spared. In other words, the Karimojong that are speaking are somehow conveying meaning in a language community that is inclusive of the Turkana. Using the concept of speech act theory, in this case, a directive speech act is established. The Karimojongs' cries exerted a force that was inherent in the language (Searle 1986).

The expressions 'leave us alone' and 'let us go' are often said by a victim to an attacker and are called *toesikinai*, the polite imperative forms of the transitive verb *aesikin*, which can be translated as 'to leave XX behind', with the addition of the suffix *ai*, meaning 'for me (or us)'. The herders call this act of speech in which individuals beg for their life *akilip akiyar*. This expression comprises the transitive verb *akilip*, which can be translated as 'to beg' or 'to request', and the object *akiyar*, meaning 'life', 'to be alive' or 'living'.

Itaru Ohta analysed the begging of the Turkana, namely, the act of speaking in the pursuit of a 'thing', such as 'give me XX', which caused him annoyance in his daily life (Ohta 1986). Ohta used the English word 'begging' rather than the Japanese equivalent, *monogoi,* for this action, and with good reason. Certainly, the Japanese word for beggar, *monogoi*, is indeed a form of begging; however, *monogoi* is a unique style of begging that is very different from the Turkana case here. The Turkana make no attempts to express humour and, by contrast, beg for what they want in a forceful tone and with the attitude that begging is natural. The Karimojong, who had to surrender to their opponent and had cried, 'We are done for,' were not obsequious toward their opponent; they neither softened their voice nor implored sobbingly about the extenuating circumstances. They stated that their encampment had been incapacitated and insisted that they should be allowed to flee. What would be more appropriate to say is that when the Karimojong or Dodoth *akilip* (or beg) to an enemy on the battlefield, they are begging for their life; thus, the Japanese word *inochigoi* should not be used, which is more akin to pleading for one's life. 'The Karimojong,' said Elamach, 'did not ask for their lives. Rather, they commanded that we allow them to live.'

2 Sparing the Lives of Prisoners of War

Individuals with inside information, such as that on the whereabouts of livestock herds and defensive positions, are a valuable resource to raiders. These informants can narrow the target for attacks. Thus, 'taking a local prisoner' is better than killing them. An example of a prisoner of war who has had his life spared is as follows.

(Let's kill them) 〔2009〕

A group of the Dodoth entered the neighbouring territory of the Jie to launch a raid. One man and five women were taken captive while the Dodoth targeted and searched for herds of livestock. Some of the Dodoth said, 'Let's kill them [the Jie]'; however, a decision was made that taking the Jie prisoner would be more useful than killing them, because they could be used as spies who could lead the looters to the cows' location.

(Our father is over there) 〔2007〕

A group of the Dodoth looters raided a Turkana settlement to steal goats. They captured a Turkana herder who had fled the initial Dodoth attack of their fellow tribesmen and forced him to lead them to a group of grazing goats. The herder told the looters, 'Go then. Go right away. And kill them. Catch up to them from behind. But our father is there. They have plenty of ammunition on their belts and guns. So, you better leave us alone.' The Dodoth looters left the area without killing the herder.

Captives sometimes escape death by spying for their enemies. When the enemy captures individuals and says things such as, 'Let's kill them,' the captives are presented with a life-or-death offer. While making charcoal, a Jie man was captured by an armed group of the Dodoth looters and immediately told them, 'I know,' when asked to provide the location of the cattle herd that the Dodoth targeted to steal. He then made an offer, 'I'll take you to the cows and show you where they are,' and the raiders responded that they would 'keep him captive until the evening.' In this case, the looters changed their mind and spared his life.

Notably, attackers do not necessarily release prisoners of war who successfully spy for them, i.e., prisoners of war are not always spared as a reward for their guidance, irrespective of whether they provide useful information. In all of the aforementioned cases, the prisoners of war were once again on the verge of death after they had fulfilled their purpose, and the attackers pronounced that they would 'kill them'. To be freed from enemy captivity, prisoners must attain the mercy of the enemy, independent of participating with them in raids, by begging again for their life.

3 Sparing the Life of the Weak

Looters spare the life of enemies in situations where their death is of no value to them. Certain categories of individuals, such as those who are disabled, elderly and poor, and those who are injured enemy warriors might have their lives spared.

（She's blind. Let's leave her.）〔Unknown〕

When the Karimojong began raiding and attacked the Turkana village, a blind woman attempted to escape, frequently stopping as she walked. However, she lost her sense of direction and headed toward the looters. The looters did not capture her and said, 'She's blind. Let's leave her.'

The physical condition of blindness puts an individual at an absolute disadvantage in lethal interactions where sight is essential, and when an individual's companions are running away, blindness constitutes an obstacle to being able to escape from the imminent life-threatening crisis. The disadvantage of the condition cannot help but be reflected and amplifies the disadvantage of the party to be murdered. Sugawara, who recorded and analysed stories on physical and mental disabilities in the Gui hunter–gatherer society in the Kalahari Desert, made two notable observations: This group believes that elderly individuals and those with disabilities should not be treated poorly, and this cultural belief is an impetus for such thoughts and feelings. In contrast with the fact that such people would be incapacitated in terms of their economic productivity, it is the Gui's belief that if they were to conduct themselves in disdainful and inhuman ways, such as by abandoning or abusing weakened individuals, it would invoke powers that would bring about some calamity (Kaba) upon them (Sugawara 2000: 203). I can assure you that among the Karimojong cluster, there is an almost universal morality, in accordance with which the tribe seek to avoid engaging in any actions that would threaten the survival of the vulnerable or disabled.

> (The old woman is just following the fence.) 〔Estimated 1975〕
>
> When the Turkana raided the Dodoth village, a blind woman who had left too late was attempting to escape along the fence. Another man said to his companion, who was attempting to stab her with his spear, 'Can't you see that the old woman is just following the fence?' And then he followed saying, 'Hey, let's go after the cows. It was the cows that we came here for. Let's make a run for the cows. They're opening the gate to the cattle enclosure and leaving for the pastures. They're opening it right now.' The Turkana did not harm the old Dodoth woman and instead rushed to the Dodoth cattle herd.

The criticism 'Can't you see that …' was referring to the disability (i.e., blindness), because he noticed his companion's unnatural lack of sensitivity, a sensitivity that everyone should possess. Individuals who are physically handicapped and too vulnerable to attack extend the value of human life in battlefield interactions. Sensing the wounds and weaknesses of others can transform the individuals whose purpose it is to kill their enemy and make them spare lives. The weakness that it embodies can cause an individual to feel new values and evoke a new conversational space and reciprocal acts in which individuals spare each other's lives. Pain, wounds and weaknesses can be used to convey, saliently and straightforwardly, without words, that the body is defective and requires the care of another. In an urgent situation that results in cruel and lethal interactions and wherein there is suffering on the attacked side, the attackers, observing the suffering of their enemy, can halt the organised actions of their group.

(Don't kill my enemy.) 〔1992〕

When the Dodoth attacked a Jie livestock camp, the Jie men, who sensed the attack, charged at the Dodoth while firing. As the Dodoth fought back and the Jie retreated, the leader of the livestock camp (Apa Lopama) was hit by a bullet and lay on the ground bleeding from his right leg. A Dodoth man, Ninyangae, who shot Apa Lopama, refused to kill him. The Dodoth then advanced further into the Jie encampment to attack the herd. After successfully raiding the cows, they returned to where Apa Lopama had fallen, but he was no longer there. Traces in the sand revealed that he had escaped by dragging himself along the ground using his hands and feet.

The following two paragraphs are part of the original transcript of the interview in December 2018 with Dodoth's old father, Loita, who participated in the raid; they were rewritten to create a single, flowing piece.

"The Story of (Don't kill my enemy.) "

'Oh, they're here,' I said. Understood! We lay down on the ground. They opened fire. Pyak, Pyak, Pyak. Pyak, Pyak, Pyak. Ninyangae spoke. Pun, pun. Apa Lopama was shot, and he fell on his back. We went over to him. Where was he shot? Here. Here, where the thigh meets the hips. Ouch! He was lying down. He fell to the ground on his back. He was lying face up. He was extremely dry. We said to one another, 'He's dead.' Another said, 'Oh! This one is still alive.' Ninyangae refused to kill him and said, 'Don't, we shouldn't kill this one.' We said, 'He's our enemy, we need to finish him off.' Ninyangae said, 'Leave this enemy alone. This one belongs to me. Don't kill my enemy.' Oh! We said, 'Okay, let's leave this one alone, we have a long way to go to catch up with the cows.' We left, and once there, divided some of the cows (stole part of the herd). Yes, after that, we came back, but he had already gone. He had gained consciousness and crawled away. What a shock!

Saying that the injured (Apa Lopama), who had been shot by a bullet in his lower body, was 'dry' meant that he was in a breathless state. Notably, although Loita and some of his comrades thought that the deeply injured, bloody and unmoving man was dead, other attackers wanted to wound him further, to ensure that they had killed him. However, the man who fatally shot Apa Lopama, now bloody and lying at his feet, suddenly stopped them from doing that, which would have ended the victim's life. That they cannot feel the fragility and transience of their enemy leads to an ethnic rift within the 'we' that is attacking the other ethnic group, between those who want to 'finish off the enemy' and the 'I' who refuses.

4 The Raiding Culture

What conclusions can we draw from these cases in which lives were spared? The culture determines the enemy and the permissibility and conditions in which an enemy can be killed. However, not all warriors always kill cultural others. Individuals who had helped an enemy on the battlefield sometimes explained to me that the only reason they refrained from killing them was to obtain the cattle (livestock). Actually, when examining the conversations between herders in the scene, a controversy over the pros and cons of killing helpless prisoners of war and vulnerable individuals is observed, and it is often the idea that the purpose of the raid was to steal livestock that highlights that they should limit their actions to those that would fulfil their goals ((The old woman is just following the fence), (Don't kill my enemy)).

P. Clastres, who has organised explanatory models in the field of social relations for uncivilised societies, examined the relationship between war and peace, and characterised the naturalist discourse of war and violence by analysing the considerations of A. Leroi-Gourhan (Leroi-Gourhan 1973). As the idea of war is inherent in human beings because violence exists in humans as it does in nature, war and hunting are considered twins; they serve as a 'purpose of being that is recorded in the core of the living body'. According to this idea, war can be defined in one sentence as 'a form of hunting that targets humans' (Clastres 2003: 27).

To the Karimojong cluster, hunting a human target, namely, an attack without a reward other than the opportunity to kill another human, is inherent to the idea of raiding, and attacks on vulnerable targets (e.g., individuals who are disabled, elderly, children or injured) can be conducted without major hindrances. However, as I have demonstrated in the aforementioned cases wherein lives were spared, raiders abruptly stop killing such innocents on the battlefield when the capture of livestock, which plays a central role in pastoral life, is the reason for the attack. In this sense, the conflict (raiding) between pastoral groups is an act that differs substantially from war (modern war). B. Straight, who conducted a survey on the Samburu pastoral tribe in Central Kenya and their experiences of collective lethal violence, indicates that the purpose of the decision not to kill the enemy on the battlefield is empathy and that cross-cultural norms are in place (Straight 2017). The sparing of life in the Karimojong cluster also occurs when an individual breaks through the social construct of 'enemy', which is created continually by the community, and the culture provides a template to elicit that action. Notably, there are things (e.g., norms) that transcend the specific context or interaction in which individuals of the Karimojong find themselves, and at those times, they do not determine their attitudes. From the attackers' perspective, there are often conflicts over the pros and cons of sparing an enemy's life (《The old woman is just following the fence》, 《Don't kill my enemy》). What do these results imply? Although instances of life-sparing acts exist, not all raiders spare lives. While cultural norms related to sparing life provide guidance on who to help, they do not always have the coercive force observable in functions that always have unique solutions.

IV Begging for One's Life

As I have demonstrated through defeated individuals and prisoners of war who have had their lives spared, the sparing of an enemy life is often in response to them begging for their life and the consequence of a desperate struggle to the death, in which individuals that take one another's lives are at that moment immersed in battlefield interactions with one another. In what follows, I discuss the forces antagonistic to forcible inclusion within the 'us'.

1 Visible Lies

I have demonstrated that when the life of a person who is weak is spared, the life sparing has been motivated by the weakness of the other. By contrast, individuals in the position of weakness who are confronted with a life-or-death situation speak of how helpless and weak they feel in begging for their life, and there are times when hearing this plea is why the listener spares their life. The following episodes were told by a young man, Loiki, who lives in the village where I stayed to conduct my research. One night, Loiki was suddenly captured by a group of Jie looters. In order to protect himself and his companions from the life-threatening ordeal, he explained to the looters that the people at whom they were aiming their weapons were helpless and only earned a meagre living making burning charcoal and grinding flour. He begged by making the case that those they were attacking were powerless and worthless but, in reality, this was a visible lie that he repeated toward the same opponent.

"The Story of (The Young Squirt) 〔2013〕"

We were drinking in a friend's village. We had been drinking alcohol, and the sun had just begun to set. We went outside. We were wrapped in cloth and singing loudly. By the time we got back to our village, the enemy was already at the entrance. One of the looters captured me and abducted me. He said to me, 'Tell me where there is a herd of cattle without any lookout.' I took them. They took away my relative's livestock. It was the night that Natori [the name for an unmarried relative] had been dancing.

'Nyengomo [the name of steer], pull the pear! You're a red steer with long horns. Pull!' the children are saying, while plowing the fields. 'Our father (referring to the steer named Nyengomo) pulls strongly.'

(Sung by the narrator Loiki)

They said, 'Let's kill this one (referring to Natori, who had been singing).' I said, 'Leave him alone. He's just a young squirt, a *nyecharioit.* He's just a drunkard. He cuts trees for charcoal for a living. Look closely. He's more like one of the women. None of the other men are singing. He's useless. Leave him alone. Go attack the village. Can it be that you're afraid to attack the village? There's nothing else for you here. Go and attack!' They attacked, and while they did, Natori ran away.

> After raiding my relative's livestock, I ran with the looters. We ran and ran. When we arrived in Lobunei [place name], another said, 'Let's kill him now.' I said, 'There's nothing I can do to you. I'm just grinding flour with Naidiid's machine. I'm a worthless man. Don't kill me. Don't kill me. I have nothing. Nothing at all.'
>
> They said, 'So, what is the *siyori* (shape of the ears of the cow in the song) that you were singing earlier?'
>
> I said, 'I'm a squirt. I've never killed a single person. I just play and sing songs.'
>
> That's when they released me. Many of them still said, 'Let's kill him,' but one of them told me to 'go away, somewhere other than here.' They released me, and I returned home.

The Jie whom Loiki had guided had set out to snipe Natori, who had been singing in the livestock enclosure, from outside the village in a place where their relatives lived. On the spur of the moment, Loiki said, 'He's a very poor man.' He spoke the words without thinking of helping his friend at whom the gun was being pointed. They then ordered the raid. After having raided the village and dispersed the settlements' inhabitants, including Natori, Loiki's story of how he discouraged the raiders who had been very close to killing them had been considered a complete fabrication. Loiki is not a wage worker. He, similar to the other men in the settlement, had sufficient cattle to feed his family. When captured that night, Loiki sang an *emon* (personal song) that was praising the altered ears (*siyori*) of his steer. *Siyori* involves the cutting of a letter into the midsection of the ear as proof that its owner has killed a man in battle defending against livestock looters. Loiki is a master of raiding and the owner of a large herd. The looters who kidnapped Loiki remembered vividly the song that they had heard when hiding to catch him. They were aware of this inconsistency in Loiki's story in which he played the role of a young squirt, but this lie did not prevent them from sparing his life.

2 Discord and Sensitivity

One day, a Dodoth woman in her fifties named Lokoru told me about a sudden attack by their enemy. Lokoru was also captured when the village was attacked by a looting group of Jie. She reported to them that she was too old to walk and that she was blind and would be lonely for the remainder of her life, and she was released.

"The Story of (Help me to leave this place.) 〔2004〕"

> I asked them, 'Will you kill me?' I said to them, 'You are burning everything and stealing the livestock, so will you kill me too? Answer me. Let me go. I am *amojong* [an old woman]. I have neither a son nor a husband. Please leave me alone. My enemies, young ones, help me to leave this place.'
>
> They said to me, 'This is the one that created our enemy.' I told them, 'I'm blind. Nobody takes care of me. I'm alone. My husband died a long time ago.'
>
> 'Why would we hurt someone so helpless,' they said. 'Let's let her go. It would be troublesome to kill her. Let her go,' the enemy said. Slowly, I made my way back to my relatives.

I removed an extract from the prior edited text, but in this episode, the enemy first set fire to the settlement. Lokoru, who fled to her thatched hut, was forced to go outdoors by the heat of the fire they had set at the fence to the site and was captured by looter men. The looters succeeded in breaking into the village, and she was overtaken by grief at the destruction they would unleash once inside. Lokoru instantly begged them to spare her life. To her surprise, the invaders stopped and listened to her. They argued over whether to kill her or help her. 'This one made our enemies.' The cries of the individuals who bore the responsibility of killing were drawing attention to the fact that she, as a local, was responsible for the birthing of their enemy through reproduction. However, Lokoru begged and urged the men to change their minds, to spare her life despite her giving birth to their enemy.

I applied the analytical framework of speech act theory to her cries, and using the categorisation proposed by John Searle, the cultural peculiarities of her statements were revealed. Individuals experiencing a predicament in which they have no hope of living immediately list the atrocities and destruction of the thieves. They ask about their intentions for the future. They prompt them to answer their questions ('Will you kill me? Will you burn everything? Will you take the livestock? Will you kill me too? Answer me.') and beg them saying, 'Please, let me go.' Additionally, after repeating descriptive illocutions to convey their condition ('I'm an old woman. I neither have a son nor a husband.'), they clearly use commandments in their speech ('Let me go. Help me to leave this place, enemies, young ones, please help me.') to cause the other to support their escape (i.e., the sparing of their life). Declarative illocutions aim to match the content of an individual's speech to a certain state of the world. Speakers are not merely examining the words (or their meanings) that they say; they are using their words to sharpen the listener's awareness of the reality that they are attempting to depict.

However, Lokoru's statement is clearly a lie. The misery she claimed to her enemy that supported the legitimacy of sparing her life was all false. Nevertheless, no interest is paid to the distinction between truth and falsehood. She has a husband, children and grandchildren. She is neither particularly old nor blind. Unlike elderly women (*amojong*) that have trouble walking, she walks normally, and she understands the Jie. However, this unmistakable discrepancy with physical reality is locked out of the conversational world.

Lokoru is the second wife of Loita, the man who said, 'Don't kill my enemy.' Loita's younger sister, Lomus, is the second wife of Lonya, the patriarch of the family with which I was living. Lokoru and Loita, together with Lonya's family, reside in a single ring-shaped settlement (*ere*). Since I had begun to take care of Lomus's *ekar* (family living space), I had met Lokoru almost every day, and we became friends. When Lokoru was telling me (Help me to leave this place), at the end of the story, I said to her, 'But you have a husband, Loita.' I said, 'You aren't blind, and don't you have a lot of children?' It was an absurd question. Lokoru, of course, knew that I knew that the statements regarding her blindness and loneliness were false. Lokoru promptly replied and refuted, 'And what about your *etau*, (or heart)? Do you have a bad heart?'

To the Dodoth, the heart is an organ that resonates with the state of the outside world. For example, an individual with a warm heart would quickly help an injured person, whereas a cold-hearted person would ponder how best to intervene and time would elapse before they acted. When an individual has lost a family member or friend and is severely depressed, they are described as 'having a closed heart'. The act of physically touching the heart (or chest) with a hand or cowbell is considered necessary to heal from any type of trauma caused by armed conflict. What she was indicating through her critical, angry and abrupt response to my foolish question was that it is nonsensical to discuss individuals' truthfulness based on objective evidence when they are being confronted by potential violence at the hands of a looter and an enemy, and that the authenticity of a victim's explanations should not be questioned. By contrast, an individual in that predicament, who is in a life-or-death situation, is appealing to determine whether the looter has sympathy for her (whether the looter is 'bad-hearted'?). That is all there is to it. The Jie thief was sympathetic to the begging of Lokoru.

3 Coexisting in the World of Communication

What can be learned from the act of begging for one's life? Koji Kitamura presents in 'Here and Now' that there are specific episodes in which the Turkana tell lies, which they know are lies, when they beg for things, and he highlights that to remain positive about 'their lived reality', a lie (or untrue words) is justifiable to them (Kitamura 1996). The Turkana refuse to form agreements on the basis of absolute standards. In the Karimojong cluster, as soon as the begging begins, the participants in the interaction relinquish their roles as linguistic agents. 'Linguistic agent', according to the moral philosopher G. Steiner, is a term that refers to a person who understands and evaluates the rationality of the other party while expressing their rationality in the form of a proposition. G. Steiner criticised mainstream political philosophy, which according to him, has unknowingly continued to exclude and discriminate by determining that only those individuals, who can use reason and carefully deliberate issues, should be able to participate in politics (Steiner 2013).

The herders, who can inspire and gain bargaining ground by begging; the beggars; and those who listen to the begging coexist in the world of communication in a spoken or 'vocal' dimension, which is more fundamental than the political dimension is. According to this concept, two individuals confronting each other in person and in a state of continual flux can negotiate the sparing of one of their lives and sympathise with one another through words that transcend meaning. In other words, when begging, a falsehood that was clear to all parties involved is not important in understanding why the Karimojong cluster's lives were spared. Rather, the primary purpose of these lies was to introduce a compelling reality into the interaction by directing a statement fraught with the turmoil of reality at the source of their urgency and breaking the maxim of 'tell the truth'.

The looter (listener) is exposed to the other's voice, a voice separated from reason. The begging inevitably attracts the former's attention. The listener begins to actively explore the relationship and context in which he and the speaker find themselves. At this point, the enemy enters into a companionship with the beggar. This companionship is a bond that differs from the one he shares with members of his (imagined) territorial group or cultural community. This difference occurs because for both parties witnessing the begging, the identity of the individual subject is established under face-to-face conditions and subjectively between the two parties.

V Making Ethnicity Flexible Again through Face-to-face Identity

In raids, different ethnicities are in contact as enemies that represent their respective communities. They are members of groups that are homogenised internally and collectivised but that reciprocally endanger each other's existence. Once they meet, the 'we', attached to a single cultural community, drifts from the reality that is categorised into mutually taxonomic groups. In a situation where individuals must beg for their lives in a face-to-face encounter, instances occur where they are not motivated by the power of the self-contained representation into which they classify each other. The interest is drawn to the act of speaking, comprising the voice and words of the enemy in front of them.

In opposition to the brute force encompassed in the ideology of sameness, the 'I' that is called to by their opponent, which is fundamental to self and to where the voice is targeted, act in concert. At this time, the begging person is heard, and the irreplaceable nature of the individual that feels supports the irreplaceable nature of the individual to whom the begging is directed. The source of the 'I' of the person who wants to have her life spared resonates with the 'I' who decides to spare her life.

I have demonstrated that physical injuries, disabilities and pain, as well as a vivid look that expresses the urgency of the crisis, constitute the gestures from which this originates. I have confirmed that to be affected by the sorrow of another is to be exposed to another who puts forward herself as being in a state of crisis and that, in such circumstances, they cannot help but be dragged into a joint present. At this point, spoken begging is not different from physical pain, and the interactions of the human beings halt their continual flux and are focused on a particular direction, in response to the call of 'we are here, at this moment'. In this manner, the body and voice, in this face-to-face interaction and on the brink of life, rebel against the self that is categorised within a social category, causing them to question the face-to-face identity of themselves and the other. In contact (tangent) with the otherness of the other, the origin of the other and the origin of the 'I' as other to the other resonate and again question the fictitious imitation of the pseudo universalised community. In other words, the specific face-to-face interaction results in a sense of incongruity, which opens a new perspective on the structure that prioritises the ethnic group, which is taken for granted in day-to-day events and repeated within the social group.

Finally, I would like to note that when I am confronted by the otherness of the other in front of me, and when a crack runs between me and them, I cannot escape the inertia of that categorisation and this is not only confined to a pure, direct relationship between the subject and myself. In face-to-face interactions, to advance beyond the culturally constructed dichotomy of the enemy and ally is to begin to experience their symbiosis and to live in a space where individuals act in concert with the characteristics of the other. The instinct of the subject at this time is not the loneliness of one's self as isolated from the other but, by contrast, the self that shuts down during intrinsic experiences of time. This is none other than a dynamic divulsion of the boundary between them and myself. A raid, as an interaction in East Africa between those that live as pastoral farmers, is a moment that causes an individual involved in the raid to return to their origin and enables ethnicity to become flexible again through discarding customs that result in the tribes' sense of belonging based on their territories. Nations and peoples take the lead in terms of ethnicity. Ethnicity is enshrined at the centre of the idea of multiethnic and multicultural coexistence in modern societies, and the world is full of conflict and destruction caused by identity politics. In this modern society, where there are few signs of hope, this source of face-to-face reciprocal identities in East African pastoral societies constitutes hope and seems to reveal possible solutions.

Acknowledgements

This work was supported by the INOUE ENRYO Memorial Grant, TOYO University, JSPS KAKENHI Grant Numbers JP18H03606, JP22H03828 and JSPS Joint Research: South Africa–Japan 'Human

Resilience in the face of man-made and natural disaster in Japan and South Africa: Ethnographic Perspective'.

References

Clastres, Pierre (2003) *Archéologie de la violence : La guerre dans les sociétés primitives*, (trans. Marimo) Tokyo: Gendaikikakushitsu (in Japanese).

Dyson-Hudson, Neville (1966) *Karimojong Politics*, Oxford: Clarendon Press.

Galaty, John G. (2016) 'Boundary-making and pastoral conflict along the Kenyan–Ethiopian borderlands, *African Studies Review*, Vol. 59, No. 1, pp. 97–122.

Gray, Sandra J. (2000) 'A memory of loss: Ecological politics, local history, and. the evolution of Karimojong violence, *Human Organization*, Vol. 59, No. 4, pp. 401–418.

Gulliver, P. H. (1955) *The Family Herds: A Study of Two Pastoral Tribes in East Africa: The Jie and Turkana*, London: Routledge and Kegan.

Hazama, Itsuhiro (2016) 'Old women's roles in a matter of life-and-death among. the pastoral Dodoth in Northeastern Uganda', *Journal of African Studies*, No. 90, pp. 59–70 (in Japanese).

___________ (2019) 'Body and Violence: Illnesses among the Karimojong and Dodoth in the Period of Disarmament', in Ohta and Soga (eds) *Nomadic Ideas: Turbulent Africa Seen from Anthropology*, Kyoto: Showado (in Japanese) pp. 169–196.

Kitamura, Koji (1996) 'Experiences of "Cooperative Presence" in Corporeal Communication: "Negotiatory" among the Turkana, in Nomura and Sugawara (eds) *Body as Communication*, Tokyo: Taishukan, (in Japanese) pp.288-314.

Korf, Benedikt, Hagmann, Tobias and Emmenegger, Rony (2015) 'Re-spacing African drylands: territorialization, sedentarization and indigenous commodification in the Ethiopian pastoral frontier', *Journal of Peasant Studies*, Vol. 42, No. 5: pp. 881–901.

Lamphear, John E. (1992) *The Scattering Time: Turkana Responses to Colonial. Rule*, Oxford University Press: Oxford.

Leroi-Gourhan, Andre (1973) *Le Geste et le Parole* (translated by Toru Araki) Tokyo: Shinchosya: Tokyo (in Japanese).

Matsuda, Motoji (1998) 'Social Theory of Ethnic Conflict: Possibilities of Africa's Organizing Ethnicity', in Takeuchi (ed.)

For Understanding Conflicts in Africa Today, Tokyo: Institute of Developing Economies (in Japanese) pp. 15-39.

Murdock, George P. (1959) *Africa: Its Peoples and Their Culture History*, New York: McGraw-Hill.

Ohta, Itaru (1986) 'Reciprocal Exchange among the Turkana', in Itani and Tanaka (eds) *Anthropological Studies on the Nature-dependent Society*, Kyoto: Academiashuppankai (in Japanese) pp. 181-215.

__________ (1989) A Classified Vocabulary of the Turkana in Northwestern Kenya, *African Study Monographs*, Supplementary Issue 10, pp. 1–104.

Roscoe, Paul (2011) 'Dead birds: The "theater" of war among the Dugum Dani', *American Anthropologist*, Vol. 113, No. 1, pp. 56–70.

Schlee, Gunther (1989) *Identities on the Move: Clanship and Pastoralism in Northern Kenya*, Manchester: Manchester University Press.

__________ (2013) 'Territorializing ethnicity: The imposition of a model of statehood on pastoralists in Northern Kenya and Southern Ethiopia', *Ethnic and Racial Studies*, Vol. 36, No. 5, pp. 857–874.

Searle, John R. (1986) *Speech Acts* (translated by Sakamoto and Tsuchiya) Tokyo: Keisoshobo (in Japanese).

Sobania, Neal (2011) 'The formation of ethnic identity in South Omo: The Dassenech', *Journal of Eastern African Studies*, Vol. 5, No. 1, pp. 195–210.

Steiner, Gary (2013) *Animals and the Limits of Postmodernism*, New York: Columbia University Press.

Straight, Billinda (2017) 'Uniquely human: Cultural norms and private acts of mercy in the war zone', *American Anthropologist*, Vol. 119, No. 3, pp. 491–505.

Sugawara, Kazuyoshi (2000) 'Social Welfare in Botswana: Psychosomatic Disorders in Bushman Society', in Wazaki, Tochimoto and Usami (eds) *Social Welfare in the World 11: Africa, Latin America, and Spain*, Tokyo: Junposha (in Japanese) pp. 187–207.

__________ (2002) *Monkey and Human with Emotions*, Tokyo: Koubundou (in Japanese).

Chapter 16

'Whose Gaze Matters?': Re-thinking the Ways in which Whiteness Studies Research has Traditionally Been Done

Zuziwe Nokwanda Msomi

Introduction

The study of what has been since the 1990s referred to as whiteness studies or critical whiteness studies is relatively young in South Africa compared to its growth in North American academia. While there is a plethora of writing on being white in South Africa, the shift in academia to look at the dominant group in understanding and ending racism is tracked primarily to 1990s North American academia. Thus, while black foundational texts on what is now referred to as whiteness studies abounded long before, it is 1990s North American academics' work from which most whiteness studies work traditionally draws, that is, focusing on the dominant group (i.e., those who are phenotypically white) to understand how whiteness is constructed, used, changes, etc., written primarily by white academics. With time, similarly, drawn from experiences, engagements and constructions etc. of whiteness from black academia would slowly increase. While there has been some contestation as to how whiteness studies research is traditionally done, these challenges arguably are too few and far between. 1990s North American ways of doing whiteness studies endures; tradition appears to pervade, and it is this resilience of traditions of doing research – particularly whiteness studies – that is explored here. This chapter looks at why the above mentioned 1990s trend of doing whiteness studies persists?

The term 'resilience' may be used in a myriad of ways as evident from how other writers in this book have defined and used the term. The term 'resilience' may generally be associated with a persistent existence of a people, practices and phenomena despite great adversity. Adversity, whether it be cultural, physical or otherwise threatens the continued existence of people, practices and phenomena, is determined to end or change the way things are. A change or eradication is sought by one or more parties for political reason. 'Political' here broadly refers to two or more parties fighting over a limited resource. This may be a physical resource but, in this instance, refers to how practices and phenomena are constructed, understood and perceived. If this was not important, then studies of discourse analysis and propaganda, for example, would not need to exist. In this chapter however, the term is used generally to refer to the continued persistence of how research is done, that is, continuing patterns of how whiteness studies research is done despite increasing voices that there have been changes for the better. The chapter argues that despite claims of changes for the better, the ways of doing whiteness studies work remains influenced by 1990s North American tradition.

This topic is particularly worth considering given changes brought on by COVID-19. While the means of collecting data may no longer be the same due to social distancing and other restrictions, the question remains: 'What is at stake if we continue to do whiteness studies research in the traditional racially polarised ways?'

Whiteness Studies without Relying on Black Experiences and Voices

After collecting nine hundred and twenty-one articles on whiteness studies which used participants, only a handful of articles drew specifically from black experiences and perceptions of whiteness. Of these articles, only one which located itself specifically within whiteness studies drew from black experiences and perception of whiteness. This was Twine's (1997) 'Brown Skinned White Girls, Culture, and the Construction of White Identity'. The question then became for me why there were not more studies drawing on black participants to inform researchers on whiteness, while there appeared to be innumerable studies drawing from white participants specifically. While it is possible that this might have been limited by what I was searching for, the wide scope of the searches in Google Scholar, Google and Mendeley under the search terms 'whiteness studies', 'whiteness studies and South Africa' should have produced more studies drawing on black participants' perceptions and experiences of whiteness. While there is admittedly much scholarship from black writers writing on whiteness (see for example Mills 2008;

hooks 1997; Morrison 1993; Yancy 2004), the question remained as to why not more of the results showed studies which used participants drawn from black participants' perceptions and experiences in the field.

This chapter tries to think through some of the reasons that whiteness studies continues largely to draw from predominantly white experiences. A review of the literature reveals that the term 'whiteness' refers predominantly to two aspects of whiteness: firstly, phenotypically white people and, secondly, whiteness having an ideological function produced and reproduced in society's institutions. While the two are not entirely separate it is argued here that having a plethora of research focusing on predominantly white experiences and perceptions of whiteness, undermines the fact that whiteness is not limited to phenotypical features as several studies suggest (see Bashkow 2006; Lopez 2005; Nyamnjoh and Page 2002; Twine 1997). In the former, white people are the focus of white privilege, white discourse and white identity. Whiteness in the latter instance can still focus on white people as the creators and benefactors of many of the social institutions which perpetuate whiteness. Lopez's (2005) collection includes an acknowledgement that whiteness when reproduced in social institutions is not limited to white people. What is needed, I argue, is looking at white identity construction, white discourse and white privilege that does not rely predominantly on white bodies. Even if there has been an increasing move away from this way of doing research, it is worth bearing in mind why there is not more of such research not connected to phenotype specifically.

The chapter thinks through some of the reasons why, in particular, are there not more studies using participants looking at black constructions of white identity, black people's usage of white discourse and what we call white privilege. Of course, then the question becomes whether we can still call it white discourse, white privilege or white identity or, for that matter, whiteness studies when we look at black usage of whiteness and white privilege? To do this a review of some of the literature on whiteness studies is used to think through why whiteness studies still relies largely on white participants when it comes to looking at white identity construction, white discourse and white privilege.

The chapter is not interested in a statistical representation of exactly how many articles draw from black participants' experiences versus how many are white but rather it is about thinking about what it does 'do' to want to engage with a scholarship that most of the articles that you find draw predominantly from white perceptions and experiences. If nine hundred and twenty-one articles are a sample of the field, despite the possibilities of the writer's way of searching, then admittedly this might point to a trend in the whiteness studies literature. The chapter is interested particularly in work that draws specifically from participants to inform us about white identity, white privilege and white discourse. In essence what does it 'do' and mean to type in 'whiteness studies' and find that the bodies of knowledge that use participants that come back to you are predominantly white.

This idea of 'do'-ing is drawn from Sullivan (2006). Sullivan (2006) argues that white identity, in particular white superiority, is learned from one's surroundings. Living in a society where you see the poorest people are not white, where the menial jobs are done by people who are not white and where the media presents the most attractive and knowledgeable bodies as white. All of this does work in socialising us to map the world racially and organise racial groups hierarchically. It is through this watching, listening and taking in as we grow up as children that tells us how the world is organised. It then provides us with a racial common sense of who is white, who is black, and how each group is valued and stereotyped. We each learn over time, just from the way that the world around us is organised, in terms of who is doing what, when, who tells them to do it, that we also begin to learn as children where we fit into the racial hierarchy and our worth in the society.

Through having predominantly white bodies in TV and literature, and spaces and places that people live such as Sullivan (2006) and McIntyre (1997) point out, then it is argued here that whiteness studies does similar work in presenting whiteness studies as a predominantly white field.[1] This is an issue that has been recognised in the work of Kolchin (2002), for example, who argued that whiteness studies will benefit more from drawing on black experiences and voices instead of predominantly white participants only. Students in South African universities have protested calling for the decolonisation of universities on the very same grounds. Lecturers need not say anything that is overtly racist, but it is enough that the bodies who are always doing the teaching are predominantly white in historically white universities (see Luescher, Lodaer and Taabo Mugume 2017: 236–240 on student calls for decolonisation and free education). This then places the expectation that knowledge holders are white bodies. Similarly, a curriculum that draws from largely white canon does work of expecting and mapping in our racial common sense that it is white bodies, Western objective epistemology that is the only acceptable and legitimate knowledge. A similar note has been made about the work that paintings, names of institutions and the material that fills the institutional space. Similarly, I argue here that finding predominantly white perceptions and experiences of whiteness do subconsciously map expectations about who can contribute to whiteness, and which bodies can contribute to the field. It also leaves an impression that the field is more concerned with skin colour rather than the ideological function of whiteness. It becomes the norm to expect whiteness studies to be about white people's privilege, discourse and their identity construction. In the same way that experiences of the author McIntyre (1997) allowed her to grow up completely surrounded by white people, without having to know or engage with black people as being indicative of white supremacy, it is argued here that whiteness studies places itself in danger of normalising, and making invisible whiteness in the field.

In other words what is of concern here is being able to do research on whiteness without necessarily having to know black representations and perceptions of whiteness on white identity, white privilege and white discourse as well. This, it is argued, is similar to Toni Morrison's (1993) critique of North American literature of constructing narratives that write out and or largely ignore black contributions to North American society. When black participants are included, it is to support the white protagonist and re-inscribe white superiority as Dyer (1997) notes in his analysis of films. Without black perceptions and experiences of whiteness forming an equally large part of whiteness studies, it is argued, whiteness studies bears the risk of reducing the field to the study of white people's experiences, perceptions, privileges and discourses of whiteness. This means falling exactly into the trap of essentialism that many who do this work fear. When we look at the institutions of whiteness as playing a part in the creation and recreation of whiteness, we will likewise continue to limit our understanding of these institutions and their effect upon people as part of the legacy of colonialism and apartheid. This is undoubtedly true, and there is plenty of scholarship to support this argument (see Nyamnjoh 2012, 2016). However, this limits the agency, inventiveness and contradictions of human beings even while they are limited by structures. We lose the stories of survival, of adaptation and sense making beyond victimhood as pointed out by Ratele (2007). It is here that the second half of the chapter turns to. The chapter recognises that white people do benefit from social institutions that continue to value and establish whiteness as the norm to the disadvantage of black people. However, it is argued that there needs to be more work recognising that there is sense making, resistance, adaptation of whiteness amongst black people that ascribes more to them than victimhood. Whiteness even amongst white people is not homogenous but there is resistance, adaptation and sense making amongst different forms of whiteness. And there are moments when whiteness, that is attaining desirable aspects of whiteness that will allow someone who is black to some extent be accepted within whiteness and accorded white privileges as shown by the work of Twine (1997). In which case whiteness is not just about mimicry, internalised oppression for black people nor a homogenous experience for white people. The only possible experience to cover all scenarios this chapter ultimately argues is that whiteness is beyond phenotype only. It also has an ideological function between white people, between black people, and between black and white people which needs even more exploration than we currently have.

Weaknesses Noted in the Literature: Whiteness not Connected to the White Body Only

When studying whiteness there is the danger of 'essentialising differences or homogeny[s]ing an admittedly diverse group' (Lewis 2004: 624). White people, in other words, are not the same, and do not have the same experiences of what it means to be white. Kolchin (2002), in a review of whiteness studies literature, notes that whiteness studies has evolved to include different nuances of whiteness. However, the field would do well, he argues, to include more research on the perceptions and experiences of whiteness from those who are not white as noted in the first half of the chapter. In line with this criticism, one of the nuances of whiteness should therefore include black perceptions and experiences of whiteness. The work of Twine (1997) in line with thinking indicates that there is limited research that looks at how black bodies can acquire a white cultural identity – even if only in part. She notes that the development of a white identity has been studied in reference to white women but not in women that are not phenotypically white. Located within North American constructions of race, the 'young black women' refers to women that have at least one parent of African or Asian descent. Within South African constructions of race, this would be referred to as coloured. Even within Twine's (1997) study there is a physical connection to whiteness, which I argue need not always necessarily be present for whiteness to continue to be created and valued. This is supported by Bashkow's (2006) study of the construction of white men by the black Orokaiva community of Papua New Guinea.

Whiteness, what it means to be white continue to be created and recreated within Papua New Guinea by the Orokaiva where almost no white people remain. Many white people have left, with many government jobs being taken over by educated new middle class Orokaivas or educated black people of African descent from outside Papau New Guinea. Rather than disappear from the Orokaiva imagination, Bashkow's (2006) study indicates a continued engagement with whiteness in the Orokiava imagination in how town, black educated foreign nationals, and food are constructed as white. Even within Orokaiva villages whiteness remains in the embodiment of what the Orokaiva value as development, and ideas that will lead to development and improvement of their lives. Interestingly Bashkow's (2006) study also highlights how the embodiment of whiteness is not the mere effect of the hegemonic nature of whiteness or colonialism. Rather whiteness is constructed by being mediated through the communities' own cultural values. Even disparaging comments of the Orokaiva can be traced to the prior presence of whiteness. It is not blindly taken and applied by the Orokaiva to themselves. Rather, the disparaging, if somewhat racist, comments on the Orokaiva's lack of control are mediated through the Orokaiva concern for the crime, and limited integration into the global economy. Similarly, constructions of whiteness are mediated in terms of the Orokiava social norms of gift exchange, and the importance of food and land in Orokaiva culture. Thus, many constructions of whiteness are related to these important aspects of Orokaiva life. Bashkow's (2006) study indicates that whiteness is not all consuming but rather in this context is used as means to think through and about local traditions, values and concerns that the community has about itself. Thus, whiteness can be localised rather than assumed that it consumes all as warned by Ratele (2007). To be white for the Orokaiva is not always limited to skin colour. Likewise, it is argued here, whiteness need not have the presence of white people to be reproduced as shown in the collection of essays by Lopez (2005). Whiteness is constructed likewise by people in terms of their experience, values, concerns and access to social goods rather than in a vacuum. Whiteness then can also be a resource of thinking through the concerns, values and imagination of those who are constructing whiteness. It is the Orokaiva cultural norms, values and concerns that take precedence in their imagination and engagement of whiteness despite the unequal power relations. Regardless of unequal power relations, the Orokaiva gave agency and ability to adapt in the face of whiteness. This connects the point that was made earlier in the chapter on how limiting whiteness to white bodies only renders black bodies as mostly the victims of whiteness. Here whiteness is localised in Orokiava discourse in their cultural values and concerns. Whiteness is also clearly not the purview of white people but rather about what the engagement of the other (i.e., white people) means to the Orokaiva within their reality. We begin to realise then that the construction of the other is not the purview of white bodies but of all people as argued by Bashkow (2006).[2] Of course, this approach does have its dangers as will be taken up further on in the article. Nonetheless Bashkow's (2006) study is useful in revealing that whiteness is not as all powerful and encompassing as one would assume because of the focus of whiteness studies on what has been described as the dominant group. A focus on whiteness from the view of those who are not white, places non-white bodies at the centre and thus places their perceptions and experiences and constructions at the centre. The protagonist in the story, so to speak, ceases to be white people and their dominance, but rather perceptions and experiences of whiteness. It becomes a story about the Orokaiva and how they localise, contextualise and mould whiteness within their own world. Whereas a focus on whiteness from white people arguably focuses on their dominant position, and thus places those who are non-white in the position of subordinate or victim, an analysis of Orokaiva constructions of whiteness places upsets or unsettles the way we think about whiteness, and thus arguably renders it at least a little less powerful in the imagination.

Continuing with a review of what the literature has said in terms of whose bodies are the focus in whiteness studies, Twine and

Gallagher (2008: 4) note that whiteness studies has developed to include analysis of 'white identity formation among members of racial and ethnic minorities'. Whiteness studies, in North America in particular, the two authors argue, has indeed started to move beyond focusing on people of European descent. Indeed, the field has faced criticism for focusing too much on the black/white binary as noted previously in the chapter (Deliovsky and Kitossa 2013: 159). However, this focus has typically shifted to Asian and Latina/o American white identity construction – in particular, light skinned Asian and Latina/o Americans rather than in the direction of white identity development by those who are phenotypically black. What still needs to be further pursued, I argue, are phenotypically black perceptions, experiences and uses of whiteness. Twine's (1997) study partly takes this up but still necessitates the presence of whiteness in the form of one white parent and being in a majority white neighbourhood. Twine (1997) none the less makes the important contribution that white identity is not only limited to those who are racialised white. It is worth noting here that although there is literature that looks at how black people assimilate into whiteness such as Fanon's (2008) *Black skin, white Masks*, this article offers a critique of studies that are specifically located within whiteness studies. As has been noted by Kolchin (2002), whiteness studies would benefit from the inclusion of experiences of whiteness from those who are not white. This however would mean looking beyond what is currently most of the whiteness studies literature. It is, in fact, possible that it means looking at older race studies work. However, this then leads to the yet unresolved question of what, if anything, differentiates whiteness studies from race studies?

Why So Little on Black Participants?

One of the reasons that whiteness studies does not focus on black participants may be because colour-blind ideology has been found to affect black people the least according to the work done by Bonilla-Silva (2014). Thus, there is less need to study black constructions and uses of whiteness as they are less vested in it according to Bonilla-Silva (2014). However, research that I recently completed reveals that like the work of Twine (1997), Bashkow (2006) and Nyamnjoh and Fuh (2014) and Nyamnjoh and Page (2002), to name a few, there is need to think about whiteness beyond the white body or including blackness as victim only.

As much as Bonilla-Silva (2014) is indeed correct about black bodies being less vested in colour-blind ideology, an analysis of the extent to which black people rely on the frames, style and racial stories of colourblindness is arguably not worth simply ignoring. As few as the cases may be, and as little as the investment in colourblind ideology may be, its presence and use are worth exploring. This is especially so if we are to move away from traditional 1990s pattern of doing whiteness studies work. This is particularly worth exploring as in reality post-apartheid youth are constructing race – including whiteness – in ways that are not necessarily along racially polarised lines. Research, in other words, needs to start following what is happening in reality – even if new constructions of race are few and far between. As few and as temporary as these racial boundary crossing constructions and use of race (including whiteness) may be, as Bonilla Silva (2014 later points out, ideology is hegemonic not because it affects all members of society in the same way or to the same degree. For this reason, it is sufficient basis to look at black experiences and perceptions of whiteness together; and at the cases of the exceptions rather simply reinforcing the racially polarised patterns in which work following the 1990s pattern arguably does. How else are we to learn new things except to look in the dark corners where the light of exploration has not yet been as brightly shone?

Another reason whiteness studies may have tended to focus on white people may be because it is not clear whether whiteness studies is an entirely new body of race work, or a continuation of older race work, as briefly mentioned above in the chapter. The literature states that whiteness studies may be differentiated from earlier race work because older race work used to focus on minority groups, whereas whiteness studies focuses on the dominant group (Doane 2003; Kolchin 2002). Previous extensive work on understanding race had been found to not adequately explain why racism continued in society (Doane 2003; Kolchin 2002: 167) – in particular the covert, subtle nature of racism could not be adequately explained – especially in anti-racist and transformation focused spaces (see Durrheim and Dixon 2000; Outlaw 2004: 166). In addition, there was disappointment over the collapse of progressive movements in North America (Kolchin 2002: 167). It was found, therefore, that while previous race work had focused on understanding racism as a matter of white racism; and prejudice which prevented black people from assimilating into North American society being attributed to lack of education, the focus needed to change. The focus changed to assuming that all of society's institutions are organised around race (Delgado, Richards and Stefancic 2001; Doane 2003). Thus, while previous race work had found limitations in focusing on minority groups, whiteness studies wished to rectify this limited study of race and racism by now turning the lens to what it refers to as the dominant group. The interpretation of who this dominant group is refers specifically to white people if one looks at the literature. The focus on white people under whiteness studies under these circumstances makes sense.

However, for Kolchin (2002) there is no decisive break from older race studies work to the relatively newer 1990s whiteness studies. Kolchin (2002: 172) argues that whiteness studies is 'less a radical new departure than an evolution of a historical scholarship that has long been preoccupied with the changing ways of making race'. Rather, argues Kolchin (2002: 172), whiteness studies uses new language, and provides 'a new way of addressing old questions'. However, the central concern of all race work – the conceptualisation and reconceptualisation of race – remains the same for both whiteness studies and older race work. What is of concern however in analysis of whiteness is that there remains little work that draws on both black and white constructions of whiteness together to better understand the continued existence of racism.

Similarly, while there is an increase of work that looks at whiteness beyond the phenotypically white body in the style of writers such as Bashkow (2006), Twine (1997), Nyamnjoh and Page (2002) and Nyamnjoh and Fuh (2014), these works still remain largely on the fringes. In addition, regardless of whether or not whiteness studies is a field, is a break from or merely a continuation of previous race studies simply taking a different turn, both whiteness studies and race studies focus on the conceptualisation and reconceptualisation of race. This according to Kolchin (2002: 170–171) is not new. It is a stance that is similarly taken in this chapter.

Nonetheless, until we can clearly determine whether whiteness studies is an evolution of race studies or is an entirely new body of knowledge, it is unlikely that black perceptions and experiences will readily form part of whiteness studies. There is also the question of whether race studies continues alongside whiteness studies today, or whether it came to an end with the establishment of whiteness studies. Not every study that looks at white people falls under whiteness studies. If there is some confusion regarding what falls under whiteness studies then it may be difficult to determine whether whiteness studies has taken over and replaced race studies, or whether race studies continues alongside whiteness studies. This, in turn, means challenging the reasons for the existence of what some call whiteness studies. Until this confusion of the boundaries is cleared up, how race is understood and studied – including whiteness – remains an issue.

Thirdly, there is a danger, of course, in the inclusion of black perceptions and experiences of whiteness. By including black experiences and perceptions of whiteness into whiteness studies, there is the danger that this may be used by white people in white discourse to spread the blame of racism (see for example Steyn and Foster 2008: 32; see also Milazzo's (2015: 10) awareness of this danger). Whiteness studies may thus cease to be a way to force white people to come to terms with their white privilege and their place within the racial hierarchy but, rather, become a case for arguing that it is not only white people that have white privileges, nor play a part in the perpetuation in whiteness, and the construction of the other. However, if whiteness is to be understood and challenged, and uprooted in the post-colonial context as a cultural norm in many of the postcolonial world's 'official and unofficial cultural practices' (Lopez 2005: 4–5) we need a broader, more relational understanding of the term 'dominant'. A similar point is made in the work of Goebel (2015) in how racialisation may be used by a few elite blacks to criminalise and marginalise the majority poor black bodies. Work on whiteness, therefore, needs to take heed of both former colonisers and colonised, now fellow citizens in a post-independent state, and their 'common dependence upon—and complicity with—the ideology of whiteness, or more specifically of white (hence Western) superiority' (Lopez 2005: 4-5). Each, states Lopez (2005: 4–5), 'must now face the unpleasant truth of their own complicity in telling, and believing in, the cultural lie of colonial whiteness'.

Circumstances, within society, no longer permit a strict polarised understanding of race because we no longer have overtly racially discriminatory laws and policies as previously mentioned (see for example Dolby 2001). Rather, the removal of overtly discriminatory laws and policies, and the growth of the black middle class in South Africa means coming to terms with the need to explore the few cases where racial boundary crossing and constructions are happening, and the continuing allure of whiteness as the norm for both black and white people in the post-apartheid context. As was noted by Twine (1997), it is the practices of whiteness such as how people speak, access to middle class interests and schools and living areas that allow the development of a white cultural identity by those who are not phenotypically white. Lopez makes a similar note regarding the role of education. Today many black people, as was mentioned before, have the capital to go the schools and live in the neighbourhoods that they previously would have been excluded from. This means many students, black and white, struggle to think of race in essentialist terms (see Seddon, 2014 on teaching the book *Beloved*[3] to a multiracial classroom). Unlike the coconut or the rainbow nation, for many students going to the same schools and living in the same neighbourhoods has helped to develop a historical amnesia of the injustices of apartheid past.[4] Thus, many students in Seddon's class are either surprised 'that this was going on' or construct the book, *Beloved*, as being 'so old'. It is not the book itself that is old but rather the relevance of its subject matter – racial injustice and segregation in the traditionally racially polarised fashion in which much work following 1990s pattern that is increasingly starting to be outdated. What articles such as Seddon's (2014) suggest is that expecting students to act and understand interracial relations in terms of the effect of the legacy of racism cannot continue to be a simple case drawn primarily on phenotypical features alone. There is ample evidence to suggest that we increasingly need more of the 'new' ways of understanding race – including whiteness and whiteness studies.

Special Knowledge? The Importance of the Black Gaze

In 'Representing Whiteness in the Black Imagination', hooks (1997) describes the knowledge that black people have of white people gleaned from years of scrutiny during slavery as 'special knowledge'.

hooks (1997) states that, 'black folks, have, from slavery on shared with one another in conversations "special" knowledge of whiteness gleaned from close scrutiny of white people. Deemed special because it was not a way of knowing that has been recorded fully in written material, its purpose was to help black folks cope and survive in a white supremacist society. For years black domestic servants, working in white homes, acted as informants who brought knowledge back to segregated communities—details, facts, observations, psychoanalytic readings of the white "Other"" (hooks 1997: 165).

There is no disagreement with the view that people, as a result of their structural position, have some special insights. This structural view of special knowledge is not disagreed with. However, as Nyamnjoh points out in his analogy of the elephant with different researchers describing an elephant based merely on what they individually touch, research that follows pre-existing patterns of how research is done can fall prey to the same trick. As one researcher feels the tail, they are of the view that an elephant is a being which is thin and wiry; while another who feels the trunk, for example, claims that an elephant is a long thick, muscular animal that can grab things; and one who feels part of the belly may claim an elephant is a round, thick skinned animal of unimaginable size. Each believes and is, in a way, correct about their findings, but would learn a lot more about what an elephant is if they were willing to draw from each other. Drawing from this analogy, this chapter acknowledges that indeed special knowledge is held because of structural position. However, in agreement with Nyamnjoh and his analogy, if we are willing to draw from different perspectives, we would perhaps have a more comprehensive idea of what, how and why race – including the privileging of whiteness persists. Let us be willing to draw from both black and white perspectives together to better understand whiteness; let us be willing to look in the dark corners of that which we ordinarily would ignore, such as partial acquisition of whiteness by those who are not black. The chapter argues, that despite the risks, what we then could potentially learn might allow insights and inroads to challenge the privileging of whiteness which has continued to exist despite attempts to bring it to an end. Likewise, this chapter does not claim to fully understand whiteness nor know all the ways to study it. But rather the chapter makes a case for attempting to gain more comprehensive understandings of whiteness. A puzzle cannot be complete or, for that matter, known what the image is, until one is open minded enough to attempt to collect as many pieces as possible. Similarly, what image of whiteness and whiteness studies emerges if we are willing to consider as many of the available pieces and patterns of doing whiteness studies research as is available could be astounding; that is, not using piecemeal approaches but rather attempting to put as many pieces together as a new approach. How much more? The chapter encourages us to imagine how much more we could possibly learn and pioneer rather than walking the well-trodden pathways – as useful and as lifesaving as they have been. This is not to argue that one wholesome approach will resolve all our race issues nor that the need for continually new approaches will end. Instead, in alignment with much of the work of Nyamnjoh, the chapter argues for a more comprehensive approach, but which is ever open ended and incomplete. As the construction, use and meaning of race changes, so too we should be ever evolving and open minded in the approaches used lest we become irrelevant as some young post-apartheid Africans have already been claiming (McKinney and Pletzen 2004; Seddon 2014).

Standing on the Shoulders of Giants

No researcher can ever claim to come with wholly new research without relying on and drawing on the wisdom of those that came before. There is the danger, however, that we may get stuck in the ways that they used instead of learning of how to think imaginatively as they had with what came before them. The need to recognise and cite what has become before can in some ways become stifling, and for the new academic, especially frightening should they dare to go against the mould. This matter that has arisen time and time again in regard to unequal power relations in knowledge production, and also what is considered valid knowledge. The stakes are high – potentially not being published and thus a stagnant career. This is particularly difficult when it comes to sensitive topics such as race. However as works such as that by Nyamnjoh (2012, 2016), Twine (1997), Bashkow (2006) and several others have shown, standing on the shoulders of giants does not necessarily always mean having to tread the same ways in which research is done. Instead, here a little, there a little may be sufficient to provide new insights on an old topic. This thankfully is ever the interest of academia despite, at times, the unfamiliarity of a new flavour to a well-known recipe.

Conclusion

This chapter has briefly argued that we need new ways of doing whiteness studies research. While COVID-19 has undoubtedly called for new ways of learning and researching, it is worth considering whether this adaptation will only extend as far as to how we find new ways of doing things the old way. In other words, for example, the use of platforms such as Zoom to hold focus groups, interviews and so on to do research but still being bound by the same way of how to think through the data. In as much as we may be putting energy into thinking of new ways to continue to do research, more creativity arguably needs to also be put into thinking of new approaches to engage with social issues such as race – including whiteness.

This chapter has looked specifically at some of the reasons as to how and why old 1990s patterns of doing whiteness studies research continue to dominate. Why, as mentioned in the introduction to this chapter, have old trodden pathways of whiteness studies research continued dominate – even as we see some moves away from this. Some of the reasons as to why this persistence of the old continues were covered. However, equally in each case the chapter also covered some reasons to look in the dark corners which have not yet had as much light. Unless we are willing to take some risk – even if it is a little – in how research is done, we may be bound by the very same fetters we wish to escape as is the case with whiteness studies and the danger of essentialism as covered in the body of the chapter.

Notes

[1] There is some contestation as to whether whiteness studies should be considered a field or not. However, there is sufficient work labelled 'whiteness studies' and 'critical whiteness studies' which implies that at least some people consider whiteness studies as a new way of engaging with the issue of race (see, for example, Twine and Gallagher 2008 and Garner 2017).

[2] See also a similar point being made in the work by Nyamnjoh and Fuh (2014) on African constructions of whiteness in the discussion of hair.

[3] Written by Toni Morrison in 1987, the book explores the ongoing effects of slavery on a family. The family had escaped the geographical area of where slavery was legal but unfortunately find themselves not only haunted by the ghost slavery in their relationships and psychology but ultimately hunted down, and found by entities sent to recapture them.

[4] Seddon's hope was to engage with the historical amnesia that her students portrayed.

References

Ahmed, S. (2007) 'A phenomenology of whiteness', *Feminist Theory*, Vol. 8, No. 2, pp. 149–168.

Ansell, Amy E. (2006) 'Casting a blind eye: The ironic consequences of color-blindness in South Africa and the United States, *Critical Sociology*, Vol. 32, No. 2–3, pp. 333–365.

Bashkow, I. (2006) *The Meaning of Whitemen: Race and Modernity in the Orokavia Cultural World*, Chicago and London: The University of Chicago Press.

Bonilla-Silva, E. (2014) *Racism without Racists: Color-Blind Racism and the Persistence of Racial Inequality in America* (4 ed.), Lanham, Boulder, New York, Toronto, Plymouth, UK: Rowman and Littlefield, http://gen.lib.rus.ec/book/index.php?md5=f583a2d3d31f02528ea4ba5901d4acb0 (accessed: April 2020).

Delgado, R. and Stefancic, J. (2001) *Critical Race Theory: An Introduction*, New York and London: New York University Press.

Deliovsky, K. and Kitossa, T. (2013) 'Beyond black and white: When going beyond may take us out of bounds', *Journal of Black Studies*, Vol. 44, No. 2, pp. 158–181.

Doane, W. (2003) 'Rethinking Whiteness Studies', in Doane, W and Bonilla-Silva, E (eds) *White Out: The Continuing Significance of Racism*, Routledge, https://doi.org/10.4324/9780203412107, pp. 3–18 (accessed: May 2020).

Dolby, N. (2001). *Constructing Race. Youth, Identity and Popular Culture in South Africa*, Albany: University of York Press.

Durrheim, K. and Dixon, J. (2000) 'Theories of culture in racist discourse', *Race and Society*, No. 3, pp. 93–109.

Dyer, R. (1997) *White*, London and New York: Routledge.

Fanon, F. (2008) *Black Skin, White Masks (Get Political)*, London: Pluto Press, http://abahlali.org/files/__Black_Skin__White_Masks__Pluto_Classics_.pdf (accessed: May 2020).

Garner, S. (2017) 'Surfing the third wave of whiteness studies: reflections on Twine and Gallagher', *Ethnic and Racial Studies*, Vol. 40, No. 9, pp. 1582–1597.

Goebel, A. (2015) *On Their Own: Women, Urbanization, and the Right to the City in South Africa*, Montreal and Kingston, London and Chicago, McGill-Queen's University Press (MQUP).

hooks, bell. (1997) 'Representing Whiteness in the Black Imagination', in R. Frankenberg (ed.) *Displacing Whiteness: Essays in Social and Cultural Criticism*, Durham and London: Duke University Press.

Kolchin, P. (2002) 'Whiteness studies: The new history of race in America', *Journal of American History*, No. 89 (June), pp. 154–173.

Lewis, A. E. (2004) '"What group?" Studying whites and whiteness in the era of "color-blindness"', *Sociological Theory*, Vol. 22, No. 4, pp. 623–646.

Lopez, A. (2005) 'Introduction: Whiteness after Empire', in A. Lopez (ed.) *Postcolonial Whiteness: A Critical Reader on Race and Empire*, New York: State University of New York Press, p. 119.

Luescher, T., Lodaer, L. and Taabo, Mugume (2017) '#FeesMustFall: An internet age student movement and the case of the University of Free State', *South African Journal of Political Studies*, Vol. 44, No. 2, pp. 231–245.

McIntyre, A. (1997) *Making Meaning of Whiteness: Exploring White Racial Iidentity with White Teachers*, Albany: State University of New York Press.

McKinney, C., & Pletzen , E. van. (2004). ' '… This apartheid story … we've finished with it': student responses to the apartheid past in a South African English studies course1." *Teaching in Higher Education.*

Milazzo, M. (2015) 'The rhetorics of racial power: Enforcing colorblindness in post-apartheid scholarship on rac., *Journal of International and Intercultural Communication*, Vol. 8, No. 1, pp. 7–26.

Mills, Charles W. (2008) 'Comments on Shannon Sullivan's *Revealing Whiteness*', *The Journal of Speculative Philosophy*, https://doi.org/10.1353/jsp.0.0005 (accessed: April 2020).

Morrison, T. (1993) *Playing-in-the-dark: Whiteness in the Literary Imagination*, New York: Vintage Books.

Nyamnjoh, F. B. (2012) "Potted Plants in Greenhouses": A Critical Reflection on the Resilience of Colonial Education in Africa. *Journal of Asian and African Studies, 47*(2), 129–154.

Nyamnjoh, F. and Fuh, D. (2014) 'Africans consuming hair, Africans consumed by hair', *Africa Insight*, Vol. 44, No. 1, pp. 52–68.

Nyamnjoh, F. and Page, B. (2002) 'Whiteman Kontri and the enduring allure of modernity among Cameroonian youth', *African Affairs*, Vol. 101, No. 405, pp. 607–634.

Nyamnjoh, Francis B. (2016) *#RhodesMustFall: Nibbling at Resilient Colonialism in South Africa*, Cameroon: Langaa RPCIG.

Outlaw Jr, L. (2004) 'Rehabilitate Racial Whiteness' in Yancy,G (ed) *What White Looks Like: African American Philosophers on the Whiteness Question*, New York and London: Routledge.

Ratele, K. (2007) 'Make indigenes unconscious of whiteness: A response to Green, Sonn, and Matsebula', *South African Journal of Psychology*, Vol. 37, No. 3, pp. 431–436.

Seddon, D. (2014) '"Be a Mighty Hard Message": Toni Morrison's beloved and the exploration of whiteness in the post-apartheid classroom, *Safundi,* Vol. 15, No. 1, pp. 29–52.

Steyn, M. and Foster, D. (2008) 'Repertoires for talking white: Resistant whiteness in post-apartheid South Africa', *Ethnic and Racial Studies*, Vol. 31, No. 1, pp. 25–51.

Sullivan, S. (2006) *Revealing Whiteness: The Unconscious Habits of Racial Privilege*, Bloomington: Indiana University Press.

Twine, F. W. (1997) 'Brown Skinned White Girls: Class, Culture and the Construction of White Identity in Suburban Communities', in Frankenberg (ed), *Displacing Whiteness: Essays in Social and Cultural Criticism*,. Durham, NC: Duke University Press, pp. 214–242.

Twine, F. W. and Gallagher, C. (2008) 'The future of whiteness: a map of the "third wave"', *Ethnic and Racial Studies*, Vol. 31, No. 1, pp. 4–24.

Yancy, G. (2004) *What White Looks Like: African American Philosophers on the Whiteness Question*, in G. Yancy (ed.), New York and London: Routledge.

Index

D

J

K

Q

R

X

Z

CPSIA information can be obtained
at www.ICGtesting.com
Printed in the USA
LVHW080647201022
731135LV00001B/17

9 789956 552238